OXFORD ENGLISH MONOGRAPHS

RADICAL SATIRE

AND

PRINT CULTURE

1790–1822

MARCUS WOOD

CLARENDON PRESS · OXFORD

1994

Oxford University Press, Walton Street, Oxford OX2 6DP

Oxford New York Toronto
Delhi Bombay Calcutta Madras Karachi
Kuala Lumpar Singapore Hong Kong Tokyo
Nairobi Dar es Salaam Cape Town
Melbourne Auckland Madrid
and associated companies in
Berlin Ibadan

Oxford is a trade mark of Oxford University Press

Published in the United States
by Oxford University Press Inc., New York

British Library Cataloguing in Publication Data
Data available

Library of Congress Cataloging in Publication Data
Wood, Marcus
Radical satire and print culture, 1790–1822 / Marcus Wood.
— (Oxford English monographs)
Includes bibliographical references and index.
1. Political satire, English—History and criticism. 2. Hone,
William, 1780–1842—Political and social views. 3. Cruikshank,
George, 1792–1878—Political and social views. 4. Politics and
literature—Great Britain—History—19th century. 5. Politics and
literature—Great Britain—History—18th century. 6. Art and
literature—Great Britain—History—19th century. 7. Art and
literature—Great Britain—History—18th century. 8. Radicalism—
Great Britain—History—19th century. 9. Radicalism—Great
Britain—History—18th century. I. Title II. Series
PR936.W66 1994
827'.709358—dc20 93-46675
ISBN 0-19-811278-5

1 3 5 7 9 10 8 6 4 2

Typeset by Create Publishing Services Ltd., Bath, Avon
Printed in Great Britain
on acid-free paper by
Biddles Ltd.,
Guildford and King's Lynn

To my Mother and Michael

ACKNOWLEDGEMENTS

I THANK the following people who have helped me to write this book: John Adams, Bob White, Alan Hurd, Michael Gearin-Tosh, Rachel Trickett, John Bayley, Jonathan Wordsworth, John Golding, Don McKenzie, Michael Turner, Peter de Francia, Adam Ashforth, John Santos, Ethan Johnson, Stephen Farthing, Fabio and Christina Lopez, Jac Leirner, José Rosendé, Jean Lodge, Lynn Murphy, Dillwyn Smith, Julius Tabaçek, Stan Unsworth, Benjamin Ross, Andrea Rausch, Debbie and David Goldie, Sarah Turvey, Rufus Wood, and Kate Wood.

I am especially grateful to Louis James, John Stevenson, Roy Park, Mark Philp, Jon Mee, Iain McCalman, Malcolm Chase, Michael Lobban, and Dick Brown, who read and criticized the manuscript, or large parts of it, when *I thought* that it was finished.

Radical Satire and Print Culture 1790–1822 was written intermittently at Worcester College, Oxford, during the course of two fellowships. As Michael Bromberg Fellow in the Study of Prints I benefited from the advice and friendship of Asa and Susan Briggs. I was also very lucky that the fellowship introduced me to Joseph and Ruth Bromberg. Their great kindness and wisdom has continually encouraged me. I would also like to thank the British Academy for awarding me a postdoctoral fellowship, which allowed me to focus on completing the book.

Finally thanks to Sarah Squire for her integrity and clear thought, and for her love.

M.W.

CONTENTS

LIST OF ILLUSTRATIONS

ABBREVIATIONS

An Admirable Satire	*An Admirable Satire on the Death, Dissection, Funeral Procession and Epitaph of Mr Pitt* (London, 1795).
Arnott and Robinson	J. Fullerton Arnott, and J. W. Robinson, *English Theatrical Literature: A Bibliography* (London: Society for Theatre Research, 1970).
Atherton	Herbert M. Atherton, *Political Prints in the Age of Hogarth* (Oxford: Oxford University Press, 1974).
Ault	Alexander Pope, *The Prose Works of Alexander Pope 1711–1720*, ed. N. Ault (Oxford: Basil Blackwell, 1936).
Baer	Marc Baer, *Theatre and Disorder in Late Georgian London* (Oxford: Oxford University Press, 1992).
BMC	British Museum Collection of Political and Personal Satires.
Bowden	Ann Bowden, 'William Hone's Political Journalism, 1815–1821', Ph.D. diss., University of Texas at Austin, 1975.
Bruttini	A. Bruttini, 'Advertising and Socio-Economic Transformations in England, 1720–1760', *Journal of Advertising History*, 5 (1982), 9–14.
Chase	Malcolm Chase, *The People's Farm*, (Oxford: Oxford University Press, 1989).
Claeys	Gregory Claeys, *Thomas Paine: Political and Social Thought*, (Boston: Unwyn Hymann, 1989).
C. of E.	Jeremy Bentham, *Church of Englandism and its Catechism Examined* (London, 1818).
Cohn	Albert Mayer Cohn, *A Bibliographical Catalogue of the Printed Works Illustrated by George Cruikshank* (London: Longmans, Green, 1914).
Crimmins	James E. Crimmins, 'Religion, Utility and Politics: Bentham versus Paley', in Crimmins (ed.) *Religion, Secularization and Political Thought* (London: Routledge & Kegan Paul, 1990).

D & H	R. Dalton and S. Hamer, *The Provincial Token Coinage of the Eighteenth Century*, 3 vols. in 14 parts (1910–18).
Elliott	Blanche B. Elliott, *A History of English Advertising* (London: B. T. Batsford, 1962).
Evans	E. P. Evans, *The Criminal Prosecution and Capital Punishment of Animals* (London: Faber & Faber, 1987).
Garrett	C. Garrett, *Millenarians and the French Revolution in France and England* (Baltimore: Johns Hopkins University Press, 1975).
Hackwood	Frederick William Hackwood, *William Hone: His Life and Times* (London: T. F. Unwin, 1912).
Hamilton	Walter Hamilton, *George Cruikshank: Artist and Humorist* (London: Elliot Stock, 1878).
Henriques	Ursula Henriques, *Religious Toleration in England 1787–1833* (London: Routledge & Kegan Paul, 1961).
Houtchens	Leigh Hunt, *Leigh Hunt's Literary Criticism*, ed. L. H. and C. W. Houtchens (New York: Columbia University Press, 1956).
Irish Tracts	Jonathan Swift, *Irish Tracts and Sermons*, ed. H. Davis (Oxford: Basil Blackwell, 1948).
Jackson	Mary V. Jackson, *Engines of Instruction, Mischief and Magic: Children's Literature in England from its Beginnings to 1839* (Aldershot: Scholar, 1989).
Jerrold	Blanchard Jerrold, *The Life of George Cruikshank in Two Epochs* (London: Chatto & Windus, 1898).
Johnson	A. F. Johnson, *Type Designs: Their History and Development* (London: Grafton, 1934).
Jones	Mark Jones, *Medals of the French Revolution* (London: British Museum, 1977).
Lilburne	*The Triall of Lieut. Collonell John Lilburne* (London, 1649).
Mack	Maynard Mack, *Alexander Pope: A Life* (New Haven, Conn.: Yale University Press, 1985).
Marlow	Joyce Marlow, *The Peterloo Massacre* ([London:] Rapp & Whiting, 1969).
ODN	Iona and Peter Opie (eds), *The Oxford Dictionary of Nursery Rhymes* (Oxford: Clarendon Press, 1952).

Presbrey	Frank Presbrey, *The Development and History of Advertising* (New York: Doubleday, 1929).
PM	*Pig's Meat; or, Lessons for the Swinish Multitude*, 3 vols. (London, 1793–6).
PP	Daniel Isaac Eaton, *Politics for the People: or, A Salmagundy for Swine* (London, 1793–5); Greenwood repr. 2 vols (New York, 1968).
Raven	James Raven, *Judging New Wealth* (Oxford: Oxford University Press, 1992).
Rea	Robert R. Rea, *The English Press in Politics, 1760–1744* (Lincoln, 1964).
Rudé	George Rudé, *Wilkes and Liberty* (Oxford: Clarendon Press, 1962).
Rudkin	Olive Rudkin, *Thomas Spence and his Connections* (London: George Allen & Unwin, 1927).
Savage	William Savage *Practical Hints on Decorative Printing* (London, 1822).
SB	*Studies in Bibliography.*
Scribner	R. W. Scribner, *For the Sake of Simple Folk: Popular Propaganda for the German Reformation* (Cambridge: Cambridge University Press, 1981).
Sherburn	G. Sherburn, *The Early Career of Alexander Pope* (Oxford: Clarendon Press, 1934).
Smith	Olivia Smith, *The Politics of Language 1791–1819* (Oxford: Oxford University Press, 1984).
SP	*Shelley's Prose*, ed. with intro. and notes by David Lee Clark (London: Fourth Estate, 1988).
ST	*State Trials: A Complete Collection of State Trials*, compiled by William Cobbett and later by T. B. Howells, 34 vols.
Spater	George Spater, *William Cobbett: The Poor Man's Friend*, 2 vols. (Cambridge: Cambridge University Press, 1982).
Straumann	H. Straumann *Newspaper Headlines: A Study in Linguistic Method* (London: George Allen & Unwin, 1935).
Tatler	*The Tatler*, ed. Donald F. Bond, 3 vols (Oxford: Oxford University Press, 1987).
Thompson	E. P. Thompson, *The Making of the English Working Class* (London: Victor Gollancz, 1966).

Trial   Daniel Isaac Eaton, *The Trial of Daniel Isaac Eaton* (London, 1812).

Turner   E. S. Turner, *The Shocking History of Advertising!* (London, 1952).

Waters   A. W. Waters, *The Trial of Thomas Spence in 1801* (Leamington Spa: Courier Press, 1917).

Whiting   J. R. S. Whiting, *Trade Tokens: A Social and Economic History* (Newton Abbot: David & Charles, 1971).

Wickwar   William Hardy Wickwar, *The Struggle for the Freedom of the Press 1819–1832* (London: George Allen & Unwin, 1928).

Wood   James Playstead Wood, *The Story of Advertising* (New York: Ronald Press, 1958).

INTRODUCTION

The Potatoes Speak
for Themselves

On 28 January 1817, as the Prince Regent returned from opening Parliament, his carriage was surrounded by an angry mob. One of the carriage windows was broken, almost certainly by a stone, but there were rumours of a bullet. Thomas Wooler, editor of the extreme radical journal *The Black Dwarf*, sprang to the government's aid. He conjectured a softer, more sinister missile and his 'High Treason: Examination of the Treasonable Potatoes' enthusiastically reported the full proceedings of the government's attempt to prosecute the culprits.

Previous suspects, the cobble-stones, were exonerated because 'no malice *propense* could be urged against them; *positively* at least; for they might have been lying there in their honest avocation of making a *firm footing* for the carriage of royalty.'[1] The potatoes had no such alibi:

In the emphatic language, however, of Mr. Magistrate Hicks,—'the POTATOES *speak for themselves*. It is not the practice to pave streets with potatoes. *Ergo*, the potatoes must have been there with some treasonable design. They could have no lawful business outside the kitchen or the market place.' (*BD* 4 (1817), 60)

Wooler's potatoes are an ideal of dumb passivity which the state then proceeds to condemn through cold-blooded legal sophistry:

When questioned, the poor potatoes *said nothing*, they had not even an excuse to offer. They were mute as death … The worthy Magistrate then proceeded to substantiate his charge.—'The Potatoes', my lords and gentlemen, '*speak for themselves!* I do not mean that they express themselves in the common forms of language. But there is my lords and gentlemen, as we all know, a *dumb sort of eloquence* that speaks louder than words and silences the

[1] *BD* 4 (1817), 59–62.

most noisy advocates ... Their language is a silent confession of their evil intentions, which as I said before is palpable from the very presence of the potatoes at such a place. (*BD* 4 (1817), 61)

The very existence of Wooler's satire proudly proclaims that the potatoes *can* speak for themselves in a very different way from that argued by his fictional advocate. Wooler's 'Treasonable Potatoes' is everything that the state hoped radical satire could not be—bold, sophisticated, jubilant, capable of conducting abstract political argument, and able to attack state appropriation of the law through parody of legal language. It takes the language of alarmist paranoia and runs with it. Wooler's parody is doubly confrontational: it mocks authority and criticizes its victims.

The defence lawyer emphasizes the docility of his clients. Without rights or will-power their only excuse is that they have been hopelessly misled by the reformers:

They have been thrown as it were in the very teeth of royalty, at a time when and in a place where it was impossible to swallow them ... my clients were evidently the tools, the dupes of some violent reformists; and from their *quiet appearance* and *humble demeanour* at present, there is every reason in the world to conclude that they have been forced into this violent attack *will they, nill they* ... Feel how soft they are my lords and gentlemen. (*BD* 4 (1817), 61)

Wooler's insight into the humiliating assumptions upon which the defence is based gives the satire its double sting. Responsibility lies not only with the powerful for exploiting the helpless but with the helpless for not helping themselves. While the people act like potatoes they have no right to be treated as anything else.

Where does this satire come from? A self-educated working-class radical takes on a tone of satiric hauteur to upbraid those without power for their passivity. He speaks to them in a language of urbane irony which is equally appropriate for another audience, his real victims, those with power. Where does this work stand in relation to a fixed notion of a language of class? What are its formal and linguistic sources? What is the basis for its knowing confidence? Where *does* Wooler's satire come from?

Such are the questions addressed in this book, which is a study of popular radical propaganda published in London, from the Battle of Waterloo to the Queen Caroline affair. Its central focus is the collaborative work produced by the reformist printer, publisher, and antiquarian William Hone, and the politically ambivalent young caricaturist and satiric printmaker George Cruikshank. This work was the most widely circulated and influential anti-government satire printed during the efflorescence of radical publicity which occurred in the years 1815–22. This period has been designated by E. P. Thompson as 'the heroic age of popular radicalism'.[2] The works and methods of the mainstream radical publicists active during these years have not so far been placed in relation to their well-springs in the popular political and social satire of the eighteenth century. My first two chapters are consequently devoted to uncovering an eighteenth-century satiric inheritance for early nineteenth-century radicalism which has, up to this point, been unevenly and sometimes fancifully mapped.[3]

Between 1815 and 1821 Hone produced 175 publications.[4] Most of these were political satires based on earlier models. Hone looked back to the propaganda of the Wilkes affair and the late eighteenth-century Westminster elections and beyond these to judicial and social satire from the reign of Queen Anne. He was also strongly influenced by the more immediate and violently radical activists of the 1790s. Thomas Spence and Daniel Isaac Eaton were the most effective political publicists to be thrown up during these years. The impact of their work on the strategies of later radical propagandists is greater than has hitherto been acknowledged. My second chapter discusses this in detail.

Hone and Cruikshank's satire grew out of the forms of sacred texts, almanacs, press advertisements, chapbooks, children's books, nursery rhymes, games, poems, songs, last wills, dying confessions, playbills, and showman's notices. Many of the biblical models which they used had been current since the Reformation, while the majority of other forms had become familiar in the eighteenth century and feature in what are normally considered the ephemeral publications of major literary figures including Defoe, Swift, Addison, and Pope. Hone was deeply versed in long-standing traditions of religious and judicial parody, which provided him with insights into the ceremonies and rhetoric of the Church, the courts, and government.

[2] For the distribution and sales of the pamphlets, see Bowden, 257–71, 304–6, 317–20. For Hone's influence see Thompson, 603, 604, 688–9, 720–3; Louis James, *English Popular Literature 1819–1851* (New York, 1976), 70–5.
[3] The shortcomings in recent works of literary scholarship are discussed below in the Conclusion.
[4] For the complicated bibliography and chronology of these titles, see Bowden.

He applied these insights to the trials and political scandals of his own day.

The radical free press, to which Hone's works were a formative contribution, became powerful and experimental in the period under consideration. The propaganda which was directed against Lord Liverpool's administration and the Prince Regent was unprecedented in its scale and diversity. This material was in part the result of developments in publishing and communications, which had in their turn fostered a variety of parodic activity which was not necessarily 'political' in its inspiration. The sudden expansion of the print trade, and the rise of the satiric etching in particular, the growth of periodical publication and of the children's book trade, all had a direct impact on the production of social satire and political propaganda.

Advertising from 1720 to 1820 occupies a prominent position in this study because of the ways in which it opened up language and communications. Hone's parody would not have taken the forms it did, or have reached the market it did, without the development of the early nineteenth-century advertising industry. Advertising popularized, appropriated, and imitated different writing styles and systems of iconography. It had the effect of loosening and challenging established linguistic divisions and notions of social empowerment. It established a range of models which were taken up and developed in political satire but it was shunned in polite literature as the most visible manifestation of the corruption of the book trade.[5]

Cruikshank's graphic work for Hone was particularly astute in the ways it combined old models and new styles. Cruikshank fused techniques developed in contemporary illustrated product advertisement with earlier graphic methods. The latter included eighteenth-century engraved copperplate book illustration, the folk style of chapbook woodcut, seventeenth-century emblem books and political engravings, eighteenth-century political satires in the Hogarthian mode, and the caricatural styles of the late eighteenth-century satiric etching.[6]

The most successful of the satiric hybrids that resulted from the Hone–Cruikshank collaboration, *The Political House that Jack Built, The*

---

[5] Raven provides a detailed account of the extreme reactions of the world of *belles-lettres* to the growth of the trade and manufacturing classes in the period 1750–1810. For the vilification of the advertising methods of the most successful new booksellers, see pp. 48–9.

[6] The technical virtuosity with which Cruikshank fused past and present graphic resources has not been discussed by art historians. His work in commercial advertising is universally passed over. See pp. 224–5 and 235–7 below.

Bank Restriction Barometer, The Man in the Moon, Non Mi Ricordo!, The Queen's Matrimonial Ladder, A Slap at Slop, and *The Political Showman—at Home!,* were produced in great quantities and distributed nation-wide. They generated innumerable loyalist and radical imitations, and they exerted a powerful effect on political satire during the post-Peterloo period of radical ferment. Hone's pamphlets were still widely used as models for anti-government and anticlerical satire in the revival of radical agitation during the two years preceding the passage of the Great Reform Act.[7]

Radical spokesmen and propagandists in the second decade of the nineteenth century came from a variety of social backgrounds and levels of political commitment. They included survivors from the heady days of the London Corresponding Society and the 1794 treason trials such as Major Cartwright, Thomas Hardy, and John Thelwall, and a range of aristocratic Whigs which numbered in its ranks Sir Francis Burdett, Henry Brougham, and on occasion even Lord Byron.[8] There were the infidel intellectual radicals led by Bentham and Godwin. There was also a vast middle ground that incorporated organizational geniuses such as Francis Place and William Gast, and popular orators and demagogues, the most notorious being Henry Hunt. Religious enthusiasm blended in and out of radicalism in various ways which have yet to be properly unravelled. Figures such as Thomas Preston fused their political vision with millennialism, while Robert Wedderburn used the language and forms of enthusiasm or Nonconformity to his own advantage, although in the final analysis the extent of his religious commitment is not easy to verify.[9]

On the publishing front the term 'radical' can take in such members of the literati as Lamb, Peacock, Hazlitt, and John and Leigh Hunt. It also describes mainstream political journalists like Cobbett, Thomas Wooler, and Richard Carlile, and the broadside, handbill, and pamphlet publishers Thomas Dolby, William Benbow, and John Cahuac. The latter category could on occasion accommo-

---

[7] For Hone and Reform literature in the 1830s see Ch. 5 n. 2 below.

[8] Ann Hone, *For the Cause of Truth: Radicalism in London 1796–1821* (Oxford, 1982); for Whig Radical relationships, 152–62, 171–6, 289–94, 334–5.

[9] Ibid. 326–9, 332–6, 340–8. The most succinct overview of the historiography treating the variegated nature of radicalism during the revolutionary period is Mark Philp, 'The Fragmented Ideology of Reform', in Philp (ed.) *The French Revolution and British Popular Politics* (Cambridge, 1991).

date elevated figures like Brougham and Byron.[10] During brief
periods of nation-wide excitement, the most significant being the
weeks directly following Peterloo and the period of the trial of
Queen Caroline, radical enthusiasm and popular outrage shaded
into one another to form an amorphous publishing front. Under
such conditions radical propaganda found an unending series of
politically ambivalent but commercially sharp allies in the gutter
press. The likes of John Pitts and Jemmy Catnach (the phenomenally
successful ballad entrepreneur of the Seven Dials publishing district
of London) profitably plagiarized the most successful radical satires.
The Queen Caroline affair in particular blurred the dividing lines
between politics, social satire, royalist enthusiasm, and pornography.
It drew in a very odd set of hacks and opportunists, many of whom,
like Cruikshank, produced vicious propaganda for both sides.[11]

Given the social and political gallimaufry which *was* early nineteenth-century radicalism it is not surprising that the satire which
was generated under the broad heading of the 'radical free press'
comprises a diverse and frequently bewildering terrain. The diffi-
culty of mapping it lies not only in the range of publications and
types of social behaviour it incorporates but in the changing contributions of individual radicals. Allegiances and energy levels altered,
as did the political goals, commitment, and self-confidence of individuals. Hone's career provides a focused way into the operations
of radical pressmen in the first two decades of the nineteenth
century. His work and friendships embraced the full range of radical
publication and opinion.

Hone was born in London on 3 June 1780, during the Gordon
Riots, and he died in 1842. The fragmentary autobiographical
account of his early years described a boy obsessed with print culture. The texts which made the greatest impact on Hone, during the
first fifteen years of his life, were the Bible, the *Pilgrim's Progress*, and
Foxe's *Book of Martyrs*.[12] As a small boy he showed an intense interest
in printed objects. He spent large amounts of time in a copperplate

[10] Brougham's ephemeral pamphlet literature is an unstudied area of his literary
output. Under the pseudonym Harry Broom he wrote several burlesques in the
Hone manner including *A King in a Pickle! With a Cabinet of Curiosities*. For Byron's
relation to popular satire and publishing, see my 'The Dedication to *Don Juan* and
Nursery Rhyme Parody: A New Satiric Context', *Byron Journal*, 20 (1992), 71–7.

[11] Iain McCalman, *Radical Underworld* (Cambridge, 1989), 162–77.

[12] Hone's unpublished and unfinished autobiography is repr. in Hackwood,
23–60. Hackwood discusses Hone's childhood reading of the Bible, Bunyon, and
Foxe on pp. 24, 28–30, and 35–6 respectively.

engraver's office and claimed to have studied every plate that passed through the place over a three-year period.[13] Throughout his adult life he maintained an interest in prints and amassed a curious collection. This contained Italian and Dutch old masters and ephemeral political satires ranging over the centuries from anonymous Lutheran woodcuts to the etchings of Gillray and his imitators. When he was 10 Hone had picked up an old printed page of scrap paper. He eventually found out that it was a leaf from *The Trial of John Lilburne*. Hone saved up and bought the book for half a crown. He read this notorious Leveller trial as an adventure story: 'since *The Pilgrim's Progress* no book had so riveted me; I felt all Lilburne's indignant feelings'. It marked the birth of his political consciousness and began a lifelong fascination with Lilburne, the Levellers, and with popular publishing.[14]

Hone passed his teens in London during the 1790s working in various offices as a clerk. At the age of 16 he became, for a brief period, a member of the London Corresponding Society, although he was forced to leave under pressure from his father, who exiled him to Chatham away from extreme radical influences. At this time he was also a disciple of Godwin's, although he abruptly dropped Godwinism. On first meeting the great man face to face a terrible display of temper had convinced Hone that there was an unbridgeable gap between Godwinian theory and practice.[15]

Hone's activities up until 1817 reflected his consistent interest in social, political, and judicial reform and his delight in public scandal. In 1807 he became friendly with a Dutchman called John Bone, who claimed to have been released from the Bastille in 1794, and attempted to launch 'Tranquillity'. This was to be a combination of national savings bank, insurance office, and employment registry— something along the lines of the Fieldings' plan for a Universal Register.[16] The most innovatory part of the scheme lay in the founding of a 'Society for the Gradual Abolition of the Poor's Rate' which would provide protection from the Poor Law system through donations from the wealthy. Despite several interviews with the Paymaster-General, George Rose, the project came to nothing. Hone ended up by selling his furniture to pay off the debts he had incurred.[17]

Hone became increasingly involved in high-profile political

[13] Smith, 172.   [14] Hackwood, 39–40.   [15] Ibid. 55.
[16] See pp. 23–5 below.   [17] Hackwood, 73–8.

activity. In 1810 a black Haitian boy, John Toussaint L'Ouverture, was being fêted in London as the son of the great slave revolutionary. Hone not only espoused the boy's cause but took him into his home to protect him from commercial exploitation. During this year he also took a prominent part in organizing the mass celebrations surrounding the release of Sir Francis Burdett from the Tower. He was also involved with the Westminster Committee during the Old Price Riots at Covent Garden.

Hone's publications from 1810 to 1817 combined a desire to bring ills to public notice with an ability to exploit the prurient interest which sensational abuses of the law could awaken. In 1815 he brought out a series of publications designed to highlight the treatment of inmates in lunatic asylums. These varied from serious reports aimed at increasing government awareness of the maltreatment of the insane, to sensational street fare lubriciously detailing the torture and brutalizing of individuals. His collaboration with Cruikshank began at this time with a commission to depict *William Norris, an Insane American, rivetted alive in Iron*.

Between July 1815 and September 1816 Hone brought out over twenty publications focusing upon murder trials, inquests into deaths during public disturbances, and a range of trial literature dealing with sex scandals, libel, the freedom of the press, and blood-money convictions. Hone also published a variety of titles, celebratory in tone and politically naïve in content, which vindicated Napoleon as a revolutionary who broke down despotism in Europe. This period also saw the appearance of Hone's first satiric broadsides illustrated by Cruikshank.[18]

By 1817 Hone had become an accomplished political publicist. He maintained a phenomenal rate of pamphlet publication and also started up *Hone's Reformist's Register*, a journal designed to fill the gap created by Cobbett's flight to America. The most sensational satire he produced at this time consisted of a series of parodies based on various forms of Anglican instructional text—the Catechism, Litany, and Creed. Three of these resulted in his prosecution by the government for blasphemous and seditious libel. Hone's triumphant self-defence and final acquittal during the three trials which followed in December 1817 briefly gave him the status of a national hero. From this point his greatly increased circle of acquaintance, and the

[18] See Robert Patten, *George Cruikshank's Life, Times and Art*, i. (London, 1992), 125–7.

national subscription taken out in his aid as part of the extensive celebrations following his trials, provided him with the basis to develop into a prominent radical spokesman. After a brief period of retrenchment in 1818 Hone re-emerged between 1819 and 1821 when he and Cruikshank created the famous series of pamphlet satires which began with *The Political House that Jack Built* and concluded with *The Political Showman—at Home!*

Hone continued to write for twenty years after the Queen Caroline affair. He converted to Nonconformist Christianity in the late 1820s and produced pioneering publications on the early history of Church festivals and Church drama in England. He became a respected antiquarian anthologist. His widely successful *Every-Day Book* (1825–6), *Table Book* (1827), and *Year Book* (1832) consistently emphasized his knowledge of the ideological and formal inheritance of anti-state agitation in the context of folklore and popular culture. He consolidated his friendship with Charles Lamb, became a correspondent and friend of Frances Douce, and even exchanged affectionate and mutually respectful letters with Southey, who was remarkably generous in his capacity to forgive Hone for his earlier satires of the Laureate.[19]

Hone's experience and knowledge of the shifting radical landscape was varied and enduring. He knew Burdett over a twenty-year period, worked with Brougham during the Queen Caroline affair, and was a friend of Hazlitt's. He brought out Hazlitt's *Political Essays* at a time when their publication required more courage than his habitual publisher cared to show. He moved in and out of Cobbett's orbit and indeed claimed that Cobbett had tried to lure him into attending the fateful final meeting of the Cato Street conspirators. He was a long-term friend and correspondent of Francis Place's. Thomas Hardy was a visitor to his shop. Hone knew Thomas Spence, by far the most imaginative radical propagandist in the period 1790–1810, collected his works, and as a young man saw Spence arrested on the street for selling Paine's works.[20]

[19] For Hone's activities as an antiquarian publisher, see J. W. Robinson, 'Regency Radicalism and Antiquarianism: William Hone's Ancient Mysteries Described (1823)', *Leeds Studies in English*, 10 (1978), 1231–44. For Hone's conversion, F. R. Rolleston, *Some Account of the Conversion of the Late William Hone* (London, 1853); *New Letters of Robert Southey*, ed. Kenneth Curry, 2 vols (Columbia, 1965), ii. 358, 26 Nov. 1830.
[20] For Hazlitt and Hone, see Bowden 232–5; Hone, *For the Cause of Truth*, 270; for Hone and Place, see Francis Place, *The Autobiography of Francis Place (1771–1854)*, ed. Mary Thale (Cambridge, 1972), 65, 68, 76.

Hone is a representative early nineteenth-century radical in the sense that it is very difficult to determine what exactly his politics were. He adopted a broadly consistent stance of radical pacifism on questions such as the freedom of the press, the law of libel, and universal suffrage for men. Hone insatiably attacked the most visible and trusted radical targets. He missed very few opportunities to ridicule the government for its maintenance of the system of sinecures and pensions. He castigated corruption within the Church and law especially in the area of clerical magistracy. He and Cruikshank developed a political bestiary headed by the Prince Regent and descending through the leading members of the Cabinet and on down through various well-established stereotypes—the time-serving courtier, the soldier, the clergyman, and the lawyer.

Hone's political writing reveals little theoretical ambition. He was at his best as a journalist responding to specific incidents—such as the passage of the Six Acts, or Peterloo—which could be interpreted as extreme manifestations of repression. As a political theorist he was not original or percipient, but then as a satirist whose main function was to attack existing evils, rather than to suggest solutions to the social and economic organization of society, he was not required to be. His thought was based in a violent satiric impulse which made possible his collaboration with the politically free-wheeling Cruikshank. A complicated and energized autodidact, Hone managed to use his extensive knowledge of, and research into, the history of parody to create political journalism and pamphlet satire with broad appeal and lasting influence.

A study of Hone and Cruikshank's work has to come to terms with the pervasiveness of parody in eighteenth-century English popular satire. There is no generally accepted working definition of parody, and I do not want to attempt one here, but it is necessary to indicate that I shall be taking parody to incorporate many different types of satire, imitation, and linguistic appropriation.[21]

[21] This expanded notion of parody is not new. Paul Lehman in his standard work on medieval parody emphasizes that it was a wide-ranging phenomenon that must be taken to include not only parodies of well-known literary works but formal imitations and even loaded quotations from a great variety of texts and from all sorts of visual material. See Paul Lehmann, *Die Parody in Mittelalter* (Stuttgart, 1963), 3. For the application of Lehmann's definition to later parody, see J. G. Riewald, 'Parody as Criticism', *Neophilologus*, 1 (1966), 125–9. The most wide-ranging contemporary

It has become a critical commonplace to see the period this book covers as a high point for literary parody. But the notion of parody emphasized and described in recent literary studies is a narrow one which centres upon travesties of elevated models such as the poetry of the *Anti-Jacobin*, the *Rejected Addresses* of Horace and James Smith, and James Hogg's *The Poetical Mirror*. There has been increasing interest in the general popularity of Miltonic and most importantly Shakespearian parody. Recent analysis of this phenomenon has extended to prints, paintings, newspapers, and the theatre. This work comes at popular publishing and parody only when it has been 'legitimized' through attachment to the Shakespeare or Milton ticket.[22]

Early nineteenth-century literary society assumed that it was only appropriate to acknowledge parodies of certain respectable texts the elevated style of which made them desirable models.[23] When the Smiths parodied popular forms in their *Rejected Addresses* they were taken to task by reviewers. A composition in the style of a street ballad entitled 'Drury Lane Hustings, A New Halfpenny Ballad By a Nic Pic Poet' was condemned in the *Edinburgh Review* as 'a good imitation of what was not worth imitating'. But what the Smiths' volume showed was that in the realm of parody 'worth' is relative and sometimes worthless. *Rejected Addresses* was threatening to literary taste in its demonstration that parody was not class-specific. Parody could, and in the prolific world of popular publishing outside the book trade *it did*, absorb anything that came its way. Whether the transforming powers of the parodist necessarily elevated what was 'bad' and debased what was 'good' is not so easily determined as the *Edinburgh Review* wished to imagine.

This book includes literary travesty as a relevant but by no means dominant part of a body of material that incorporates graphic satire and the appropriation for satiric purposes of various forms of language developed by institutions such as law, Church, and government. In adopting this latitudinarian approach to what constitutes parody I follow Hone's lead.

discussion of parodic theory is Linda Hutcheon, *A Theory of Parody* (New York, 1989). The most recent theoretical survey of the history of parody, Margaret Rose's, *Parody, Ancient, Modern, and Post-modern* (Cambridge, 1993), makes no reference to Hone.

[22] For a case in point, see Jonathan Bate, *Shakespearian Constitutions* (Oxford, 1990), 104–26; also Bate, 'Shakespearian Allusion in English Caricature in the Age of Gillray', *Journal of the Warburg and Courtauld Institute*, 49 (1986), 196–210.

[23] For an example of the unquestioning continuation of this assumption, see Bate, *Shakespearian Constitutions*, 106–9.

Hone and parody were inextricably connected. In 1832 *The Examiner* pleaded 'Profane parodical muse of Hone, Be pleased to keep your distance', although the subject of the request had not written a parody for ten years.[24] Hone commanded, and commands, a pivotal position as both parodic theoretician and practitioner. He had a wide-ranging conception of parody that was not primarily literary in its emphasis or in its influence on Regency political satire.

Hone's interest in the subject began when he put together a collection of parodies in order to construct the defence for his trials in 1817. In court he read out, or in the case of satiric prints and playing cards, held up, dozens of examples of religious, political, and social parody. These blur formal and linguistic categories. Parody emerges as a great leveller throwing archbishops, poets, statesmen, and anonymous balladeers into the same tub. In the material he presented in his trial, and in the parodies which he obsessively amassed for his proposed *History of Parody* over the next twenty years, Hone tapped into a great reservoir of popular dissent. His parodic theory and practice were informed by the anonymous satires which for centuries had proliferated around public events, scandals, and institutions.

The law and the Church had inspired a mass of mockery based on their institutional language and ritual. Last dying speeches and a variety of trials and cross-examinations had been commonly travestied since the seventeenth century. Parodic litanies and catechisms had been part of popular entertainment over an even longer period.[25] These forms were widely used for satires during the American War, and radicals had picked up on them in the early 1790s. Big elections had also greatly contributed to the incorporation of commercial advertising methods into political campaigning in the second half of the nineteenth century. They were great show-cases for popular satire of all sorts and fed directly into the work of early nineteenth-century radical publicists. Francis Place, as well as Hone, built up an extensive personal collection of this material.[26]

This study establishes that parody of this scale and diversity was not a tame phenomenon—merely a ridiculing outgrowth of serious literature. Parody was knocking away continually and uncontrol-

---

[24] Quoted in *OED* under 'parodical'.

[25] Mikhail Bakhtin, *The Dialogic Imagination: Four Essays* (Austin, Tex., 1981), 51 ff.

[26] Francis Place Collection (1792–1852), vol. xx. William Hone Papers, *BL* MS Add. 4071.

lably at the notion that language reflected class and social position, that polite and literary forms of language could be set up above, and separate from, what Hone termed 'the literature of the multitude'.

Parody in all its forms and variations was a living proof that the rigid linguistic hegemony, which scholars such as Olivia Smith have argued was increasingly implemented and stabilized during the latter half of the eighteenth century, did not hold absolute sway.[27] Parody suggests mastery of linguistic convention and style, to produce parodic variations of a trial, a sermon, or a fable, the workings of the original have to have been thoroughly digested. Parody may work in different ways upon its model, sometimes ridiculing, sometimes complementing, but beyond these effects it gives proof of the linguistic availability of the original to the parodist. When commandeered by radical propagandists parody may become an act of linguistic acquisition and simultaneous subversion.

Hone developed a sophisticated understanding of the social basis of religious and judicial parody which reached beyond his explicitly political work. His 1824 publication *Ancient Mysteries Described* was an anthology consisting of excerpts from medieval pageants, mysteries, and miracle plays. The collection has a political edge; its inspiration is laid with consummate irony at the hands of Lord Ellenborough the Chief Justice, who interrupted Hone's defence during his second trial to inform him that 'the first scenic performances were mysteries or representations of incidents in holy writ'. Hone stresses both the parodic content of his material and its function as the common people's appropriation of the language and myth of the Bible. His own research is described as an act of linguistic liberation 'violating step after step, the circumscription by which the aristocratic compasses were again and again, with reluctant extension to successive greater distances, defining the scope of the knowledge proper for a man of my condition'.[28]

Hone's view of parody as a form of linguistic appropriation and expansion practised by the people defines and explains his success as a political satirist. He appropriated earlier friendly radical satires and neutral social satires. Hone could read the trials of John Lilburne and use their parody of judicial form and ceremony as a framework for his own trials. As my first chapter demonstrates, the

---

[27] Smith, 1–35.
[28] William Hone, *Ancient Mysteries Described* (1824), p. ii. These words are footnoted by Hone as an ironic quotation from Foster.

satire of Hone and his imitators is saturated in the forms of Augustan
Grub Street parody—the mock advertisements, burlesque gallows
literature, and phoney almanacs produced by literary minnows and
whales alike in the first decades of the eighteenth century. Hone took
up and developed the parodic experiments of satirists over the preceding century. His works include reworkings of Defoe's parodic
hymns and poems. Wilkes's parodies of religious forms, and the whole
range of Thomas Spence's imitations and travesties, whether of
children's books, biblical texts, or the national coinage.

Most importantly of all Hone could see sources for parody in
society at large, both in the tastes of the poor and in the way the
privileged classes expressed their power. Any institution or social
ceremony could become a parodic vehicle. In this area his association
with Cruikshank was vital. Funerary monuments, public statuary,
public buildings, coats of arms, and the language and ceremony of
Church and court were all grist to Hone and Cruikshank's mill.

Undoubtedly their greatest asset was the Prince Regent himself.
Once he had abandoned the Foxite Whigs, his corpulence, his tastes,
his habits, his disastrous marriage, his spectacular amours with married mistresses nearly as vast as himself, and his increasing
inhabitation of a fantasy realm which found its concrete embodiment
in the bizarre Brighton Pavilion, had moved the Regent so far towards
self-parody that it was difficult for the radicals to know how to
approach him. 'Prinny' was metamorphosed into a bewildering variety of forms. Cruikshank's prints alone present him as, among other
things, Henry VIII, an enormous baby, a whale, Apollo, a cannon, a
green bag, a night-watchman, Guy Fawkes, a load of cat's meat, a
teapot, and a Chinese mandarin.[29] The Brighton Pavilion could not
be seen for what it was but only in terms of what it parodied. For
Cobbett it was 'a little Kremlin'; for Hazlitt, stone pepperpots and
pumpkins; Sydney Smith saw unnatural architectural procreation:
'the Dome of St Pauls went down to Brighton and Pupped'.[30] Hone
and Cruikshank went further: the Prince and his building become one
and the same—a Teapot (Fig. 1):

> The queerest of all the queer sights I've set sight on;—
> Is, that *what d'ye-call'-t thing*, here, THE FOLLY at Brighton

---

[29] *BMC*, nos. 11877, 12041, 12746, 12800, 13735, 13764, 13843. William Hone,
The Queen's Matrimonial Ladder (London, 1820), B8^v, C1^r, C4^r, D1^v.

[30] These examples and others appear in J. H. Plumb, 'The Brighton Pavilion', in
Men and Places (London, 1966), 106.

FIG. 1. George Cruikshank. Wood engraving. THE JOSS AND HIS FOLLY
(C4ᵛ). For *The Queen's Matrimonial Ladder*. 1820.

A living teapot stands, one arm held out,
One bent ; the handle this, and that the spout.
Rape of the Lock.

FIG. 2. George Cruikshank. Wood engraving. THE JOSS AND HIS FOLLY
(D1ᵛ). For *The Queen's Matrimonial Ladder*. 1820.

The outside huge teapots, all drill'd round with holes,
Relieved by Extinguishers, sticking on poles:
The inside—all tea things and dragons, and bells,
The show rooms—all show, the sleeping rooms—cells.
But the grand curiosity's not to be seen—
The owner himself—an old fat MANDARIN;
A patron of painters who copy designs,
That grocers and tea dealers hang up for signs
Hence teaboard taste artists gain rewards and distinction
Hence his title of 'TEAPOT' shall last to extinction
I saw his great chair into which he falls—*soss*—
And sits in his CHINA SHOP, like a large JOSS,
His manikins round him in tea tray array,
His pea hens beside him to make him seem gay.[31]

Produced within a year of the Peterloo massacre this is as much a satire on taste, or the lack of it, as a reformist's assault on a corrupt government. Hone uses the elaborate new ritual of Regency England, tea-drinking, and the advertising surrounding its sale and consumption, as the basis for extended parody, although Hone's association of the Regent with tea would also have had a political edge. Because of the tax on it tea was a politically charged substance at this time; radicals were marketing alternatives such as Orator Hunt's 'Radical Breakfast Powder'.[32] The Pavilion is a huge but functionless teapot. Full of holes it cannot contain what it should. What it does contain is more tea things, and pictures painted in the style of tea advertisements; the whole interior is a china shop, the servants are set out in 'tea tray array', the Prince himself is a TEAPOT. The satire ends with a Popeian vision of a world where the objects of fashion have become animated, and beneath Cruikshank's plate of the Regent transformed into a teapot is a quotation from *The Rape of the Lock*: 'A living teapot stands, one arm held out, One bent; the handle this and that the spout' (Fig. 2). The Popeian qualities of the satire extend into a general assault on the false taste of the age. The Regent is attacked not in the direct terms of Painite anti-monarchism but on what he considered his home ground—fashion and aesthetics. Pampered, over-elaborate, joyless, and above all un-English, the Pavilion and its creator are a disgrace.

[31] Hone, *The Queen's Matrimonial Ladder*, D1^r.
[32] For the sudden increase in tea consumption and the development of the tea-drinking ceremony and advertising, see Dan Cruikshank and Neil Burton, *Life in the Georgian City* (London, 1990), 27–31, 42, 43, 45.

In the way it combines high and low publishing, literature and advertising, image and text, caricature and illustration, this little satire highlights the diverse qualities which gave Hone and Cruikshank's publications such appeal. They constantly incorporate developments from the commercialization of leisure industries and a working knowledge of new advertising techniques. There is also a tone of civilized urbanity, an ability to approach politics obliquely and jauntily, to embarrass the King and the government by taking a moral middle ground rather than some extreme political high ground. Hone delights in meeting his opponents rather closer to half way than they would like. As we shall see he had the common touch but only when he wanted it.

I

Advertising, Politics, and Parody
1710–1780

ADVERTISING occupied a significant place in popular print culture by the second decade of the eighteenth century. Its growth in the press had not been seriously hampered by the 1712 Stamp Act. By June of 1720 the investment frenzy which directly preceded the collapse of the South Sea Company had led to big increases in advertising, and the extravagantly competitive market inspired formal experimentation.[1] As the century progressed advertising came to occupy an increasing amount of space in newspapers. The harsh tax increases of 1725 had the immediate effect of causing several papers to close down, but the idea of advertising in the press was firmly established and, despite their cost, advertisements began to dominate in surviving papers. During the 1730s the dailies would commonly devote 50 per cent of their space to advertisements.[2]

Advertising outside the press was developed on a mass scale in the first half of the eighteenth century. The earliest agencies, or as they were termed 'registers', were set up to organize the collection and distribution of advertisements. Book trade advertising developed many of the techniques now associated with 'hard sell'—money back and quality guarantees, sales representatives, and so on.[3] Entrepreneurs such as John Newberry, the owner of the most prolific children's book publishing company of the century, and later George Packwood, the self-styled 'celebrated razor strop maker', organized individual publicity campaigns, the scale and

---

[1] Bruttini, 9–14.
[2] Stanley A. Morison, *The English Newspaper* (Cambridge, 1935), 159–201; R. Munter, *The History of the Irish Newspaper* (Cambridge, 1967), 57–66; Presbrey, 74–9; Bruttini, 11.
[3] Raven, 61–6.

nature of which were new.[4] Prints and print satires, from the time of Sir Robert Walpole onwards, reveal that posters, handbills, and placards were pasted and hung all over the capital.[5]

In terms of its volume, its language, and its physical make-up, advertising provided new models, and even suggested new methods, for satirists prepared to use them.[6] Advertising parodies were soon commonly used in the political propaganda surrounding election campaigns and political scandals. They appear frequently in the satires that proliferated following the South Sea Bubble disclosures.[7] Various types of satire formally based on advertisements were a central weapon in the personal wars of Grub Street from as early as the 1720s.

The development of new advertising methods in the period 1710–80 had an immediate and lasting impact on political propaganda. Agitators and satirists adopted and parodied many forms of advertisement, and this propaganda was, in its turn, used and developed by subsequent radical satirists in the period 1790–1820. The widespread use of the new advertising technologies in the 1784 Westminster election, and most significantly during various stages of the Wilkes affair, demonstrated the effectiveness with which political proselytizing could be married to the devices of commercial puffing.

Mainstream political and literary authors including Defoe, Swift, Addison, Pope, the Fieldings, Dr Johnson, Wilkes, and Junius

[4] John Pendred, *The Earliest Directory of the Book Trade*, ed. with intro. by Graham Pollard (London, 1955), pp. ix–xxiii; Elliott, 58–90; D. and G. Hindley, *Advertising in Victorian England 1837–1901* (London, 1972), 32–40; Wood, 71–86, 113–19; George Packwood, *Packwood's Whim* (London, 1796); C. Welsh, *John Newbery: A Bookseller of the Last Century* (London, 1885), 107–15; Presbrey, 76–8; G. J. Kolb, 'John Newbery, Projector of the Universal Chronicle: A Study of the Advertisments', *SB* 11 (1958), 249–52: J. D. C. Buck, 'The Motives of Puffing: John Newberry's Advertisements', *SB* 30 (1977), 196–210. The most detailed discussion of Packwood's advertising campaigns is Neil McKendrick, 'George Packwood and the Commercialization of Shaving', in Neil McKendrick, John Brewer, and J. H. Plumb (eds.), *The Birth of a Consumer Society* (London, 1982), 146–97.
[5] *BMC*, nos. 1807, 8981, 10727, 11047, 11441; T. R. Nevett, *Advertising in Britain* (London 1982), 16–27.
[6] Johnson, 201–7; C. Bradshaw, 'An Infamous Typographer', *Printing News* 1957, 15–17; Vincent Figgins, *Vincent Figgins: Type Specimens 1801–1805*, ed. with intro. by B. Wolpe (London, 1967); S. A. Morison, *Politics and Script* (Oxford, 1972), 327–31.
[7] T. Wright, *Caricature History of the Georges* (London, 1865), 41–59. Also, George William Reid, *Catalogue of Prints and Drawings in the British Museum. Division 1: Political and Personal Satires*, ii (London, 1870), nos. 1625, 1627–9, 1636, 1638, 1651, 1664, 1690, 1700, 1711, 1713.

analysed and experimented with advertising in a variety of contexts. An analysis of this material provides one way of uncovering the relationship between advertising and political satire in the eighteenth century. Another way is to look at the impact of advertising on visual satire. The rise of the satiric print in the latter half of the eighteenth century is closely related both in formal and economic terms to the rise of advertising forms outside the press. Hogarth's attitudes to and use of advertising provide a convenient focus for the study of this area. Hogarth trained as a commercial engraver and brought out satiric advertising throughout his career. He used advertising campaigns to further his aesthetic and political battles and incorporated advertising forms such as the shop sign into the didactic structure of his work.

The critical insight of the early eighteenth century into the language and mechanisms of advertisements, and into their potential as a resource for satire, was considerable. Joseph Addison's essay on press advertising appeared in September 1710 and in it Addison lays bare the subversive and potentially anarchic effects which the forms and rhetoric of press advertising had on other types of journalism.[8]

Addison's essay raises issues which have a direct relevance for the practical experiments of his contemporaries and also for later satirists who used advertising. The essay opens:

It is my custom, in a dearth of news, to entertain myself with those collections of advertisements that appear at the end of all our public prints. These I consider as accounts of news from the little world, in the same manner that the foregoing parts of the paper are from the great. If in one we hear that a sovereign prince is fled from his capital city, in the other we hear of a tradesman who hath shut up his shop, and run away. If in one we find the victory of a general, in the other we see the desertion of a private soldier. (*Tatler*, iii. 166)

Addison articulates through a series of striking juxtapositions the reductive capacity of advertisements. There is a paradox, of which the author seems only half aware. While he stresses the distinction between the 'great' and 'little' worlds the very pairing of victorious general and deserting private, or of runaway tradesman and sovereign prince, subverts this division. The formal make-up of the papers of his day enforced the blending of social strata. Journals

---

[8] The essay has been referred to in every major history of English advertising: Presbrey, 64–8; Elliott, 104–7; Turner, 25–7; Wood, 37–41. All these critics are seduced by the whimsical tone of the original and have not considered how Addison reveals the violent and ironic dialogue which advertising had set up with literature.

could be divided as much as half-and-half in terms of the space devoted respectively to news and advertisements.[9] As Addison's reactions suggest, in a 'dearth of news' the advertisements would assume a more dominant position.

Addison takes his interest in juxtaposition of great and small further: 'An advertisement from Piccadilly goes down to posterity with an article from Madrid; and John Bartlet of Goodman's fields is celebrated in the same paper with the Emperor of Germany. Thus the fable tells us that the wren mounted as high as the eagle by getting upon his back' (*Tatler*, iii. 166). The concluding fable presents a reassuring vision where the insignificant has been raised to prominence through a lucky association with the great. Addison attempts to impose a reassuring elegance on the pairing of high and low, yet this seemly conclusion is undermined by earlier statements. The sentence 'An advertisement from Piccadilly goes down to posterity with an article from Madrid' articulates a bibliographical fact. Both elements appear in the same ink and type and on the same piece of paper—press advertisement has levelled them.

Advertising is not passive, as Addison's fabular conclusion so gracefully implies, but actively disruptive. Indeed throughout the eighteenth and into the nineteenth century advertisement provided a popular forum for public argument and Addison addresses this issue when he complains that 'above half the advertisements which one meets nowadays are purely polemical'. The controversies between rival advertisers created an arena in which new techniques of propaganda developed. The similarities between the advertising campaigns of rival haberdashers or razor-strop makers and those of politicians in later eighteenth century election campaigns are significant.[10]

Addison's understanding of the rhetorical strategies of advertisers comes out in his discussion of style: 'I must not pass over in silence an advertisement which has lately made its appearance, and is written altogether in a Ciceronian manner. It was sent to me, with five shillings, to be inserted among my advertisements; but as it is a pattern of good writing in this way, I shall give it a place in the body of my paper' (*Tatler*, iii. 166–7). Addison makes an identification between his own style and that of this advertisement through the gesture of absorbing it into 'the body of my paper'. Addison is, of course, flattered by the way the advertisement mimics the style

---

[9] See Morison, *The English Newspaper*, 123–57.
[10] See Bond's notes in *Tatler*, iii. 166–7.

which he had popularized, but this only emphasizes the protean nature of advertising language. Any popular form can be assumed if it is thought that it can effectively sell the product. Addison continues, however, by setting up this advertisement as a standard of excellence against which other advertising is to be condemned:

At the same time that I recommend the several flowers in which this spirit of lavender is wrapped up ... I cannot excuse my fellow labourers for admitting into their papers several uncleanly advertisements, not at all proper to appear in the works of polite writers. Among these I must reckon the Carminative Wind-expelling Pills. If the doctor had called them only his carminative pills, he had been as cleanly as one could have wished; but the second word entirely destroys the decency of the first. (*Tatler*, iii. 170)

The prescriptive attitude highlights Addison's stylistic rigidity. The terms in which he attempts to impose a linguistic norm upon advertisements raises the fascinating possibility that the linguistic resources which advertising was prepared to draw upon were richer than those of Addison's proper literary style. The advertisement for pills uses the latinate medical term 'carminative' and then immediately renders the colloquial English translation 'wind-expelling'. The method has similarities with Shakespeare's frequent 'translations' from one register to another as in, 'multitudinous seas incarnadine, making the green one red'. Addison's good taste is restrictive and allows only the first term in the advertisement any legitimacy. It is a final irony that the *OED* cites Addison's quotation of this advertisement as the first use of the word carminative outside a specifically medical context. Addison has gone down to posterity as the author of a compound which he singled out for its tastelessness.

Despite his attempts to impose a linguistic standard on advertising, Addison had an unusual understanding both of its essentially heterogeneous nature and of its unique economic position in the publishing world: 'a collection of advertisements is a kind of miscellany; the writers of which, contrary to all authors, except men of quality, give money to the booksellers who publish their copies. The genius of the bookseller is chiefly shown in his method of ranging and digesting these little tracts' (*Tatler*, iii. 170). The jesting comparison between the stylistic freedom enjoyed by both gentlemen and advertisers uncovers a vital truth: the authors of advertisements had paid for the privilege of writing in any manner they pleased. Advertisers borrowed or parodied anything which would help to sell the product. Addison's insight in fact anticipates Stanley Morison's analysis of the econ-omics of press advertising.[11]

When Dr Johnson came to consider advertising, as he did quite frequently in his journalism,[12] he was writing some fifty years after Addison, during the period when newspapers were starting to become dependent on advertising. Methods of copywriting had become psychologically sophisticated using techniques based on in-timidation, snobbery, and paradox. Johnson reacts in detail to these methods in *The Idler*, 40, ironically underlining the claims of adver-tisers who 'know the prejudice of mankind in favour of honest sincerity'. He lays bare the manipulation of sentiment and fear: 'The true pathos of advertisements must have sunk deep into the heart of every man that remembers the zeal shewn by the seller of the anodyne necklace, for the ease and safety "of poor toothing infants", and the affection with which he warned every mother, that "she would never forgive herself" if her infant should perish without a necklace' (*Idler*, 40: 126).

Johnson adopts a probationary tone towards the new industry, which he takes as an established part of journalism and public life: 'The trade of advertising is now so near to perfection, that it is not easy to propose any improvement. But as every art ought to be exer-cised in due subordination to the publick good, I cannot but propose it as a moral question to these masters of the publick ear, whether they do not sometimes play too wantonly with our passions' (*Idler*, 40: 127). Assuming a degree of irony the passage is still remarkable in implying that advertising can be seen in terms of its own history and that it develops according to the laws of art and aesthetics—even aspiring towards the ideal. As his discussion develops, however, Johnson displays an increasing uneasiness with regard to how adver-tisement may be categorized and controlled. His worried question 'whether the advertising controvertists do not indulge in asperity of language without any adequate provocation' leads into the general question of how advertising deploys language emotionally to its own ends. Its moral content does not affect its persuasiveness, a fact of great import for later political propagandists.

The extent to which advertising was beginning to assert itself on the literary and journalistic scene of Johnson's day comes out clearly

[11] Stanley A. Morison, *The History of* The Times: '*The Thunderer in the Making*', *1785–1841* (London, 1935), 14.
[12] *Idler*, 7, 12, 40; *Rambler*, 105.

in the experiments of Henry and his blind brother John Fielding to set up the Universal Register Office. This was intended to be a centralized London agency combining the functions of employment centre, estate agent, travel office, and exchange market. The scheme was launched with a substantial campaign involving the publication of thousands of letters, plans, and hand-outs. When Phillip D'Halhuin set up a competing enterprise, the Public Register Office, a bitter campaign was conducted in the press with the Fieldings resorting to 'asperity of language' in the form of crude and xenophobic assertions. The affair had a direct effect on the literary output of Henry Fielding, for his last sustained effort at periodical journalism, *The Covent Garden Journal*, was motivated by a desire to help the Register Office during a period of crisis.

The Fieldings' experiment inspired Johnson to his most deeply felt response to the arrival of the advertising industry, *The Rambler*, 105. Johnson's essay opens with a utopian vision of the ultimate advertising agency: 'A place where every exuberance may be discharged, and every deficiency supplied, where every lawful passion may find its gratifications ... where the stock of a nation, pecuniary and intellectual, may be brought together, and where all conditions of humanity may hope to find relief' (*Rambler*, 105: 195). Johnson parodies a passage from Henry Brookes's *The Fool of Quality*, a widely sold defence of the new eighteenth-century trading class: 'The merchant ... is he who furnishes every comfort, convenience, elegance of life; who carries off every redundance, who fills every want, who ties country to country, clime to clime'.[13] Beyond this specific context, Johnson looks back to a tradition of philanthropic thought which had long envisaged such an institution. The Fieldings' was the latest practical manifestation of a series of grand schemes which begins with Montaigne and continues via Theophrastus Renadaut into English Projectors such as Samuel Hartlib.[14] Johnson goes on to present a satiric dream vision in which he imagines himself inside such a universal registry and proceeds to use this framework to attack the abuses of contemporary advertising. The first figure

[13] Quoted in Raven, 87–8.
[14] For Johnson's references to the Fieldings' Register, see Bate's notes to *Rambler*, 105, in *The Yale Edition of the Works of Samuel Johnson*, ed. W. J. Bate and Albrecht B. Strauss, 8 vols. (New Haven, Conn., 1969), iii. 105. The history of the concept of a universal registry is laid out in Henry Fielding, *The Covent Garden Journal, and A Plan of the Universal Register Office*, ed. Bertrand A. Goldgar (Oxford, 1988), pp. xv–xxviii. See also Elliott, 120, 133, 134–5.

Johnson meets is 'shaking a weighty purse' and turns out, perhaps predictably, to be a patron. On finding, however, that he can only be registered as such on condition that he should 'never suffer himself to be flattered, never delay an audience ... and that he should never encourage followers without intending to reward them' he refuses and 'is posted upon the gate among cheats, robbers and public nuisances'. Johnson proceeds to attack in a similar vein most common forms of contemporary advertisement: there are inventions such as miraculous telescopes, vehicles for surviving floods, quack medicines, and the tale of a miser who marries late and advertises a lack of children. The contrast between a benevolent ideal of trade and its reality in the greed and deceptions of the *nouveaux riches* is central to a variety of late eighteenth-century literature.[15] Johnson attacks the way advertising uses fantasies and panders to fear, greed, and envy. It was, however, these very qualities which were to make advertising forms such attractive vehicles for social and political satires. The majority of advertising forms which Johnson isolates had been popular in various parodic forms since the 1720s. These early eighteenth-century experiments established both a publishing background and a set of models for subsequent political and social satire.

The Spectator, 547, demonstrates the familiarity of polite society with the strategies of the advertisers. This issue was given over to a series of parodies in which essays of Addison's from former editions of the paper are presented as quack advertisements. The introductory paragraph states that the parodies were written as an amusement by a 'private assembly of wits of both sexes' and sent in to Addison. Again advertising forms have been subsumed into the main body of the journal. The correspondent's introduction states that 'everyone in the Company retired, and writ down in the Stile and Phrase of the like Ingenious Compositions, which we frequently meet with at the end of our News Papers'. The parodies underline the versatility of advertising language, its ability to adopt a sentimental tone or an elegant locution very much in the Addisonian manner. Their style and tone are, in Addison's terms, respectable.[16] The parodic exploitation of coarser and more sensational advertising forms can be found in the broadside and pamphlet wars of Grub Street. The formal variety of advertising, its eclecticism, and

[15] Raven, 82–112.
[16] *The Spectator*, ed. Donald F. Bond, 5 vols. (Oxford, 1965), iv. 459–60.

its lack of literary pretension made it peculiarly suitable raw material for the framing of inflammatory personal attacks unconstrained by notions of literary propriety.

Daniel Defoe used advertising in a number of different ways to further his political and personal battles. His vast pamphlet and broadside output reveals him to have been an inspired self-publicist. One of his earliest and boldest experiments in this line was *A Hymn to the Pillory*.[17] This pamphlet satire was hawked about to the crowds while Defoe served his sentence on the pillory for having angered Queen Anne with the pamphlet *The Shortest Way With Dissenters*. The use of popular journalism to celebrate his own trial and punishment anticipates the methods of late eighteenth- and early nineteenth-century radicalism. Horne Tooke, Thomas Hardy, Thomas Spence, Daniel Isaac Eaton, William Cobbett, Henry Hunt, Robert Wedderburn, Richard Carlile, and of course William Hone, all brought out popular publications in connection with their trials.

In his ability to move between different areas of publishing, in his willingness to use many forms considered ephemeral or lowbrow, in his awareness of contemporary whims or crazes, and in his experiments with the literature of crime, Defoe was in many ways an important forerunner of William Hone. Defoe also anticipated Hone in using advertising in a variety of ways in his political journalism. Hone for his part was intimately familiar with Defoe's work.[18]

Unlike Addison, Defoe had no rules about the rigid separation of advertising from the main text of his journal. He often used the advertisement section in his *Review* to develop, unexpectedly, political debate. Sometimes he would head his advertisement section with a notice of his own directed at an enemy. Advertisements attack such various subjects as the price of bread, the Suffolk justices for interfering with army recruitment, and Dr Sacheverell, and there is even one addressed to the 'street gentry', in which he tells the mob of the Queen's support for the clergy. There are several long advertisements concerning himself which combine the functions of political

[17] Presbrey, 62–3; also F. Bastian, *Defoe's Early Life* (London, 1981), 32–40; Daniel Defoe, *A Hymn to the Pillory* (London, 1703).

[18] Hone published a heavily reworked version of Defoe's satiric epic *Jure Divino* in 1821, under the title *The Right Divine of Kings to Govern Wrong*. He was also an enthusiastic reader of Defoe's *A Review* (repr. as *Defoe's Review*, 22 vols. (New York, 1938)) and approved of him as a journalist. The title-page of Hone's pamphlet *The Political Showman—at Home!* carries a prefatory quotation from Defoe's introduction to the first issue of *A Review*: 'To exalt virtue, expose vice, promote truth, and help men to serious reflection, is my first moving cause, and last directed end.'

diatribe and genuine commercial advertising. They commonly begin with attempts to clear both the author and the journal of scandalous charges and end with a listing of new sales outlets.[19]

Defoe's satiric use of advertising reached a climax in his response to the attacks made upon him in *The Observator*. His initial response was an advertisement in the form of a beast fable. This concerns a noble mastiff, Defoe's *Review*, which is 'insulted continually by a little whiffling yelping Cur', *The Observator*. The parable ends with the mastiff confronting the little dog 'and finding him not worth his Anger, tho' he could have torn him in pieces at one Gripe, lifted up his Leg, piss'd upon him, and went in-a-doors'. This coarse but homely parody was then followed up with a series of mock advertisements designed to be inserted in *The Observator* in which Defoe attempts to clear himself of the charge that he is a bankrupt and that no one will trust him with a shilling.[20]

The energy and ingenuity with which Defoe used advertisements in satire was not unique at this period. Among Pope's literary enemies there were several who used the genre with malicious commitment. Perhaps the most inventive was the notorious publisher, plagiarist, and libeller Edmund Curll. Curll had been the victim of a particularly elaborate and cruel practical joke of Pope's. Having arranged a meeting Pope slipped an emetic into Curll's glass and then produced a pamphlet, *A Full and true Account of a Horrible Revenge by Poison on the Body of Edmund Curll*, detailing its effects.[21] Pope was to be dogged by Curll's bitter retributive campaigns over the next thirty years. He used pamphlets, broadsides, handbill lampoons, and even republished obscene poetry of Pope's which the author would rather have forgotten. He made 'Pope's Head' the title of his shop and hung a sign outside it showing a caricatured head to celebrate what he considered a great victory over Pope—the publishing of his plagiarized letters.[22]

[19] For the Suffolk justices, see Defoe, *A Review*, 154 (26 Dec. 1706), 616. For Sacheverell, *A Review*, 47 (13 July 1710), 184; also 51 (22 July 1710), 199. For the Queen, *A Review*, 146 (14 Mar. 1710), 583. For advertisements concerning himself, *A Review*, 149 (21 Mar. 1710), 596, and 184 (16 May 1710); also 2nd Ser., 2 (12 Jan. 1711), 83–4.

[20] *A Review*, 2nd ser., 120 (29 Dec. 1711), 484; 2nd series, 123 (5 Jan. 1712), 495–6.

[21] The biographical background has been treated in detail by several scholars: Sherburn, 162–85; B. Dobrée, *Alexander Pope* (London, 1951), 59–60; R. Halsband, 'Pope, Lady Mary, and the Court Poems', *PMLA* 68 (1953), 237–50; Ault, pp. xliv–xlx; Mack, 294–6.

[22] Mack, 653–7.

Curll launched a sustained attack on Pope's edition of Homer spearheaded by a series of savage advertisements. Pope's translation appeared not long after the Preston rebels had been tried and when anti-Catholic feeling was running particularly high.[23] In 1716 *The Flying Post* carried a long advertisement in the following style:

> This Day is publish'd, The second part of Mr. Pope's POPISH Translation of Homer ... N.B. Mr. Pope has translated one Verse of *Homer* thus: The *Priest* can pardon, and the God appease. Next Week will be publish'd An Excellent New Ballad call'd *The Catholick Poet*, or Protestant *Barnaby's Lamentation*. To the Tune of, *which nobody can deny*.[24]

The Flying Post carried another advertisement, part of which read:

> To prevent any further Imposition on the Publick, there is now preparing for the Press by several Hands, Homer Defended: Being a Detection of the many Errors committed by Mr. *Pope*, in his pretended translation of *Homer*.[25]

Curll invited contributions from anyone who wished to defame Pope. The project, if serious, never bore fruit, but indicates Curll's ruthless approach. A letter of Gay's gives further evidence of Curll's pre-eminence in the field of advertising directed against Pope: 'All I could hear of you [Pope] of late hath been by advertisements in news-papers, by which one wou'd think the race of Curls was multiplied; and by the indignation that such fellows show against you, that you have more merit than any body alive could have.'[26]

For his part Pope appears to have been careful to play down the extent of his engagement with Grub Street satires, including parodic advertisements. Pope was publicly dismissive of advertising. He produced a lengthy critique of the style of contemporary newspapers in *The Spectator*, 452, which included the following discussion of the subject: 'Men who frequent Coffee-houses, and delight in News, are pleased with everything that is Matter of Fact ... They read the Advertisements with the same interest and Curiosity as the Articles of Public News; and are as pleased to hear of a Pye-bald Horse that is strayed out of a field near Islington, as of a whole Troop that has been engaged in any Foreign Adventure.'[27] On one level, that of his public criticism, Pope clearly regarded advertisements as not worthy

[23] Sherburn, 173.   [24] *Flying Post* (7 Apr. 1716).
[25] Ibid. (10 Apr. 1716).
[26] John Gay, 2 Aug. 1728, letter 53 of *The Letters of John Gay*, ed. C. F. Burgess (Oxford, 1966), 77.
[27] Ault, 56.

of serious attention. His attitude does, however, reveal his insight into their potential as a vehicle for satire. He corroborates Addison's attitude, drawing attention to the fact that, simply by existing alongside reports of major events, advertisements can achieve an intrusive significance.

Pope's piece in *The Spectator* demands the restitution of order and propriety to the contents of newspapers, an attitude which is close to that of Addison. He concludes, none the less, with a series of parodic proposals for the content of a newspaper and these demonstrate his expertise in the methods of contemporary advertising copy. He suggests items of intelligence which mimic the style of information columns. The trick is to raise the reader's curiosity by appearing to withhold information, while in fact having nothing to say: 'By my last Advices from *Knights-bridge* I hear that a Horse was clapped into the Pound on the third Instant, and that he was not released when the Letters came away ... They advise from *Fulham*, that things remained there in the same State they were. They had Intelligence just as the Letters came away of a Tub of excellent Ale just set abroach at Parson's Green; but this wanted confirmation.'[28]

The majority of Pope's early pamphlets mimic various types of popular literature and incorporate a wide range of advertising forms. The earliest of these is *A Critical Specimen* of 1711, a mock publisher's specimen advertising a forthcoming folio. *The Narrative of Doctor Robert Norris* appeared in 1713 and masquerades as the announcement of a real quack doctor to clear his name. In 1716 Pope produced *A Full and True Account of a Revenge by Poison on the Body of Edmund Curll* in mimicry of the style of contemporary murder pamphlets. He followed up later that year with *A Further Account of the Deplorable Condition of Mr. Edmund Curll*.

These works may be considered as a group of prose experiments which explore the formal and linguistic aspects of the early eighteenth-century gutter press, especially as they manifested themselves in various forms of advertising. Pope's early prose satires are unashamedly coarse and absorb the forms of street literature upon which they are based with delighted gusto and great precision. Scholarly interest in these publications has been restricted to the light they cast upon Pope's biography, or on the background to the poems. Even recent discussions, such as those of Pat Rogers and W. Kinsley, which treat the Grub Street context of Pope's pamphlet

[28] Ault, 57–8.

satires, do not locate or examine the popular models which Pope was parodying.[29]

Pope's first published prose was the pamphlet *A Critical Specimen.* His immediate motive for writing it was to avenge the attacks upon himself and his work in John Dennis's *Reflections Critical and Satirical Upon a Late Rhapsody Called an Essay Upon Criticism.* The *Critical Specimen* takes the form of a four-page preface followed by a digest of a proposed quixotic romance. The subtitle, *A Specimen of A Treatise in Folio, to be printed by Subscription,* draws attention to the model. Pope constructed his parody with great attention to the details of genuine publisher's prospectuses.

Because of their ephemeral nature only a small number of publishing prospectuses have survived from this period; it is consequently not possible to tell in what volume they were being produced. The great increase, however, in the process of publishing books by subscription at the beginning of the eighteenth century would suggest that the numbers were considerable, and they were written according to certain formulas. The most common word describing these publications was 'proposal', although 'address', 'prospective', and 'specimen' were also used. The title would then normally be followed by a set of conditions which were set out as a guide and a guarantee for prospective subscribers.[30] This would be followed by a list of final short advertisements. Several of these elements are incorporated into Pope's *Critical Specimen.* He discusses the terms for subscription in realistic detail: 'It will be publish'd either by single Chapters, or in the whole, as the Majority of Subscribers shall be pleased to Appoint; who are desir'd to pay half a Guinea down, and the other half when the Book is delivered. The Author gives Notice, that when his Subscriptions are full, he will (like most of his Contemporaries) begin the Work.'[31] He then gives a list of contents, which constitutes the meat of the satire, and ends with a set of short bookseller's advertisements.

While adopting several of the common features of publisher's prospectuses in general the *Critical Specimen* travesties a quite specific type of publisher's advertisement. Pope's second title-page runs, 'A /

[29] See Pat Rogers, *Hacks and Dunces* (London, 1980); Rogers, *Grub Street: Studies in a Subculture* (London, 1972); also W. Kinsley, 'The Dunciad as Mock Book', in J. A. Wynn and W. Kinsley (eds.), *Pope: Recent Essays by Several Hands,* (Hamden, 1964).

[30] John Feather (ed.), *Book Prospectuses before 1801 in the John Johnson Collection* (Oxford, 1976).

[31] Ault, 7–8.

SPECIMEN / OF / A Treatise in *Folio*, to be printed by Subscription, /
ENTITULED, / *The Mirror of Criticisme*: / OR, / The History of the
Renown'd *Rinaldo Furioso*, Critick of the Woful Countenance'.
'Specimen' was an uncommon title for publisher's prospectuses and
was conventionally used to describe those advertising translations of
epic poems. These included specimens of the translations in a parallel text.[32] Typical titles run *Specimen for a translation of the third book of
Tasso's Jerusalem, Proposals for Publishing a Translation of Virgil's Aeneids in
blank verse. Together with a Specimen, A Specimen; consisting of extracts and
episodes from a poem called Gideon; of the restoration of Israel.* Pope's parody
adopted all the salient features of this type of advertisement: the pair
of title words, the provision of alternative titles, the synopsis, and the
provision of specimens of verse.

Pope turns the grandiose associations of his model to cruel
account. After discounting the notion of treating the subject—the
life and career of Dennis—in the form of a blank-verse epic, he
proposes a romance inspired by *Don Quixote*. He then gives a synopsis
of the entire contents of this work which reduces Dennis's life to the
space of a few sentences. The satiric potential latent in the process of
narrative compression is carefully exploited. Some of the chapters
are merely one-liners aimed at Dennis's ignorance and recent
failures on the London stage:

> *Chapter 6*
> How the *Critick* read *Milton* Backward.
> *Chapter 10*
> How he wrote a Dialogue, which he fancied to be a Comedy.
> *Chapter 12*
> Of the Critick's *mortal* aversion to the *Catt call*.[33]

The final chapter acts out the death of Dennis in much the same way
as Swift's *The Accomplishment of the First of Mr. Bickerstaff's Predictions* had
done for John Partridge: 'How, and what Year, Month, and Day,
the Critick is to dye, what Will he is to Make, and what dying Words
he shall utter, where, and by whom he is to be buried, and what
Funeral Orations and Elegies will be made upon him, with his Epitaph a Prophecy, by the *True Individual* Isaac Bickerstaff, *Esq.*'.[34]

---

[32] It does, however, appear quite regularly in several items listed in D. F. Foxon,
*English Verse 1700–1750: A Catalogue of Separately Printed Poems with Notes on Contemporary
Collected Editions*, 2 vols. (Cambridge, 1975), i, items, B 319, B 374, H 218; ii, items P
592, R 43, Y 105.
[33] Ault, 12–13.   [34] Ault, 17.

Pope focuses on the ceremonies surrounding death, and the printed matter which is generated in the forms of dying speeches, funeral sermons, elegies, epitaphs, and, of course, the self-congratulatory announcements of almanac-makers. This part of the work possesses a stark finality which reverberates beyond the personal satire. Society is shown as capable of responding to death primarily in terms of extravagant publicity.

It may well be that Pope set a fashion in literary circles for the use of the publisher's prospectus as a satiric vehicle. A year after his piece came out a similarly realistic parody appeared bearing the title *Proposals for Printing . . . A Treatise on the Art of Political Lying.*[35] This takes the form of a twenty-two-page pamphlet followed by two unnumbered pages of short parodic advertisements. The work opens by giving 'Proposals' for subscribers. There is then a synopsis of the proposed work consisting of pseudo-scientific classifications and quasi-philosophical analyses of the 'art of lying'. These travesty the style of a prospectus for a natural-science treatise.

Pope's experiments with mock advertisement were continued two years later in his next prose attack on Dennis, *The Narrative of Doctor Robert Norris*. The pamphlet is well known to have had its origins in the advertising campaigns of a genuine quack doctor of the day.[36] He had been advertising his miraculous cures of lunatics in several newspapers for about three years. Then in July 1713 he changed his address and advertised the move in a flurry of advertising in *The Daily Courant*, *The Post Boy*, and *The Guardian*:

Robert Norris, on Snow-hill, having had many Years Experience and good Success in the Cure of Lunatics, is removed to the Pestle and Mortar, near the middle of Hatton-Garden, where he hath a very convenient large House and Garden, Airy and fit to receive Persons of the best Rank of either Sex, with suitable Attendance. Any Person applying themselves as above, may there be satisfied, that the Cure shall be industriously endeavoured (and by God's blessing effected) on reasonable terms.[37]

On 28 July the following advertisement appeared in *The Post Boy*: 'The Narrative of Dr. *Robert Norris*, concerning the strange and deplorable Frenzy of Mr. *John Denn–s* ——, an Officer of the Custom

---

[35] This has been recently attributed to Pope's friend John Arbuthnot, and it was clearly popular since editions with both a London and an Edinburgh imprint have survived; see Feather (ed.), *Book prospectuses Before 1801 in the John Johnson Collection*, items I B09/31, I D02/32.

[36] Sherburn, 106–10.   [37] *Post Man* (25 Dec. 1713).

House: Being an exact account of all that pass'd betwixt the said Patient and the Doctor, till this present Day; and a full Vindication of himself and his Proceedings from the Extravagant Reports of the said *Mr. John Denn–s* ——'.[38] This was an advertisement for Pope's pamphlet using almost exactly the same wording that the title-page was to carry. The pamphlet purports to be an account by Norris of the insane conduct of Dennis. Pope's direct motive was a desire to avenge the attacks which Dennis had made on Addison's play *Cato*, although Pope no doubt still remembered Dennis's earlier criticisms of his own work.

The satiric method is again similar to that of Swift in the Bickerstaff pamphlets. Swift presents an outraged astrologer defending his honour and puffing his reputation: Pope adopts the persona of a quack in a similar predicament. Pope's satire is even bolder, for in adopting the name of a genuine doctor, and bringing out mock advertisements alongside Norris's real ones, truth and fiction become hilariously entangled.

Dennis's humiliations are described in the self-celebratory prose of the quack. The doctor affects a bogus medical jargon: 'If the Patient, on the third Day, have an Interval, suspend the Medicaments at Night; let Fumigations be used to Corroborate the Brain; I hope you have on no Account promoted Sternutation by Hellebore.' The parody draws on a rich popular tradition. Rochester's notorious success in the previous century in impersonating a mountebank inspired a glut of satirical prints on the theme of medical charlatanry, and print satires in the late eighteenth and early nineteenth centuries often attacked figures by presenting them as quacks.[39]

Pope criticized the disruptive and linguistically invasive aspects of advertising yet ingeniously exploited the phenomenon in pamphlet satires. A similar contradiction between theory and practice may be observed in Swift, who disapproved of advertisements and was particularly concerned about their relationship with the main text of newspapers. He discusses the issue at some length in a letter to *The Tatler*:

Those who were condemn'd to Death amongst the *Athenians*, were obliged to take a Dose of Poison, which made them die upwards, siezing first on

---

[38] *Post Boy* (28 July 1713).
[39] Elliott, 102–12; *BMC*, nos. 1406, 1689, 8821, 11916, 12267, 11549: Roy Porter, 'The Language of Quackery in England 1660–1800', in Peter Burke and Roy Porter (eds.), *The Social History of Language* (Cambridge, 1987), 73–95.

their Feet, making them cold and insensible, and so ascending gradually until it reached the Vital Parts. I believe your Death ... will fall out the same Way, and that your distemper hath already siez'd on you, and makes Progress daily. The Lower Part of you, that is, the *Advertisements*, is dead; and these have risen for these Ten Days last past, so that they now take up almost a whole Paragraph. Pray, Sir, do your Endeavour to drive this Distemper as much as possible to the extreme Parts for if it once gets into your stomach it will soon fly up into your Head, and you are a dead Man.[40]

For Swift there is an absolute division between the substance of advertisements and that of the main body of the paper. The metaphor of disease infecting and destroying a healthy form expresses a fear of the invasive capacity of advertising and a simultaneous recognition of its potency. Despite his adoption of a hostile stance towards advertising, and his erection of a theoretical division between it and the language of reputable journalism, Swift's recognition of the power of advertising is revealed in the different ways he used advertisement in his own satires. The form in which the Bickerstaff papers are set, that of the astrologer's almanac, is itself a form of popular advertising, and one which had been absorbed into political satire from the time of the Civil War.[41] Almanacs were remarkably popular in the early eighteenth century, and men such as Partridge were among the foremost puffers of their day. While Swift was sending the form up he was also harnessing the very power which such publications exerted over the reading public in order to get the serious aspects of his satire across.

The extent to which the almanac, and the almanac author, were enmeshed in the world of eighteenth-century advertising is both revealed and sent up in the pamphlet *An Account of the Proceedings of Isaac Bickerstaff Esq.* This piece of Partridgeana is a testament to both the versatility and the satiric energy of the form Swift had developed. In its final stages the pamphlet parodies Partridge's methods of self-advertisement. He is presented attempting to confirm his continued existence despite the announcements of his decease in Swift's earlier satires: 'Tho' I print Almanacs, and publish Advertisements; tho' I produce certificates under the Minister and Church Warden's Words, I am alive ... out comes A Full and true Account of the Death and Interment of John Partridge'. The forms of burlesque

---

[40] *Bickerstaff*, 236–7.
[41] James, *English Popular Literature*, 51–7; J. F. C. Harrison, *The Second Coming: Popular Millennarianism* (London, 1979), 45–52; John Lewis, *Printed Ephemera* (London, 1962), 58–63.

advertisement multiply. Partridge ends by announcing his own existence as a natural wonder of the age in the sales patter of a showman:
'Now can any Man of common sense think it consistent with the
Honour of my Profession ... to stand bawling before his own
Door—Alive! Alive! Ho! The famous Dr. *Partridge*! No Counterfeit
but all alive!—as if I had the twelve Celestial Monsters of the *Zodiac*
to show within.'[42] The pamphlet concludes with a bizarre advertisement in which Partridge identifies himself with Christ: 'and through
my side there is a wound given to all the Protestant Almanac-Makers
in the Universe'. The grotesque exaggerations of contemporary
advertising polemic are taken to the final extreme, the advertiser
becomes the Saviour. Yet this imagery is located in the religious
concerns which originally sparked off the Bickerstaff pamphlets. Not
only did Partridge coarsely and continually attack the High Church
but he and his fellow almanac writers appeared to Swift as a debased
popular surrogate for genuine religious feeling.[43]

Swift adopted a similar moral approach in his parodic use of other
forms of advertising. His contributions to *The Dublin Exhibition* for 4
and 18 January 1736 carried a lengthy 'ADVERTISEMENT For the
honour of the Kingdom of Ireland':

This *is to inform the Publick, that a Gentleman of long Study, Observation and Experi-
ence, hath employed himself for several Years in making Collections of Facts, relating to the
Conduct of* Divines, Physicians, Lawyers, Soldiers, Merchants, Traders, *and*
Squires, *containing, an Historical Account of the most remarkable* Corruptions,
Frauds, Oppressions, Knaveries *and* Perjuries; *wherein the names of all the Per-
sons concerned shall be inserted at full Length, with some Account of their Families and
Stations* ... It *is intended to be printed by Subscription in a large Octavo; each volume to
contain five hundred Facts, and to be sold for a* British Crown ... *Whoever shall send
the Author any Account of Persons who have performed any Acts of Justice, Charity,
Publick Spirit, Gratitude, Fidelity, or the like* ... the said facts shall be printed by
Way of *Appendix* at the End of each Volume ... But, lest such Persons may
apprehend, that the relating of such facts may be injurious to their Reputa-
tions, their names shall not be set down without particular Direction.[44]

Curll had used similar methods when he was compiling his edition of
Pope's letters. He put out a series of advertisements requesting his
readers to send in material with which he could attack Pope. Again
Swift is expressing his opinions on the corruption of society by

---

[42] *Bickerstaff*, 222–3.   [43] Ehrenpreis, ii. 197–202.
[44] Jonathan Swift, *Miscellaneous and Autobiographical Pieces*, ed. H. Davis (Oxford,
1962), 346–7.

adopting in a precise manner the conventions of a particular type of advertisement. He impeccably observes the exterior form of his model and it is only with the final comments on the appendix that he completely springs the trap.

Swift's attacks and hoaxes on individuals were almost always motivated by a desire to call attention to some serious social problem, the individual forming a convenient focal point for a general satire.[45] In his experiments with various sorts of popular publishing Swift anticipates, more precisely than Pope, the satiric methods of late eighteenth- and early nineteenth-century radicals such as Thomas Spence, Thomas Dolby, William Benbow, and William Hone.

In 1722 Swift produced a number of broadsides purporting to give *The Last Speech and Dying Words of Ebenezor Elliston*. These were probably hawked about beneath the gallows alongside the 'genuine' last speeches which the criminal had penned for the occasion of his execution. Swift's macabre broadside, and the accompanying satiric advertisements in the newspapers, were directed against a serious crime wave which Dublin was facing due to the desperate condition of large numbers of unemployed weavers. Swift observes the form of his model with great ingenuity and adopts thieves' cant and the sort of factual detail relating to the process of hanging which was typical of the gallows broadsheet. The parody, however, uses this familiarity with the conventions of the criminal world to bring home to a popular audience a series of contemporary crimes ranging from street robbery to informing for blood-money.[46]

Another example of Swift's adoption of a popular advertising medium for purposes of political satire is his pamphlet *The Wonder of all the Wonders that Ever the World Wondered At*. The title plays upon a word which Swift had clearly come to associate with the gutter press, for the fictional persona in his first Bickerstaff pamphlet describes himself 'seized upon by four interloping printers of Grub-Street, the title stuffed with the matter together with the standard epithets of Strange and Wonderful'.[47] *The Wonder of all the Wonders* is one of a series of squibs with which Swift attacked the project for establishing a national bank in Ireland. At the time when Swift composed his

[45] For the differing attitudes to social satire and to 'realism' in the black journalism of Pope and Swift, see Ronald Paulson, *The Fictions of Satire* (Baltimore, 1967), 150–62.

[46] G. P. Mayhew, 'Jonathan Swift's Hoax of 1722 upon Ebeneezor Elliston', in A. N. Jeffares (ed.), *Fair Liberty Was all his Cry* (London, 1967), 299–302, 307–8.

[47] *Bickerstaff*, 197.

satire the bill to establish the bank had already been rejected by both houses of the Irish parliament. The bankers, however, still possessed a royal charter for the project and were hunting around for subscribers. Swift's satires were aimed at burying a scheme which he believed would benefit only corrupt financiers.[48]

Swift parodies the broadsides which magicians and mountebanks handed out, listing the fantastic dangers which they apparently put themselves through during their performances. In Swift's advertisement, however, it is the spectators themselves who are performed upon. Each of the showman's tricks involves violent physical mutilation, although the victim is apparently unharmed:

HE takes a Person of Quality's Child, from two Years old to six, and lets the Child's own Father and Mother take a Pike in their Hands; then the Artist takes the Child in his Arms and tosses it upon the Point of the Pike, where it sticks, to the great Satisfaction of all the Spectators; and is then taken off without so much as an Hole in its Coat.[49]

A complicated relationship between the duped and the duper is articulated. There is an implicit criticism of the Irish people, who, as an enthralled audience, demonstrate a willingness to be practised upon amounting almost to complicity. The final and most damning implication is that it is the helpless children who will be the real victims of the parent's ruin. Swift's satire goes on to articulate the compulsive attraction which exotic financial schemes can exert on the victim's imagination through a prose that is intensely visual: 'With his Fore-finger and Thumb he thrusts several Gentlemen's and Lady's Eyes out of their Heads, without the least Pain; at which Time they see an unspeakable Number of beautiful Colours; and after they are entertained to the full, he places them again in their proper Sockets.'[50] Swift's fantasy relates to the effect whereby slight pressure on the eyes causes halations and abstract colour patterns to obscure the field of vision. The process of temporary painless blinding is developed into a brutal metaphor for the fraudulent activities of the bankers. Much of the effectiveness of the passage comes from the way Swift maintains the tones of mystery and exultation typical of the sales rhetoric of the mountebank.

Pope and Swift's experiments with advertising operate in a tradition that was essentially popular and anonymous. During the eighteenth and early nineteenth centuries there are many instances

[48] Ehrenpreis, iii. 158–65.   [49] *Irish Tracts*, 285–6.   [50] Ibid. 287.

of events of national and international importance, of which wars and elections were the most significant, which led to the organized production of popular propaganda including large amounts of parodic advertising. The new forms of commercial organization which emerged as the century progressed, and the trade clubs and societies in particular, allowed for the development of a genuinely popular mass market for political propaganda by the 1780s.[51]

Advertisement parody was a constant and increasingly significant element in this growing market for political publicity. Certain types of advertisement parody were well established by the eighteenth century and continued to develop their parodic pedigrees throughout the century. The parodic almanac flourished both here and in France during the revolutionary era and was still providing a vehicle for radical print and pamphlet satire in the post-Peterloo period.[52]

The mock funeral announcement and the last will and testament had been popular for centuries. The most celebrated example was probably the last will and testament of Pope Leo the Tenth's pet elephant Hanna by Pietro Aretino.[53] Swift produced several broadsides using related forms, and directed against the project for establishing a National Bank of Ireland. The titles give their flavour: *The Last Speech and Dying Words of the Bank of Ireland*, and *An Account of the Short Life, Sudden Death and Pompous Funeral of Michy Windybank*.[54]

Mock funeral processions, wills, and funeral advertisements continued to be widely used during the late eighteenth century. One loyalist broadside advertised *The Last Dying Speech, Confession, Behaviour, Birth, Parentage and Education of* THOMAS PAINE, Late Member of the French National Convention, and went on to advertise his death at Taunton for high treason on 18 December 1792. The radicals responded with gusto. *The Telegraph* brought out satires describing Pitt's death from an attack of diarrhoea (brought on by excessive consumption of *French* claret) and his subsequent dissection and funeral. These squibs appeared on consecutive days

---

[51] The central discussion of the impact of 18th-cent. trade clubs and societies on advertising, electioneering, and political propaganda is John Brewer, 'Commercialization and Politics', in McKendrick *et al.* (eds.), *The Birth*, 197–262.

[52] Lise Andries, 'Almanacs: Revolutionizing a Traditional Genre', in Robert Darnton and Daniel Roche (eds.), *Revolution in Print: The Press in France 1775–1800* (Berkeley, Calif., 1989), 203–22.

[53] J. Cleugh, *The Divine Aretino* (London, 1965), 40–2.

[54] *Irish Tracts*, 285–7, 305–10.

in August 1795 and were then brought out as a pamphlet.[55] The elaborate account of the dissection methodically follows the coroner's revolting voyage of discovery. The author stops short at the genitals, pleading a sense of propriety: 'The delicacy necessary to be observed in a public print, does not permit us to enter minutely into the remaining part of the Report. Suffice it to say that the marks of *sexual* distinction in this case were not easily to be discerned.' There is a savage delight in the process of dismemberment. This would have been pointed for a society where folk belief maintained that the bodies of the deceased appeared on the Day of Judgement in the state in which they were interred. The public dissection of criminals still carried the terrifying association that this part of the punishment would carry into the next life. The *Telegraph* satire takes up this belief in its comparisons between several of Pitt's organs and those found during the dissections of criminals at Surgeon's Hall:

On sawing through the *cranium*, the first thing that struck an observer, was a remarkable accumulation of the brain on the *left* side of the scull, while the cavity on the *right* side was almost empty. The whole organ seemed to have an involuntary tendency to press in that direction ... So remarkable a deviation the reporter had never seen, except in one subject dissected a great many years ago at Surgeon's Hall. It was a fellow who was hanged at Tyburn.[56]

Mock wills and epitaphs proliferated during the period of Napoleon's threatened invasion and were then taken up in reform agitation in the early nineteenth century. Hone made his own contribution to the form with a 2*d.* broadside attacking the property tax and titled *The Will of a Great Personage who Died of 37 Mortal Stabs, on Friday, the 5th of April, 1816.*[57]

Similarly Swift's *The Wonder of all the Wonders that Ever the World Wondered At* is part of a subgenre of parody. There were follow-up pamphlets to Swift's piece and the mock showman's notice became a standard form in print, handbill, and pamphlet satire in the late eighteenth and early nineteenth centuries. Anti-Napoleonic government propaganda included many examples, one of which was titled MOST WONDERFUL WONDER OF WONDERS. *Just arrived at Mr. Bull's*

[55] *An Admirable Satire.* I am most grateful to Jonathan Mee for introducing me to this satire.

[56] *An Admirable Satire,* 11–13.

[57] The broadside is repr. and discussed in David Bindman, *The Shadow of the Guillotine*, exhibition cat. (London, 1989), 21, 110.

MENAGERIE, *in British Lane the most renowned and sagacious* MAN
TIGER, or *Ourang Outang called* NAPOLEON BUONAPARTE.[58] Both
Spence and Hone used the form in satires that were in their turn
widely imitated. The most celebrated example in the late eighteenth
century was *Signor Gulielmo Pittachio*, which came out as a handbill, as
an article in Spence's journal *Pig's Meat*, in several broadside forms,
and as a print.[59] It led to imitations by Daniel Isaac Eaton, one of
which, entitled *More Wonderful Wonders*, clearly echoes Swift's piece.
The theme of the showman practising his dangerous and brutal feats
on a gullible public was also developed by Hone and Cruikshank.[60]

There were further uses of the theme during the agitation
surrounding the Queen Caroline affair. The idea of the
sword-swallower was cleverly applied to the lying Italian witnesses
who had been disastrously introduced by the government in an
attempt to prove the Queen's adultery. One broadside announced:
'The New Indian Jugglers surprised the town by swallowing a sword;
but they (Count Milani and Countess Colombier) undertake to make
their friends swallow anything, how preposterous soever'.[61]

The advertising industry accelerated its large-scale growth during
the period from 1780 to 1820, and certain radical satirists exploited
the new forms and methods of publicity which became available as a
result of this expansion. Figures such as Spence and Hone might be
seen as representing a radical avant-garde in terms of the way they
absorbed the new forms and resources of the advertising industry
into their political publications. Yet the novelty of this work should
be qualified, for the material presented in this chapter suggests that
most of the satiric models connected with advertising, both inside
and outside the press, had been taken up in earlier satire. Much of
the success of the work of the later satirists resulted from the way it
adapted new publishing techniques and subject-matter to well-established forms of street literature. This relationship between
established content and novel form has particular importance for the
expanding market in prints.

The single-sheet etching became increasingly significant for
satirists in the early nineteenth century, yet it had been maturing
during the previous sixty years. The period 1720–80 saw the politi-

---

[58] The text of the broadside is reproduced in John Ashton, *Caricature and Satire on
Napoleon I* (London, 1888), 200–1.
[59] *BMC* no. 8500. Also *PP*, ii. 406–7.   [60] *A Slap at Slop*, 1r.
[61] *The New Italian Jugglers* (London, 1820), printed by O. Hodgson, One Penny.

cal print develop in both formal and economic terms. It moved from the stiff, emblematic, text-laden engravings of the 1720s to the fluid and complicated art of Gillray, Cruikshank, and their imitators. At the beginning of the eighteenth century the market for print satires was small and ill-defined; by the end of the American War of Independence graphic satire had become one of the most potent ingredients in political propaganda. Although the poor could only gain access to etchings and engravings in shop-window displays or on coffee-house walls prints became popular with all levels of London society.[62]

The career of Hogarth gives a series of precise demonstrations of the ways in which new and old methods of advertising interacted with formal and economic developments in the print industry. Hogarth's influence on the development of the satiric print in both technical and economic terms was substantial and complicated. He developed the vocabulary of graphic satire combining the old methods of emblematization and symbolization with social description, sequential narrative, and caricature. He produced prints which worked on a number of narrative levels and were designed for extended circulation. He attempted to appeal to connoisseurs interested in aesthetic and artistic questions, and also to fashionable society interested in scandal and topical political questions. Beyond this he reached out to a vast and undefined public who could, if nothing else, relish elements of coarse humour and crude morality in the prints. To embrace these markets he was forced to experiment in different forms of print-making, production, and distribution. His prints were produced as etchings, engravings, and mezzotints. He even tried to reach the cheap broadside market by bringing some prints out as woodcuts.[63]

The roots of Hogarth's involvement with the forms of commercial graphic art run deep. The first years of his life were spent as apprentice to a silver-engraver learning the standard forms of commercial decorative engraving—emblems, coats of arms, and ornamental borders. The first independent prints which he produced as copper-plate engravings were advertisements for tradesmen and performers. He continued throughout his career to produce print advertisements

---

[62] Michael Wynn Jones, *The Cartoon History of the American Revolution* (London, 1974); Atherton, 27–83.

[63] The best survey of Hogarth's complicated relationship with print technology is Ronald Paulson, *Hogarth: His Life, Art, and Times*, 2 vols. (New Haven, Conn., 1971).

such as shop cards for his sister's millinery business, engraved subscription tickets for Garrick, and philanthropic works such as the
engraved subscription for the Foundling Hospital in 1739.[64] It is,
however, in the methods chosen to promote his own work, and in
his utilization of contemporary advertisement within his own paintings and prints, that he made the most significant contribution to
the ways graphic satire could incorporate advertising methods.

The process of combining advertisement with graphic satire began
for Hogarth in 1727 with the *Large Masquerade Ticket*, a satire in the
form of a mock ticket showing worshippers paying homage to Priapus.
The print was a general attack upon the corruption of the Walpole
administration but also a specific hit at the Prince of Wales's recent
obsession with extravagant masquerades.[65] Periodically throughout
his career Hogarth produced satires in the forms of mock advertisements. He brought out a subscription notice for a six-volume work
'The Perriwigs of the Ancients' titled *The Five Orders of Perriwigs*. This
satirized the recent coronation and the academic pretensions of the
Society of Arts.[66] Hogarth's mock advertisement was in its turn taken
up as the basis for travesties. These appeared as part of the mass attack
launched on Hogarth once he had become embroiled in the production of anti-Pitt propaganda near the end of his life.[67]

Hogarth's use of advertising in satire before the 1760s tended to
follow the same pattern as his satire generally. It steered away from
specific political attacks on party or political policy and concentrated on more general social satire. *The Company of Undertakers* was
a print in the form of a mock coat of arms and was a general attack
upon the self-promoting methods of socially well-positioned doctors. In *Cunicularii* he ridiculed the King's physicians for their
gullibility and dishonesty in cashing in on the public interest surrounding Mary Toft and her claims to have given birth to rabbits.
An earlier print, *Royalty, Episcopacy, Law*, which shows three emblematic figures, the King with a guinea for a face, a bishop with a
Jew's harp, and a judge with a gavel, was both a general political
satire and a satire on quack advertising. The subtitle takes the form
of an advertisement for a telescope perfected during the last eclipse
and refers to the advertising campaigns of rival doctors who

---

[64] For Hogarth's engraved work as an apprentice, see ibid. i. 50–3; for early print
advertisements, see i. 67–9; for his sisters, i. 207–8; for Garrick, ii. 22; for the
Foundling Hospital, ii. 38–9.

[65] Ibid. i. 172–4.   [66] Ibid. ii. 34–41.

[67] *A Set of Blocks for Hogarth's Wigs* (1762); repr. in Paulson, *Hogarth*, ii. 378.

attempted to make money out of peddling optical aids for the recent phenomenon.[68]

The great profusion of mountebank and showman's advertising, which was to underpin so many of the later satires based upon the forms of beast menageries and showman's performances, also featured in Hogarth's mature art. National consciousness and suspicion over the methods of advertising had been greatly increased by the South Sea Bubble. Although the affair led to a plethora of prints, nearly all of them were based on rather staid emblematic French and Dutch originals.[69] Hogarth produced the only important print to break with the foreign models. *The South Sea Scheme* was the first treatment of what was to become a lifelong fascination with public deceptions and public entertainments, with the gulf between appearance and reality, the deceiver and the deceived. It is also Hogarth's first great treatment of the theme of the fairground and its attractions.

Actors, showmen, masqueraders, and the concomitant signs, booths, and displays used to advertise them proliferate in Hogarth's prints. His greatest variations on this theme are in *Southwark Fair* (Fig.3) which is both a celebration and an exposé of the various types of puffing in a big London fair. Advertising enforces a hectic conjunction between the most riotous behaviour and the elevated subjects of mythology and history. The enormous signs, placards, and banners which rise above the crowd in this print take up and travesty the classical and Christian myths which formed the subjects of the grand schools of painting. The print is a furious meditation upon human vanity, which is shown metaphorically in images of rising and falling. The false claims of advertisers, the puffing, the raising of spectres, are placed next to the squalid realities of theft and deception going on at ground level.

Nothing is safe from the advertiser's voracious craft. The fall of Troy, the rise and fall of imperial monarchies, and the fall from grace of Adam and Eve are all engulfed in the hectic drive for publicity. On the left-hand side of the print the company advertising *The fall of Bajazet* enact their own literal fall as their booth collapses. Below a sign showing the temptation of Eve is Punch wheeling Judy in a barrow; the original occasion for strife between the sexes, the first human tragedy, finds its consummation in the farcical rituals of domestic violence which characterize the puppet-show—a fall from

[68] Paulson, *Hogarth*, i. 127–8.   [69] Atherton, 260.

grace certainly. Above Adam and Eve a latter-day Icarus attempts to fly from a rope attached to a church steeple and descends headlong, his own fall is imminent. Hogarth probably had in mind the recent sensational death of the flying man who fell attempting a leap from Greenwich Church, yet the image has universal appeal and a general status in the satire of the day.

In *Gulliver's Travels* the rope-dance was to become a central metaphor for the dangers of powerful office and the political shenanigans of the Lilliputians. It was then taken up in political satires from the mid-eighteenth century onwards.[70] The fairground with its sudden jumps between appearance and reality, and with its combinations of glamour and squalor, danger and disaster, beauty and brutality, was to provide the metaphorical basis for innumerable print satires in the late eighteenth and early nineteenth centuries. Prints such as Williams's *A Political Fair* of 1807 (*BMC*, no. 10763) are still directly related to Hogarth's *Southwark Fair*. In *A Political Fair* the original rope-dancers have survived intact while the overall scene surveys developments in international politics through the presentation of a series of booths and placards. Williams's print leads in its turn to Hone's *The Political Showman at Home* of 1822.

Contemporary attacks on Hogarth were not slow in taking up the showman metaphor. In December 1753 Paul Sandby produced *A Mountebank Painter*, which presented Hogarth in the guise of a showman and mountebank. Sandby's attack concentrated on Hogarth's extravagant and novel methods of self-publicity and suggests that he had become notorious as a puffer in his own right. The charges were not without foundation, for Hogarth had become one of the most celebrated self-publicists of his day. Hogarth combined satire and advertisement in the engraved subscription tickets for his own print series and in the advertising surrounding his controversial picture auctions. He advertised his new subscription for *The Rake's Progress* and *The Humours of a Fair*, in 1733, in the terms: 'half a guinea to be paid at the time of subscribing, for which a receipt will be given on a new etched print describing a pleased audience at a theatre'. The print, *The Laughing Audience*, showed a cross-section of society and included mild social criticism, the

---

[70] For *Gulliver's Travels*, see John Traugott, 'The Yahoo in the Doll's House: *Gulliver's Travels*, the Children's Classic', in C. Rawson (ed.), *English Satire and the Satiric Tradition* (Oxford, 1984), 140–4. For print satires based on the rope-dancing metaphor, see *BMC*, nos. 1337, 1689, 3486.

Fɪɢ. 3. William Hogarth. *Southwark Fair.* Etching and engraving. 1733–4.

groundlings laughing heartily in the pit, the orchestra tired and bored, and the aristocrats attempting to seduce the flower-girls and wholly ignoring the play. Later series included subscription tickets that confronted politics and aesthetics more straightforwardly. He produced *Characters and Caricaturas* as the sales ticket for *Marriage à la Mode.*

With *Marriage à la Mode* Hogarth's ability to combine aesthetic argument with successful advertising reached a new intensity. He went to Paris to secure the services of top French engravers, feeling that their refinement and skill would better capture the intricate interiors and concern with fashionable detail in his new paintings. But at this point the war with France broke out. Hogarth turned the deal to his advantage by advertising his relations with the French engravers in a long advertisement in *The Daily Advertiser*. Orator Henley then replied with a mock advertisement attacking Hogarth as 'the little Game Cock of Covent Garden'. A series of ripostes and counter-ripostes followed couched in the phraseology of cock-fighting. While the whole business was very effective publicity it demonstrates that complicated debate in artistic circles could be conducted via the conventions of a particularly disreputable type of advertising.

Hogarth's most notorious sales pitches centred around the exhibitions which he organized from the mid-1740s. In January 1745 he launched a series of proposals advertising the sale by auction of the sets of paintings for *The Harlot's Progress, The Rake's Progress, The Times of Day, The Strolling Actresses in a Barn,* and advertising an imminent auction for the sale of the paintings for the recently completed *Marriage à la Mode.* The first auction was to be preceded by a month during which a book would be opened and the sums from bidders recorded. During February Hogarth refined and developed his auction proposals through an advertising campaign in the press. He also brought out an auction ticket, *The Battle of the Pictures,* an etched satire to be given to each bidder who had entered their name in the book, and who would be permitted entry to the final auction. The sale ticket is a political and aesthetic satire in which Hogarth develops Swift's *Battle of the Books* into a pictorial battle. Hogarth's modern history paintings are shown slashed and assaulted by inferior imitations of old masters, the type of painting then flooding the market. The auction and the advertising surrounding it were seen as vulgar and Hogarth gained a reputation for arrogance and a generally unrealistic approach to his own art.[71]

[71] Paulson, *Hogarth*, i. 472–9.

As his career progressed, however, Hogarth increasingly concentrated on the production of work which would have a mass appeal and which would not be constricted within the circles of connoisseurship and polite society, the markets in which he had tried so hard to gain a reputation. *Beer Street, Gin Lane,* and *The Four Stages of Cruelty*—the great social satires, advertised together in 1751—were adapted for a popular market and were intended to be polemical. These works were the climax of Hogarth's attempts to disseminate large cheap editions of his prints. *The Four Stages* relate directly to the mass success of Hone and Cruikshank's illustrated satires of the years 1816—22.

In the very popular portrait caricature *Lord Lovat,* which pictured the recently arrested rebel of the 1745 uprising, Hogarth had begun to experiment with a coarse style of deeply bitten etching. Such prints could be cheaply produced in enormous editions: the depth of line allowed the plates to stand up to a very long run. The print combined the caricature of a topical figure with powerful but simplified draftsmanship and is a direct prefigurement of late eighteenth-century satire. Its fluidity emanates from its origin in a caricature sketch from life and in this it shares the vitality of Gillray's closely observed caricature portraits. From this base Hogarth went on to experiment with the production of different editions of his next print series, *Industry and Idleness,* advertising both a cheap popular edition and one on good paper for the connoisseurs. In *Beer Street* and *Gin Lane* he continued the experiment, only now adapting his drawing style back to the bold simplifications of the *Lovat* print.

With *The Four Stages of Cruelty* stylistic and formal simplification were taken further and Hogarth attempted to adapt the prints to the popular form of woodcut. Ironically only two of the four plates were ever produced in this way, for the large and still intricate blocks finally cost more to produce than copper engravings. Yet John Bell's woodcut impressions of the last two stages of cruelty are formally far more suited to express the horror and melodrama of these social satires. The woodcuts were seventy years ahead of their time and closely anticipate Hone and Cruikshank's satires in the period 1819–22. Hogarth's woodcuts are, in terms of scale and technique, perhaps of even more significance in the way that they anticipate the large woodcuts which C. J. Grant produced as part of the print propaganda directly preceding the First Reform Act.[72]

[72] The bibliographic background to the printing of the various series is given in *Hogarth's Graphic Works,* ed. and comp. with intro. and comm. by Ronald Paulson, 2 vols. (New Haven, Conn., 1971), ii. 213–15.

Hogarth's involvement with popular art was both theoretical and practical. This comes out plainly in his complicated relationship with the most visible and dominant advertising displays of his day, shop signs. Hogarth sought to bring the sign-painters within the fold of serious art through his organization of and participation in the sign-painters' exhibition of 1762. Beyond this, however, the trades-man's signs and notices increasingly influenced both the form and content of his own satire.

The sign-painters' exhibition opened in April 1762 and consisted entirely of shop signs, either borrowed from their normal positions, or from the stock of sign-painters' businesses. It is difficult to know to what extent the exhibition was intended as a satiric gesture ironically commenting upon what Sir James Thornhill, another of the exhibi-tion's organizers and Hogarth's father-in-law, described as 'the want of Taste among my countrymen, and their prejudice against every artist who is a native'.[73] As it turned out, however, it was to be Hogarth's final public exhibition of painting. It was, on one level at least, a gesture of solidarity with English popular and folk art and with the narrative structures of the sign. The symbols, rebuses, and visual puns which operated in the shop signs fed into Hogarth's own work and into the political prints of the next half-century. Hogarth's contributions entered the show under the transparent pseudonym of Hagarty. They featured images which already were established in political satire and which would continue as part of the core vocabulary of the political print over the next five decades.

Exhibit 5, *The Light Heart, A Sign for a Vintner*, showed 'a feather weighing down a heart in a pair of scales'. Although the exhibition catalogue refers this device back to Ben Jonson's *The New Inn*, vari-ations on the trope of the fantastic scales were frequent in Lutheran anti-papist prints, and the device was used in later English political prints. Cruikshank employed it on the cover of the most widely selling political satire of the early nineteenth century, *The Political House that Jack Built*.[74]

Exhibit 19 showed an 'Officer, all Head, Arms, Legs and Thighs'. This was a time-honoured graphic device for negating a political opponent. With the arrival of personal caricature it became even more popular in political prints—an enemy's features could be

[73] Quoted in Ronald Paulson, *Popular and Polite Art in the Age of Hogarth and Fielding* (Notre Dame, Ind., 1979), 36–7.
[74] See pp. 238–9 below.

shown attached to arms and legs with no torso—he became literally 'nobody'. Exhibit 64, *View of the Road to Paddington, with a Presentation of the Deadly Never-Green that bears Fruit all the Year round*, featured Tyburn and is typical of the grim gallows humour which remained central to later political graphics.[75]

The exhibition incorporated the retouching of signs and stylistic juxtapostions that brought them close to the ironies and puns of later caricatures. Hogarth was directly involved in these processes of readaptation. He reworked two old signs of the Saracen's Head and the Queen's Head; making the eyes glare at each other and sticking out the tongues he also reinscribed them 'the Zarr' and 'Empress Queen'. The old signs became a comment on the relations between the Tsar and the Queen of Hungary.[76] This bold defacement of a monarch's head brings to mind the brilliant reworking of the official state portrait of Louis XVI by French printmakers in the 1790s. The simple addition of a *bonnet rouge* in opaque red gouache achieved a semiotic transformation.[77]

Although shop signs were about to disappear (their size, number, and insecure hanging made them a public nuisance and an act for their suppression passed later that year) the exhibition demonstrates how their content and humour operated in ways that were to make their absorption and reinvention in the political etching inevitable. The shop sign exhibition is one indication of the resources Hogarth was to provide for subsequent print satire. The works he produced in the last two decades of his life had an even more direct bearing on the development of the political print. They were concerned with popular politics and this interest found its major manifestation in the election series of 1753. Ronald Paulson has gone so far as to see these works as deliberately painted in the crude flat style of sign-boards and reads them as an attempt to find a painted equivalent to Bell's woodcuts for *The Four Stages*.[78] This is difficult to substantiate: the highly elaborate and delicate print versions of the paintings are very far removed from the hard outlines and uncluttered compositions of *The Four Stages* and *Gin Street*. Paulson is right, however, to emphasize the popular political nature of the content of the election series and to consider the ways in which

[75] See p. 80 below.   [76] Paulson, *Hogarth*, ii. 350–1.
[77] *French Caricature and the French Revolution 1789–1799*, exhibition cat. (Los Angeles, 1989), 103, 179.
[78] Paulson, *Hogarth*, ii. 196–7.

depictions of sign-boards operate on a number of levels within the series.[79]

The increasing tendency towards facial caricature, the concentration on the phenomenon of the mob and on procession, and the introduction of fantasy elements (such as the lion eating the fleur-de-lis in *Canvassing for Votes*) are elements which anticipate print satires in the period of Gillray. Hogarth's *An Election Entertainment* provided the basis not only for Gillray's *The Union Club* but for a whole host of prints presenting political celebrations in the form of orgies. The climax of these elaborate reworkings of Hogarth's print came with Cruikshank's rabidly anti-abolitionist satire of July 1819, *The New Union Club*.

While the election series indicates Hogarth's growing involvement with specific political issues, the Jew bill in particular providing a topical focus for the series, he was still operating as an elevated Augustan. The satirist provides a satiric disquisition on the corruption of electoral procedure. It was only at the end of his career with the two prints entitled *The Times*, and the prints growing out of the Wilkes affair, that Hogarth ushered in the populist and frequently cynical methods of graphic satire that dominated the period 1790–1820.

The Times, plate I, was, in personal terms, the most disastrous print of Hogarth's career. It brought down on him the wrath of Pitt's followers and created a rift between the artist and his two former friends Charles Churchill and John Wilkes. It is a hectic political allegory presenting London aflame as a result of a war it should not be fighting. Hogarth's crowded urban scene of disaster, in which each participant performs an act which reveals his political orientation, provided a model which was to be taken up by Gillray and his imitators. Sign-boards and placards proliferate identifying the possessors of the burning houses, the role of West India wealth, and the corrupting nature of faction. The only quality this print lacks to make it quite typical of a great Gillray is the element of personal caricature. Hogarth made good this deficiency with the production of the monumental portrait caricature *John Wilkes Esq*. Hogarth's lethal response to Wilkes's attack on him in *The North Britain*, 17, was drawn from the life. It anticipates Gillray's habit of preying on the living bodies of Fox and the younger Pitt. The print represents a loss of satiric purity. Hogarth was submerged in a world where personal

[79] Ibid. 222–3; Paulson, *Popular and Polite Art*, 29–30.

vituperation and ridicule supplanted elevated social satire and where politics were synonymous with party and personal enmity. This satiric environment was to feed the anarchic mind of Gillray. The personal attacks on the Regent and the members of the Liverpool administration made by radicals in the first two decades of the nineteenth century also grew out of it. Its final efflorescence was the satiric mythologizations of the Queen Caroline affair.

In taking on Wilkes and Churchill Hogarth was entering the arena with a new style of satirist. Wilkes's campaign methods from 1760 to 1772 influenced radical publicity methods in the post-Peterloo period. He was a campaigner who claimed to be the people's representative, upholding liberty and the freedom of the press. Yet he did not appear to have a moral centre: he joked about the gullibility of the freeholders of Middlesex and the mob, and he used scurrility, pornography, and violence in his publicity campaigns.[80] Wilkes was the focus for, and to some extent the director of, a tumultuous propaganda campaign which used the press, and the print trade, with a wily awareness. In its spirit, methods, and wide popular allure Wilkite activism anticipated ultra-radical publicity methods in the second decade of the nineteenth century.

Wilkes is a central figure in the history of English radicalism. George Rudé describes him as 'one of the founders of a mass radical movement in Britain'.[81] Both Rudé and H. T. Dickinson stress his importance as a figure linking late eighteenth- and early nineteenth-century radicalism.[82] John Brewer has demonstrated that Wilkes's supporters drew on the already powerful and well-established London network of trading clubs and societies. He argues that it was the campaigning and publicity skills of these organizations that underpinned many of the elaborate festivities, demonstrations, and ritual celebrations which occurred at key moments during the Wilkes affair.[83] It has recently been shown that these developments were not completely unprecedented. Kathleen Wilson's analysis of the Admiral Vernon celebrations has shown that nation-wide demonstrations of support for a popular hero, who was seen to stand against an unpopular administration, occurred as early as 1739–40. The Vernon case involved the mobilization of many of the struc-

---

[80] Paulson, *Hogarth*, ii. 368–9.   [81] Rudé, 196.

[82] Rudé, 56, 59, 190–8; Thomas Spence, *The Political Works of Thomas Spence*, ed. with intro. by H. T. Dickinson (Newcastle, 1982), pp. vii–ix.

[83] Brewer, 'Commercialization and Politics', in McKendrick *et al.* (eds.), *The Birth*, 201–48.

tures and resources which are now associated with the Wilkes affair. These included the harnessing of the organizational skills of the trade societies, the mass production of ceramic propaganda, and the mobilization of the press, which produced a mass of pro-Vernon ephemera.[84] Wilkes was, however, fresher in the memories of early nineteenth-century radicals, and his relationship with the press offered lessons which the Vernon affair did not.

Wilkes's greatest importance for this study lies in his impact on the operation of the political press in this country. The publicity campaigns surrounding his various trials and election victories fundamentally altered the relations between the government and the political press, between the government and public opinion, between the press and the London mob, and between the law and the press. In the 1750s and early 1760s the political press had certainly become more active as a force influencing the decisions and perceptions of politicians. The various campaigns directed against Bute showed how a concentrated campaign of invective could affect the country's and the Cabinet's confidence in an individual.[85] The volume of publications increased and the political print came to fill a more central role, but the debate was still about personal influence within the royal Court and Cabinet, not about a basic reappraisal of the rights of the popular press and the people. The personal publicity machine which Grenville put together in the early 1760s pointed the way for Wilkes. Grenville's unofficial team consisted of William Knox, Thomas Whately, and John Almon—a journalist, an editor, and a political scout were co-ordinated and informed by an influential politician.[86] Yet the publications of Grenville's team operated within a proscribed publishing arena which was limited in circulation, in the forms it was prepared to adopt, and in the readership which it hoped to reach. It was the educated and informed who were targeted and the politicians who were the inspiration for the thought and polemic of the writing. Wilkes, in adopting the role of people's champion, in becoming a very lively symbol of the abused rights of the freeholders of Middlesex, and in enmeshing a large number of London printers and publishers in litigation on his behalf, transformed the political arena.

[84] Kathleen Wilson, 'Empire, Trade and Popular Politics in Mid-Hanoverian Britain: The Case of Admiral Vernon', *Past and Present*, 121 (1988), 74–111.

[85] Rea, 20–23, 34–6, 123–9. See also *BMC*, nos. 4840–2, 4416, 4883, 4885, 4949–61, 5124–35, 5226–9, 5667–71.

[86] Rea, 140–1.

Wilkes learned his trade as a propagandist in the period leading up to his flight to Paris in 1762. Tried for seditious and blasphemous libel for writing *The North Briton*, 45, and the pornographic *Essay on Woman*, he brilliantly controlled the timing and volume of the media coverage of the various legal proceedings. Poetry, prints, handbills, broadsides, songs, and processions all contributed to the creation of the Wilkes myth. Handbills were even distributed within the court during hearings. After the government's failure to prove their case against him Wilkes managed to gain sufficient financial backing to prosecute the government for trespass and wrongful arrest of all the booksellers and publishers who had been arrested for suspected involvement in the printing and selling of *The North Briton*, 45. Wilkes exploited these trials for months and nearly all of them involved the government in paying damages to the pressmen.[87] On his release Wilkes set up a press in his own house and sent out a steady flow of handbills, pamphlets, and public letters. It was only in the area of the satiric print that he lacked fire: not surprisingly he was unable to find a graphic satirist who could adequately combat the effect of Hogarth's work.

It was, however, after his return to England, with the criminal charges of 1763 still hanging over him, that Wilkes became the focus for an enormous propaganda campaign which was to have a lasting effect on popular radicalism. Throughout 1767 he had been preparing London and the government for his return with public letters, one of which had led to Lord Temple brandishing his sword at Lord Talbot in the House. Wilkes returned in time for the spring elections, boldly stood for Middlesex, and scored a resounding victory in a campaign of sustained intimidation. He was subsequently tried and convicted for the pending charges and imprisoned in St George's Field. His support at this point was genuinely popular and extended through the merchant classes into the mob. General discontent flared into direct confrontation between troops and the mob resulting in the St George's Field massacre. From this point on Wilkes was at the centre of a controversy involving a confrontation between government and the electorate, and the aspiring electorate. Expelled from the House of Commons on the grounds of his criminality he was immediately re-elected by the freeholders of Middlesex. The whole procedure was repeated when the Cabinet insisted on a second expulsion. Finally the government put up its

[87] Rea, 68–9.

own candidate, Henry Lawes Luttrell, who lost disastrously to Wilkes yet was allowed the seat although he had polled only a miserable 300 votes. The government's recognition of Luttrell elevated the Wilkes affair into a national debate on the rights of the electorate and led to nation-wide petitioning on constitutional issues.[88]

Wilkes's prison cell became the central press office for a propaganda campaign which, in its diversity, its duration, and the way it captured the interest of all types and classes of Londoner, was not to be rivalled until the Queen Caroline affair. Wilkes did not gain the support of the respectable and commercially the biggest printers, booksellers, and publishers, yet the majority of established opposition printers became loyal and enthusiastic supporters. They marketed pro-Wilkes material on a very big scale and in formally imaginative ways.[89] While the Wilkes craze lasted he was also popular among the anonymous producers of ballad and street fare. As John Brewer stresses, one of the most significant aspects of the popular support which Wilkes attracted lies in the way it shaded off into all sorts of commercial opportunism. The distinctions between political propaganda and popular entertainment became intriguingly blurred. Wilkes and *The North Briton*, 45, were celebrated through a merchandizing campaign that drew in a variety of industries including ceramics, fashion, brewing, catering, jewellery, tobacco, cosmetics, and printing. Publicans went to great lengths to manifest Wilkite sympathies to their clientele, people donned Wilkite-colours buttons and brooches, transfers decorated almost every type of ceramic tableware, pewter and silverware were stamped with the number 45, and perukiers brought out Wilkes wigs with 45 curls.[90]

The government attempted to respond to the enormous volume of publicity with its own propaganda but this frequently combined scurrility and high-handedness in a most detrimental manner.[91] When the prosecution of printers or authors was attempted it only served to cement a growing and dangerous alliance between political radicalism and the free press. Wilkes had proved the catalyst for developments which were to be of central and lasting significance for

[88] Rudé, 106–10; also J. R. Pole, *Political Representation in England and the Origin of the American Republican* (London, 1966), 427–9.

[89] Brewer, 'Commercialization and Politics', 254–8.

[90] All details of the merchandizing of Wilkes are drawn from Brewer's account, ibid. 236–49.

[91] Rea, 166–8.

radical propagandists up until the passage of the First Reform Bill. From this perspective it was not what was said about Wilkes or Lut-trell that mattered but the alignment of the press with general popular discontent. The trial of printers became closely connected with the rights of all men to trial by jury, and the general hatred of the government's proceeding by information. The significance of the co-ordination of the popular press with the process of public petitioning is rightly stressed by Robert Rea.[92]

The periodical press burgeoned, and concomitant forms of ephemeral publishing mushroomed around it. The volume and di-versity of the productions generated by the Middlesex elections made them unprosecutable. While the scandal was at its height people could publish pretty well what they liked and this was a pat-tern which was to repeat itself in the second decade of the nineteenth century during subsequent media celebrations of govern-ment-inspired or mismanaged scandal. The Wilkes affair saw popular satire assume a new force in politics. Its volume and mass appeal briefly transformed the free press into a force that proclaimed its liberty and did not request it as a privilege sanctioned by govern-ment. The alliance of popular radicalism with the concept of the freedom of the press was to repeat itself with unerring consistency over the next fifty years during periods of unrest. Wilkes seems to have had a fairly well-defined notion of what the popular political press had achieved during the years of his celebrity. It not only educated the people but empowered them, or at least created a fic-tion of empowerment which in the long run was to prove as useful: 'The people are now made the Judges of the conduct of their rep-resentatives, and the full exertion of the liberty of the press, the great bulwark of all other liberties, in support of the constitution, with the other acquisitions for the public, will render this aera ever memor-able in our annals.'[93] The claim is inflated but subsequent radical propagandists owed Wilkes a lot and they were not slow to learn from his methods. Hone was particularly astute in this respect. He was prosecuted for his publication of a reworked Wilkes satire, and he studied Wilkes's methods of propaganda generally.[94] It was above

[92] Rea, 163–4.   [93] *Town and Country Magazine*, 4 (1772), 220–1.

[94] The book sale catalogues of 1824 and 1827, which detail the contents of Hone's print and book collections, list the following material by or about Wilkes: 'Wilkes's Genteel and Moral Advice to a Young Lady 1748' (1824 cat., item 2147); 'Wilkes John. Letters to and from. 3 vols. 1769–71' (1827 cat. item 6); 'The North Briton. 2 vols. Very curious edn. by Bingley, with much private history of the affairs of the

all the popular appeal and formal eclecticism of Wilkite propaganda that was of use to ambitious publicists such as Spence and Hone. The Wilkes affair showed that, under certain conditions, the new printing and manufacturing technologies, and the organizational skills of the trading classes, could be tapped by political radicalism.

times' (item 341); 'English Liberty. A collection of Tracts relating to John Wilkes, from 1762–99' (item 342); 'A Form of Intercession for the delivery of John Wilkes' (item 647).

2

Eaton, Spence, and Modes of Radical Subversion in The Revolutionary Era

THE propaganda generated by the Peterloo massacre and the Queen Caroline affair demonstrated that between 1819 and 1822 the radicals were able to produce anti-state publicity that in the variety of its forms, and in its sheer volume, was unprosecutable. The groundwork for this most visible demonstration of the freedom of the press had been laid in the years 1790–1815. It was not merely the product of experiments with political publication, but grew out of adaptations and refutations of the forms of loyalist publicity, and out of apolitical developments in the publishing industry.

The extent to which radical propaganda in this period was shaped by loyalist forms of publication should not be underestimated. *The Rights of Man*, arguably the most effective work of popular radical polemic, would not have taken the form it did, and might never have been written, but for Burke's *Reflections*. Radicals saw this immediately and even wrote bitingly to Burke to congratulate him on stimulating this 'magnificent reply'.[1] But cause and effect operated on the propaganda of both loyalists and radicals in less obvious ways and over a protracted period. From 1792 to 1795 the propaganda war greatly accelerated in terms of its forms and distribution; but who fed off whom, and why propaganda adopted the forms and iconography it did, are complicated questions. They relate to the history of popular satire and popular disturbance as well as to the direct stimuli of events in France or on the domestic front.[2]

The pamphlets and broadsides published and distributed by the Reevesite Associations were popular, but when successfully innovative they provided new models for the radical publicists. The series

[1] John Cannon, *Parliamentary Reform 1640–1832* (Cambridge, 1972), 120.
[2] Robert Hole, 'British Counter-Revolutionary Propaganda in the 1790s', in Colin James (ed.), *Britain and Revolutionary France: Conflict, Subversion and Propaganda*, (Exeter, 1983).

of broadsides in the form of letters between John and his cousin Thomas Bull is a case in point.[3] Even when set in traditional forms, such as ballads, hymns, songs, trial reports, and catechetical dialogues, loyalist satires increased the public appetite for entertaining political literature in ways which the radicals would inevitably capitalize upon in the decades to come. In one sense the immediate political content of Association propaganda was irrelevant, for its very existence was an acknowledgement of a generally politicized reading public which needed to be wooed and warned.

The production of mass propaganda by both loyalists and radicals was also affected and even directed by developments in publishing. Advertising inside and outside the press, the children's book industry, and the print trade all mushroomed from 1780 to 1820. Consequently, in the 1790s propagandists had unprecedented opportunities to exploit these new formal and methodological resources. All these publishing environments were up for grabs and in the initial stages it was loyalist propaganda which colonized them most efficiently.

The greatest long-term impact came not from the politically specific publications of the Association but from the new educationalists' infiltration of the lower reaches of the publishing market. In the 1790s children's literature, and the production of cheap didactic religious Church and King tracts, became a loyalist stronghold and triumph. The activities of Hannah More, Sarah Trimmer, and their numerous imitators were manifested in the success of the *Cheap Repository Tracts* and of the new prayer guides and instructional textbooks of the Church of England.

A serious radical counter-offensive to this publishing barrage was not in motion until the period 1816–22 when intellectual radicals, outraged at the loyalist infiltration of the market in educative texts, combined with popular publishers to develop alternative forms of children's book and to convert the children's book and the forms of religious ceremonial into popular parody.[4]

An equally complicated interplay emerges for the political print. During this period the market for prints developed. Although beyond the price range of the poor, they became increasingly accessible through public displays in taverns and coffee-houses, or in print-shop windows. The satiric etching was predominantly anti-

---

[3] See Smith, 71.
[4] For loyalist educational texts, see Claeys, 60–6; Crimmins, 169–79.

government during the American war, then became primarily a loyalist weapon during the period of the French Revolution and the war with France. Yet all these prints came to provide both a stimulus and a set of models for radical satirists after Peterloo. The ramifications of the rise of the political print, and its unpredictable effects, can be succinctly indicated in the career of the most influential of the English satiric etchers, James Gillray. It was Gillray's satiric experimentation during the American war, from 1774 to 1782, that provided him with the technical resources for the dense stylistic and narrative fusions which typify the great prints he produced from the mid-1780s until 1810. Political satire did not predominate in the 1770s, as it had done during the previous fifteen years, yet the period of the American war, all of which Gillray probably spent in London, set crucial precedents for the development of the print as propaganda.[5]

The vital point is that almost all the print satires opposed the war. The prints did not treat the Americans, at least until their alliance with France, as foreigners, but as Englishmen who were the victims of invasive government legislation and finally of tyrannical actions which threatened their freedom. As the war went on the targets which the prints were aimed at became more and more daring. While ministers such as Grenville, Townsend, and North continued to be attacked, the prints also turned on military figureheads, particularly Howe and Burgoyne, and finally on the King. These prints set up a pattern that was to bear upon subsequent anti-government print campaigns. The opposition became involved in the co-ordinated production of visual propaganda to attack the government's foreign policy. Hard-hitting and indeed libellous accusations could be made through print satire which the government would be reluctant to prosecute, partly because print satire had become associated with respectable political dissent on the part of the opposition, and partly because of the obvious difficulties surrounding the introduction of prints into a court as evidence.

Gillray matured in this environment and the majority of political prints he produced in the 1770s and early 1780s follow the dominant patterns of opinion. Initially they are anti-state, then anti-military, and finally attack members of the royal family, ending with the King. By the end of the American War Gillray had developed a formidably varied graphic vocabulary. He had mastered the stiff

[5] *BMC* v, pp. xvi–xxvi.

ideographic conventions of the prints of the 1750s and 1760s. He had also developed his own fluid style of personal caricature based on a distortion of the academic conventions of figure-drawing. His American war prints also testify to his intellectual ambition, his ability to encapsulate complicated political situations within enormous metaphors.

If the American Revolution provided the catalyst for the formation of Gillray's style, the French Revolution was the historical framework responsible for its mature expression and for the prints which were to provide the radicals in the first two decades of the nineteenth century with a lethal satiric vocabulary. The Revolution gave him an ideal environment for the exploration of his morally decentred vision. In *Representations of Revolution* Ronald Paulson has made a determined effort to locate a moral core to Gillray's satire. It was a worthwhile venture, for Gillray seems invariably to attack even that which he claims to defend. Despite the government pension, awarded him in 1797, he stands outside party and political creed, and his savagery is indiscriminate and delights in the depiction of violence, particularly sexually charged violence.[6] Paulson was finally reduced to reading John Bull as the only affirmative characterization in Gillray's entire cast. In Paulson's words he 'represents for Gillray the impervious core of human nature: innocent, dumb and intractable but ultimately enduring'. John Bull is also, unlike most of Gillray's targets, an abstract personification, not a real figure.[7]

Gillray's negativity takes a variety of forms. There are the straightforward examples of defamatory attacks on the King and Queen—*Sin Death and the Devil* is perhaps the most notorious—and his innumerable attacks on the Prince of Wales's preference for older women. Yet even Gillray's concentrated assaults on the English radicals during the French Revolution, which Marilyn Butler has taken to be the quintessence of nationalistic propaganda, can be read as even more subversive than the unambiguous attacks on royalty.[8]

Gillray's favourite method for warning of the dangers of revolution was to create visions of the country overrun by the leading radicals and members of the Whig opposition. The French are fre-

[6] For the history of the pension, see Draper Hill, *Mr. Gillray the Caricaturist* (London, 1965), 56–72.

[7] Ronald Paulson, *Representations of Revolution* (New Haven, Conn., 1983), 190 12.

[8] Marilyn Butler, *Romantics, Rebels, and Reactionaries* (Oxford, 1981), 53–7.

quently an incidental addition. A successful revolution is carried through in the caricaturist's imagination in the most fantastic and extreme forms. As early as 1791 Gillray came out with 'The HOPES of the PARTY, prior to July 14'th' (Fig. 4). The title, *From such wicked CROWN & ANCHOR Dreams, good Lord, deliver us,* refers to a notorious radical tavern and purports to be loyalist in sentiment, but it is set out as a mock litany, and this was a favourite form of radical religious parody. The indignity and extremity of the outrages committed against the King and Queen cast further doubt on the patriotic inspiration of the print and undermine the victims more than the revolutionaries. The King is shown with shaved head and still insane, oblivious of his situation and repeating himself, a conversational tic for which he was notorious. Horne Tooke's position as he hoists the King up and presses into him is charged with obscene sexual tension—he appears to be raping a lunatic. There is an equally perverse innuendo in the postures of the hanged figures of Pitt and Queen Charlotte. The scene is encircled by an ecstatic crowd.

Later prints such as *Promis'd Horrors of the French INVASION,—or— Forcible Reasons for negotiating a Regicide PEACE* (Fig. 5) repeat this tension between a pretended warning and Gillray's evident delight in depicting the imagined destruction of the English system of government and of its figureheads. The revolution has come—a swarthy Charles Fox determinedly thrashes Pitt, who is lashed to the liberty pole, the Prince of Wales is cut in half and his head and the lower part of his body are hung from a scales, his guts spilling down on to the crowd. There are heads everywhere, on plates, in baskets, floating down the gutter. Gillray's fury was beyond the call of duty well before he went mad in 1811.

When radical satire finally exploded on a somewhat bewildered administration in 1820, during the Queen Caroline affair, the government had contributed to its humiliation in more far-reaching ways than the simple mishandling of the Queen's return. Cruikshank's formulaic depictions of the Regent and leading politicians, his very willingness to work for whoever would pay him, and to play both sides off against the savage nihilism of his own satiric vision, find their legitimization in Gillray's mature work. In the sphere of publishing it was the popular works of the evangelical educationalists, the Reevesite Associations, and the vast quantities of government-backed anti-Napoleonic satire which had been more

FIG. 4. James Gillray. Coloured etching. The HOPES of the PARTY, prior to July 14th—'*From such wicked* CROWN & ANCHOR *Dreams, good Lord, deliver us.*' 1791.

FIG. 5. James Gillray. Coloured etching. *Promis'd Horrors of the French INVASION—or—Forcible Reasons for negotiating a Regicide PEACE.* 1796.

instrumental than the more fitful propaganda assaults of the radicals in opening up both the readership and the print environment. And yet the final irony may be that all this sound and fury merely signified the increasing scepticism of a public over-familiar with the conventions and increasing volume of political propaganda. It was a case of too much, too late.

Historians increasingly emphasize the extent of radical fragmentation throughout the period 1790–1820 and stress the diversity of the social, intellectual, and geographical histories of radical organizations and individuals. The dramatic shifts in the reception of the different stages of the French Revolution in England, the ideological inheritance of different classes of radical, and the problems of differentiating between political intent and political rhetoric are concerns which increasingly inflect all attempts to generalize about the nature of popular radicalism.[9]

Radical propaganda from 1790 to 1820 has become problematic. While one must not underestimate the various effects of loyalist propaganda on the radical publicists, direct links can be established between certain forms of radical propaganda which were developed in the 1790s, kept alive during the fallow periods between 1796 and 1815, and then fed directly into the massive propaganda campaigns of the post-Peterloo years. It is a mistake to look for the continuation of radicalism in this period as manifested exclusively in organized activity. John Dinwiddy, with typical subtlety, has indicated, for example, the consistency with which radicals continued to give the basic symbols of the French Revolution a casual airing from 1795 to 1815.[10]

No organizations equivalent in size or impact to the London Corresponding Society and the Society for Constitutional Information sprang up from 1800 to 1815, yet the inheritance of the 1790s had changed not only what radicals thought but how they could communicate their thought. Radicalism in the first decade of the nineteenth century was blessed with inspired propagandists who not only kept radical ideology alive but who developed publicity techniques which subsequent radicals, Hone is exemplary, took into a mass market. The rest of this chapter is devoted to a detailed consideration of Thomas Spence and Daniel Isaac Eaton. These men

[9] Philp, 'The Fragmented Ideology of Reform', provides an excellent summary.
[10] John R. Dinwiddy, *Radicalism and Reform in Britain 1780–1850* (London, 1992), 207–29.

stand out in terms of the way they consistently latched on to and politicized new formal developments in publishing and advertising. Their most lasting contribution to English radicalism lay in the extension and mobilization of radical thought through propaganda.

Despite the considerable attention he attracted in his lifetime, Spence was neglected until the 1960s when his agrarian theory was taken up in the work of Marxist historians. He has been consistently reassimilated into various areas of English radical and labour historiography since, and there has been a corresponding growth of interest in Spence as a linguistic theorist.[11] None of this recent work has, however, concentrated on Spence's activities, methods, and influence as a propagandist. Iain McCalman has traced the activities of Spence's varied disciples and adherents in the politics and thought of the radical underworld from 1795 to 1840 and has shown how ultra-radicals infiltrated institutions. Thomas Evans, Robert Wedderburn, John Cannon, William Benbow, and Samuel Waddington, who were all at various times Spenceans, used the debating society, the chapel, and the trial as forums for political satire, publicity, and self-expression. Certain of the extreme Regency radicals were also prepared to use sensational methods including blackmail, extortion, and pornography, yet Spence, working primarily in the very different publishing environment of the 1790s, was a good deal more ingenious and less superficially shocking than his followers. He generally steered clear of openly blasphemous or obscene expressions in his propaganda while he looked to the infiltration of rapidly developing communications networks such as token coin production, the political print, the advertising industry, and children's book publishing. This is a crucial distinction because the satires of Hone and his numerous imitators who were not Spenceans but who take up Spence's methods had much greater impact than the published works of any of Spence's immediate political disciples.

It is necessary to place Spence's works in this wider context in

[11] For a contemporary biography of Spence, see T. Evans, *A Brief Sketch of the Life and Times of Thomas Spence* (1821). See also E. Mackenzie, *A Memoir of Thomas Spence* (1826); A. Davenport, *The Life, Writings, and Principles of Thomas Spence* (1836); Francis Place, 'A Collection for a Memoir of Thomas Spence' BL MS Add. 27808, fos. 138 ff. For Marxist interest in Spence in the 1960s, see Thompson, 138–9, 161–3, 175, 497, 613; P. M. Kemp-Ashraf, 'Selected Writings of Thomas Spence 1795–1814', in P. M. Kemp-Ashraf (ed.), *Essays in Honour of W. Gallacher* (East Berlin, 1966). For the cultural and intellectual context for Spence's thought, see Chase. For Spence's experiments in satire and language theory, see Smith, 90.

view of the way that historians continue to examine his influence simply in terms of the personal following he was able to command. H. T. Dickinson wrote recently that by the 1800s Spence 'still peddled his Land Plan, but his works had a tiny circulation, and he was only able to influence a small group of disciples who met with him in a London tavern'.[12]

Thomas Spence was born in Newcastle in June 1750, one of nineteen children in a poor family, and he was impoverished throughout his life.[13] The most profound influence on his early intellectual development was the Revd James Murray, an extreme Presbyterian who had moved down to Newcastle after his dismissal from a pastoral position in Alnwyck. Murray was something of a local celebrity whose highly inflammatory sermons and political journals, *The Freeman's Magazine* and *The Protestant Packet*, took a firm stand on several issues connected with radicalism. He condemned heavy taxation, land enclosure, and the American war. In the early 1770s Spence and his mentor Murray were active in the agitation surrounding the fight by local inhabitants to prevent the enclosure of the Newcastle town moor. This affair was central to Spence's development as a radical and to his political thought. From the mid-1770s Spence developed the ideas relating to land reform which were to form the basis of his 'land plan' and which were to underpin his political thought from then on.

In 1755, speaking to the Newcastle Philosophical Society, Spence put forward his land theories for the first time in a paper entitled 'The Real Rights of Man'. Here he advocated common ownership of land, the organization of society according to a set of communally owned parishes, and the abolition of all rent and taxes with the exception of a tax paid equally by all members of the parish. Spence's subsequent publishing of the paper in the form of a cheap broadside led to his expulsion from the society. From 1775 to 1792 he remained in Newcastle where he continued to publish tracts, chapbooks, and pamphlets advocating his land reform plan and the plan for language reform which he also developed. During this period things went badly for him: he lost his job as a local school-

---

[12] H. T. Dickinson, *British Radicalism and the French Revolution 1789–1815* (Oxford, 1983), 69.

[13] Spence's 'career' and various activities are described in Rudkin; P. M. Kemp-Ashraf, *The Life and Times of Thomas Spence* (Newcastle, 1983), 11–41; Chase, 18–77; McCalman, *Radical Underworld*, 1, 4, 7, 17–25, 42–9, 117–19.

teacher and his political views and difficult temperament prevented the school he attempted to set up himself from being a success.

Murray died in 1782, Spence's publisher Thomas Saint in 1788, and his wife, with whom he had not been happy, in 1792. Spence decided to move to London and consequently arrived in the capital when the effects of the French Revolution on English political thought were at their height. Both reform and anti-reform societies flourished, and Paine's writings were published. *The Rights of Man*, for the sale of which Spence was to be arrested, appeared in two parts in 1791–2. From 1792 to 1803 Spence, despite continual government harassment, arrest, and imprisonment, produced his most significant publications, prints, and token coinage.

He was involved in radical activity across a wide area, and the government took a keen interest in his activities, regarding him as a dangerous agitator. While certainly in contact with respectable and mainstream radicals such as Francis Place, who wrote an unpublished biography of Spence, he also interacted with other areas of radicalism where politics and underworld criminality could not easily be disentangled. He organized graffiti campaigns, debating societies, and free-and-easies, and by the early nineteenth century had acquired a committed if small circle of disciples who were to form the nucleus of the Society of Spencean Philanthropists set up by Thomas Evans immediately following Spence's death in 1814. The society flourished over the next six years, attracting quite a large following in the capital and increasingly became associated with revolutionary radicalism. Spenceans were actively involved in the planning of two attempts at instigating a popular insurrection, the Spa Fields riot of 1816, and the Cato Street conspiracy of 1817. The government had become concerned enough with the activities of the revolutionary Spenceans to include reports on their gatherings in committee meetings in both the Lords and Commons in 1817. Spence's influence carried beyond the first two decades of the nineteenth century and he exercised a considerable influence on Chartist thought and writing.[14]

During his career he was a token dealer and manufacturer, a philologist and phonetician, a graffiti artist, a journal editor, a leader of debating societies in London and Newcastle, a printmaker, and a publisher of extraordinary courage and ambition. He edited two journals, *Pig's Meat* and *The Giant Killer*, and his numerous chapbooks,

[14] Chase, 173–9.

broadsides, pamphlets, and handbills contained songs, hymns, poems, showman's notices, marginalia, advertisements, letters, declarations, and constitutions. He was tried and imprisoned twice, and conducted his own defence and published his own trials.

Behind all these activities lay the desire to publicize his ideas and to educate the public. Spence's propaganda exerted a significant influence both in formal and methodological terms on subsequent radical agitation. His methods were quickly absorbed by some of his contemporaries in the 1790s, and most noticeably by Daniel Isaac Eaton. More significantly the propaganda of Spence and Eaton provided a framework and a set of models for radical agitation in the period 1816–22.

Spence's influence on and relevance for early nineteenth-century radicalism lay not so much in what he thought but in how he attempted to disseminate that thought. He was prepared to look at any available means of reproduction as a vehicle for his ideas. Conventional aesthetic notions involving hierarchy and quality, or distinctions between beauty and ugliness or literature and pulp, are difficult to apply to his works. His work showed that in popular political satire anything might be joined with anything else.

Most of his contemporaries, including radicals, presented Spence as politically naïve, hopelessly eccentric, and unworldly—a view that has remained surprisingly resilient.[15] It finds much of its justification in the surviving biographical recollections of his contemporaries. The engraver Thomas Bewick knew Spence while he was still living in Newcastle, and his account of a political argument which he had with Spence reveals the violent obsession with which he adhered to his theories. After a meeting in which Bewick, together with most of the company, had voted against Spence's 'plan' he found Spence

became swollen with indignation which, after all the company were gone, he vented upon me, to reason with him was useless—he began by calling me (from my silence) a sir Walter Blackett, and adding 'If I had been as stout as you are I would have thrashed you'—indeed! said I 'it is a great pity you are not'—but said he, 'there is another way in which I can do the business, and have at you!' he then produced a pair of cudgels—and to work we fell, after I had black'ned the insides of his thighs and Arms, he

[15] T. R. Knox, 'Thomas Spence: The Trumpet of Jubilee', *Past and Present*, 76 (1977) 75–99: 'his obsession with his [land reform] "plan", well rooted by his middle age, stunted Spence and produced a radical crank'.

became quite outrageous, and behaved very unfairly, which obliged me to give him a severe beating.[16]

Francis Place summarized Spence's character and politics in a passage in his unpublished biography of Spence:

He was a very simple, very honest single minded man, querulous in his disposition odd in his manners, he was remarkably irritable. He was perfectly sincere, unpractised in the ways of the world, to an extent few could imagine in a man who had been pushed about in it as he had been, yet what is more remarkable this character never changed, and he died as much of a child in some respects as he was when he arrived at the usual age of manhood.[17]

Spence's refusal to compromise his ideas or his life and his unflinching commitment to idealistic egalitarian notions certainly make him appear naïve from the perspective of a worldly political operator such as Place; yet Spence's works reveal him to have been anything but a political innocent. The different ways in which he attempted to disseminate his theories, using as many commercial forms as possible, show him to have been a shrewd and sophisticated thinker capable of great satiric tact.

One of the most successful and surprising of Spence's operations as a radical propagandist was his production of token coinage. In England during the last two decades of the eighteenth century copper currency was in such a neglected condition that various forms of alternative token coinage were struck independently in enormous quantities.[18] The coins had several functions. While usually struck simply as currency, they were also produced for commemorative reasons or by individual businesses as advertisements.[19] The potential of the tokens for political propaganda was exploited to a limited extent before Spence's activities in the field. Medals and tokens had been struck on a large scale to celebrate Wilkes's victories in the Middlesex elections of 1768 and 1773. Tokens of Pitt, Fox,

---

[16] Thomas Bewick, *A Memoir of Thomas Bewick Written by Himself*, ed. Iain Bain (Oxford, 1975), 53. For the opinions of Pitt and Southey, see McCalman, *Radical Underworld*, 66.

[17] Francis Place Papers, BL MS Add. 27808, fo 152.

[18] D & H, i, intro.; *British Numismatic Journal and Proceedings of the British Numismatic Society*, vols. *1–3* (London, 1904–6), 1: 299–332, 2: 369–97, 3: 271–81; Waters, 9–11; R. C. Bell, *Commercial Coins 1787–1804* (Newcastle, 1963), 9–11; Whiting, 13–31; Newark, 3–8.

[19] Newark, 7, 14–18; Whiting, 99–112, 119–120; D & H, v. 144–6; R. C. Bell, *Tradesman's Tickets and Private Tokens 1785–1819* (Newcastle, 1966), pp. xi–xii.

and Sheridan were brought out as part of the propaganda during the King's illness of 1789. Further patriotic tokens were brought out by the Pittites after the King's recovery. The trial and acquittal of the leaders of the London Corresponding Society in November 1794 led to a mass of celebratory tokens. All these examples are unambitious in terms of the way they used the form and mostly consisted of portraits which accompanied uplifting inscriptions. It was left to Spence to use the token as a satiric vehicle, and to exploit its different functions, in trade, advertising, and the collector's market.[20]

Spence designed a range of dies and with these struck many different series of coins of penny, halfpenny, and farthing denominations. These combined folklore, proverbs, and literary quotation. They also developed the popular imagery of chapbooks and late eighteenth-century children's emblem books. He produced them as currency, for the collector's market, and as a form of free advertising.[21] He is described as throwing large numbers of them out of the windows of his shop to passers-by on the London streets, much in the manner of a free advertiser's hand-out of today.[22] The extent to which Spence's tokens were distributed on a national scale, both as currency and as free propaganda, has not been sufficiently analysed. E. P. Thompson's conclusion that 'his propaganda was scarcely likely to win any massive following in urban centres, and never seems to have reached any rural districts' does not hold up for the tokens. Spence's coins reached a variety of counties apart from Middlesex. They were circulating in different forms in London, Newcastle, Hastings, Birmingham, and all over Worcestershire, and in Ireland and France. A contemporary description of Spence's token business suggests that it was a considerable operation:[23]

[20] Whiting, 121–30; Newark, 8. For Pitt, Fox, and Sheridan's tokens, see Whiting, 121–4. For Wilkes, see Laurence Brown, *A Catalogue of British Historical Medals* (London, 1980), 27–35, 42.

[21] The best discussion of this question is still that of Waters, 9–11. See also Kemp-Ashraf, *The Life and Times of Thomas Spence*, 194–5.

[22] Francis Place Papers, BL Add. MS 27808, fos. 182–5.

[23] Thompson, 162. For the distribution of Spence's tokens in the British Isles, see D & H i. 7, no. 35; 30, no. 1; iv. 95, no. 39; viii. 217, no. 20; ix. 251, no. 2; 257, no. 33; x. 285, nos. 230, 239; 317–18, nos. 7–31. Spence's tokens even got to Munster; see xiii. 521, nos. 14–15. For France, see Christopher Brunel and Peter Jackson, 'Notes on Tokens as a Source of Information on the History of the Labour and Radical Movements', pt. 1, *Bulletin of the Society for the Study of Labour History*, 13 (1966), 27. See also *Seaby's Coin and Medal Bulletin* (June 1964), 229.

It is not long since I called at Spence's shop, and saw many many thousands of different tokens lying in heaps, and selling at what struck me to be very great prices. These, therefore, could not be considered as struck for a limited sale. I confess, considering the number of them I saw struck, and what the subjects of them were, I thought myself justified in supposing that it was the intention to circulate them very widely.[24]

Spence knew a lot about the token-collector's market. He produced limited editions of several of his tokens in silver or white metal, a practice which catered for the specialist market. He also produced *The Coin Collector's Companion, Being a Descriptive Alphabetical List of the Modern Provincial Political and other Token Coinage*, which includes an introduction in which Spence states that the printing of tokens was often inspired by popular reactions to such events as the French Revolution or the Birmingham riots. This suggests that Spence was familiar with the popular propaganda which came out of France during the Revolution and which provided brilliant examples of the conversion of the iconography of traditional state propaganda into revolutionary satire. Coins and medals were particularly charged in this context. They had been considered such a potent weapon of propaganda that Louis XIV declared them a royal monopoly. When the Revolution came masses of medals and tokens were produced commemorating historic episodes such as the storming of the Bastille, the King's enforced return to Paris, and the execution of the King and Queen. Many were designed and signed by the common artisans and labourers who produced them and were a direct celebration of the destruction of the *ancien régime*. The fall of the Bastille was by far the most popular subject to appear on tokens and in prints and Spence produced a token of this subject himself for the English market.[25] Spence's *Companion* and his activities in the coin-collector's market are typical of his infiltration and politicization of publishing environments normally considered to be apolitical. There was strong contemporary reaction. The attacks on him in a series of articles in *The Gentleman's Magazine* show

[24] *Gentleman's Magazine*, 67 (Apr. 1797), 269.
[25] Jones, 1–3. For the image of the Bastille in revolutionary propaganda, see Claude Langlois, 'Counter-revolutionary Iconography', in *French Caricature and the French Revolution 1789–1799*, exhibition cat. (Los Angeles, 1988), 42–3; Michael Beurdeley, *La France à l'encan: exode des objets d'art sous la Révolution* (Fribourg, 1981), 18–20; Jean Jacques Levêque, *L'Art et la Révolution française 1789–1804* ([Neuchâtel,] 1987), 55–74. For its influence on English radical literature and thought including Blake and Erasmus Darwin, see Albert Boime, *Art in an Age of Revolution* (Chicago, 1987), 330–1. For Spence's Bastille token, see Waters, 23; D & H vi. 166, no. 692.

the efficacy of his token propaganda. One contributor complains: 'His dies were numerous; and they were interchanged almost beyond the powers of calculation. The designs of many of his pieces were contemptible and illiberal in the extreme ... they have not either taste or beautiful execution to recommend them, but are struck in a very careless and awkward manner upon the most corrupt copper.'[26] The outrage is directed against the method of production. The very crudity of Spence's coins is seen as reprehensible and threatening. The statement 'his dies were numerous and interchanged almost beyond the powers of calculation' unwittingly reveals the efficient way Spence exploited the processes of manufacture and the double-sided nature of the coin. His dies were designed so that they could be recombined with each other to create a series of different messages. Almost any combination for the obverse and reverse of a token was both possible and effective. Spence developed a visual and verbal medium that would creatively combine set elements. In ringing the changes 'almost beyond the powers of calculation' Spence promulgated his ideas through an ever varying series of juxtapositions.

Spence's tokens mirror his publications in incorporating a bewildering mixture of material. They include satire, straightforward statements of political belief, and many non-political images. Several tokens appear to have been produced as popular entertainment and some even take the form of occasional celebrations of victories in the French wars. It is probable that Spence produced these to entice an audience that would have found the political tokens unacceptable.

By far the majority of Spence's token output was aggressively political presenting the essence of his views on slavery, taxation, land reform, and the French Revolution. His uncompromising opinions adapted well to the combination of image and aphorism on a coin. The picture of an American Indian with a bow encircled by the words 'IF RENTS I ONCE CONSENT TO PAY MY LIBERTY IS PASSED AWAY' (Fig. 6) is a good example of the way Spence could anchor his theory in popular imagery. Indians were a fairground phenomenon as well as serving in the context of political debate as representatives of the natural man. Spence may also have been familiar with examples of the copper currency struck in New York and Massachusetts by the victorious colonists in the late 1780s. Several coins carried the image

26 *Gentleman's Magazine*, 68 (Feb. 1798), 122.

Fig. 6. Thomas Spence. Trade token. American Indian. Inscribed if
RENTS I ONCE CONSENT TO PAY MY LIBERTY IS PASSED AWAY. 1794.

Fig. 7. Thomas Spence. Trade token. A cat. Inscribed MY FREEDOM
I AMONG SLAVES ENJOY. 1796.

of a brave carrying a bow and arrow as an expression of the fierce independence of the new nation.[27]

Spence produced several tokens which turn the tables on the viewer revealing satire beneath what appears to be almost simple entertainment. Animal imagery is used particularly effectively in this context. A token showing a cat bears the inscription 'MY FREEDOM I AMONG SLAVES ENJOY' (Fig. 7). This makes a general point about liberty similar in its effect to that of the Indian token. Here the message is that the domestic pet has more freedom than the people who keep it. Spence is both asserting his own freedom (he regarded the token as his personal symbol) and accusing his audience of being unaware of their thraldom. Many tokens question the acquiescent servitude of the British public, a satiric stance which is probably inherited from the sermons of James Murray. One shows a dog with a stick in its mouth and is inscribed 'MUCH GRATITUDE BRINGS SERVITUDE' (Fig 8), another shows a snail crawling along in a pastoral landscape with the inscription 'A SNAIL MAY PUT HIS HORNS OUT' (Fig. 9). This is informed with a gentle but taunting sarcasm. The primary thrust of the satire is against the oppressors for tyrannizing the people to an extent where they cannot go their own slow way or express themselves, but the comparison of the people unfavourably with a mollusc is again challenging their docility. Spence has the boldness as a satirist to attempt to stir up his audience by insulting them for their failings while simultaneously sympathizing with their sufferings. The homely animal imagery enjoys an unspecified status; the semiotic implications of the tokens remain fluid, for it is only the aphoristic inscriptions that anchor them in a specific meaning.

Many of Spence's coins consisted of images and proverbs which were open-ended and which could react in different ways if connected to more specific political messages on the other side of a token. Powerful and often hilarious effects could result. One of Spence's tokens shows a guillotine standing in stark outline on a platform. The design is unadorned except for three steps, the empty basket awaiting the victim's head, and a distant building. The token

---

[27] R. D. Altick, *The Shows of London* (Cambridge, Mass., 1978), 46–8, 276–9, 286–7. For Spence's discussions of the Indian and land ownership, see Thomas Spence, *The Political Works of Thomas Spence*, ed. H. T. Dickinson (Newcastle, 1982), 41–4. For the American coins, see Cory Gillillano, 'Early American Copper Coinage in Relation to the Art and Taste of the Period', in *America's Copper Coinage 1783–1857* (New York, 1985), 77–9.

Fig. 8. Thomas Spence. Trade token. A dog. Inscribed MUCH GRATITUDE
BRINGS SERVITUDE. 1795.

Fig. 9. Thomas Spence. Trade token. Snail. Inscribed A SNAIL MAY PUT HIS
HORNS OUT. 1795.

FIG. 10. Thomas Spence. Trade token. A guillotine. Inscribed HALPENNY.
1793.

was simply inscribed HALPENNY (Fig. 10). The image was ambiguous.
In loyalist propaganda it had become the central symbol of the
Terror and of the collapse of the French Revolution into blood-lust
and recrimination.[28] Negative associations for the image were standard in the political prints of Gillray and his imitators. In radical
circles, however, the image had maintained its significance as a
triumphant expression of liberty. It was an explicit reference to the
culminating event in the death of the old order, the decapitation of
the King, its symbolic head. More extreme radical publications of
the 1790s had alluded to the desire to see George III suffer a similar
fate. One of the most inflammatory pieces of evidence brought forward by the prosecution during Thomas Hardy's trial for high

[28] Gillray's *A View in Perspective* (*BMC*, no. 8300), *Destruction of the French Colossos*
(*BMC*, no. 9260), *Apotheosis of Hoche* (*BMC*, no. 9156), and Cruikshank's *The Radical's
Arms* (*BMC*, no. 13275), *A View of the Grand Triumphal Pillar* (*BMC*, nos. 12541,
12541a) and *A Radical Reformer or a Neck or Nothing Man* (*BMC* no. 13271). For the
English obsession with the image of the guillotine, see Ronald Paulson, 'The Severed
Head', in *French Caricature and the French Revolution*, 55–65.

treason was a handbill which opened 'A New and Entertaining Farce Called la GUILLOTINE or George's head in a basket'.[29] Spence's token developed the theme with great vivacity, for he issued it with the conventional portrait of the King's head on the reverse. Juxtaposed with the guillotine the image ceases to be read as a classical bust of the King and is inverted into a celebration of the destruction of the monarchy. Spence's token has a laconic simplicity which relates to the grim humour of popular French prints brought out after the King's execution. One bipartite print shows a crown suspended in mid-air with the inscription 'I have lost a head'. On the right, below a crudely drawn guillotine, is the rejoinder 'I have found one'.[30] Spence engineered his own assault on state-sanctioned images of the royal head through his counter-striking of legal tender. Although rare, a few examples survive where Spence has stamped a slogan such as 'No Landlords You Fools, Spence's Plan Forever' across the King's face.[31]

Spence was a multi-media satirist. Several of his most outspoken tokens were simultaneously produced as prints either by him or by other publishers. The token showing a man walking on all fours with the inscription 'IF THE LAW REQUIRES IT WE WILL WALK THUS' (Fig. 11) also came out as a small format caricature etching (Fig. 12). Sometimes the imagery from two tokens would be conflated into one print. The token showing an ass loaded with a double set of panniers inscribed 'rents' and 'taxes', and bearing the title 'I WAS AN ASS TO BEAR THE FIRST PAIR' was also brought out as part of a print caricature (Figs. 13 and 14). This contains the figure of the American Indian on the left who looks at the ass on the right. The text has been altered from the token so that the Indian now exclaims, 'Behold the civilized Ass / Two pair of Panyers on his back / The first with Rents a Heavy Mass / With Taxes next his Bones do Crack'. The Ass replies 'I'm doom'd to endless Toil and Care, I was an Ass to bear the first pair.'[32] The choice of the image of the overloaded ass as a metaphor for the burdens of the common man indicates Spence's instinctive feeling for popular culture. It had been

[29] Quoted in John Wardroper, *Kings, Lords and Wicked Libellers: Satire and Protest 1760–1837* (London, 1973), 165–6.
[30] Waters, 19. For humorous French prints dealing with the king's decapitation, see Daniel Arasse, *La Guillotine dans la Révolution*, exhibition cat. (Paris, 1987), 127–31.
[31] *The Shadow of the Guillotine*, exhibition cat. (London, 1989), items 206–06.
[32] Waters, 13; Kemp-Ashraf, *The Life and Times of Thomas Spence*, 193. For Murray's influence on Spence, see ibid. 17–25; Chase, 40–7.

FIG. 11. Thomas Spence. Farthing trade token. Man walking on all fours.
Inscribed IF THE LAW REQUIRES IT WE WILL WALK THUS. 1796.

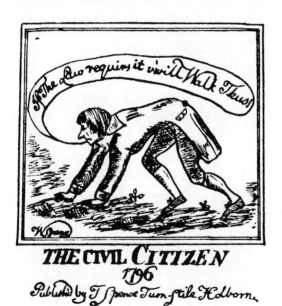

FIG. 12. Thomas Spence. Etching. *The Civil Citizen*. 1796.

Fig. 13. Thomas Spence. Trade token. Ass with double panniers. Inscribed I WAS AN ASS TO BEAR THE FIRST PAIR. 1796.

Fig. 14. Thomas Spence. Etching. *The Contrast*. 1796.

used on the engraved frontispiece to all early editions of James Murray's *Sermons to Asses*. The image also ran throughout the heyday of the satiric print from the 1780s until the 1820s. It was to be the basis of Cruikshank's celebrated print *Poor Bull and his Burden; or, The Political Murraion* and continued to be a staple in political prints in England and France throughout the nineteenth century.[33] Spence also brought out a token showing a pig trampling on emblems of the Church and state. This image related to his journal *Pig's Meat; or, Lessons for the Swinish Multitude* and to the whole body of prints and journals that had capitalized upon Burke's notorious reference to the common people in *Reflections*. The various forms of advertising which Spence used to sell his publication highlight his formal versatility as a political satirist. A bubble coming from the pig's mouth in the token announced 'PIG'S MEAT PUBLISHED BY THOMAS SPENCE LONDON'. Spence produced *Pig's Meat* firstly in weekly penny numbers then in bound editions in single- and three-volume form. Spence also produced handbills which he called *Loose meat for the Pigs* and which contained songs and other material extracted from the journal. He even brought out a caricature of the pig developed from the token and carrying the jingle 'This is that matchless Pigs meat / So famous far and near / Oppressors hearts it fills with dread / But poor men's hearts does cheer'. Sometimes copies of this caricature would be bound into copies of the collected edition of *Pig's Meat*.[34]

Spence's tokens and publications provided specific models for a multitude of radical pamphlets and prints in the second decade of the nineteenth century.[35] It is above all the ebullience and bravura of Spence's satiric stance that make him such a significant antecedent of the next generation of radical publicists. Spence's contemptuous and hilariously irreverent attitude to what he considered the figureheads of corrupt state power are increasingly mirrored by the later radicals, who similarly launched concentrated campaigns of ridicule at individual members of the Liverpool administration and with most fervent irreverence at the Regent. The basis of much of Cobbett's satire in attacks on the corruption and

---

[33] *BMC*, nos. 6962, 13288. for a discussion of the allegory of the social pyramid in the political print, see Robert Philippe, *Political Graphics: Art as a Weapon* (Oxford, 1982), 15–16.

[34] Waters, 21.

[35] Marcus Wood, 'Popular Satire in Early Nineteenth-Century Radicalism, with Special Reference to Hone and Cruikshank', D.Phil. thesis, Oxford University, 1989, 82–4.

luxury of individuals, his genius for creating nicknames, which Hazlitt picked out as one of the glories of his prose style, and the basis of
his political argument in a stolid egoism can all be related back to
Spence. In his hate campaign against Pitt Spence pointed the way
for the later radicals. Spence's attacks on Pitt present a remarkable
example of a self-educated working man in the 1790s using all the
resources of the contemporary media at his disposal to attack, as a
personal enemy and equal, a major political figure.

Spence wrote the pamphlet *A Letter from Ralph Hodge to his Cousin
Thomas Bull*. This ironically attacked Pitt's financial policies and its
form was craftily based on the Reevesite Association's series of
letters between Thomas and John Bull. He also produced a series of
tokens attacking Pitt in the most personally violent terms. One
showed Pitt's head on the top of a pole under which four rustics
dance holding hands in a circle. The caption reads 'TREE OF
LIBERTY' (Fig. 15). Two tokens use the famous Janus head, a satiric
medallic device which dates back at least to the time of Luther. One
shows the head of Pitt looking out to the left and conjoined to that of
the Devil, whose face also resembles that of Pitt only it carries two
horns. The caption reads 'EVEN FELLOWS'. The identification of Pitt
with the Devil was a general one in the radical press of the day. The
device on the medal had, however, a specific history in Lutheran
anti-Catholic satire, where the conjunction of the head of the Pope
with that of the Devil was standard, and this identification had been
absorbed into English eighteenth-century broadsides and caricature
satire and would not have been lost on Spence's audience.[36]

Spence's other anti-Pitt tokens go even further in the virulence of
their satire. In one Pitt is presented hanging on the gallows (Fig. 16).
The inscription 'END OF PIT' includes a pun that is both graphic and
linguistic. The I in the middle of Pitt's name is presented literally as
an open eye. This image revivifies popular iconographic tradition.
The discovery of the Gunpowder Plot, the destruction of the
Armada, and the execution of enemies of the state were conventionally presented in prints from the seventeenth century onwards as

---

[36] For the identification of Pitt with the Devil, see Waters, 30. Waters claims that
Spence may be the author of the squib he quotes but gives no evidence beyond the
similarity of the token and the verse. For another squib on the Pitt–Devil theme, see
PP ii. 54. For the history and continuing influence of the Janus head motif, see F. P.
Barnard, *Satirical and Controversial Medals of the Reformation: The Biceps or Double Headed
Series* (Oxford, 1927), 1–45; Scribner, 166, 233–4; E. H. Gombrich and E. Kris,
Caricature (Harmondsworth, 1940), 8. For the development of the image in English
graphic satire, see *BMC*, nos. 319, 1505, 6234, 6570, 8433, 13290.

FIG. 15. Thomas Spence. Trade token. Four men dancing round Pitt's head on a pole. Inscribed TREE OF LIBERTY. n.d.

FIG. 16. Thomas Spence. Farthing Token. Pitt on the Gallows. Inscribed END OF PIT. n.d.

divinely ordained events. God's approval in the destruction of evil was shown by the depiction of the all-seeing eye of God, placed above an illustration of the events concerned. Spence's token satirically exploits the convention. In presenting the Prime Minister as an enemy of the state executed beneath the eye of God Spence ironically redirects a powerful image of state propaganda. There is sheer daring in such a reversal and refined dexterity in a pun that is both orthographic and typographic.[37]

Spence's attacks on Pitt were carried into his journal *Pig's Meat* and he incorporated mock advertisements with great skill. He reproduced a handbill supposedly advertising a performance by 'Signor Gulielmo Pittachio'. Spence's was one of several reprintings of this celebrated squib by the satirist and jacobin sympathizer Robert Merry. The piece was brought out in several periodicals and appeared as a broadside carrying an illustrated headpiece which showed a caricature of Pitt ringing a bell. Merry's piece is a revealing example of the extreme satiric experimentation which the French Revolution generated in England in the early 1790s. Merry and Spence were, on the face of it, strange satiric bedfellows, but the Revolution brought them briefly within the same ideological pale.

Educated at Harrow and King's College, Cambridge, after unsuccessfully trying careers in the law and the Army, Merry squandered a substantial inheritance at the gaming-tables and then travelled Europe. In Rome he met, and was befriended by, the painter David. Merry ended up in Florence where he became a notorious figure in the English colony, writing verses and carrying on an open affair with Countess Cowper. Back in England by 1787 he embarked on a literary career writing plays, verse tales, and journalism. The events in France in 1789 suddenly changed his life: he was smitten with the ideals of the Revolution and travelled immediately to Paris. He made another trip there in 1791 and, renewing his friendship with David, found himself at the hub of revolutionary activity. His celebratory poetry, and his writings on the nature of government, were favourably received by the French National Convention, and Merry was in Paris throughout the period of the King's flight to Varennes and of his subsequent capture and eventual trial. A ticket for a seat at

[37] For the satiric history of the image of the hanging man, see Gombrich and Kris, *Caricature*, 9: E. Kris, *Psychoanalytic Explorations in Art* (New York, 1964), 192–4; Scribner, 78–80. For the device of the eye of God, see *BMC*, nos. 13, 41, 45, 10737, 10738.

the King's execution was even reserved for Merry, although he declined to take it up. On his return to England in 1793 he became a fierce satiric opponent of Pitt, and of his war policy in particular. It was at this period that he composed *Sigor Pittachio*.[38]

Merry's willingness to use lower forms of publishing, his accessible satiric style, and his utter hostility to the Pitt administration allowed working-class radicals to take him up. In using the mock showman's notice Merry was adapting a popular satiric form that had been used by Rochester, Swift, and a host of anonymous eighteenth-century pamphleteers. *Signor Pittachio* opens

WONDERFUL EXHIBITION!!!

SIGNOR

Gulielmo   Pittachio

The SUBLIME WONDER of the World!!!

Condescends to inform the Public at large, and his friends in particular, that he has now opened his

Grand Hall of Exhibitions at Westminster, with a grand display of his

ASTONISHING AND MAGNIFICENT DECEPTIONS; . . .

First—The Signor will bring forward

A Magical ALARM BELL,

At the ringing of which all the Company will become mad or Foolish.

Secondly he will produce his justly Celebrated CURIOUS SPY GLASSES,

which distort and misrepresent all Objects that are looked at through them . . .

Thirdly—by means of an ENCHANTED DRUM, he will set all the Company a

FIGHTING, for the avowed Purpose of preserving

ORDER AND TRANQUILLITY.

During the Battle Signor Pittachio will convey their MONEY OUT of their

POCKETS in a New and Entertaining Manner . . .

In the Course of the Entertainment the Sublime Pittachio will exhibit

UPWARDS OF TWO HUNDRED AUTOMATA, OR MOVING PUPPETS,

who will rise up, sit down, say Yes, or No, Receive Money, Rake among the

Cinders, or do any Dirty Work he may think proper to put them to[39]

---

[38] For Merry's life see entry for Robert Merry in *DNB*, *The Monthly Magazine*, 7 (1799), 255–8, and P. W. Clayden, *The Early Life of Samuel Rogers* (1887), 283–4.

[39] For the broadside, see *BMC*, no. 8500; see also George's discussion of this print in *BMC*. The print was produced in a great number of different versions and forms. Its authorship is, with somewhat overblown praise, attributed to Robert Merry in an obituary notice in *The Monthly Magazine*, 7 (1799), 258. 'His [Merry's] Signor Pittachio . . . must ever be considered a most happy production of keen satire, unsurpassed by anything in ancient or modern times.'

Of all forms of advertisement the mountebank's and quack doctor's were the most disreputable. By the end of the eighteenth century there was a history of hostile criticism attached to them and Merry brings this opprobrium down on Pitt's head.[40] The satire operates on a number of narrational and fictive levels and uses the rhetoric of this form of advertising with surprising delicacy. While the primary narrative voice is supposed to be that of the fictive Pittachio, the author's voice breaks through the surface at times in undisguised outrage. The description of the control which Pitt exerts over the House of Commons is a good case in point: 'In the Course of the Entertainment the Sublime Pittachio will exhibit UPWARDS OF TWO HUNDRED AUTOMATA, OR MOVING PUPPETS, who will rise up, sit down, say Yes, or No, Receive Money, Rake among the Cinders, or do any Dirty Work he may think proper to put them to.' The first sentence exhibits a latinate and circumlocutory diction, the tone of grandiose patronage reaching a climax with the translation of the word 'automata' into the plain English 'moving puppets'. This is immediately succeeded by the introduction of a series of short, sharp clauses peppered with verbs that describe the helpless responses of the politicians. A mechanical rapidity and awkwardness of movement is suggested through verbal mimesis: 'rise up, sit down, say Yes, or No, Receive Money'. It is as if the speed with which the figures go through their paces destroys all power of individual conscience. The list of orders is carefully arranged as it moves from the purely physical actions of sitting and standing, in themselves not morally charged, to the pairing of 'say Yes, or No', which describes an absolute abuse of language. Sycophancy and moral blindness operate to a degree that confounds semantic content and words which should possess precisely opposite meanings—Yes and No— become interchangeable. From here the development of the inventory into more overt accusations of bribery ('Receive Money') and corruption ('do any Dirty Work') appear inevitable. By this stage the narrational voice is clearly that of Spence, and the fury is expressed without irony.[41]

Such narrational duality allows certain lines to operate a lethal

---

[40] For Swift's use of the form, see *Irish Tracts*, 285–7. For the general background, see *The Wit of the Day; or The Humours of Westminster* (London, 1784), 88–9; Altick, *The Shows of London*, 307; James, *English Popular Literature*, 245; Elliott, 102–13.

[41] Spence's conversion of politicians into puppets may relate to Samuel Foote's controversial use of actors to play puppets on the London stage in the 1790s. See Percy Fitzgerald, *Samuel Foote: A Biography* (London, 1910), 318–34.

ambiguity. Later a 'Dramatic piece in One Act, called The Humbug: Or John Bull a Jack Ass' is proposed. This title can be taken in two ways. Spoken by Pitt it articulates his callous contempt for the British public. Spoken by the author it expresses the anger that Merry felt towards the people for letting themselves be imposed upon.

Merry's piece is a good example of the way his work was absorbed into, and developed by, the radical press. Signor Pittachio inspired a number of sequels including one published by Eaton in his journal *Politics for the People, or, A Salmagundi for Swine*. Eaton's piece is called *More Wonderful Wonders* and echoes the titles of Swift's earlier parodies of the mountebank's broadsheet.[42] In satiric method, however, it is more reminiscent of the Bickerstaff pamphlets. As Swift and his imitators followed up the first Bickerstaff pamphlet with a series of fictional denials of and ripostes to their own earlier satire, all supposedly by Bickerstaff himself, so Eaton presents Pitt replying indignantly to his public in *More Wonderful Wonders*. The process of satiric dialogue and interchange generated by Signor Pittachio was unusual in such popular models in the 1790s but was to become a common and celebratory practice in radical satire by the second decade of the nineteenth century.[43]

Spence constantly questioned and stretched the resources of late eighteenth-century English. His poetry, hymns, and songs are composed in an impressive variety of metric forms. He had a gift for compact and striking language: the inscriptions on the tokens and the titles of his works use proverb, aphorism, and linguistic features which are now associated with the headline and the block language of advertising, but which were only just being developed in the broadside in the 1790s. It is impossible, for obvious reasons, to study the forms of graffiti which Spence chalked over London walls, yet this enterprise again suggests his open approach to language, nor should the graffiti be written off as an impotent or small-scale operation. As late as 1812 Lord Sidmouth sent a circular letter to the police calling attention to the chalking of slogans such as 'Spence's Plan Full Bellies' on walls in London, and Home Office spy reports suggest that Spence, and after his death the Spenceans, organized

---

[42] *PP* ii. 406–7. Eaton also reprinted a version of Signor Pittachio, *PP* ii. 388–9. Compare Swift's titles *The Wonderful Wonder of Wonders* and *The Wonder of all the Wonders that Ever the World Wondered At*, in *Irish Tracts*, 281–7.

[43] Bowden, 257–78.

co-ordinated graffiti campaigns which reached out into the sub-
urbs.[44]

Spence saw language as a political and class weapon and linguistic
reform as an essential stage in political reform. His concern with the
development of a phonetic system that would standardize pronunci-
ation and eliminate class distinctions based on dialect was linked
with his notions of the coming of the millennium. The link is made
explicit in several of the editions of his works which he had printed
according to his phonetic system. The dedicatory poem to *A Supplement to the History of Robinson Crusoe* puts the thesis into urbane
doggerel the full effect of which is only apparent when the text is
seen printed in his specialized alphabet, which he termed the
Kruzonian Manner:

> And dho mi bwk's ĭn kwer Lĭngo
> I wĭl ĭt send tw St. Dŏmĭngo
> Tw dhĕ Rĕpŭblĭk ŏv dhĕ 'Inkăz
> Fŏr ăn ĕgzămpl hŏw tw fram Lŏŏz
> Fŏr hw kăn tĕl bŭt dhĕ Mĭlĕneŭm
> Ma tak ĭts riz frŏm mi pwr Krăneŭm

Spence's concern with the political implications of mass literacy
led him to publish a dictionary, *The Grand Repository of the English
Language*, explaining the conventions of his phonetic system and
printing his new alphabet. He published the majority of his works
both in conventional form and according to his system. And in London in the mid-1790s he tried to launch a phonetic Bible to be sold
in penny numbers.[45]

The variety of published forms in which Spence's work appeared
worked alongside his mastery of vernacular rhetorical modes. In *The
Restorer of Society to its Natural State* he experimented with epistolary
forms, writing a series of open letters to the citizens of England.[46]
Several of his Newcastle publications are in the form of children's
chapbooks, and he wrote these in a style of unembellished simplicity
which complements the vehicle and anticipates the parodic
children's books which the radicals used after 1819. He used various
popular biblical styles connected with the prophetic and millennial

[44] Rudkin, 45, 126–7, 146; Chase, 74.

[45] By far the best account of Spence as linguistic reformer is that of Anthea
Shields, 'Thomas Spence and the English Language', *Transactions of the Philological
Society* (1974–5), 33–45. Shields quotes Spence's dedication to *A Supplement to the
History of Robinson Crusoe*, 42.

[46] *The Political Works of Thomas Spence*, 73–92.

pamphlet literature of London in the 1790s, including *A Fragment of an Ancient Prophecy*.

Spence's millennialism dates from the period of his move to London in late 1780s. At this time the popular interest in millennialism and millenarianism in the capital had led to a publishing boom in astrological, homoeopathic, prophetical, and mystical chapbooks.[47] Spence's stylistic absorption of this material is a complicated affair. Most popular prophetic pamphlets during the mid-1790s, under the initial impact of events in France, had a pre-millennialist basis, that is they assumed the millennium would arrive as a cataclysmic and final event, a day of judgement. Spence appears to have tended towards a more respectable post-millennial position in terms of his eschatology. He believed that the millennium would precede the Second Coming, and manifest itself as an idyllic period, the Spencean Jubilee, which was to be achieved through the mass adoption of his policies of land and language reform.[48]

Spence frequently uses the sensational and apocalyptic style of popular pre-millennialist literature for his own ends, often in surprising contexts. Jon Mee has argued that Blake is doing much the same thing with the rhetoric of his early prophecies.[49] *The Rights of Infants* is a typically strident Spencean chapbook in which the theme of the rights of women and children is explored in a furious dialogue between a working-class mother and an aristocrat. It ends with an attack on Paine's *Agrarian Justice* but the first part of the work, a more general defence of the individual's right to own property, falls into two halves. In the first the woman triumphs over the aristocrat in a debate, in the second she logically and calmly sets forward the basic ideas of Spence's land plan to her vanquished opponent. The climax of the argument in the first half is distinguished by the woman's increasing use of the diction of popular prophecy. Spence's preparedness to adopt this language again both anticipated and provided a method for later radical satire. The woman's outburst climaxes:

Hear me! ye oppressors! ye who live sumptuously every day! ... ye, for whom the heavens above drop fatness, and the earth yields her encrease; hearken to me, I say, ye who are not satisfied with usurping all that Nature

[47] Chase, 47–9.

[48] Malcolm Chase, 'The Concept of Jubilee in Late Eighteenth- and Early Nineteenth-Century England', *Past and Present*, 129 (1990), 138–43.

[49] Jonathan Anson Mee, *Dangerous Enthusiasm: William Blake and the Culture of Radicalism in the 1790s* (Oxford, 1992), 29–39, 52–7.

can yield; ye who are insatiable as the grave ... Your horrid tyranny, your infanticide is at an end! Your grinding the faces of the poor and your drinking the blood of infants, is at an end! The groans of the prisons, the groans of the camp, and the groans of the cottage, excited by your infernal policy, are at an end! And behold the whole earth breaks into singing at the new creation, at the breaking of the iron rod of aristocratic sway, and at the rising of the everlasting sun of righteousness![50]

Spence's journal *Pig's Meat* provides further evidence of his unconstrained approach to the way language could be used in political debate. It was an influential publication. The collected editions sold over a long period.[51] Its form was innovatory. Spence described it as 'the honey or essence of politics' and 'the political bible'. It was a creative anthology of texts concerning liberty, oppression, taxation, revolution, reform, and the luxury and corruption of rulers. Its content varied in style and chronology to an astonishing degree. It included substantial quotations from Civil War and Interregnum texts including Cromwell, Harrington, and his follower William Sprygge. It included pieces of Locke and Berkeley, passages from Shakespeare, Swift, James Thomson, and Goldsmith. There are texts from more contemporary sources, Priestley, Richard Price's lecture on civil liberty, and several quotations from Volney's fashionable *Ruins of Empires*. There is a translation of the French Constitution of 1793, which Spence was to use as the basis for his own utopian *Constitution of Spensonia*, and an account of the dismantling of the Bastille. The journal also took up a number of popular and satiric forms, reprinting songs, hymns, squibs, and showman's notices, and it is of course sprinkled with a good number of Spence's own compositions. Recent commentators see *Pig's Meat* as an anthology of sources for late eighteenth- and early nineteenth-century radical thought.[52] The journal certainly made otherwise expensive and obscure earlier writings available, but it also performed an archaeological function, uncovering a political content in works which were conventionally interpreted in aesthetic terms. The political basis of Goldsmith's *Deserted Village* and the increasing politicization of James Thomson's poetry are emphasized by the texts they are sandwiched between and surrounded by.[53] Spence

[50] *The Political Works of Thomas Spence*, 50.   [51] Chase, 18–19.
[52] Smith, 105–7; Chase, 60–2.
[53] For Goldsmith, see *PM* i. 33–5. The text is placed between an extract from Richard Price, 'On the Excellency of a Free Government', and a tract titled 'On the Responsibility of Kings' by a 'Candid Philosopher'. For Thomson, see *PM* iii. 117.

also prints particularly absurd examples of loyalist propaganda and converts them into his favourite polemic form, the dialogue, by adding his own interjections. There is, for example, a hilarious inter-textual version of Sir John Sinclair's *An Antidote Against Revolutions*, which is now published 'with remarks by a Spensonian on the same' and the title text from St Mark 'out of thy own mouth will I judge thee thou wicked servant'. Sinclair's piece, a fantasy showing how if the king falls society will immediately degenerate into anarchy, ends with a prophet being sent by God to restore society to its former monarchical state. Spence responds with an outburst thoroughly reminiscent of Blake's marginalia: 'Is it not a shame, Sir John, to father such lies upon God, and make him the author of such ridiculous sophistry in favour of oppression?'[54]

The form of the journal has a levelling effect on the content. Spence treats his sources with a utilitarian panache as he applies a cut-and-paste technique indiscriminately to Milton, Shakespeare, anonymous balladeers, and loyalist propagandists. He questions and redefines the notion of a political text, he breaks down boundaries between disciplines and schools of thought, above all he celebrates the accessibility of the English language, an accessibility which, as Olivia Smith has argued, the state rigorously attempted to obfuscate and deny.[55] His confidence and omnivorous approach to form and chronology were increasingly mirrored in Daniel Isaac Eaton's *Politics for the People*. The influence of these journals on radical publications from 1815 to 1822 is pervasive. Wooler's 'Black Neb' feature in *The Black Dwarf* and Hone's collage approach to journal, pamphlet, and book production grow directly out of this tradition.[56]

Eaton was, next to Spence, the most significant and adventurous of the radical satirists prepared to use popular models in the 1790s.[57]

The text is placed between a tract titled 'On the Trust, Power and Duty of Grand Juries' and a passage 'The Ambiguity of Kingly Titles' from Harrington's *Oceana*. For contemporary reactions to the political content of these texts, see Oliver Goldsmith, *Collected Works of Oliver Goldsmith*, ed. Arthur Friedman, 5 vols. (Oxford, 1965), v. 278–9. James Thomson, *Liberty, The Castle of Indolence*, ed. James Sambrook (Oxford, 1986), 37–9.

[54] *PM* iii. 188–92.   [55] Smith, 1–32.

[56] Wood, 'Popular Satire', 119–48, 248 n. 10.

[57] Very little work has been done on Eaton's life or writings. The best account of his career and publications is Daniel M. McCue's splendid article in D. Baylen and Norbert J. Gossman (eds.), *A Biographical Dictionary of Modern British Radicals* (Brighton, 1979), 140–4. My biographical detail has been extracted largely from this source. Smith, 85–7, provides a short discussion of the developing satiric method of *Politics for the People*.

Unlike Spence he did not develop a personal radical philosophy but he shared with him an indomitable courageousness. Eaton was born in 1751 or 1752 and from 1786 until he died in August 1814, just a few days before Spence, he indefatigably wrote and published for the radical cause. He was tried eight times during his career, and endured temporary exile to America, imprisonment, and, as late as 1812, the public pillory.[58]

From 1792 to 1794 he was at the hub of radical activity. By 1793 he had set up his own press and was publishing pamphlets; one of these, *The Pernicious Effects of the Art of Printing upon Society, Exposed*, was a particularly hard-hitting exercise in sustained irony. At the end of 1793 he was arraigned for having published a satire presenting the King as a game-cock which is decapitated. On his release in 1794 he showed his calibre as a publicist by setting up the Cock and Swine as his shop sign. During the 1794 treason trials the government searched his house and business and seized his papers. This did not prevent him from taking a leading role in stirring up support and collecting funds for the imprisoned treason suspects.

In 1797, facing prosecution and certain conviction for publishing the second part of Paine's *The Age of Reason*, Eaton fled to the United States where he remained for at least three years. He was back in England by 1803 and tried and imprisoned on the charges he had fled six years before. He was released on a pardon from the King in 1805, having sworn to desist from political publishing. By 1810, however, he was publishing as energetically as ever, and in 1813 was tried and imprisoned again, this time as a result of publishing the third part of *The Age of Reason*. This trial was a bad mistake on the government's part in terms of the widespread and sympathetic publicity which it earned Eaton. The government was not, however, deterred from indicting him again only a few months before his death.

It was in his writings and publishing activities that Eaton made a lasting contribution to radicalism. He was an indefatigable popularizer of banned and seditious literature. In 1792 he was publishing in pamphlet form Henry 'Redhead' York, James Parkinson, and most importantly the second part of Paine's *The Rights of Man*. Eaton continued to publish and sell Paine throughout his career. Paine authorized him to bring out the 'official' edition of the second part of *The Age of Reason* in 1795. Eaton was passionate in promoting this

[58] For Eaton's exploitation of his trial of 1813, see my discussion, p. 138-40 below.

text in its various parts up to his death. No man suffered as much for disseminating Paine's writings, including Paine himself.

As a republisher Eaton's taste was as eclectic as that of Spence. In August 1794 he began his series of *Political Classics*, which in its short life included texts by Thomas More, Algernon Sydney, and Rousseau. From 1795 to 1796 he published Thelwall's journal *The Tribune*. In this year he also published Pigott's *Political Dictionary*, a witty assault on Pittite political double-talk in the form of a lexicographic parody, and Iliff's *The Duties of Citizenship*. When he re-entered the publishing arena in 1810 he brought out his translation of Helvetius's *The True Sense and Meaning of the System of Nature*, the latest contribution to a career as translator-publisher that had already produced Volney's *The Law of Nature*.

Eaton's achievements were also considerable as a writer and satirist in his own right. His approach to political satire underwent a fundamental change after his detention and subsequent acquittal on three charges of seditious libel in 1794. After his release his journal *Politics for the People* became increasingly experimental in terms of its methodology, and the type of material which it used as the basis for its satires. Like *Pig's Meat* it is a gallimaufry, the very form of which was politically charged. Its mixture of ballads and popular songs (including a reworking of the national anthem beginning, 'God save great Thomas Paine, / The Rights of Man explain / To every soul'), fables, dream visions, mock news-sheets, quack advertisements, and children's games appeared all the more striking in the light of the literary company they kept in the journal, for Eaton continued to reprint texts on such subjects as corruption, injustice, and liberty from a range of sources that included Pindar, Rhianus, the Bible, Shakespeare, Dryden, Butler, Swift, Voltaire, Addison, Wilkes, Dr Johnson, Robespierre, Rousseau, Thelwall, Priestly, and Godwin. There are mock book catalogues and pretended lists of resolutions for Loyalist Associations.[59]

Eaton's contribution to the anti-Pitt campaign included a *Te Deum Pitticus*, which was advertised as a 'Litany to be used every Sunday by the Swinish Multitude'. Parodies of religious forms constituted an ancient tradition of popular satire which first exploded in publishing terms during the pamphlet battles of the Reformation and which was thereafter part of the standard vocabulary of popular political satire. Eaton's work provides further evidence of the popularity of

[59] Smith, 80–9; Wood, 'Popular Satire', 91–6.

the genre in eighteenth-century radical satire: *Politics for the People* is
pitted with mock litanies, catechisms, creeds, and hymns.[60]

As with Spence it is the general tone of Eaton's publication which
is important in demonstrating the confident and independent way in
which radical journalism in the late eighteenth century found its feet
and increasingly built satire out of the most heterogeneous cultural
material. One of the most effective of Eaton's experiments is a curious poem composed according to the game of crambo and titled 'A
Crambo Epistle to Mr. Pitt, on his memory failing him at a late
trial':

> OH! Pitt, lately
> Thy memory
> Gave thee the lie
> Most treacherously,
> When wilfully,
> And craftily,
> With effrontery,
> To the Jury
> Thou didst reply
> To them falsely . . .
> I heartily
> And constantly,
> Pray fervently,
> Thou Pitt may'st hie,
> To the old Baily . . .
> And the Jury
> That shall thee try,
> Find thee guilty.
> So may'st thou die,
> Despicably,
> On gallows high.   (*PP* ii. 368)

The name crambo originates from the Latin phrase 'crambe re-
petita' meaning 'cabbage served up again'. By the early seventeenth
century 'crambe' had come to mean repeated punning or quibbling
on the sound of a word. The game crambo developed out of this. By
1800 it was a children's game. Strutt's *Sports and Pastimes* describes it
as a 'Term used among schoolboys when in rhyming, he is to forfeit
who repeats a word that is said before'. Eaton's rhyme is constructed
according to the rules of this game. The form has great advantages

---

[60] *PP* ii. 353–5. Eaton also included 'The Republican's Creed', which is not
satiric; see *PP* ii. 356–7.

as a political weapon. The rhyme will only stop when a word is repeated and so the poem is charged with the tension of this implicit competition. If the poet has to repeat himself in his criticisms of Pitt he must stop. Hence each new insult is a victory and as the poem totters and stutters its way through its inventory of accusation it appears that there is no end to the evils of the Pitt administration.

Spence and Eaton's publications of the 1790s should be viewed against the background of loyalist propaganda. No clear pattern seems to have emerged for the period after the initial burst of activity from 1792 to 1795. It is certain, however, that during this early period enormous amounts of loyalist propaganda were produced in response to events in France, and more immediately in response to the phenomenal success of Paine's writings and the sudden and organized spread of radicalism through the Corresponding Societies.[61]

Pitt and Dundas built up a propaganda machine which attempted to discredit radical thought and to magnify the dangers of radical activity, and of armed insurrection in particular. The founding of the Association for the Preservation of Liberty and Property against Republicans and Levellers, and its rapid spread through local branches, greatly facilitated the mass dissemination of state-backed propaganda. The government had a very tight hold over the stamped press: Dozier argues that the majority of news bulletins in the established newspapers in London and the provinces were extracted from the government organ *The London Gazette*.[62] There were, however, areas of the publishing trade which the government could not control through the stamp taxes and which became increasingly influential in the 1790s. Radical propagandists increasingly used forms such as the pamphlet, the handbill, the chapbook, and the broadside. Paine had been aware from the start of the way these areas of the media had to be exploited. The second part of *The Rights of Man* came out in February 1792 and was a publishing phenomenon. Paine was writing a few months later of the necessity for following up this advantage through the mass distribution of cheap, simplified editions of the text: 'As we have now got the stone to roll it must be kept going by

---

[61] Austin Mitchell, 'The Association Movement', *Historical Journal*, 4 (1961), 56–77. H. T. Dickinson, 'Popular Conservatism and Militant Loyalism', in Dickinson (ed.), *Britain and the French Revolution 1789–1815* (London, 1989), 105–17.
[62] R. R. Dozier, *For King, Constitution and Country* (Lexington, Ky., 1963), 15.

cheap publications. This will embarrass the Court gentry more than anything else, because it is a ground they are not used to.'[63]

It has not been sufficiently recognized that for working people in the 1790s *The Rights of Man* would frequently have been read not in the form of the lengthy pamphlet, which in its combined form ran to some 120 tightly printed pages, but in highly simplified forms which included broadsides, chapbooks, handbills, and selections. In Paine's trial the Attorney-General complains that *The Rights of Man* was 'thrust into the hands of subjects of every description, even children's sweetmeats being wrapped in it'.[64] Spence's works with their stress on cheapness and variety should be seen as a contribution to this sudden radical exploitation of popular publishing forms. Loyalists rapidly took up the challenge. The Association commissioned pamphlets which were printed in enormous editions and circulated through its local branches with the aid of the Post Office. It is also important to realize that many areas of loyalist opinion merged into genuine popular opinion. H. T. Dickinson and Robert Hole have recently produced work which warns against the dangers of underplaying the intensification of anti-gallic feeling as the 1790s progressed. The evidence that has survived of the spectacular pageants and publications directed against Paine late in 1792 and into 1793 demonstrates the variety and energy of popular reactions against the notion of revolutionary radicalism.[65]

Spence's works in the 1790s must in part be seen as reactions to this publishing environment. He was in London by the early 1790s and was right at the centre of the controversy surrounding the banning of *The Rights of Man*. He was arrested and imprisoned for selling a cheap edition of it. His own publications played a part in the radical attempt to produce a counter-rhetoric to combat government-backed propaganda. His achievement lies partly in the fact that he continued to produce work during the fallow period from 1796 to 1814, when government repression attempted to force radical activity underground and when a definite gap opened up between 'respectable' or intellectual radicalism and popular forms of revolutionary radicalism. Spence was consistently opportunistic and intelligent in the way he looked at publicity; he aimed at producing works with genuine popular appeal that did not patronize the audi-

[63] Thompson, 121; Smith, 68–70; Mark Philp, *Tom Paine* (Oxford, 1989), 41–5.
[64] Thompson, 118.
[65] Dickinson, *British Radicalism*, 26–43; Hole, 'British Counter-Revolutionary Propaganda in the 1790s', 53–69; Bindman, *The Shadow of the Guillotine*, 21, 110.

ence. Spence opened his career as a political activist by reading a lecture on radical agrarian reform to the Newcastle Philosophical Society and was expelled from the society, in the words of Mackenzie, his earliest biographer, 'not for printing it [the lecture] only, but for printing it in the manner of a halfpenny broadside and having it hawked about the streets'. His heroic and efficient career as a grassroots publicist followed him quite literally into the grave. A pair of scales was carried before his coffin. It bore white ribbons in token of his purity and was filled with equal quantities of earth as a symbol of the fairness of his land reform plan. His favourite tokens, those showing the cat and the meridian sun of liberty, were thrown on to his coffin and distributed among the mourners.[66] The Festal Day of the Society of Spencean Philanthropists was Spence's birthday, and the celebratory hymn which Thomas Evans composed to be sung on these occasions emphasizes two things, the variety of Spence's publications and the way he suffered for them:

> His books and songs for forty years,
> He's published many ways.
> For which he oft was sent to Jail
> Grant him your mead and praise.[67]

---

[66] For Spence's sale of Paine, see Rudkin, 78–86; Kemp-Ashraf, *The Life and Times of Thomas Spence* 44–6. for Spence's sale of his lecture, Mackenzie, *A Memoir of Thomas Spence*, 5: and for Spence's funeral, Rudkin, 142–3; McCalman, *Radical Underworld*, 99.

[67] Quoted in Rudkin, 161.

3

Radicals and the Law: Blasphemous Libels and the Three Trials of William Hone

> How majestic is Law! How it swells and looks big;
> How tremendous its brow! and how awful its wig!
> But the frown of a Judge was not valued a fig——
> By the Verdicts of Three Honest Juries, huzza!
>
> (*The Verdicts of Three Honest Juries*, broadside, 1817)

In 1817 Hone became a figure of national celebrity as a result of his three trials. Throughout March and April he had written violently anti-government articles in his periodical *Hone's Reformist's Register*. These attacked the Cabinet's recent suspension of Habeas Corpus and Lord Sidmouth's circular letter sent out to Magistrates in March 'to prevent, as far as possible, the circulation of blasphemous and seditious pamphlets and writings'.[1] Hone had also brought out a series of parodies which used the forms of sacred texts in order to attack the government. Early in May he was arrested on three separate *ex officio* informations for having published three of these, namely *The Late John Wilkes's Catechism*, *The Political Litany*, and *The Sinecurist's Creed*. After two months' imprisonment without trial he was released only to be informed that he would have to face trial in December after all.[2]

In the first two trials Hone was charged with blasphemous and seditious libel and in the third simply with blasphemous libel. The trials were held on consecutive days and Hone conducted his own defence. On each occasion the judge stated that the publication was

---

[1] Quoted in *Hone's Reformist's Register and Weekly Commentary* (12 Apr. 1817), i, cols. 354–5.
[2] For Hone's reactions prior to his trials, see *Hone's Reformist's Register*, i (21 June 1817), col. 679; William Hone Papers, BL. Add. MS 40120, fo. 73; draft of autograph letter, signed from William Hone to Sir Samuel Shepherd, 23 Nov. 1817; Bowden, 159–62.

in his opinion libellous. Hone's defence rested on the claim that his parodies did not ridicule the scriptures but the politicians who formed the real targets for his satire. As evidence he produced a mass of earlier, and unprosecuted, scriptural parodies. At this time a jury was in the position of having to determine from the given evidence in a case not simply a verdict but the law with regard to libel. They agreed with Hone and acquitted him.[3]

Hone's trials bring into focus a number of questions relating to the status of popular radicalism. To what extent did, or even could, working-class radicals control their public image? Were they capable of operating political fictions in order to manipulate public and governmental conceptions of radical thought, organization, and goals? Did they have any idea what their political status should be? What insight did they have into the interactions of Church and state in the area of prosecutions for blasphemy? The official stance towards reform activism was ideally one of distanced calm and patrician disdain, although a pumped-up rhetoric of alarmism could be employed during periods of extreme instability such as the early 1790s or the months following Peterloo.[4] The demands and political manifestos of reformers were consistently marginalized when presented formally. Petitions, no matter what the size or the variety of signatories, were discarded without being read on the grounds that they were couched in an inappropriate, 'vulgar' language.[5] Reform demands were presented as fanatical, anti constitutional, and irreligious. Given the fact that it was in the state's interest to present, and to treat, reform agitation as at best eccentric and at worst the product of a Francophile revolutionary fanaticism, it was a continual struggle for working-class radicals to have themselves and their publications taken seriously by those with power. The respectable literary journals in the first two decades of the nineteenth century reserved their analytical wrath for the productions of socially and linguistically acceptable figures such as Hazlitt, the Hunts, and Brougham. They paid very little attention to the content of the publications of Wooler, Carlile, Benbow, Hone, or even Cobbett. When the writings of these figures were mentioned it was usually in terms

---

[3] William Hone, *Trial by Jury and Liberty of the Press* (London, 1818), 21.

[4] Thompson remains the central study of the formation of radical political consciousness and of government strategies to combat it.

[5] Smith, 30–4; Ann Hone, *For the Cause of Truth*, 144, 157, 159, 261, 264, 269, 278. For the linking of 'vulgar' language with socially unacceptable behaviour in the latter half of the 19th cent., see Raven, 138–41.

of an outraged and undiscriminating opprobrium. Hone and Carlile came in for particularly blind attack. They were singled out by the loyalist press as atheist bogymen on account of their blasphemy trials. Their work and ideas were never seriously addressed by their critics outside the court room.[6]

It is in this context that libel and sedition trials were central to radical debate and self-definition. They were an official acknowledgement that grass-root radical activity, and more significantly that radical thought and publication, had been taken seriously by the government. They provided an officially sanctioned context in which the state, under public scrutiny, had to justify its attitudes. Radical writings and theories were quoted, recited, and discussed seriously by both defence and prosecution. Inside the court room radical publicists could bring their considerable propaganda skills to bear in a setting long established as a focus for public debate and entertainment.

In cases where the accused conducted or contributed to their own defence the inheritance of Protestant martyrology could be utilized and redefined in a variety of ways. The state was presented as aggressor and persecutor attempting to abuse the constitution, to stifle the sacred rights of the free-born Englishman and to stamp out the freedom of the press. Victories such as Hardy's in 1794, or Hone's in 1817, were presented as ordained by Divine Providence. If the state bungled a particular prosecution, the results could be far-reaching. Hone's trials were the most seriously misjudged government prosecutions of a radical since those of Thomas Hardy and Horne Tooke. His acquittals caused a national sensation and so shook government confidence that there were almost no libel trials throughout 1818.[7]

Hone's career as a political journalist spanned the years 1816–22. This period saw sudden increases in government prosecutions for blasphemous and seditious libel and a series of radical counter-offensives which demonstrated the increasing confidence and ingenuity with which they took on the courts. Hone was an inspiration to radicals in his confrontation with the language and procedure of the judiciary. His trial defence consisted of a creative exegesis of the history of religious parody since the sixteenth century, and also related to the early nineteenth-century debate

[6] Crimmins, 130–48. For Carlile, see Henriques, 239, 242–3, 248.
[7] Wickwar, 315.

upon the function of the Catechism, Creed, and Litany within the Church of England. Hone's parodies of the texts and his defence of them should be seen as a contribution to the mainstream intellectual radical attack on the policing role of the state Church. Hone also drew more extensively than any other early nineteenth-century radical on the rich inheritance of Marian heresy trials and Civil War treason trials.

Between the 1794 treason trials and the mass production of radical and loyalist propaganda which came out of the trial of Queen Caroline in 1821 the radical press steadily enlarged the scope and ingenuity of its attacks on the state judiciary. Hone made a major contribution to the development of this branch of propaganda. His trials should not be seen in isolation but as part of a host of experimental publications which came out between 1816 and 1822. The court room came to provide radical publicists with a core structure around which to arrange publishing activities, and Hone was particularly aware of the different types of parody which surrounded the trial. Between 1816 and 1821 he produced and frequently developed almost every available form of legal satire. Radical publication focusing on trials came to include the exhaustive reprinting of each day's events in journals and newspapers, the production of print caricatures featuring the major combatants and events leading up to the final appearance in court, and the concoction of street ballads, songs, and pamphlet squibs. On top of this the text of the trials themselves, often in a carefully worked-up form, was brought out before public interest in the events had cooled. Many of these forms incorporated materials developed out of long-established types of popular satire and gallows literature.

The production of judicial satire climaxed in the exuberant pamphlets and prints which mushroomed around the trial of Queen Caroline. Several of the most notorious and widely imitated of the satires based on legal forms were produced by Hone, and his work emphasizes that it is profitable to consider the background to the judicial parodies of 1821 in the light of earlier radical exploitation of the political show trial.

Church and Law, Blasphemy and Parody

The charge against which Hone had finally to defend himself was for blasphemous and seditious libel. The emphasis both for defence and prosecution was almost exclusively on the blasphemy charge. The trials were both affected by, and were a contribution to, the special history of blasphemy trials and the parodies which these trials gave rise to.

The Church and courts in England had a long tradition of working together. During the Marian heresy trials conviction and examination took place before an ecclesiastical court which would pass sentence of excommunication. The physical side of the sentencing and punishment was left to a secular court. The Church and the law continued their intimate connection even when blasphemy superseded heresy in state prosecutions for abuse of the Church or scripture. Blasphemy and heresy prosecutions had in turn generated many trial parodies.[8]

Hone was familiar with the most widely used tropes attacking the Pope and Catholicism. He owned an 1806 reprint of *The Trial of Antichrist*, a lengthy anti-Catholic pamphlet in which the Pope under the appellation of Antichrist is put on trial for 'High Treason against His Most Sacred Majesty, King of Heaven and Earth'. The legal forms for a treason trial are followed closely. The indictment is read, the accused is asked to raise his hand and to plead, the jurors are sworn, and Antichrist objects to several of them. The witnesses consist of historical personages giving evidence of the Catholic Church's undeviating history of crime. Many of the witnesses are resurrected martyrs from the Marian persecutions, and the overall effect of the work is not unlike an abbreviated dramatization of Foxe's *Actes and Monuments*. The climax of the work comes with the Pope's elaborate sentencing:

you shall be drawn upon a hurdle to the place of execution, where you shall be hung with the chain of restraint, but not until you are dead; but while you are yet alive, your church, which is your body, shall be taken down and you deprived of the vitals of your religion. Then a mighty Angel shall proclaim from heaven, louder than the most tremendous peal of thunder, *Babylon the great is fallen, is fallen*, and that the hour of your judgement is come. Your head or dominion shall then be struck off with the sword of God's inflexible justice, when the Lord of Hosts himself *will consume it with the spirit of his mouth*.[9]

The official punishment of the traitor—to be hanged, drawn, quartered, and decapitated provides the underlying structure. The official

[8] Henriques, 5–17, 54–99. Crimmins, *Secular Utilitarianism*, 160–82.
[9] *The Trial of Antichrist* (London, 1806), 191. For Hone's copy, see 1827 book sale catalogue, item 218.

terms of sentencing are followed minutely but are married to a biblical allegorical interpretation which incorporates Protestant readings of the Last Judgment through the Book of Revelation. Fragments from the prophecies of Revelation concerning the whore of Babylon are worked into the pamphlet to produce a hybrid that combines biblical and judicial language.

Hone was also aware of the trial parodies which surrounded more down-to-earth blasphemy trials, several of which remained in print throughout the eighteenth century. By far the most popular publication of Thomas Sherlock, Bishop of London and friend of Robert Walpole and Queen Caroline, was his *Tryal of the Witnesses*, which came out in 1729.[10] It grew out of the general interest surrounding the blasphemy trial of Thomas Woolston. Woolston had published a series of attacks on the miracles of Christ which argued that they should be interpreted as metaphors not as events. Sherlock's mock trial attempts to vindicate a literal reading of the miracles by bringing the Apostles to trial over the charge of 'giving false evidence in the case of the Resurrection of Jesus'. This rather laboured parody was frequently reprinted in the eighteenth and early nineteenth centuries and upholds a stiffly establishment line on state religion. Other parodies were of more direct use to Hone and radicals interested in formulating a practice for ridiculing repressive aspects of state religion.

William Whiston, millenarian, philosopher of science, convinced enemy of Trinitarianism and of the Athanasian Creed in particular, was thrown out of his Cambridge professorship in 1710 for his blasphemous publications. A parody soon appeared: *The Tryal of William Whiston, Clerk, for Defaming and Denying the Holy Trinity, Before Lord Chief Justice Reason*. This defends Whiston and presents his prosecutors as having monotonous recourse to the Church and King mob to prove its case when reason fails. Dr Trip of Oxford is the most outrageous of the ecumenical advocates. The following address encapsulates his hysterical claims to represent the people: 'If I cannot have justice from the court, I will have it from the people. Fire; Murder; The Church is in Danger; down with the Heretics; Tear them to pieces; Beat their Brains out.'[11] Just over a century later Thomas Love Peacock, in his most explicit attack upon the repressive Liverpool

[10] Hone, 1827 book sale catalogue, item 221.
[11] *The Tryal of William Whiston, Clerk* (1740), 13. For Hone's copies, see 1827 book sale catalogue, items 381, 383.

administration, repeated the joke in more expansive but strikingly similar terms. *Melincourt* features a discussion of the volatile political situation in the years directly after Waterloo. Mr Vamp, Mr Anyside Antijack (Canning), Mr Derrydown (Castlereagh), and Mr Paperstamp, the principal inhabitants of Mainchance Villa, constantly blank out problems and justify extreme action through recourse to the chant 'The Church is in danger'. The cry had survived unadulterated since Whiston's day and in Peacock's hands attains the status of a pavlovian panacea to justify any coercion:

MR. VAMP.   Moral philosophy! Every man who talks of moral philosophy is a thief and a rascal, and will never make any scruple of seducing his neighbour's wife, or stealing his neighbour's property.

MR. FORESTER.   You can prove that assertion, of course?

MR. VAMP.   Prove it! The editor of the *Legitimate Review* required to prove an assertion!

MR. ANYSIDE ANTIJACK.   The church is in danger! ...

MR. FEATHERNEST, MR. KILLTHEDEAD, AND MR. PAPERSTAMP.   Nothing can be more logical. The church is in danger! The church is in danger!

MR. VAMP.   Keep up that it is an infallible tocsin for rallying all the old women in the country about us when every thing else fails.

MR. VAMP. MR. FEATHERNEST. MR. PAPERSTAMP, MR. KILLTHEDEAD, AND MR. ANYSIDE ANTIJACK.   The church is in danger! The church is in danger![12]

Peacock satirizes the government's insistence that state religion was essential if social order was to be maintained. Mr Vamp's cynical belief that the church can be 'infallibly' exploited to whip up solidarity in the political ranks relates to the state's recent harnessing of blasphemy charges to libel prosecutions. Hone's trials should be seen in the context of the greatly increased government confidence that religion could be used as a tool to aid the suppression of seditious libels. The activities of the Vice Societies are central to this development and led in their turn to a radical intellectual counter-attack. Hone's trials relate to these developments in direct ways.

William Wilberforce, generally remembered as an abolitionist, was a man with two missions. Once converted to his passionate brand of Evangelicalism he was one of the Common's most consistent spokesmen on public morals. He constantly asserted the necessity for the Church to control the lower orders. He was instrumental in the foundation and workings of the Proclamation Society

[12] *The Novels of Thomas Love Peacock*, ed. David Garnett, 2 vols. (London, 1963), i. 312–13.

and its early nineteenth-century successor the Society for the Suppression of Vice (SSV). His Commons speeches frequently summarize with brutal clarity the theory justifying the spiritual policing of the lower orders. This attack on the reformers contains the essential ingredients: 'Heretofore they [the reformers] inveighed against the inequality of property, and used every artifice to alienate the people from the constitution of their country. But now they are sapping the foundations of the social edifice more effectually by attacking Christianity. The high and noble may be restrained by honour; but religion only is the law of the multitude.'[13] Such a passage is underpinned by the following assumptions: the only aim of reformers is the destruction of social order and they will do anything to gain this end; the multitude are protected by their Church and their constitution, without which they are helpless; the ruling class do not require religions because they have a code of honour which controls their behaviour, while without the constraints of state-administered religion the multitude would run riot. Adopting these attitudes it was possible to excuse the godless libertinism of the upper classes and to advocate the zealous imposition of morally strict state religion. This position could also be extended to justify the prosecution of any political figure who could be linked with the promulgation of blasphemy, defined in the broadest sense, among the poor.

The Proclamation Society and even more directly the SSV worked very closely with the government to secure state convictions.[14] What made the situation even more dangerous for political radicals was the way the SSV in its proselytizing zeal made little distinction between the activities of radical propagandists and straightforward criminals. The leading Evangelicals coincided with the Tory Anglican Establishment in seeing obedience to Church and state as central premises for the conduct of the lower orders. This belief in blanket obedience had the practical effect of clouding distinctions between political agitation and criminal activities concerning breaches of the peace. The various 'crimes' for which the SSV was vigilant grouped prostitution, Sabbath-breaking, profane swearing, and obscenity together with political manifestations of blasphemy and sedition.[15] When Hone was tried for blasphemy

[13] I. R. and S. Wilberforce, *Life of William Wilberforce*, 5 vols. (London, 1838), v. 40.
[14] For Wilberforce and the Vice Societies, see Henriques, 217–30; John Pollock, *Wilberforce* (London, 1977), 58–67.
[15] Henriques, 234–5. Crimmins, *Secular Utilitarianism*, 150.

he was a victim of the 'Church in danger' theory of political prosecution. It now appears an astonishing lack of judgement on the government's part to have continued with Hone's trials through a second and third prosecution. This can, however, be explained by the fact that it had never as yet failed to exploit a blasphemy charge brought against a radical. Where Hone differed from previous and subsequent victims of blasphemy charges was in his ability to capitalize on the specific material upon which the charges had been based.

Blasphemy trials from the early 1790s to the early 1820s fell into two categories. Firstly there were trials brought for the use of profane and blasphemous language. A trial such as that of Robert Wedderburn, the mulatto preacher who set up in the notorious Hopkin's Street Chapel, shows the complicated way in which both government and radicals were capable of exploiting religion to their own ends. Wedderburn appears to have procured a dissenting minister's licence in the wake of the revised Test Act in order to set up what was basically as much a political debating society as a church. Ultra-radicals in the second decade of the nineteenth century used the protection afforded dissenters increasingly as a smoke-screen for political meetings.[16] The government sent spies to record Wedderburn's utterances and then tried him for 'having used blasphemous language with intent to excite impiety and irreligion in the minds of his majesty's subjects and to vilify the Christian religion'.[17] Wedderburn preached a primitive Painite deism couched in ribald profanity. He could consequently be convicted as a blasphemer on account of both his ideas and the language they were framed in.

The second type of blasphemy case was usually straightforward for the government. It consisted of prosecution for publishing or selling material held to be blasphemous because it attacked the legally constituted Church. Prosecutions were normally framed against texts which had already been proved blasphemous in previous cases. The majority of convictions were brought against radicals for publishing or selling Paine's *Age of Reason* or any part of it.[18]

The prosecution condemned blasphemous libel through two basic

[16] McCalman, *Radical Underworld*, 129–50.
[17] *The Trial of the Rev. Robt. Wedderburn* (London, 1820), 3.
[18] For early state prosecutions of *The Age of Reason*, see Claeys, 185–9. For early 19th-cent. prosecutions, see Wickwar, 67–73.

arguments. Firstly that it threatened the security of the nation because both the law and the constitution were based in scripture. Secondly that it endangered public morals because religion constituted the cement holding society together and without it the lower orders could not be controlled. The first assertion was proved through the citation of legal precedents beginning with Sir Matthew Hale. These charges were expressed with an elaborate rhetoric which was designed to overawe a jury. In Hone's first trial Hale's 'part and parcel' dictum is not simply cited but Hale himself is introduced in overblown, not to say hagiographic, terms as 'the most learned man that ever adorned the bench—the most even man that ever blessed domestic life—the most eminent man that ever advanced the progress of science—and also one of the best and most religious men that ever lived' (1st trial, 14). The second position allowed for a variety of strategies both for blocking the defendant and for asserting the dangerous nature of the crime. One of the most persistent arguments presented the ridicule of state religion in France as the primary cause of the excesses of the Terror. As late as 1820 James Tucker was successfully prosecuted in Exeter for republishing the parodies of the Catechism for which Hone had already been acquitted. The prosecution was still harping upon the salutary lesson which the French Revolution offered: 'our religion has been retained whole and unsullied but in a neighbouring nation, disrespect and ridicule of religion led to scenes of bloodshed and confusion more dreadful than ever disgraced the most savage people. No cause was so proximate to that horrid revolution as the early attempts to vilify religion and destroy its deputy.'[19] Because of the necessity for protecting public morality judges would deny the legitimacy of any evidence in court which questioned the truth of Christianity. Consequently, a defence such as that of Eaton or Carlile which attempted to argue for the intellectual veracity of a particular form of free thought was considered completely inadmissible and the jury was instructed to rule it out.

Hone's defence brilliantly evaded this conventional form of government attack and indeed appropriated and parodied the attitudes and language of the prosecution vying with them for the moral high ground. In all three trials the government's case was founded on the well-tried precepts set out above. When describing the effect of Hone's parodies upon the public a tone of paternal outrage was

[19] *Woolmer's Exeter and Plymouth Gazette* (Jan. 1820).

adopted. Justice Abbot summed up in the first trial: 'The pamphlet before the jury was so injurious in its tendency, and so disgusting in its form, that any man, on the first reading, would start (he had almost said) with horror from it; it was like an infecting pestilence, which every man shunned that valued his safety' (1st trial, 65).

Hone countered this moral attack in each trial by switching the technical ground. Unlike free-thinkers such as Eaton and Carlile he did not present himself as an opponent of state Christianity but as an upstanding Christian himself: 'He professed himself to be a Christian: and he would be bold to say, that he made that profession with a reverence for the doctrines of Christianity which could not be exceeded by any person in that Court' (1st trial, 14).[20] He then continues his defence by outdoing the rhetoric of horror with which the prosecution reacted to the notion of a blasphemer: 'He had, however, been held up as a man unfit to live, as a blasphemer, a monster ... it was the proudest day of his life to stand there ... putting in a plea of not guilty against a charge of infamous and blasphemous libel; for if he were guilty of blasphemy he would go to the stake and burn as a blasphemer, at the same time avowing the blasphemy' (1st trial, 18). He denied both the blasphemous content and intent of his parodies, and as evidence read out example after example from the rich history of biblical parody which pervades Western European culture from the Middle Ages. The judges in all three trials attempted to enforce an argument that the citation of previous offences similar to his own did not mitigate his crime but compounded it. Every time Hone could reply that none of the parodies he read out had ever been prosecuted, and he used each intervention by the judge to highlight the persecutory nature of his case.

In basing his defence of biblical parody upon the citation of a multitude of other parodies Hone was able to confound the prosecution. The trials are almost choreographed in terms of the complex ways in which Hone creates parodies of parodies within the court and can extrapolate from one parodic model into another. The

---

[20] Several scholars have misjudged Hone's own religious position at the time of his trials. J. C. D. Clark wrongly calls him an atheist (*English Society 1688–1832: Ideology and Social Structure during the Ancien Régime* (Cambridge, 1985), 431, 481) and Smith, in reading Hone's trial as 'a literary event' (p. 178) and the trials as 'a literary artefact' (p. 179), bypasses Hone's motivation to clear his name as a Christian. He was clearly traumatized by the accusation of blasphemy and by the public calumny that resulted even after his acquittal; see Robert Hole, *Pulpits, Politics and Public Order in England 1760–1832* (Cambridge, 1989), 215–16, 225–8.

sophistication and topicality with which Hone regenerated and in-
vestigated the workings of parodic forms comes out in his comic
treatment of the topical issue of the Church and education.

The parodies for which Hone was prosecuted, a catechism, a litany, and a creed, were modelled on texts central to the education
of children in the Anglican Church. In the second decade of the
nineteenth century the Catechism in particular was at the centre of
a hot controversy. The increasing anxiety over the necessity for the
Established Church to exercise social control over the lower orders
had immediate repercussions in the area of children's education.

The Bible, always a potentially revolutionary text, was felt to be
open to misinterpretation by the poor and by unlicensed Methodist
preachers. The fear of Nonconformist appropriation of the Bible
had been exacerbated in 1805 when George III subscribed to
schools established by the Quaker John Lancaster in which the
Bible was the only teaching text. The founding of the Royal Lancastrian Institution in 1809 was quickly countered by the founding
of the National Society for Promoting the Education of the Poor in
the Principles of the Established Church. The foundation of the
British and Foreign Bible Society in 1804, and the sudden activity
of Wilberforce's supporters, including Hannah More, in the founding of schools and religious centres, were the most visible
manifestations of the increased interest in religious education. One
of the chief aims of the Bible Society was the sterilization and control of the Bible for consumption by the lower orders. The Bible
Society promoted and distributed large amounts of religious propaganda intended to provide a sanitized version of the scriptures
which would encourage obedience and trust in the existing Establishment. Prayer books, litanies, martyrologies, tracts, tales and
school books were designed and distributed to further this end and
to encourage the safe and time honoured religious prejudice
against popery.[21]

In parodying didactic Anglican religious forms Hone was not
only taking up popular models which had been often parodied
before but was contributing to the widespread criticism of the educational practices of the Established Church. The Church of
England Catechism had been singled out for criticism by intellectual radicals. Shelley makes an explicit connection between

---

[21] For the dispute within the Church on the formation of the Bible and school
societies, see Hole, *Pulpits, Politics and Public Order in England*, 187–200.

government repression and the Catechism in *Swellfoot the Tyrant* as
Mammon describes his grandchildren at play:

> And then my little grandchildren, the gibbets,
> Promising children as you ever saw,—
> The young playing at hanging, the elder learning
> How to hold radicals. They are well taught too,
> For every gibbet says its catechism . . .
> Before it goes to play.[22]

The most thorough and damaging attack was produced by
Bentham's *Church of Englandism and its Catechism Examined*. The
Church had recently produced a set of catechisms and catechetical
instructors. Bentham uses a variety of satiric methods to expose what
he saw as the hypocrisy and manipulative strategies of these texts.
He sets the dispute over the Catechism in the context of the general
corruption of the Church and its role in blocking reform. Bentham
adopts a Lancastrian approach, stating that the Bible should be the
'only lesson book used for religious instruction' (*C. of E.* 5).[23] He sees
the Catechism as displacing the Bible and is worried by the
thoroughness of the displacement. He dislikes both the varieties in
which the Catechism is printed and the manner of instruction 'by
question and answer and by *challenging*, alias, competition and place
taking, *injected*' (*C. of E.* 16). Bentham's polemic takes a lethal turn
when he describes the content and origin of the various editions of
the Catechism. His contumacious attack on the authors begins with
the observation that their work is a substitution for the religion of
Jesus:

> as if by the shuffling of a pack of cards, the works of the '*Blessed Saviour*' are,
> without any the smallest distinction, huddled together in a promiscuous
> bundle with those of *the Rev. Mr. Ostervald*, and the anonymous author of the
> CHIEF TRUTHS. Not so those of MRS. TRIMMER. Her more Holy name is
> distinguished and illustrated by capitals. What the *Blessed Virgin* is to the
> Church of Rome, this *Blessed Matron* is to the *Church of England*. In the
> Mother the son finds a rival and that rival, is a preferred one. (*C. of E.* 19)

Bentham turns protector for the dignity of the scripture. The
metaphor of the card-game is developed into a social discussion. The
mixed pack becomes a group of paupers 'huddled together' in a

---

[22] Shelley, *Poetical Works*, ed. Thomas Hutchinson, 2nd rev. edn. (Oxford, 1970),
396.
[23] For Bentham's general critique of the Church of England, see Crimmins,
166–80.

'promiscuous bundle' consisting of Christ, Mr Ostervald, and an anonymous hack. Yet Christ is presented as fortunate to get any recognition at all as Bentham goes on to work a subtle papist reference against Sarah Trimmer. Canonized as the Church of England's answer to the Virgin Mary she becomes a symbol of the state Church's mystification and substitution. The final sentence shifts into a sardonic tone presenting the whole affair in terms of debased family rivalry. The arguments concerning the dangers of disrespect towards the language of the scriptures, which were so favoured in state prosecutions for blasphemy, are here turned upon the propagandists of the Established Church.

Bentham's anger is directed at the anti-intellectual and extortionate language. Again and again he pinpoints and translates the coercive terms hidden in the new catechisms. He turns to the title-page of the simplified version, which announces that 'The CHIEF TRUTHS of the CHRISTIAN RELIGION, are explained to the MEANEST CAPACITY' (C. of E. 17), and points out that this is a transparent formula for the creation of blind fear given that no child or adult wishes to admit that their understanding is below 'the meanest capacity'. The Church is curtly condemned as the 'instrument of corruption' and the Bishop as a manipulator of public morals: 'and thus the grand and avowed object of the Bishop of London's labours—the prostration of understanding and wills—is accomplished' (C. of E. 40).

The abuse of the unprotected minds of the young is described with mounting outrage through a series of metaphors which work cumulatively around the imagery of force-feeding. The teaching of the Catechism is 'forcing into the mouths of babes, almost as soon as they cease to be sucklings, the pill, the bitterness of which is all the while endeavoured to be gilded over by a covering of praise' (C. of E. 32). The full version of the Catechism is 'unminced', but the simplified 'broken catechism' is 'minced', and there is yet a third, intermediate, form so that 'before they [the children] are allured thus to feed upon the mass, in the shape of minced meat, they are forced . . .—these tender mouths—to swallow it whole. Yes: twice to swallow it whole. Such is the relief afforded by the breakage' (C. of E. 42). The originators of the Catechism are shown as bad parents deliberately and knowingly forcing unsound food down the children's throats, 'the thing, viz. the Old Catechism, is bad in matter. Those by whom it is thus forced into the mouths of those innocents are conscious of its being so. The proof of evil consciousness is their forcing into the same tender and much injured mouths their newly made up bolus—"*the Catechetical Instruction*".'

The general attack on the educational texts of the Church of England, for which Bentham was the radical intellectual spearhead, lies behind Hone's use of religious parody. Recent scholarly treatments of Hone's trials present him as a victim of government oppression and hypocrisy wrongly prosecuted for creating purely political parodies based on the forms of religious texts.[24] This is to present Hone in terms of his own defence: the situation is far more complicated. Hone constructed a defence based on historical parodic precedent. While this had the practical effect of showing up the hypocrisy of his judges, it should be seen in more general terms as a major contribution to the radical attack on the educational publications of the Bible societies.

Hone's parodies confront and subvert the instructional texts of the Established Church in a more direct manner than the critical anatomizations of Bentham. Yet they are inspired by a similar radical hatred for the Church in its role as an organ for state control of the poor. Rather than formulate a head-on attack in the manner of *Church of Englandism*, Hone has the Church hoist with its own petard through his ironic appropriation of its instructional forms. Bentham had already in fact taken this course in constructing his *Catechism of Parliamentary Reform; or, Outline of a Plan of Parliamentary Reform*.[25] When the prosecution opens its case by reading out Hone's parodies, and the crowd laughs, there is a peculiar and celebratory poignancy:

Q. Rehearse the Articles of thy Belief.
A. I believe in GEORGE, the Regent Almighty, Maker of New Streets, and Knights of the Bath.
    And in the present Ministry, his only choice, who were conceived in Toryism, brought forth by WILLIAM PITT, suffered loss of Place under CHARLES JAMES FOX, were execrated, dead, and buried. In a few months they rose again from their minority; they reascended to the Treasury benches, and sit at the right hand of a little man with a large wig; from whence they laugh at the Petitions of the People who may pray for Reform. (1st trial, 8)

[24] Hackwood, 133–8; Bowden, 158–67; Smith, 176–201.
[25] Hone produced a serious political catechism influenced by Bentham's model: *A Political Catechism, Dedicated Without Permission, to his Most Serene Highness Omar Bashaw Dey* (London, 1817).

The pounding question-and-answer formula designed to force children into a state of obedience is turned on its head and becomes an ironic testimony to the blind political creed of the placeman and pensioner. The fictional catechant appears as the obedient child of the ministry dutifully reciting the rules of a corrupted faith. Hone claimed consistently throughout the trials that the whole aim of the parodies was political and that at no point was Christianity mocked. He scrupulously avoided criticism of the Church in his trials, yet it is impossible to see how the parodies could avoid constituting a comprehensive attack upon the much-maligned instructional forms of the Established Church.

The skill with which Hone exploited the didactic base of his satiric vehicle developed as the trials progressed. Litanies and catechisms set out the rules of belief which a teacher could then enlarge upon either in the form of his own explanations or through the use of a printed commentary. In his second trial Hone developed his defence by taking up this opportunity for providing a formal commentary upon his own anti-ministerial litany. In order to prove the political basis of his work he reads his parody out again and provides a detailed analysis of its content. It is a cheeky satiric ruse. Hone reads out as part of his defence the very lines which the prosecution had earlier recited as the evidence for its case. He then demonstrates the veracity of his satire through a close commentary in which he amplifies his criticisms.

As Hone takes the court and jury through the satire step by step, his explanations fuse a variety of information drawn both from his own experience and from events of the day. When his parody prays for delivery from 'an unnational debt ... unmerited pensions ... sinecure places ... an extravagant Civil List ... and utter starvation' the final element, which suddenly switches attention from the corruptors to the victims of corruption, is illustrated through a personal anecdote. Hone describes how he 'had himself indeed seen two persons who had actually expired in the streets from absolute want' (2nd trial, 121). When he refers to the supplication 'that ye spend not extravagantly the money raised from the production of our labours, nor take for yourselves that which ye need not' he goes on to defend it with an illustration featuring Canning: 'This was surely not to be condemned especially after the government had sanctioned the scandalous Lisbon job, in which Mr. Canning took from the public purse not less than £14,000 for doing nothing ...

and Mr. Canning accepted the bribe without the excuse of necessity, for his means were ample' (2nd trial, 125).

Having advanced a certain distance through the disquisition on his parody Hone provides the jury with a further commentary on his commentary, spelling out the morally corrective basis of the satire:

If they required it, he would go through every supplication to our rulers in the parody, to show that what he said he was justified in saying—that it was true, and not libellous—that if there was ridicule, those who rendered themselves ridiculous, however high their station had no right to cry out because they were ridiculed. He *intended* to laugh at them. They were his vindictive prosecutors and his hypocritical persecutors, and laugh at them he would, till they ceased to be the objects of his laughter by ceasing to be Ministers. (2nd trial, 126)

Hone's manner of conducting his defence is so full of inversions that it threatens to turn the trial itself into parody. Tried for writing a parody he cites a huge number of parodies as his defence. He provides a parodic exegesis of the very parody for which he is being tried in which he concludes by accusing the government ministers of parodying their function as public guardians and the ministers of justice of inverting their function as upholders of public liberty. Hone even manages at one point to invert the position of judge and judged, to the delight of the packed court. During the second trial he held up that morning's copy of the *Day* newspaper in which Lord Sidmouth's opinion that Hone was a blasphemer was quoted. He stated that he hoped the jury would 'dismiss the unfair prejudice which might have been excited against him from the highest authority', at which point Ellenborough interrupted:

LORD ELLENBOROUGH——Why, nobody can have read that newspaper you speak of; what have I or the jury to do with——
MR. HONE——My Lord! My Lord! it is I who am on my trial, not your Lordship. I have to defend myself, not your Lordship.
Long-continued acclamations here interrupted the proceedings of the Court. (2nd trial, 98)

While Hone's parodies of the Litany, the Creed, and the Catechism related to recent developments in the debate over the Church's role in politics, they also show Hone's familiarity with the history of popular and radical religious parody. Birmingham radicals took up these forms during the American war and political writers in the 1790s had made extensive use of them. Eaton's *Politics for the People* is strewn with religious parodies of all sorts and includes not only parodic litanies, creeds, and a *te deum*, but parodies of various forms related to scripture such as hymns and prayers.[26] By the second decade of the nineteenth century radicals became increasingly inventive in terms of the models they were prepared to use. The Spenceans Evans and Wedderburn were involved in the establishment of chapels which were used as a social focus for the dissemination of their political theories. In his preaching Wedderburn used sermon literature, prophetic discourse, and biblical quotation and exegesis with particular success. Both Wedderburn and Samuel Waddington used their experience with various forms of biblical rhetoric to great effect in their trials for sedition realizing the emotional power which scriptural quotation could have over a jury.[27]

Maybe because of these developments Hone was careful to distance himself from the specific radical associations of scriptural parody and when defending himself sensibly avoided the quotation of any other radical examples. The main thrust of his argument in the trials lay in his presentation of the language of the scriptures as a common literary heritage which had been and could be exploited in parody without belittling the model:

> The first productions of genius ... were parodied because they were generally known, and were in themselves original and beautiful, obtaining for that reason an extensive popularity. The thing was not done from motives of contempt—quite the contrary. If parodies on Scripture were criminal, they must have been so at all times, whoever might have been the author, and whoever might have been Attorney-General. (3rd trial, 153)

Many of the examples from previous parodies which Hone quoted were taken from authors of undoubted authority whom the court had to respect. These included Luther, Latimer, Archdeacon Paley, and Dr Boys, and among literary figures Jonson, Milton, and Burke. Hone included a number of parodies produced in support of the government as loyalist propaganda. These included pieces from *The Edinburgh Magazine, The Anti-Gallican,* and *The Anti-Jacobin,* and he produced caricatures by Gillray involving parodic quotations from, and travesties of, religious paintings. Hone also introduced examples of religious parody drawn from more popular culture such as carols and hymns, ballads dealing with religious subjects, and several catechisms and litanies.

[26] Mee, *Dangerous Enthusiasm*, 175.
[27] McCalman, *Radical Underworld*, 133–51.

In parodying the catechism Hone was using a model of great linguistic power. The catechismic formula of question and answer can be used to create effects ranging from aggressive interrogation to ironic understatement. By the early nineteenth century parodic catechisms had become a widely used form of popular entertainment and were brought out in the lowest areas of publishing. Drunkards', soldiers', and old wives' catechisms are to be found among the single-sheet productions of John Pitts and Jemmy Catnach. Hone's book sale catalogues reveal that his interest extended into these areas. Hone possessed sheets produced by John Pitts and David Brown, which include *The English Lady's Catechism* and *The Coachman's and Footman's Catechism*. These pieces were essentially non-political and produced as popular entertainment.[28]

Parodic litanies were common in verse form and Hone introduced a striking example of the latter as evidence. This was a halfpenny ballad entitled *The Poor Man's Litany*. Written in a coarse but effective rhyming doggerel it underlies the manner in which street publishing had absorbed the educative texts of the Church:

> From Forestallers, Regraters, and all that curs'd train,
> Who, to swell up their bags, will hoard up the grain,
> Against which we cry out with our might and main,
>   Good Lord, deliver us!

> From a Workhouse where hunger and poverty rage,
> And distinction's a stranger to birth, sex, or age;
> Lame and Blind all must work or be coop'd in a cage,
>   Good Lord, deliver us! (2nd trial, 119)

Such work is a very long way from the sophistication of Hone's parodic catechism and litany yet carries through in crude form a similar attack on the abuse of privilege.

The examples used by Hone in his trials were a carefully calculated mixture of styles—good, bad, high, and low. The startling variety of this material and the way it forms a coherent and threatening pastiche relates directly to Hone's methods of parodic composition generally. His satiric method in the religious parodies comes out clearly in the text for which he was initially tried.

Hone's first prosecution was for the publication and possible authorship of a parody titled *The Late John Wilkes's Catechism of a*

---

[28] Hone, 1828 book sale catalogue, item 224.

Ministerial Member. Hone claimed on the title-page that it was taken from 'an original manuscript in Mr. Wilkes's Handwriting, never before printed, and adapted to the present occasion'.[29] The manuscript referred to was not produced in court by Hone and up to this point had not been located. An account of how Hone came to possess it and of how he altered it is given in a pamphlet *Some Account of the Conversion of the Late William Hone* published in 1853 and written by Frances Rolleston, a friend of his later years.[30]

Hone gave various accounts of his trials to Rolleston and it is these that provide detailed material relating to the satire. Rolleston states that 'previous to his trial of 1817 he had a small booksellers shop, occasionally publishing small pamphlets: he received by post a parody written by the late Mr. Wilkes ... a most disgusting thing it is'.[31] I discovered the manuscript referred to among Hone's collection of papers relating to his *History of Parody*.[32] This manuscript is of some importance. Hone's claim that it was not previously published appears to be valid; therefore it provides the only version of Wilkes's original. Parts of this had survived unaltered in Hone's extensively reworked published version yet it has not previously been possible to tell who wrote which parts.[33]

---

[29] William Hone, *The Late John Wilkes's Catechism of a Ministerial Member* (London, 1817), title-page. Hone stated during his third trial that a man had entered his shop and told him that the manuscript 'had been printed and published before ... in the first volume of *The Morning Chronicle*' (3rd trial, 151). Hone apparently never saw the publication and I have not located it.

[30] Rolleston, *Some Account of the Conversion of the Late William Hone*, 434.

[31] Ibid.

[32] *BL* MS Add. 40108, fos. 134–9. The whole forms a consecutive parody of the catechism as it appears in The Book of Common Prayer, large parts of which are quoted verbatim. All these sheets are written in Wilkes's hand; his text has then been substantially reworked by Hone. In accordance with the account given by Rolleston, Hone's deletions and additions produce the text which he later published as *Wilkes's Catechism*. Item 139 is composed of a separate sheet of smaller writing-paper and is entirely in Hone's hand. It is a draft of the final answer in *Wilkes's Catechism*. Wilkes's original has many topical references and a final list of contemporary 18th-cent. figures. Hone consequently needed to redraft this part completely.

[33] All of the many scholarly accounts of *Wilkes's Catechism* are badly flawed. James Routledge, in *Chapters in the History ... of the Freedom of the Press* (London, 1876), states that in Hone's trials 'the first charge was made on *The Political Catechism*, including the *Lord's Prayer* and the *Ten Commandments*' (p. 373). *The Political Catechism* was a separate work published by Hone in Jan. 1817, of which he was not the author. It does not include a parody of the Lord's Prayer or the Ten Commandments and it was not cited in his first trial. Hackwood, in his critical biography of Hone, similarly confuses the two titles, and in his bibliography gives *The Political Catechism* as one of the three

The government had good reasons for making *Wilkes's Catechism* the basis for Hone's first trial. The parody follows precisely the form of the Catechism which appears in the *Book of Common Prayer* and consequently includes parodies of two of the most central statements of Christian belief, namely, the Lord's Prayer and the Ten Commandments. Both these texts were part of the Holy Scriptures and could not be dismissed by Hone in his defence, as the rest of the text of the Catechism technically could, as the mere creation of interested churchmen. The prosecution were consequently confident that in publishing *Wilkes's Catechism* Hone had circulated a text which was irrefutably libellous, 'with design and intent to promote impiety and irreligion'.

The two texts of *Wilkes's Catechism* can be used to highlight many aspects of Hone's satiric practice. Throughout his career as a political journalist Hone adapted and republished earlier popular satires and those of his radical predecessors in particular. He possessed an unusual capacity for spotting and exploiting historical parallels and saw the potential topicality of several earlier satires besides *Wilkes's Catechism*. In 1816 he brought out two publications focusing on the conviction of the thief-takers Vaughan, Mackay, Brown, and Donnelly for a conspiracy to obtain blood-money. The second of these was a reworked republication of a mid-eighteenth century pamphlet

pieces for which Hone was prosecuted. Neither Routledge nor Hackwood take up Hone's claim that his publication was based on an MS by Wilkes; indeed they do not address the problem of Hone's authorship at all. The most misleading discussion of *Wilkes's Catechism* is that Wardroper in *Kings, Lords and Wicked Libellers*. Wardroper asserts, without evidence and incorrectly, that 'the catechism was an adaptation of a piece published during the Wilkite uproar of 1769'. Hone correctly states on the title-page of *Wilkes's Catechism* that his parody is adapted from an MS in his possession, 'never before published'. Wardroper then states that 'Parts of it [*Wilkes's Catechism*] needed not a word changed' (p. 22) and illustrates this statement by quoting several passages from Hone's publication, making no further reference to the supposed Wilkes publication. There are, in fact, only two passages of any length which Hone did not substantially alter, these being lines 36–61 and 119–35. All the passages which Wardroper quotes in his discussion differ substantially from Wilkes's MS version. The most comprehensive discussion of *Wilkes's Catechism* is Bowden's. She does, however, take an ambiguous stance over the question of whether Hone was the exclusive author, or whether he was, as he claimed, adapting an original. Smith, in her chapter on Hone's trials, does not discuss the composition and authorship of *Wilkes's Catechism*, assuming that the parody is Hone's. Patten takes a similarly unquestioning stance in *George Cruikshank's Life*, (p. 128). The discovery of Wilkes's original makes it possible to show exactly what part Hone played in the composition of the piece.

about four earlier blood-money racketeers.[34] In 1821 he brought out *The Right Divine of Kings to Govern Wrong*, an abridgement of Defoe's *Jure Divino* of 1706, a poetic satire in twelve books which had attacked the concept of the Divine Right of Kings. Hone reduced the poem to three books and extensively altered it so that it could form part of the radical assault on the newly formed Holy Alliance between Austria, Prussia, and Russia after Waterloo.

In his lengthy preface to *The Right Divine* Hone gives a detailed account of his approach to adaptation and of his creative relationship with the original:

De Foe ... was the ablest politician of his day, an energetic writer, and, better than all, an honest man; but not much of a poet. The *Jure Divino* is defective in arrangement and versification. It is likewise disfigured by injudicious repetition ... The present is an attempt to separate the gold from the dross ... It is a forcible and argumentative satire against the *nonsense* from hole-and-corner and lawn-sleeve men; and presents a series of peculiarly strong and quotable lines, to engraft on the common sense of the free-minded, honest and open hearted of my country men.[35]

Hone's confidence in the relevance of a political satire that was over a century old is typical of his strong identification with, and use of, the traditions of radical thought and popular publishing. The very fact that these texts, although adapted, had a precise contemporary relevance indicated the power and accessibility of their style and the unchanging nature of the injustices which they attacked. Hone's act of republication is legitimized by the continuity of corruption.

Both in satiric terms and in terms of sales *Wilkes's Catechism* was by far Hone's most successful readaptation. Hone realized the way the form had been produced in different publishing contexts and the appeal which his publication of the revised Wilkes satire would consequently be likely to have. The insight which Hone brought to the parodic catechism is best revealed by examining the changes he made to key parts of the Wilkes text. The passage in *Wilkes's Catechism* which is most heavily reworked is the parody of the Ten Commandments.

Most of the alterations are directed either at the Regent per-

[34] William Hone, *The Whole Four Trials of the Thief Takers and Their Confederates* (London, 1816). Hone's annotated and reworked version of the earlier pamphlet carried the extravagant title *Hone's Interesting History of the Memorable Blood Conspiracy, Carried on by S. MacDaniel, J. Berry, J. Egan, and J. Salmon, Thief-Takers, and their Trials and Sentences, in 1756*.

[35] William Hone, *The Right Divine* (London, 1821), 10–11.

sonally or at clarifying the extent and nature of the abuses inflicted on the people. So Wilkes's fifth commandment, 'Honour the Minister and his Mistress that thy Day may be long in the Place which the Lord thy Minister giveth thee', becomes 'Honour the Regent and the Helmets of the lifeguards, that thy stay may be long' (Appendix, p. 279). It was well known that the Regent took particular pleasure in designing exotic uniforms, both for himself and for his guard.[36] The seventh commandment is changed from 'Thou shalt commit adultery' to 'thou shalt not call Royal Gallivanting adultery' (Appendix p. 279). This is a subtle change. The negative command of the original biblical text is restored in order to underline the compromised double-talk of the 'placeman or pensioner'. The phrase 'Royal Gallivanting' is particularly charged, for the word gallivanting was new and is not recorded in the OED until 1819. The OED gives its first use as a verb for 1823 and its first adjectival use for 1819. Hone's usage precedes both of these by several years. Hone demonstrates great linguistic astuteness in translating the imaginary placeman's jaunty periphrasis 'Royal Gallivanting', with its flashy novelty, into the grave and biblically sanctioned term 'adultery'.

There is a similar restoration of the 'Thou shalt not' formula in the eighth and sixth commandments. 'Thou shalt do murder' is changed to 'Thou shalt not call starving to death murder' and Wilkes's 'Thou shalt steal' is changed to 'Thou shalt not say that to rob the public is to steal' (Appendix, p. 279). Again the negative formula is being used to imply exploitative double standards. In the Bible the command 'Thou shalt not' means exactly what is says, and stands as a simple and absolute prescription. Hone has his imaginary minister use it to introduce circumlocutions which damn him out of his own mouth. Both of Hone's rewritten commandments disclose the individual responsibility of the politician for the general distress of the nation. There is a dramatic extremity in the implied accusation that every person who starves to death has been murdered by the politicians, and similarly that every sinecure given to a placeman or pensioner is taken from the people and therefore an act of theft. Many of Hone's alterations take Wilkes's original away from the scriptural text and embed it more firmly in the corrupt details of contemporary political life. In the second com-

<hr>

[36] Arthur Bryant, *The Age of Elegance* (Harmondsworth, 1958), 126. Christopher Hibbert, *George IV* (Harmondsworth, 1976), 232–4.

mandment Wilkes simply reproduces the original with virtually no alterations.

Thou shalt not make to thyself any Graven Image but mine, nor shalt thou frame the Likeness of any Thing that is in Heaven above or in the earth beneath or in the Waters under the earth except mine thou shalt not bow down to them [illegible] nor worship them for thy God art a jealous Minister and visits the sin of the Father upon the Children unto the third and fourth Generation of them that hate me.

There is only one substantive alteration to the text of the commandments as it appears in the *Book of Common Prayer*: 'I the Lord thy God am a jealous God' becomes 'for thy God art a jealous Minister'. This section of Wilkes 'satire' is simply quotation. The passage is not effective, for the minister is allowed to speak scripture to such an extent that the beauty and authority of the language come to be identified with him. Hone's alterations to this section are extensive. His final version reads:

Thou shalt not make to thyself any measure but mine, nor shalt thou frame Clauses of any bill in its progress to the House above, nor in the Committee beneath, or where the Mace is under the Table, except it be mine. Thou shalt not bow to Lord Cochrane, nor shake hands with him, nor any other of my real opponents, for I, thy Lord, art a jealous Minister, and allow not familiarity of the Majority with the Friends of the People, unto the third and fourth Cousins of them that divide against me.

The parody suddenly comes alive as Hone throws the trivialities of partisanship and the absurdities of government procedure up against the awfulness of the original text. The vast elemental perspectives of 'Heaven above ... Earth beneath ... and Waters under the Earth' are hilariously converted into an inventory that becomes increasingly silly 'The House above ... the Committee below ... the Mace ... under the table'. The final phrase is particularly lethal in its absurdist irreverence. The mace is an ancient symbol of sovereignty and power (*OED* 2A), and its specific connotations in the House of Commons relate chiefly to its use as 'a warrant demanding obedience to the House' (*OED* 2B). The linking of the mace with the homeliness of the phrase 'under the table' up-ends its status. Although funny, this image also contains slightly sinister intimations of concealed power which are an effective reminder of the hidden threat of corrupt government. Hone's alterations make the power of the original sacred text work for him and against his political enemies. The terrifying dictum that 'the sins of the fathers will be visited on the sons even to the third and fourth generations' is altered to stress the viciousness of the minister. His power, limited by both his and his victim's corruption, can be expressed only in the extortionate persecution of the families of his underlings.

In using the Catechism Hone was working in a satiric form which had a long and complicated history, and he had an unusually thorough, indeed probably unique, knowledge of previous biblical parody. W. A. Coupe has argued that the parody of a religious form when carried out in the context of a society that was devout denoted respect for the original.[37] Hone's alterations to the text of the Lord's Prayer and the Ten Commandments can be read as respectful. The original text is shown perverted, and its precepts misapplied, by the politicians and placemen. It is the difference between the way taught by the Bible and the way the time-servers lead their lives which Hone's alterations emphasize.

While I have argued that Hone's attitude towards the educative forms of the Church was hostile, his attitude towards scripture itself was not. This distinction largely bypassed his contemporaries for he was writing at a point when the feeling that parody inevitably belittled both the form it was composed in, and the subject it attacked, was gaining ground. The mass of biblical parodies, which Hone presented as the core of his defence, were necessary in order to educate the jury in this older attitude to parody. Coleridge's reaction to Hone's trial demonstrates the extent to which parody, as early as 1817, was seen as contaminating and derivative. Coleridge articulates the confusing emotions which Hone's trials consequently gave rise to even in a sympathetic mind: 'I loathe parodies of all kinds, and hold even "To wed or not to wed", "To print or not to print", not altogether guiltless, as disturbing the simplicity of feeling and imagination; and parodies on religion still more. Yet I exult in Hone's acquittal and Lord Ellenborough's deserved humiliation.'[38] For Coleridge all parody, even the contemporary journalistic parodies of Hamlet's soliloquy which he quotes, are imaginatively corrupt.[39] Coleridge's reaction is prescrip-

---

[37] W. A. Coupe, *The German Illustrated Broadsheet in the Seventeenth Century*, 2 vols. (Baden-Baden, 1966–7), i. 214–15. Coupe, 'Political and Religious Caricatures of the Thirty Years War', *Journal of the Courtauld and Warburg Institutes*, 25 (1975), 74.

[38] Samuel Taylor Coleridge, 25 Jan. 1818, letter 1101 of *The Letters of Samuel Taylor Coleridge*, ed. E. L. Griggs, 6 vols. (Oxford, 1959), iv. 814.

[39] For an account of the popular Shakespearian parodies of this period and their political associations, see Bate, *Shakespearian Constitutions*, 105–26.

tive and limited to a contemporary reading of parody as a parasitic form which preys on, but which is ultimately powerless to hurt, its pure literary host. Elsewhere Coleridge defined parody as essentially harmless, stating that the passage of time transformed it from a satire of the original to a gesture of compliment: 'Parodies on new poems are read as satires; on old ones (the soliloquy of Hamlet for instance) as compliments. A man of genius may securely laugh at a mode of attack by which his reviler, in half a century or less, becomes his encomiast.'[40] This attitude is very much of its time and does not do justice to the complexity and political realism of Hone's satiric method, let alone to the complex operations of parody in Georgian life and art.

Hone, Lilburne, and Radical Martyrology

Questions of radical status and self-image are intimately bound up with the extent to which radicals had formulated their own historical inheritance. Hone's behaviour, arguments, and even his language during his three trials constantly echo and quote from John Lilburne's 1649 treason trials. Hone was deeply versed in the popular pamphlet literature of the Civil War. He owned many tracts by or about the Levellers printed between 1647 and 1659 and another set written by the Surrey Diggers in 1649. He had all the major writings of Gerard Winstanley and several anonymous parodic pieces including a number of travesties based upon the forms of religious texts and court trials. Hone had also amassed a comprehensive collection of over eighty texts by or about John Lilburne.[41] Hone's interest in Leveller writings is striking because it does not appear to be typical of working-class radicalism at this time. His immediate radical predecessors and contemporaries had used the popular satirists and polemicists of the Civil War in limited ways, if at all.

Certain late sixteenth- and early seventeenth-century texts by Protestant dissenters had remained popular. Foxe's *Acts and Monuments*, familiarly known in its condensed cheaper form as the *Book of Martyrs*, and Bunyan's *Pilgrim's Progress* were in print in a variety of

---

[40] Samuel Taylor Coleridge, *Omniana* (Oxford, 1917), no. 105.

[41] Details of Hone's Civil War pamphlets are contained in both his 1822 and 1827 book sale catalogues. The most complete listings are in 1827, although these are apparently fuller listings of the materials from the 1822 sale which were not sold. For the Surrey Diggers, see 1827, item. 616; the Levellers, item. 617; Lilburne, item. 636; Winstanley, item. 170; anonymous satires, item. 204.

forms throughout the eighteenth century and were fundamental to
the development of radical thought and language in the first half of
the nineteenth century.[42] The continuing effect of the multitude of
popular political theorists, who were also dissenters, which the Civil
War and its aftermath produced is more difficult to determine.

It is surprising to find that despite the fillip which the publication
of Paine's *Rights of Man* gave to the re-examination of earlier writings
on constitutional and civil rights issues, the writings of such figures as
Winstanley, Lilburne, Overton, and Walwyn do not seem to have
been reprinted in the period 1790–1822. The periodicals of Spence
and Eaton, which appeared in the early 1790s, included serialized
republications of previous authors felt by the radicals to be useful.
This practice was continued in several of the more successful radical
journals in the period 1816–22. Yet with this exception, and even
here political writings from the Civil War are a rarity, the later
radicals appear to have exhibited little interest in the popular rheto-
ricians connected with such movements as the Ranters, the
Levellers, or the Diggers. Radical thought between 1688 and 1790
appears to have looked for its inspiration to John Locke, Algernon
Sydney, and James Harrington.[43]

Bearing in mind this background Hone's obsession with Lilburne
was eccentric. The questions how and why Hone should have
chosen to use the published accounts of Lilburne's 1649 trial as the
basis for much of the argument and rhetoric in his own trials remain
unanswered. Smith's treatment of the trials in *The Politics of Language*
remains the only attempt to explain Hone's interest in Lilburne. The
discussion suffers from a lack of familiarity with the very different
legal backgrounds of the two trials. There is also no awareness of
Hone's extensive familiarity with Leveller tracts. His relationship
with Lilburne's text during the trials is presented as one of undiscriminating self-identification: 'despite Lilburne's exceptional
audacity (he can take one's breath away) he and Hone share a
similar style of language and behaviour which denies the two
hundred year interval between the trials. It is as if reading Lilburne's
text taught Hone how to manage the dialogue, as if he had read it
for that purpose the day before.'[44] Hone's use of the material was in
fact highly discriminating and grew out of a firm grasp of the signifi-

[42] James T. Boulton, *The Language of Politics in the Age of Wilkes and Burke*
(London, 1918), 141.
[43] See Claeys, 6–10.   [44] Smith, 198.

cance of the Lilburne trials in the context of the history of jury law. Hone was also aware of the continual incorporation of the tropes of Protestant martyrology into political show trials from Lilburne's time to the early nineteenth century. The martyrological tradition provided Hone with a way of marrying his historical interest in the Civil War martyrs with early nineteenth-century radicalism.

Hone had collected almost every important publication associated with Lilburne's career, and his use of this material was complicated. Lilburne's 1649 trial was of particular use to Hone in the context of an early nineteenth-century libel trial because of the claims which Lilburne had made for the power of a jury. The title-page of the 1649 trial shows Lilburne fashionably attired, standing pleading his defence at the bar (see Fig. 17). Above his head to right and left float engraved versions of the recto and verso of the medal struck to commemorate his acquittal. Around the border is engraved the motto 'IOHN LILBORNE SAVED BY THE POWER OF THE LORD AND THE INTEGRITY OF HIS IVRY WHO ARE IVDGE OF LAW AS WELL AS FACT'.[45] This aphorism encapsulates the most sensational aspect of Lilburne's defence. His absolute claims for the judgemental powers of a jury astounded and infuriated his judges. At one point Judge Jermin burst out 'that the Jury are Judges of the Law ... is enough to destroy all the Law in the Land; there was never such a damnable Heresie broached in this Nation Before' (*Lilburne*, 123). Where Lilburne got this notion from and what exactly he meant by it is not clear and still puzzles legal historians.[46] The trial is seminal in the history of English jury law and gave rise to a plethora of publications for and against Lilburne's arguments.

The essential message, however, was very simple in terms of the way Hone could use it. The power to judge the general questions of legality as well as simple matters of fact, had been given over wholly to the jury. Lilburne frequently states this claim to Lord Keble: 'The Jury by Law are not onely Judges of fact but of Law also, and you that call yourselves Judges of the Law and indeed and in truth if the Jury please, are no more but Ciphers, to pronounce their Verdict' (*Lilburne*, 122). Hone's statements concerning the jury's power are couched in similar terms: 'Gentlemen it is you who are trying me

---

[45] *Lilburne*, frontispiece.

[46] By far the best discussion of the origin of Lilburne's aphorism and of its subsequent incorporation into criminal jury law is in Thomas Green, *Verdict According to Conscience: Perspectives on the English Criminal Trial Jury 1200–1800* (Chicago, 1985), 152–99.

FIG. 17. Anon. Engraving. Frontispiece to *The Triall of Lieut. Collonell John Lilburne*. 1649.

today. His lordship is no judge of me. You are my judges, and you only are my judges. His lordship sits there to receive your verdict' (3rd trial, 148). In Hone's case, however, the legal situation had been clearly and notoriously defined by the Act to Remove Doubts Respecting the Functions of Juries in Cases of Libel, now commonly referred to as Fox's Libel Act, in a way that gave Lilburne's dictum a precise contemporary application. The Act stated that in a trial for criminal libel: 'the jury sworn to try the issue may give a general verdict of guilty or not guilty upon the whole matter put in issue upon such indictment and information; and shall not be required or directed by the court or judge'.[47]

Both Hone and Lilburne realized the advantages to be gained by emphasizing the absolute power of the jury and the judge's second-ary position as legal adviser to the court. Fox's Libel Act acknowledged the judge's right to 'give their or his opinion and direction to the jury ... according to their or his discretion'. This could not disguise the fact that the act gave an absolute power to a criminal libel jury analogous to that which Lilburne inspirationally and irrationally claimed for his jury.[48] This common legal ground made it possible for Hone to use many of the strategies employed by Lilburne despite the 200 years separating the trials. Lilburne con-stantly questioned the language and structures of formal court proceeding and Hone acutely took up this approach. In both trials the defendants use a variety of ploys to bypass the judges and appeal directly to the jury.

Using well-tried popular myths and stereotypes which had become attached to the legal profession, Lilburne and Hone care-fully create a world that is separated by absolute ethical and formal divisions. The labyrinthine language of the legal profession is set against the common sense and colloquial diction of the defendant. The defence and jury are cast as the representatives of a vulnerable state of honesty that is uncalculating and very English, while the law is a dark and degraded lower region which uses obscure ancient and foreign languages and divisive trickery. Time-honoured metaphors

[47] Quoted in Wickwar, 42.
[48] Erskine used similar arguments about the jury's power in libel cases before 1792, most importantly in the case of The Dean of St Asalph. Erskine's arguments and importance for later radical approaches to the law of libel are discussed in Michael Lobban, 'From Seditious Libel to Unlawful Assembly: Peterloo and the Changing Face of Political Crime *c.* 1770–1820', *Oxford Journal of Legal Studies,* 10 (1990), 315–18.

of the law as a trap which inevitably drags the common man down frequently surface in both trials. Both men compare themselves to a fly in a web and refer to the Pharisees attempting to ensnare Christ. Both present themselves as vulnerable victims in a world where the odds have been stacked against them. 'My Lord I am making my case as well as I can under a thousand disadvantages' (2nd trial, 92) exclaims Hone on being interrupted by the judge. When Lilburne sees the judge and Attorney-General whisper, he presents the exchange as an internecine and illegal plot. The judges attempt to justify themselves:

Judge Thorpe——*Sir Edwd. Cook is law and he says the Attourney generall or any other prosecutor may speak with us in open Court*
Lt. Coll. Lilb.——Not in hugger mugger or privately or whisperingly.
Judge Thorpe——*I tell you sir the Attourney generall may talk with any in the Court by law as he did with me.*
Lt. Coll. Lilb.——I tell you Sir it is unjust, and not warrantable by Law, for him to talk with the Court … in my absence, or in hugger-mugger, or by private whisperings.
Lord Kebble——*No (Sir) it is no hugger-mugger for him to doe as he did. Spare your words. (Lilburne, 35–6)*

Lilburne succeeds in reducing legal disputation to a squabble. His language dominates and in their exasperation the judges begin to quote Lilburne's own charged phrase 'hugger-mugger' in an attempt to defuse its power.

Nearly all the strategies are designed to build up a personal relationship between the defendant and his jurors. As the names of the jury are read out Lilburne exclaims to the judge 'Sir, I beseech you let me but see these gentlemens faces' (p. 53). The jury is frequently addressed directly as a group of friendly and honourable people completely distinct from the court officials. Lilburne moves on from addressing his comments to 'the Jury, my Countrymen' (p. 121) to a triumphant substitution of the possessive 'my Honest Jury, and Fellow-Citizens' (p. 141), and he continually advises them to look out for deception: 'I shall desire my Jury to take notice that I aver that you rob me of the benefit of the law and go about to murder me' (p. 140). His final address is a fervid celebration of the Jury's power. It is set out as a prayer which presents them as divinely ordained saviours:

You Gentleman of the Jury, my sole Judges, the Keepers of my life; at whose hands, the Lord will require my bloud, in case you leave any part of the

indictment to the cruell and bloudy men: And therefore, I desire you to
know your power, and consider your duty, both to God, to Me and to your
own Selves, and to your Country; and the gracious assisting Spirit, and the
presence of the Lord God omnipotent, the Governour of Heaven and
Earth, and all things therein contained, go along with you, give councell
and direct you, to do that which is just and for his glory.

   [*The People with a loud voyce cryed Amen Amen, and gave an extraordinary great
   hum, Which made the Judges look something untowardly about them.*] (*Lilburne*, 141)

   Similarly, Hone frequently turns to address the jury directly as his
deliverers. He creates an opposition between the way he relates to
the jury and the way the state does through a tactical use of language:

My prosecutors have laid a wager with public opinion; but they will lose it
to their irretrievable shame. 'Skin for skin (*he exclaimed vehemently*), all that a
man has he will give for his life' I am here on trial for my life. If you, the
Jury do not protect me, my life must fall a sacrifice to the confinement that
will follow a verdict of guilty ... I talk to you as familiarly as if you were
sitting with me in my own room; but then, gentlemen of the jury, I have not
seats for you; I have not twelve chairs in my house; but I have the pride of
being independent. (3rd trial, 159)

Hone works the jury over to his position with great ingenuity. The
prosecutors are set up as sinister gamblers betting on their ability to
manipulate public opinion in order to legalize a murder. The
biblical quotation from Job (2: 4) refers to Satan's second interview
with God. Having already destroyed Job's wordly possessions and
family Satan gains permission from God to torment Job physically
through the following cynical logic: 'skin for skin, all that a man has
he will give for his life, but put forth thy hand now and touch his
bone and his flesh and he will curse thee to thy face'. Hone's prosecutors are given the role of latter-day Satans plotting to turn him
from his ideals through the bodily affliction of imprisonment. The
jury are Hone's only chance against this plot. Hone fictionalizes his
own predicament in terms of a martyrdom, for he was not on trial
for his life, as Lilburne was, except in the rather extended sense that
a prison sentence might have ruined his health.
   At this point, however, Hone shifts from a passive appeal to the
jury as his judges to a positive identification with them as his equals
and friends. This is achieved through an astonishing domestic metaphor. When Hone talks to the jury the intimidating and treacherous
environment of the court suddenly melts into the solid comfort of

'my own room'. Then in an act of bizarre literalization Hone enters into the role of host and even apologizes for his lack of hospitality in not providing sufficient seating. The constant allusions to the acts of standing and sitting which both Lilburne and Hone use to emphasize their discomfort and intimidation during the trials are attached to this image of social embarrassment. Hone's inability to provide for others surreptitiously reintroduces the theme of the poverty which resulted from his protracted arrest and prosecution. Such language and thought has nothing to do with the facts of the case or with orthodox legal defence but goes beyond these confines to work strangely on the emotions of the jurors in a language of devastating availability.

Throughout their trials Hone and Lilburne focus upon the formal surroundings of the court and upon the forms of language and ceremony in which legal procedure is bound. They do this in the full knowledge that the environment is as alien to the jury as to the accused. Even before his trial has properly opened Lilburne launches into a furious attack upon what he sees as the dangerous forms of the law. He presents himself as ever vigilant for snares and tricks. Asked to raise his hand and state his name, Lilburne thinks he sees a trap: 'But Sir, to save my self from your fore-lay'd snares and desired advantage against me, I will come a little closer to the business: You demand I should hold up my hand at the Bar, and I know not what it meanes, neither what in law it signifies' (*Lilburne*, 21).

When the jury are one's judges, ignorance of the law may technically be no excuse, but in Lilburne's hand(s) it certainly has advantages. Having seized on this detail Lilburne expands it into a general argument.

those lawes which are in the English Tongue that I have read, although I find mentioned maid of holding up the hand, yet I cannot finde much of the full signification of it, onely I find it to be of a large extent, and as for those lawes, or rather the practick part of the law, that are in *French* and *Lattin*, I cannot read them, and therefore much less understand them; in which regard for me to hold up my hand at the Barre before I understand the true signification of it in law, (which tells me it is in it self a ticklish thing) were for me to throw away my own life upon a punctillio or nicity. (*Lilburne*, 22)

His favourite terms and ideas resurface. Plain common English is overpowered in legal discourse by impenetrable foreign tongues. What in everyday life is a harmless and friendly gesture, the raising of the hand, takes on a sinister and unfathomable complexity in the court room. Lilburne raises the spectre of a world of infinite complications where nothing is as it seems. A man may condemn himself through a simple gesture, for the law has its own unfathomable ways of interpreting signs. While the whole speech is to the judges a huge fuss about nothing, they are forced to reply to this plea for information in order to dispel the notion of entrapment. The judges attempt to counter Lilburne on this point by stating that the only function of the hand-raising is to identify the individual on trial and go on to state that he need only call his name and that will suffice. This gives the impression that Lilburne was justified after all. If the hand-raising was not necessary then why was it demanded? It has been shown up as a piece of ceremonial trumpery designed to overawe the witness.

Hone learned from Lilburne how powerful the stance of defiant ignorance could be in winning over a jury. In one of his opening exchanges with Lord Ellenborough he counters the argument that his citation of parody is inadmissible as evidence with the stark repetition of his incomprehension:

Mr. Hone (after a pause)———I really do not understand, your lordship; I state it seriously, that I am not sure of the exact meaning of your Lordship's intimation.
Lord Ellenborough———I think what I have stated is intelligible enough to every other person in Court.
Mr. Hone———It is certainly not intelligible to my humble apprehension.
Lord Ellenborough———I can't help it.
Mr. Hone———I really don't clearly understand what your Lordship means by the word *evidence* ... I don't know, as a man of plain understanding, what may and what may not be given in evidence. But my intention is to read to the jury certain other publications which I consider absolutely essential to my defence. (2nd trial, 86–7)

Ellenborough's 'I can't help it' is an admission of defeat and a tactical disaster. Forced to abandon the language of the law and talk in Hone's terms Ellenborough's response appears inarticulate and is ineffective, for Hone continues to read his parodies as evidence anyway.[49] Again ignorance of the law becomes a deadly defensive

---

[49] At this time rules of evidence were still in flux. Because of this Ellenborough is able to present as a ruling on the admissibility of evidence what is really a surreptitious legal ruling on previous publications which he has decided are libellous. He has no right under Foxe's libel act to make such a legal ruling. No wonder Hone was

weapon. 'I do not understand the law, but explain it to me' is the stance that triumphantly underpins the defences of both Hone and Lilburne. If the law cannot be translated into common sense then it is no good to them or the jury.

The strain of wronged innocent is frequently worked up by both men into that of martyr. They repeatedly express their predicament explicitly within the tradition of Protestant martyrology. Lilburne was an eminent model for Hone to have taken in this respect. He possessed something amounting to a martyrdom complex which he developed throughout his long career of litigation. Prosecuted by the Bishops of Star Chamber, then by royal command before the House of Lords, then by the cavaliers when captured during the Civil War, then by the government of the Commonwealth on three separate occasions, and banished twice 'beyond the seas', it appeared there was no government 'the Self Afflicter' could not turn against himself.[50] His first trial and punishment could come straight out of the *Acts and Monuments*. Sentenced to be whipped behind a cart, and then pilloried, he was finally gagged because he refused to stop haranguing his persecutors. After his punishment he brought out a series of lurid and outraged accounts of his sufferings and his career as a trial publicist was launched. His writings provided Hone with a virtual blueprint on how to play to the gallery and influence public opinion.

A degree of self-consciousness and self-dramatization surrounded Lilburne's adoption of a martyrological stance throughout his career.[51] Both in his trials and in his pamphlets he continually mythologizes himself and his actions. In the pamphlet *The Just Defence of John Lilburne Against Those Who Charge him with Turbulency of Spirit* Lilburne produced his most extended discussion of the tradition of Protestant martyrdom with which he identified. He counters the charge that he is absurdly contentious by stating that the Pharisees tried to defame Christ, 'giving out that he was a wine bibber, and a

confused! For the rules of evidence in the early 19th cent., see Bentham's *Rationale of Judicial Evidence*, ed. J. S. Mill, 5 vols. (London, 1827), and Julius Stone, *Evidence: Its History and Policies*, rev. W. A. N. Wells (Sydney, 1991).

[50] For a manifestation of the long-standing popular appreciation of Lilburne's contentious life, see *The Self Afflicter. Lively Described in the whole course of the Life of Mr. John Lilburne*, a posthumous chapbook biography published in 1657.

[51] Nigel Smith rightly stresses the pre-eminence of Lilburne amongst Puritans who deliberately adopted a martyrological stance during the Civil War and Interregnum. See *Perfection Proclaimed: Language and Literature in English Radical Religion* (Oxford, 1989), 44, 64, 69.

friend of publicans'. He moves on from this to a discussion of the role of martyrs throughout history to conclude: 'thus in every age ever since hath it been, as witness all the volumes of the *Book of Martyrs*', and makes special reference to the Marian persecutions.

In his 1649 trial for high treason Lilburne used many of the tropes of martyrdom. The continual comparisons of himself with Christ's treatment at the hands of the Pharisees, the images of assault, murder, and the spilling of innocent blood, the exaggerated references to his exhaustion and physical suffering, the use of prayers and the curse, and his constant profession of his true faith before the eyes of God—every one of these can be related to Foxean paradigms for the behaviour of Protestant martyrs during heresy trials. Foxe casts a long, deep shadow which stretches from Lilburne to blasphemy and libel trials throughout the eighteenth and early nineteenth centuries.[52]

The trial itself played a special and rigorously defined role in the popular conception of the Christian martyr. The trial of the innocent before corrupt judges, who he then proceeds to outwit and ridicule through God's help, was central to the rhetorical structure of the *Acts and Monuments*.[53] Foxe describes dozens of heresy trials in which humble and frequently uneducated people astound the ecclesiastical tribunals, who eventually convict them, with the subtlety and bravado of their arguments. The basic patterns and tensions in many of these cross-examinations strikingly anticipate the exchanges in the trials of Lilburne and Hone. Foxe provided basic patterns for the presentation of judicial encounters in which the simple and righteous man triumphed over the massed intellectual and coercive power of the state. In Foxe's elaborate choreography of martyrdom the intellectual testing and trial of the martyr follows the account of initial apprehension and torture and performs a proleptic function in relation to the martyr's physical suffering during execution.[54]

The *Book of Martyrs* continued to provide the basic rules in both

[52] Daniel Defoe, for example, aligned himself with the tradition of the Protestant martyrs in his 1703 *A Hymn to the Pillory*, written to celebrate his pillorying for seditious libel.

[53] The best account of the structural and rhetorical operation of heresy trials in the *Actes and Monuments* is in Warren W. Wooden, *John Foxe* (Boston, 1983), 60–9.

[54] The *Book of Martyrs* was cited as special traverse evidence in the late 17th cent. See R. M. Helmholtz and Thomas A. Green, *Juries, Libel and Justice: The Role of English Juries in Seventeenth- and Eighteenth-Century Trials for Libel and Slander* (Los Angeles, 1984), 15.

behavioural and psychological terms for popular political martyrs in the early nineteenth century. It is an ingredient in the blasphemy trials of figures as diverse as Eaton, Carlile, and Wedderburn. All these men defended their infidel and deist beliefs through sophisticated arguments concerning freedom of thought and of religion. They presented themselves not merely as political but as religious martyrs, persecuted for their faith. The government's enthusiastic misuse of blasphemy prosecution facilitated the incorporation of the tropes of Christian martyrdom in the context of radical trials, yet the tradition could be, and was, successfully incorporated into purely political trials as early as the 1790s. The 1794 treason trials provide the most significant demonstration of this process and beyond this they can be seen to have provided later radicals with a demonstration of what stagecraft and rhetorical experimentation could achieve within the court-room.

The importance of the 1794 treason trials for later radical run-ins with the government over sedition, blasphemy, and libel prosecutions is a complicated affair. The acquittals of Hardy, Tooke, and Thelwall, each on a charge of high treason, had a lasting impact on several aspects of radical interaction with the law. The trials of Hardy and Tooke in particular had riveted the attention of the nation and had given these men, however briefly, the status of martyrs. The trials demonstrated that if the government overplayed its hand radical activists could overnight become popular national heroes.

One thing, however, that is not sufficiently recognized is how different each of the 1794 trials was from the others. These differences are indeed so extensive as to make it unwise to read the three trials as a congruent group.[55] The language used in the trials and the external reactions to them went through various transformations. The trials of Hardy and of Tooke were to a large extent *sui generis* and each one had different things to teach later radicals. The trial of Thelwall was much shorter than the other two and generated nothing like the same interest.

Hardy's trial was the longest and the most tense of the three. It was also the most conventionally legalistic, decorous, and arid in terms of the forms and language observed in court. It is noticeable

---

[55] This indiscriminate lumping together of the trials is a continuing fault in academic discussions of them. The most recent example is John Barrell's 'Imaginary Treason, Imaginary Law: The State Trials of 1794', in *The Birth of Pandora* (London, 1992), 119–45.

that Hardy kept his head well down and did not cross-examine any of the witnesses. Unlike the ebullient Tooke he made no speeches to the court even after his acquittal. His defence was left in the technically and rhetorically expert hands of Erskine.

It required remarkable intellectual stamina and clear-headedness on the part of Erskine, and the other defending lawyer John Gibbs, to refute the mass of evidence which the Crown prosecution brought in during a trial which lasted nine days. This evidence was intended to prove through its associative weight that Hardy had been conspiring to overthrow the constitution and hence by extension had been (in the phrase of the statute which constituted the precise treason with which he was charged) 'encompassing and imagining the death of the king'. With indomitable patience the defence lawyers stuck at the job of questioning every Crown witness and every piece of written evidence to demonstrate that none of it constituted hard proof that the radicals were planning to instigate a mass insurrection that would result in the death of the King. Without such proof the case crumbled: the sheer mass of inconclusive evidence dragged it down. Even before the evidence was introduced a feeling had been created that the Crown prosecution were having to try too hard. After John Scott, later Lord Eldon, made his interminable opening speech Thurlow reportedly declared, 'Nine hours. Then there is no treason, by God!'[56]

Hardy's trial provided lessons in common sense and passivity—in the value of obtaining a good professional defence, of keeping a low profile, and of allowing the prosecution to hang itself with its own enormous rope. Tooke's trial took place in a wholly changed atmosphere in which Hardy's trial is frequently referred to and in which Hardy is mythologized as a new radical martyr. An air of righteous triumphalism is frequently present in Erskine's speeches. Tooke adopted a prominent part in the cross-examinations and used a variety of satiric and comic techniques, eccentric to customary legal practice, to mock the prosecution and impress the jury. Tooke's trial constituted a more active and inspirational model for subsequent radicals. It must not only have encouraged Hone, but provided him, in much the same way that Lilburne's trials did, with working techniques for winning over a jury and undermining the confidence of the prosecution.

[56] Quoted in Philip Anthony Brown, *The French Revolution in English History* (Edinburgh, 1918), 127.

Erskine markedly altered his tactics in Tooke's trial. He spent a lot of time referring back to the ways in which Hardy's acquittal had transformed the present situation. He reinvented his defence of Hardy in terms of a narrative of divine intervention. His main address to the jury after the presentation of the Crown evidence was theatrical. It drew on the language of popular enthusiasm and on appeals to divine providence derived from the popular martyrologies. He opened with an extended peroration which bypassed legal details and Hardy's suffering and which emphasized the lawyer's emotional state: 'when I reflect upon the emotions which at that time [Hardy's trial] almost weighed and pressed me down into the earth, with those which at this moment animate and support me, I scarcely know how to bear myself, or in what manner to conduct my cause.' (ST 25: 257).

As the speech develops it becomes clear that Erskine is presenting not only Hardy, but himself, as martyr. He asserts that he had to deal with 'circumstances of distress and agitation . . . which even now I tremble to look back on'. He describes how he 'had to bear up against a pressure with which no advocate in England ever before had to contend'. As he continues he moves into a strain that becomes increasingly apocalyptic. The pressures he had to endure are not only specific—the Crown, the law, the government—but terrible and general. He presents England as a country run mad in the midst of its own terror:

I had to contend too with all this in a most fearful season; when the light and humanity, even of an English public, was with no certainty to be reckoned on—when the face of the earth was drawn into convulsions—when bad men were trembling for what ought to follow, and good men for what ought not—and when all the principles of our free constitution, under the dominion of a delusive or wickedly infused terror, seemed to be trampled under foot. (ST 25: 258)

On one level this is a triumph of wit and inversion, the 'terror' of the French Revolution, the chimera which is constantly called up to justify the prosecution's horror of popular insurrection, is replaced by Pitt's new English 'terror'. The suspension of Habeas Corpus and the treason trials are substituted for the 'swinish multitude', and where the latter would, in Burke's famous phrase, have 'learning . . . trodden down under the hoofs of a swinish multitude', Pitt's terror will have the 'free constitution . . . trampled under foot'. Yet this speech is simultaneously operating a strain of popular millenarian rhetoric.

There is nothing to match this language in Hardy's trial. Erskine anticipates the tone which Hone was increasingly to adopt in his second and third trials. The battle between the state and the radicals is presented as the battle between good and evil, and the victory of radicalism is presented as divinely inspired, as the work of a protecting providence. Erskine's marvellous jury address builds to a climax in which he not only claims divine guidance but actually suggests that he speaks as a prophet, as God's expressive instrument, and that the jury are the instruments of divine providence:

When, in spite of all this mighty and seemingly insuperable pressure, I recollect that an humble and obscure individual was not merely acquitted but delivered with triumph from the dangers which surrounded him;—when I call to mind that his deliverance was sealed by a verdict, not obtained by cabal, or legal artifice ... and which accordingly HAS obtained the most marked and public approbation; when I consider all this—it raised up a whirlwind of emotions in my mind, which none but HE who rides the whirlwind could give utterance to express. In that season of danger, when I thought a combination of circumstances existed which no innocence could overcome, and having no strength of my own to rely on, I could only desire to place the jury under the protection of that benevolent Providence ... I wished that a verdict should be given, such as a jury might look up to God ... when they pronounced it. Gentleman that verdict is given;—it is recorded—and the honour and justice of the men, who as the instruments of Providence, pronounced it, are recorded, I trust, for ever along with it. (ST 25: 260)

Yet Erskine is quite aware of the dangers of adopting the language of enthusiasm. He immediately distances himself from his earlier impassioned rhetoric with an aside which allows for an elegant transition back into the language of legal analysis: 'It may be said that this way of considering the subject is the result of a warm enthusiastic temper, under the influence of a religious education—and it may be so' (ST 25: 260).

Tooke adopts a number of dramatic stances throughout the trial. He plays by turns the outraged yet sardonic innocent, the eccentric scholar, and the pitiable invalid. He is a bit of a joker when he first appears with the other prisoners to plead before the first trial, and like Lilburne he demonstrates the value of introducing human elements into the general proceedings. Standing by an open window he tells the court 'as far as I myself am concerned I am prepared to plead, though I have not had the opinion of my counsel, rather than

be exposed any longer to the wind' (*ST* 25: 24). He constantly brings
in references to his very human reaction to his predicament. In the
same way that Lilburne calls for a chamber-pot at a climactic
moment of his trial, or Hone tells of falling insensible because he was
prevented from performing an office of nature for several days,
Tooke refers to his rectal complaint. This, he tells the court, necessi-
tates a five-hour preparation each morning before his appearance in
court.[57] Tooke's methods for discrediting witnesses are at times
hilariously unorthodox. Cross-examining a Mr Beaufoy, who he believes to be a lying government spy, he opens by telling the court,
'this gentleman's remembrance requires so much *flapping*, that I must
beg leave to wake it once more', and he becomes so infuriated that
he ends by telling the court he is prepared to place a bet on the man
having lied:

> in the presence of persons of the description that I see round, able to
> inform themselves on the subject hereafter, I will venture a wager!
> Lord Chief Justice *Eyre.*—A wager!
> Mr. Tooke.—I am wrong—I forgot myself.

Tooke's mode of address to his own character witnesses is equally
original. He clinches the harmless nature of his religious views by
asking William Sharpe, 'But you do not suppose I would eat little
children without being dressed?'

Tooke was also capable of applying his expertise as a linguist and
historian of language to the evidence. His interest in semantics had
enabled him to defend himself unsuccessfully but spectacularly on a
charge of seditious libel in 1777. He based his defence on the interpretation of the word 'that'[58] and after his treason trial he continued
his complicated examinations of the relationships between law and
language in his great work *The Diversions of Purley*. In the 1794 trial he
used a semantic argument to discredit a crucial note he received
which was presented by the prosecution as a call for insurrection.[59]
He also employed an ingenious palaeographic argument to discredit
a rough draft of his writing which was read out in court. His argument centres on his habit of encircling words to signify their
excision. The court took the encircling to communicate emphasis

---

[57] *Lilburne*, 120; Hone, 1st trial, 15; *ST* 25: 132.
[58] See Smith's excellent discussion of Tooke's analysis of law and language,
pp. 110–53.
[59] Ibid., 114.

and he claimed that they had consequently misrepresented his writing and thought.[60]

Tooke's trial anticipates Hone's in the way it increasingly moves out of the control of the language and intellectual assumptions of the lawyers. In trying to prove treasonous intent through the citation of a mass of contradictory evidence derived from Tooke's private papers, the prosecution was forced to enter into debating political questions at almost every turn. Tooke's London Corresponding Society correspondence, and correspondents, focused upon such questions as government reform, freedom of speech, the right to public meetings, the rights of man, and the works of Paine. The vast majority of the printed evidence consisted of minutes and resolutions from London Corresponding Society and Society for Constitutional Information meetings and of radical satires. Much of this material was funny but none of it proved Tooke guilty personally of 'encompassing or imagining the death of the king'. Radical ideology had never had such a good public airing. Tooke's trial provided a lesson in the value and methods of trial publicity for generations of subsequent radicals.

After the débâcle of 1794 the government showed an increased sophistication in terms of the type of state prosecutions which they brought against radical activists. During the first fifteen years of the nineteenth century there were an increasing number of successful convictions on charges of seditious blasphemy. There were several reasons for this. Firstly there was the well-founded assumption that a jury would be far more likely to find a verdict of guilty on the grounds of traducing sacred texts than of those of ridiculing the government and its ministers. 'The Church in danger' was still a useful tool for rallying Establishment support.[61] Secondly there was the legal fusion of religion and law which had been established by Sir Mathew Hale in 1676. Hale's statements were the oldest and most specific justification for an ecclesiastical case to be heard before a law court. Hale was consequently quoted or alluded to by the prosecution at the opening of virtually every early nineteenth-century blasphemy trial: 'to say "religion is a cheat" is to dissolve all the obligations whereby the civil societies are preserved, and Christianity is part and parcel of the laws of England, and, therefore to reproach the Christian Religion is to speak in subversion of law.'[62] Variations on Hale's 'part and parcel' dictum were used by judges

---

[60] *ST* 25: 226–7.   [61] See pp. 101–4 above.   [62] Quoted in Wickwar, 25.

over the succeeding century. A publication which could be shown
to attack any aspect of the scriptures or treat them with undue disrespect was a criminal libel because the scriptures and the law were
one and the same.[63] This situation made the establishment of blasphemous libel in law far more straightforward than was the case
with a charge of seditious libel. In the latter case the jury had to
decide whether the publication under question was legally a libel or
not. Thirdly there was the publication of Paine's *Age of Reason*. The
publication of this book became something of a suicidal crusade
with certain radical publishers and printers. Once it had been
established as a blasphemous libel, in several successful prosecutions in the early 1800s, the government could be sure of gaining
a conviction on charges of printing, publishing, or selling this work
in any form.

The trial of Daniel Isaac Eaton in 1812 for publishing the 'third
and last part of Paine's *Age of Reason*' was perhaps the government's
most ill-judged blasphemy prosecution before that of Hone. It demonstrates the acumen with which radicals used Protestant
martyrology. Eaton was 60 years old, yet on being found guilty he
was sentenced not only to eighteen months' imprisonment but to
stand in the pillory. This ritualistic punishment provided an ideal
stage for his political martyrdom. Shelley was inspired to write and
have printed *A Letter to Lord Ellenborough*. This passionate address to
the presiding judge at Eaton's trial focused on the absolute right of
the individual to freedom of religious opinion and it is shot through
with martyrological references. Ellenborough is presented as a rein-
carnation of the spirit of Marian persecution: 'If the law *de heretico
comburendo* has not been formally repealed, I conceive that, from the
promise held out by your Lordship's zeal, we need not despair of
beholding the flames of persecution rekindled in Smithfield' (*SP*
75). Shelley goes further and sees the unfortunate judge as equivalent to the barbarian persecutors of the early Christians:

Wherefore, I repeat, is Mr. Eaton punished? Because he is a Deist? And
what are you, my Lord? A Christian. Ha then! the mask is fallen off; you
persecute him because his faith differs from yours. You copy the persecutors of Christianity in your actions and are an additional proof that
your religion is as bloody, barbarous, and intolerant as theirs. (*SP* 74)

[63] Ibid. 25–30. For Bentham's insights into this situation, see Crimmins, *Secular
Utilitarianism*, 152–7.

Shelley was, however, to be proved wrong when he went on to state that 'in a civilized and enlightened country, a man is pilloried and imprisoned because he is a Deist, and no one raises his voice in the indignation of outraged humanity' (*SP* 75). Cobbett looking back in 1820 recalled a triumphant scene where a cheering crowd offered Eaton gifts 'while the executioner and judges of office were hooted!'[64] Eaton had earned this victory. His defence in court had carefully set up the platform for his subsequent reception as a radical martyr.

The prosecution's strategy for winning the support of the jury relied on their appealing to the sacred union of the Church and the law. It was stated that the object of Paine's book was to 'lay the axe to the root of the Christian Religion'.[65] Eaton was presented as an infidel threatening to destroy a faith which held society together. Both at the opening, and with crushing repetition in his summing-up, Ellenborough repeats to the jury that they have taken an oath which officially proves their belief in the indivisibility of law and Christianity and goes through the legal precedents from Hale onwards which had made this so. Eaton's defence anticipates the pattern to be followed by Carlile and Wedderburn in their blasphemy trials. Far from denying the charges, in terms of either the blasphemous contents of Paine's work or the fact of selling it, Eaton defends and even celebrates his actions. He presents himself as a martyr upholding the individual's right to free religious opinion in the context of a general argument for the necessity of toleration.

Eaton's defence is constructed with the anticipation that he will be found guilty. He goes so far as to present himself in the guise of religious martyr, protecting the true faith from papist adulteration: 'I was in hopes of convincing the Court and Jury, that the simplicity and beauty of the primitive Christians, unadulterated by *Popish Mummery*, was, and is the Christian religion I profess; however they have not received it in that light, and I am found guilty' (*Trial*, 44). Having considered the history of religious persecutions, his defence concluded with a passionate assertion of 'the impossibility of enforcing religious opinions by judicial prosecution' and stressed that 'the days of burning are now over'.

At the same time Eaton employed a number of more blatantly

---

[64] For Shelley's *Letter* see David Lee Clark's introduction, *SP* 72–3. Cobbett is quoted in Thompson, 605.
[65] *Trial*, 8.

theatrical devices, very much in the Lilburne–Tooke–Hone tradition, in order to play upon the jury's sympathy. He had his defence read out because of 'a very heavy cold' and states that 'neither providence nor education have designed me for an orator'. When pleading for a light sentence he gives pitiful biographical details full rein:

Daniel Isaac Eaton saith, that having brought from America a recipe for the manufacture of a certain soap, which is a specific and cure for the scorubic eruptions, which he lately sold with public approbation and increase of sale, for his support and maintenance, he had designed in future wholly to desist from the publication and sale of political pamphlets. And further this deponent saith that he is of the age of sixty, very infirm in body, as well from an affliction of the stone as also from an obstinate and inveterate cough, which deprives him of nightly rest, and appears to have fixed upon his lungs, and which makes him greatly apprehensive that his life will be endangered by close confinement. (*Trial*, 68–9)

Eaton was a strange kind of martyr, pleading infirmity and requesting leniency, yet celebrating his position as an infidel prepared to suffer for freedom of thought.

Similarly, Carlile saw his trial in terms of a politico-religious martyrdom. The intoleration and witch-hunting attitudes which the SSV, with the encouragement of the government, had introduced in the years after Waterloo had created an atmosphere which Carlile was able to exploit. In his journal *The Republican* Carlile yearns for the return of the faggot and the stake. Supported by Godwin, Bentham, and the intellectual infidels, he attained the position of popular martyr for a few weeks after his trial. In the words of Henriques, 'infidelity had found its martyr, and the government and its allies an opponent who combined the thirst for publicity and the Puritan determination of an honest John Lilburne'.[66]

Even extreme and methodologically more primitive radicals such as Wedderburn and Samuel Waddington had martyrological pretensions, although the extent to which they systematically related to role models from the history of Protestant persecution is less easy to establish.[67] Wedderburn's pre-written and suspiciously erudite defence in his blasphemy trial argues forcefully for toleration. He

[66] Henriques, 246. Henriques discusses the role of infidelity and deism in radical political circles and the Vice Society's collaboration with the government to suppress it (pp. 234–46). For a detailed discussion of Carlile's trial from the perspective of radical propaganda and the law of libel, see Wickwar, 68–85.

[67] See McCalman, *Radical Underworld*, 139–147.

makes the classic martyr's identification of his persecution with Christ's, although he does it very cheekily via Voltaire: 'If they would resemble Jesus Christ' says VOLTAIRE 'they must be *martyrs* not *executioners*' and every person of common sense must see, that it is the same spirit which persecutes, me that brought the founder of Christianity to the cross'.[68] Martyrdom through blasphemy and infidelity became increasingly central to radical publicity after Peterloo. There was intense interest in the religious states of mind of the Cato Street conspirators, and in the days before their execution they were assigned a clergyman who not only attempted to bring them to Christianity but analysed their sceptical positions. The conspirators, with the exception of William 'Black' Davidson, were all executed without seeking the benefit of clergy. This was seen in some radical quarters as a victory over the coercive power of state religion.[69]

Hone's relation to martyrology is more complicated than that of the atheist or deist radicals. He did not attempt to present himself as a religious martyr in the sense that he was defending and would suffer for his religious position. Throughout his trials he presents himself as persecuted for his political ideas alone. Yet he had absorbed the literature of Protestant martyrology since his infancy and applied its tropes to a political context. He had been fascinated by the *Book of Martyrs* as a child. His father gave him a copy directly after the death of his little brother and 'the plain narrative of their [the Martyr's] sufferings and fortitude animated me to enthusiasm'. The influence of the book is evident in the published accounts of his trials.[70] Once the government insisted on bringing on the second and third prosecutions, despite Hone's acquittal on the first day, his exploitation of the martyr's persona becomes more and more pronounced. In all three trials Hone gives detailed accounts of his arrest under *ex officio* information and his subsequent maltreatment during the months leading up to the trial (1st trial, 14–17; 2nd trial, 92–7; 3rd trial, 149–53). In doing this he moves close to a Foxean balance whereby the martyr's initial suffering and persecution provide a moving context for the trial proper. The published accounts of

---

[68] *The Trial of the Rev. Robt. Wedderburn*, 11.

[69] For the relationship of blasphemy to extreme radical and revolutionary activity, see McCalman, *Radical Underworld*, 145–50.

[70] Hone gives an account of his early relationship with the text in his fragmentary autobiography, repr. in Hackwood, 35–7.

Hone's trials are carefully constructed artefacts which incorporate well-tried formal elements from the martyrologies. The assertions that Hone's prolonged defence is miraculous and providentially ordained (3rd trial, 159), the comparisons of himself with Christ and his judges with the Pharisees (3rd trial, 158, 159), the presentation of his defence as an armed conflict between good and evil (3rd trial, 154), and the constant accusations that his judges are bloodthirsty tyrants intent on trapping and then murdering him find a common heritage in Foxe.

Hone's elaborate construction of the role of secular martyr was ideally suited to radical trial propaganda and was carried through into the popular press in a variety of ways. The worked-up account of the opening of his first trial, for example, gives an account of his arrest and initial pleading:

Whilst one of the informations was being read, a mist came before his eyes, he felt giddy and applied for leave to sit. The answer of Lord Ellenborough was 'NO;' and it was pronounced with an intonation that might have been heard at the other end of the hall ... He was then taken to the King's-Bench, and was afterwards found senseless in his room there, not having performed an office of nature for several days. That arose out of the in-humanity of Lord Ellenborough. (1st trial, 15)

The image of Ellenborough shouting at the defenceless Hone was immediately taken up in a caricature which uses the speech-bubble to marvellous effect as it balloons out over the entire court room finally shattering a window to express the judge's bellicose NOOOOOOO (Fig. 18). Hone's frequent references to his physical frailty (his need to sit, his convulsions, and to his bodily functions) introduce material and details which have no place in conventional judicial proceedings but which form a sometimes comic parallel with Foxe's shocking descriptions of the physical sufferings of his martyrs. Virtually every major newspaper of the day covered Hone's trial, and several of them did so in great detail.[71] Hone's role as martyr was elaborated upon in several of the more radical journals, and Cobbett's coverage adapted this theme with particular gusto:

---

[71] See Bowden, 161–77, for a listing of the major press coverage of the trials. For Cruikshank's delighted contribution to the literature celebrating the trial, see Patten, *George Cruikshank's Life, Times and Art*, 139.

Fig. 18. George Cruikshank. Etching. *LAW VERSUS HUMANITY.* 1817.

Mr. Hone's trial and his meritorious conduct will be long remembered. They will stand, in better times, along with those of William Penn, Stephen Bushell, Bingley, Lilburn, Prynne, Bastwyck, Burton, and the rest of the brave men who have resisted tyranny's favourite weapon ... Mr HONE has to thank *himself*, and the nation have to thank *him*, for this victory over Corruption arrayed in her most deadly armour, armed with her prison and her hidden dagger.[72]

Cobbett takes up Hone's lead and places him in a direct line descending from early seventeenth-century heroes of free speech and victims of Star Chamber prosecution. The pillorying, mutilation, and branding of these figures for their unlicensed writings is presented as a model for radical publishers in the early 1800s. The law is presented as a corrupt weapon of tyranny and Hone's presentation of the fatal effects of imprisonment is also developed by Cobbett through his metaphorical reading of the law as corruption's armour and prison as its dagger. The mythologization of Eaton, Hone, and Carlile as martyrs in the radical press indicates the thoroughness with which the radicals had absorbed and come to identify with the traditions of seventeenth-century Protestant martyrology. The tradition had been so thoroughly appropriated that it could even be used as the basis for satiric attack. In 1818 Wooler ridiculed Southey's political apostasy by quoting with appropriately barbed commentaries the Laureate's monumental inscriptions to the memory of Latimer, Ridley, and early Protestant martyrs which had appeared in his youthful Jacobin publication *Poems of 1797*.[73]

Hone and the Tradition of Trial Parody

Hone was acutely aware that parody was not restricted to literary models. State authority is enshrined within, and defined by, the forms of official language and ceremony. The language of the courts and the language of the Church have their own conventions and forms. It is no coincidence that the vast majority of popular parodies which Hone collected were based upon litanies, catechisms, creeds, biblical narrative, and trials. Hone had a varied knowledge of the vast literature of trial parody. His book sale catalogues show him to have owned many mock trials. These ranged from chapbook versions of animal trials to

---

[72] William Cobbett, *Cobbett's Weekly Political Register, 1802–1835*, 33 (30 May 1818), cols. 631–2.
[73] *BD* 29 (1818), 404.

the mock trials written around certain notorious eighteenth-century blasphemy trials.[74]

Trial parody was embedded in folklore and the popular imagination. The court is a public and theatrical space which tried the integrity and quick-wittedness of all involved. It is an environment where no one has the right to remain silent and where the coercive and manipulative powers of spoken language are strangely emphasized. The potential for humiliation is tremendous. One way to diffuse the fear and to tame the strange entangling conventions of legal discourse was to parody them.

By the early nineteenth century probably the simplest and certainly the most popular trial parodies involved animal trials. Although apparently primitive pieces of burlesque, these works are more complicated than they might appear to a twentieth-century audience. *The Trial of an Ox for Killing a Man with the Examination of the Witnesses before Judge Lion* is an illustrated chapbook which came out at about the same time as Hone's trials. It is a typical example of the folk survival of the animal trial. It grows out of a tradition which reaches back into the ancient and medieval worlds and which has been authoritatively uncovered by E. P. Evans. The trials of various types of insect pest for destroying crops, of domestic and farm animals for attacking or killing people, or for being unwittingly involved in cases of buggery, were carried through according to the legal systems used for humans. Evans also refers to the development of satiric animal trials by the latter half of the seventeenth century, the most celebrated example

---

[74] It is possible to gain some idea of the collection of trial parodies which Hone had built up from his book sale catalogue for 1827: item 218, *Trial of Antichrist for High Treason*, 1806; item 219, Brooke's *Tryal of the Catholics of Ireland*, a parody, 1770; item 221, Sherlock's *Trial of the Witnesses*, 1800; item 228, *Trial of Farmer Carter's Dog Porter for Murder*, by Mr Lond, 1771; item 237, *Trial of J—— P——l, Esq &c. commonly called E—— of E——, on the 22nd of February at the old Bayley before L. C. J. Truth, Baron Reason and Mr. Justice Honesty*, 1749; item 239, Neville (Henry), *Parliament of Ladies at Sprint Garden 1647 and Isle of Pines 1668*; item 282, *The Prisoner Against the Prelate; or, A Dialogue between the Common Gaol and Cathedral of Lincoln, written by a Prisoner of the Baptised Churches in Lincolnshire*; item 291, *Arraignement of Mr. Persecution, by Rev. Yongue Martin Mar-Priest son to old Martin*, 1645; item 293, *The Parliament, Arraigned, Convicted Wants nothing but Execution*, 1648; item 306, *Tryal, &co. of Occasional Conformity*, 1703; item 377, *Prisoner's Remonstrance with their New Litany to be said or sung during their confinement*, 1732; item 381, *Tryal of Will. Whiston, with a new catechism for the fine ladies*; item 410, *Tryal of the Lady Allurea Luxury, a parody*, 1757. Hone also included fairly complete transcripts from three early parodic trials in *The Every-Day Book* (1827), ii: *The Trial of Farmer Carter's Dog Porter* (99–105), *The Dog at Heriot's Hospital* (380–2), *The Arraignment, Trial and Condemnation of Squire Lottery* (712–17).

being Racine's *Les Plaideurs* where a dog is tried for stealing and eating a capon.[75]

The *Trial of an Ox* demonstrates that even in chapbook form the burlesque animal trial had acquired quite a political edge. The ox is tried for his life for goring his owner to death. There were many earlier examples of oxen being tried and executed for this offence. In this example other animals plead for the ox.[76] There are references concerning the introduction of corrupt witnesses: the dogs are not admitted because 'they were thief takers and interested', while the ox and tiger justify the killing on the grounds of inhuman exploitation. The tiger makes a general speech about oppression to other domestic animals the political implications of which are crude but unmistakable: 'what have you Mr. Horse; for carrying the boobies on your back, but stripes and ill treatment? And what have you, Mr. Ass, who are their nurse and doctor, but lashes and ill language?'[77]

Hone took up the animal trial chapbooks as the model for a pamphlet satire *Another Ministerial Defeat! The Trial of the Dog for Biting the Noble Lord* which came out in the same year as his trials. In choosing this model Hone was taking up one of the most popular types of animal trial burlesque. Trials of dogs for theft and murder were quite common and examples still survive into the seventeenth century.[78] Racine's dog trial in *Les Plaideurs* had its counterparts in English seventeenth-century satire. In 1682 appeared *An Account of the Arraignment, Tryal, Escape, and Condemnation of the Dog of Herriot's Hospital in Scotland*. Hone based a long article in his *Every-Day Book* on this broadside satire.[79] The piece was a political satire which gave an account of a mock trial attacking the Crown lawyers for their decision to hang the Duke of Argyle for high treason because he refused the test oath. In the parody the boys of Herriot's Hospital in Edinburgh considered their house-dog to hold a public office and to be obliged to take the test. The dog would only swallow the paper on which the test was written after it had been rubbed in butter. It was consequently accused and condemned for having taken the test with a qualification. This was the same charge which had been brought against the Duke. The lawyers in the trial argue in elaborate legal terms about the niceties of the dog's action: 'one fancied, that "the tyke might take the test *secundum quid* though not *simpliciter*," ... A

[75] Evans, 166, 312.   [76] Ibid. 168–9.
[77] *The Trial of an Ox* (Banbury, n.d.), 16.
[78] Evans, 176–77.   [79] *The Every-Day Book*, ii. 380–2.

fourth thought that "Though his stomack did stand at it, *in sensu univoco*, yet it might easily digest it *in sensu et aequivoco*".'[80]

The eighteenth century saw the appearance of even more sophisticated dog trial parodies, the most elaborate was well known to Hone.[81] *The Trial of Farmer Carter's Dog Porter for Murder* was an attack on the severity of the game laws written in 1771 by the Jamaican lawyer Edward Long. The dog is accused of murdering a hare and the charge is brought in with the ferocious piling-up of opprobrious adjectives which formed part of the legal formula in indictments for murder and treason:

> he the said prisoner did him the said deceased, in the peace of our lord of the manor then and there being, feloniously, wickedly, wantonly, and of malice afore-thought, tear, wound, pull, hall, touzle, masticate, macerate, lacerate, and dislocate and otherwise eavilly intreat, of all of which tearings, woundings, pullings, haulings, touzleings, mastications and so forth, maliciously inflicted in manner and form aforesaid, the said *Hare* did languish, and languishing did die, in *Mr Just-ass Ponser's* horse pond.[82]

The elaborate linguistic plays and sophistries used by lawyers, which so delighted Racine, also form the basis for much of the satire here. The heinous nature of the crime is brought out through a bizarre etymological pun: 'To *murder* may it please your worships in Latin, is—is—*Murederare*;—or in the true and original sense of the word, *Murder-ha-re*'. This ludicrous premiss is then developed with a quite Swiftian subtlety whereby the advocate argues for a return to the purity of the original concept of murder as relating only to '*hare-murderer*, or *murder-hare*'. Later devolved forms 'such as *killing a man, a woman, or a child*' are grudgingly passed over. The effect is to introduce with great irony the central argument of the satire, the appalling nature of a law that can place a nobleman's game and livestock on a par with, or even above, human life.

In 1817 Hone used the rumour that Lord Castlereagh had been bitten by a mad dog to create his own dog trial. *Another Ministerial Defeat!* works in tandem with another pamphlet *Official Account of the Noble Lord's Bite* which came out a matter of days before. The latter is very much in the style of Pope's *A Revenge by Poison on the Body of Edmund*

---

[80] Ibid. 381.

[81] *The Trial of Farmer Carter's Dog Porter* was owned by Hone (1827 book sale catalogue, item 228) and he used the text as the basis for another long article in *The Every-Day Book*, ii. 99–105.

[82] *Every-Day Book*, ii, 101.

Curll in that it gives a humiliating fictional account of the victim's physical sufferings in his home surrounded by his acquaintance. The dog's attack is set out in the form of a crude political allegory. Castlereagh is bitten by a dog 'of the old *Bull* breed, called *Honesty*' which is 'supposed to have entered the house with Sir F————s B——d——t and his friends'. *Another Ministerial Defeat!* followed up with an account of the trial of Honesty. The charge is introduced with a frenzied piling up of formulaic adjectives reminiscent of the earlier parody:

Honesty, being notoriously, or otherwise, an animal of a wicked, depraved, and most malicious mind and disposition, and most unlawfully, wickedly, impiously and maliciously envying the peace of mind, and high happy estate of the Noble Lord, and devising, contriving, and intending to disturb, worry, hurt, harm, maltreat, injure, abuse, annoy, torture, and do bodily wrong or other mischief to the said noble lord.[83]

Hone also takes up the manner of attacking packed juries which appears in many earlier trial parodies. The jury comprises a list of satiric names and addresses: ' Peter Pension of the Regents Park Esq ... Ephraim Eitherway, of Turnstile, Dealer in Sweets'. For the most part the exploitation of legal forms and rhetoric is primitive and the parody does not play with legal discourse as effectively as either of the earlier models. It shows Hone cutting his satiric teeth and producing broadly comic effects out of the question-and-answer framework of a cross-examination.

When Hone came up for trial in 1817 the language and forms of treason and sedition trials were being widely satirized in the radical press. Wooler's *Black Dwarf* for 1817 included several extended experiments, the most hilarious of which was centred on government over-reaction to the mobbing of the Regent's coach.[84] Trial parody continued to surface in the popular press from 1817 to 1819 and it was given an increased relevance with the unprecedented glut of state prosecutions for seditious and blasphemous libel which occurred amid the mounting disaffection of 1819.[85] Wooler reacted in July by publishing *The Trial of Mr. Parliament for various acts of High Treason, Sedition and Swindling, and other Misdemeanours committed against the Majesty of the People*. As the title suggests, this was a detailed attack on state libel prosecutions. The parody addresses several of the continuing state abuses in libel trials including the judge's leading of the jury

[83] William Hone, *Another Ministerial Defeat!* (1817), 2.   [84] See pp. 1–2 above.
[85] Wickwar, 315.

during the summing-up. In this trial the jury is addressed by 'Common Sense', who stresses that the judge's opinion is irrelevant: 'Gentlemen of the Jury, you have heard the accusation and the defence. As you are the judges, and not me, it is my duty to leave the decision in your hands. There has been nothing so complicated as to require any illustration from me.' Mr Parliament is, of course, found guilty. His sentence cleverly fuses the traditional punishment for high treason (hanging, drawing, and quartering, the body disposed of according to the King's pleasure) with the reformer's demands for a representative parliament: 'Mr. Parliament should be instantly *suspended*——afterwards dissolved in the water of authority, then to be divided into six hundred and fifty-eight pieces, and sent to the various divisions of the country *entitled* to representation—to be exhibited—as the law directs.'[86]

Peterloo added to the mass of trial publicity produced by the radicals. There were exhaustive reprintings and examinations of coroner's reports and inquests into various deaths resulting from the massacre. A great deal of capital was also made out of Orator Hunt's treason trial for his part in the meeting that led to the massacre. The disastrous performance of the government's witnesses and Hunt's merciless skewering of them constituted something close to judicial parody even before a delighted radical press took them up.[87]

It was, however, the Queen Caroline affair of 1820–1 that provided the climactic context for post-Waterloo radical exploitation of the trial and the literature it generated. Hone was inspirational in his production of pro-Caroline propaganda. Caroline had featured as a useful focus for Whig political manœuvres and radical propaganda since the 'delicate investigation' of 1805–6. The radicals had maintained an interest in her during the years following her 'exile' in 1814. She returned to England in June of 1820 to demand her rights as Queen and to contest George's demands for divorce and accusations of adultery. Her cause was delightedly espoused by the entire radical popular front. The vexed question of the extent to which certain of the radical leaders and journalists

---

[86] *BD* 30 (29 July 1818), 465–72.

[87] For trial parodies attacking the government's mishandling of the prosecutions, see *BD*, no. 15 (1820), 537–40, 'Trial Extraordinary—Mr. Canning Versus the Radical Reformers'; *BD* 16 (1820), 541–56, 'The State Trials contrasted with the Manchester no Trials'.

who took up her cause believed in her innocence is not relevant.[88] What matters here is the way her case was politicized. Caroline was appropriated by the radical propaganda machine and was used as a stick with which to beat the King and his ministers. She was also harnessed to the reform cause generally and became a symbolic victim of the government's manipulation of law, and an emblem of the power of the freedom of the press. As the scandal developed this was increasingly presented as the lone force which could protect her from the machinations of her enemies.[89]

Interest in the Queen's case reached fever pitch when George finally coerced the government to proceed with his divorce claim by introducing a Bill of Pains and Penalties. This would deprive the Queen of her title and privileges and dissolve her marriage. The passing of the bill involved a protracted trial in the House of Lords. The notorious green bag, supposedly containing a mass of evidence proving the Queen's infidelity while abroad, was finally opened. The trial was the central focus of the Queen Caroline affair and was a can of worms with an apparently limitless capacity. It provided satirists from both sides with an embarrassment of riches. The radicals were particularly spoilt in terms of the way the developing case provided opportunities for trial parody.

Perhaps the government's greatest error of judgement throughout the disaster was its decision to base the prosecution evidence on the testimony of Italian witnesses, formerly in Caroline's service. These had to be brought over especially for the trial and were largely believed to have been bought by the Crown with massive bribes. In the months leading up to the trial the radical press had consistently attacked the use of these witnesses. Bought, it was claimed, with taxpayers' money, they were going to betray their former mistress with the villainy typical of their race. The first witness to appear for the Crown, Signor Majochi, had clearly been prepared with set answers. Under Henry Brougham's unrelenting cross-examination he fell apart and was soon reduced to repeating the refrain 'NON MI RICORDO' to question after question that was fired at him. Several of the other witnesses went the same way but it was Majochi who

[88] By far the best overview of the motives of London radicals during the Queen Caroline affair is Ann Hone, *For the Cause of Truth*, 307–19, 356.

[89] John Stevenson, 'The Queen Caroline Affair', in Stevenson (ed.), *London in the Age of Reform* (Oxford, 1977), 141–5; McCalman, *Radical Underworld*, 169–77; Anna Clark, 'Queen Caroline and the Sexual Politics of Popular Culture in London, 1820', *Representations*, 31 (Summer 1990), 47–68.

became notorious. He was immediately taken up by the press and 'non mi ricordo' became the catch-phrase for perjury overnight. It formed the basis for a whole batch of satires and there was even a *Non Mi Ricordo Song Book*. This contains a number of popular songs which play elaborately upon the phrase and indicate the ingenuity with which language and meaning inside and outside the court room could be discussed in popular satire. In one song, 'Memory and Want of Memory, or Rather No than Yes', Majochi's increasing confusion and final collapse in the witness box are re-enacted in ballad form:

> You liv'd on air?——'Oh Signior si'
> 'No No! Upon my vord O,
> You put *soach confuse* in to me,
> That'——'What'——'*Non mi ricordo*'[90]

There was considerable debate during the course of the trial as to exactly what the phrase meant. Brougham went into the issue with delighted irony: 'He considered the correct translation of the words to be of much consequence; ... if it appeared that they [the interpreters] always translated "non mi ricordo", "I don't recollect", it seemed to him that it might be allowable for a person—even, who was only a Tramontane like himself—to doubt whether the same words could sometimes mean "I don't recollect" and at others "I don't know".'[91] The linguistic confusion within the court room was taken up in another number from *The Non Mi Ricordo Song Book*, which takes the form of a general disquisition on the theme 'most people have a favourite phrase':

> Some say By George, and some By Gosh,
> Some put their trust in Goles,
> And many of superior rank
> Delight to damn their souls ...
>
> But Lord of all the precious words
> That ever memory stored O,
> Commend me to that pregnant phrase,
> Divine Non mi Ricordo ...

The poem then pursues the question of what 'non mi ricordo' really means through eleven stanzas that express increasingly complicated self-contradictions with a sophisticated gusto. These describe not only the confusion and mounting desperation of the perjured witness

---

[90] *The Non Mi Ricordo Song Book* (1820), 9.   [91] Quoted in Bowden, 327.

but the satirist's outrage at the perjury and his delight in Brougham's
victory. The poem attempts to explain the mystery of the famous
phrase. Its massive signification is revealed and finally laid before the
British public in the form of a dead rat:

> Sometimes it stands for one that lies,
> Sometimes for day and night,
> Sometimes for having *cash* from Brown
> To swear that black is white.
>
> Sometimes it is ingratitude,
> Sometimes expresses fear,
> And then it goes for something hot
> And for a pot of beer.
>
> Sometimes with very little help
> It means both No and Yes,
> Or sometimes rather less than more,
> Or rather more than less.
>
> Sometimes it stands for such a time
> Betwixing and betweening,
> That being well interpreted
> It means it has no meaning.
>
> It means a thief, it means some beef,
> It means a shabby villain;
> It means mine host of the Garter here,
> Who longs to bring his Bill in.
>
> In short, it means that Mr. Brougham
> Has laid *Non mi Ricordo*
> As flat upon the Parliament boards,
> As ever rat was floored O.[92]

Legal cross-examination attempts to control meaning and force language to perform according to certain rules of logic while 'non mi
ricordo' represents the linguistic anarchy of the lie. The phrase in its
blatant evasiveness and tangible foreignness signifies the entire complex of corruption and double standards which lie behind the
government's prosecution. 'Non mi ricordo' takes on a life of its
own, it becomes a linguistic factotum for bemused corruption. It
confounds semantic meaning and natural phenomena—under its
spell 'yes' and 'no' and 'day' and 'night' become interchangeable. As
the poem reaches its climax the phrase becomes all things to all men.
It describes the corruption, greed, and stupidity of the witness, the

[92] *The Non Mi Ricordo Song Book*, 14–15.

" NON MI RICORDO ! "

&c. &c. &c.

" This will witness outwardly, as strongly as the conscience does within "

Cymbeline.

" Who are you ? "

FIG. 19. George Cruikshank. Wood engraving. Frontispiece for *NON MI RICORDO!* 1820.

plots of the King, and even the triumph of Brougham and the Queen's cause. The harsh statement of what the phrase had actually come to mean in political terms for the British public: 'It means a thief ... a shabby villain ... mine host of the Garter here, / who longs to bring his Bill in' suddenly fuses Majochi and the King, who is shown standing behind the whole trial. Majochi's humiliation is the King's humiliation, and 'non mi ricordo' his catch-phrase.

Hone took this fusion of Majochi and the King much further in his mock trial based on the case and inevitably entitled *Non mi Ricordo!* The title-page carries a woodcut by Cruikshank which presents a caricature of the bloated King conjoined with the figure of Majochi through the addition of black curly hair and enormous black muttonchop sideburns (Fig. 19). In the pamphlet the King undergoes a vigorous and ribald cross-examination relating to his past history of extravagance and fornication. The King's–Majochi's misunderstanding of the questions put to him opens the way for ludicrous punning:

> Are you a Member of the Society for the Suppression of Vice?
> Yes (*with great energy*).
> The Cross-examining Council said that the Interpreter had materially altered the sense of the last question; he had in fact asked, if the Witness was a Member of the Society for the Suppression of *Wives* (*a loud laugh*) which Witness had eagerly answered in the Affirmative.[93]

There was great popular disgust at the King's refusal to appear in public during the Queen's trial and the mock trial pamphlets fed the desire for public revenge.[94] Hone's pamphlet is a testament to the delighted ferocity with which the radical press put the King through its own fantastic rituals of legal retribution. King, court, Cabinet, and the law were ridiculed day after day during a trial which they had themselves instigated. The Queen Caroline affair was a final demonstration that the courts could be a dangerous place for loyalism. They could be as much a catalyst for radical propaganda as a tool for the intimidation of reformers.

---

[93] William Hone, *Non Mi Ricordo!*, (London, 1820), A4^{r-v}.

[94] There were several other extended trial parodies presenting the imagined cross-examination of the King. *Examination Extraordinaire of the vice R——y of B——d——y Boro! Alias the Handsome Gentleman* (London, 1820) is, next to Hone's, the most ingenious.

4

Radical Puffing: Parodic Advertising and Newspapers

HONE's publications from 1815 until 1821 frequently use advertising. They incorporated all major forms of press advertisement and many types of illustrated product advertising outside the press including handbills, pamphlets, broadsides, pasteboard handouts, and even illuminated windows. Hone's experiments with advertising reached a climax from 1820 to 1821. In 1820 he brought out *The Queen's Matrimonial Ladder*, a satiric pamphlet which was accompanied by a free toy ladder based on a children's toy. His 1820 pamphlet *Non Mi Ricordo* concluded with three pages of parody handbill advertisements. In 1821 his two final and most elaborate satires were published. *A Slap at Slop* was a burlesque folio newspaper. *The Political Showman—at Home!* used many of the formal aspects of hand-out advertisements for beast menageries. Both publications enjoyed spectacular sales.[1] As with all Hone's illustrated satires they were produced in close collaboration with George Cruikshank. All of these experiments relate directly to new developments in the early nineteenth-century advertising industry. They bring into focus the relationship between radicalism and developing print technologies in the early nineteenth century.

From 1780 to 1820 the advertising industry in England began to assume its modern shape. Charles Barker and Samuel Deacon set up agencies as early as 1812 and went on to run the big agencies in the 1840s and 1850s.[2] Press advertising, despite the restrictions of the

---

[1] *The Political Showman* and *A Slap at Slop* both went through 27 edns. See Bowden, 518, 523.

[2] V. P. Norris, 'Advertising History according to the Textbooks', *Journal of Advertising History*, 4 (1981), 9; Bruttini, 8–9; D. S. Dunbar, 'The Agency Commission System in Britain: A First Sketch of its History to 1941', *Journal of Advertising History*, 2 (1979), 19–20; T. R. Nevett, 'London's Early Advertising Agents', *Journal of Advertising History*, 1 (1977), 15–18.

stamp and advertisement taxes, thrived, and the leading daily papers became increasingly dependent economically upon advertising revenue. The quarterly and half-yearly journals developed their own advertising methods. John Bell pioneered the co-ordination of advertising and main text in his lady's fashion journal *La Belle Assemblée*. Book advertising expanded in terms of both its scale and methods.[3] The children's book industry was particularly pioneering in terms of the way it used advertising inside and outside the press.[4] The printing industry was undergoing fundamental changes. From 1810 to 20 the distinctive display faces known as fat-faces or Egyptians were widely introduced. They were used in areas of advertising outside the press, giving rise to printing works specializing in packaging and placards. By the second decade of the nineteenth century bill-posting was a large and well organized trade. Southey commented on the situation in London: 'whenever there was a dead wall, a vacant house, or a temporary scaffolding erected for repairs, the space was covered with printed bills'.[5]

The volume of advertising and the parodic tendencies of many forms of advertisement led to its early incorporation into satire. Mock newspapers mainly composed of advertisements had appeared in both these contexts by 1820. As early as 1785 the antiquarian and amateur caricaturist Francis Grose brought out *A Guide to Health, Beauty, Riches and Honour*. Hone owned a copy of this anthology of preposterous advertisements.[6] In the political sphere advertising forms were adopted in the government-backed propaganda brought out against France during the Napoleonic wars. The *Anti-Gallican* is strewn with mock playbills, book advertisements, and showman's announcements. Much of this material was also brought out in poster form.[7]

---

[3] For a detailed study of Bell, see Stanley A. Morison, *John Bell, 1745–1831* (Cambridge, 1930; repr. New York, 1981), 61–71. For the book trade, see the study of the advertising methods of John Murray in E. D. Mackerness, 'End Paper Advertising', *Journal of Advertising History*, 9 (1986), 57–9.

[4] M. Fearn, ' "For Instruction and Amusement": The Publishing and Advertising of Nineteenth Century Children's Books', *Journal of Advertising History*, 5 (1982), 31–5.

[5] Savage, 21; A. F. Johnson, *Type Designs*, 201–3; Morison, *Politics and Script*, 326–7; J. A. C. Brown, *Techniques of Persuasion* (Harmondsworth, 1963), 168. For print satires showing bills, see *BMC*, nos. 10441, 10763.

[6] F. Grose, *A Guide to Health, Beauty, Riches and Honour* (London, 1785). The title is detailed in Hone's 1822 book sale catalogue, item 2358. For single-sheet print satires using advertising forms, see *BMC*, nos. 6322, 6327, 6362, 8548–9, 8981, 10727, 11047, 11056, 11249, 11528, 12751, 12886.

[7] *The Anti-Gallican; or, Standard of British Loyalty, Religion, and Liberty. Including a Collection of the Principal Papers, Tracts, and Songs that have been Published on the Threatened*

Radicals in the 1790s were quick to pick up on developments in advertising. The press and pamphlet campaigns of Martin Van Butchell—doctor, inventor, and radical sympathizer—demonstrate the subtlety and vigour with which advertising could be incorporated into political propaganda.[8] Van Butchell brought out a variety of publications celebrating his cure for fistulas, his invention of elastic bands, which were to become a dandy fashion accessory, and his splendid beard. His 1795 pamphlet *Diverting Pages* included a defence of the millenarian prophet Richard Brothers and concluded with a selection of Van Butchell's most successful advertisements. These use the conventions of quack advertising to introduce political arguments. Politics seep into the publications in unexpected ways. Even Van Butchell's method of charging had a fundamentally levelling tendency. He demanded 'two percent of five years wages', and in one of his advertisements this system is related to *The Rights of Man*:

> Fee—is—according—to Ability!
> Let those—who have much
> Give—without grudging! . . .
> Plain Folk—do comply—very readily:
> So shall—the Gaudy:—
> Or keep their Complaints!
> Many—are in want—of Food;—and Raiment,
> For large Families;
> Such,—will be made whole—Just so speedily
> As the most wealthy;
> 'THAT'S one RIGHT of MAN
> And HE shall have IT

(Diverting Pages, 43)

Advertisements for his medical services are peppered with political asides. At one point he attacks the jail allowance of bread, at another

---

Invasion (London, 1804), 14, 16, 18, 148–154, 165, 221. For the publication of these parodies in the form of broadsides see BL, 'A Collection of Squibs on Buonaparte's Threatened Invasion', 1, item 4 (= *The Anti-Gallican*, 16); item 5 (= *The Anti-Gallican*, 165); item 95 (= *The Anti-Gallican*, 292). For Hone's familiarity with the material, see his 1843 book sale catalogue, item 219. The entry reads 'NAPOLEON. An extensive and curious collection of Popular Sheets relating to Napoleon Bonaparte, and especially those printed to incite the people to resist the intended invasion of England'.

[8] I am grateful to Iain McCalman for introducing me to this extraordinary figure.

he recommends that magistrates read Junius' letters (pp. 35–6, 39–40). He breaks off to warn of the dangers of war with France and to demand that the war be stopped (pp. 29, 38). In a particularly cheeky advertisement he offers his services to the royal families of Europe. He states that he will not only operate on the ignominious complaints of various monarchs but that he will protect them from the attentions of government spies and informers:

> If the Empress of Russia,—The Emperor of Germany,—The King of Prussia,—*An Immaculate*, or the Pope of Rome; were sorely Smitten in their hinder Parts, with bad FISTULAE and tormenting PILES,—Visited MARTIN— to be made quite whole ... Nor would he suffer a third person to be in the Room. Not wanting help he would not be hindered; By half witted spies; Slavish Informers: Nor Sad Alarmists. (*Diverting Pages*, 23–4)

Another advertisement is framed as an official petition to the King. This opens in self-celebratory mode: 'Your Majesty's Petitioner is a British Christian Man aged Fifty-nine—with a comely beard full eight inches long', but soon moves on to petition for the Scottish reformers who had recently been sentenced to long terms of transportation. The question is formulated in an almost over-elaborate style of ingratiation:

> That your most gracious MAJESTY will be most graciously pleased (Like— the—'PRINCE—of—PEACE'—) to extend your Majesty's ROYAL MERCY to Messieurs Muir, Palmer, Skirving, Margarot And the Loving wife of meek Margarot. Who are on the way to Botany Bay. Spare David Downie. (*Diverting Pages*, 27)

Van Butchell uses a different mode when he pledges his support for Thomas Hardy after the 1794 treason trial:

> Not grudgingly,—or—of necessity, For the KING loveth a cheerful Giver; I would most gladly have volunteered, (Tho—no—party—man) Loud to speak in Praise of Thomas Hardy: with Emphatic Voice! (*Diverting Pages*, 25)

He then states that he was prevented from accomplishing this bold gesture by his popularity as a physician for he was overloaded with patients. An affirmation of radical sympathy dissolves into a personal puff.

Van Butchell's publications demonstrate that advertising was a fertile habitat for political satire by the close of the eighteenth century. Yet this resource was only developed in certain areas of radical publishing. Intellectual radicals such as Coleridge and the

Hunts were openly hostile to advertising, and even Cobbett had an ambivalent approach. His working relationship with advertisements was typically antagonistic and riddled with contradiction. His public pronouncements were always hostile. As early as 1800 he thundered in the preface to his American journal *The Porcupine*: 'Not a single *quack* advertisement will on any account be admitted into the *Porcupine*. Our newspapers have too long been disgraced by this species of falsehood, filth and obscenity. I am told that, by adhering to this resolution, I shall loose five hundred a year, and excite the resentment of the numerous body of empirics.'[9]

Cobbett never allowed *The Political Register* to carry advertisements. At the heart of his outrage was the fear that advertisements would compromise the main copy. Despite this attitude Cobbett was a brilliant self-publicist who frequently made public his beliefs and discoveries through what would now be termed personal advertising campaigns. He predicted disaster for Peel's 1819 Finance Bill by hanging a seven-foot gridiron outside his print-shop. Cobbett then claimed that he would submit himself to public grilling if his predictions failed. His *Register* carried a woodcut of a gridiron for several years and the image came to symbolize Cobbett in the popular press for decades.[10]

Cobbett's wild enthusiasm for his inventions expressed itself in ingenious sales gambits. In the 1820s he launched his 'American Stove' and produced an illustrated handbill complete with diagrams and an engraving of the stove blazing away.[11] He had come across a number of agricultural products during his time in America which he hoped to introduce into England. American corn or maize was, he believed, a revolutionary alternative to English grain crops. He began demanding that farmers take up its production. His campaign was ferocious. He took a farm at Barn Elm and claimed that the yield of what he now termed 'Cobbett's corn' was three times larger than that he would have got from any English grain crop. He published a string of articles in his *Register* on the subject and the first pages of *A Treatise on Cobbett's Corn* were made out of corn husk paper. He accompanied his letters to the editors of all the leading newspapers with ears of corn and corn loaves.[12] His published claims for the product outstripped those of the most optimistic quack: 'it will prevent the labourers from ever being slaves again; it will inevitably

[9] Quoted in Turner, 51.   [10] Spater, 410–15.   [11] Ibid. 431–3.
[12] Ibid. 436–7.

reproduce small farms; it will make the labourers more independent of their employers; it will bring back, it will hasten back, the country to its former happy state'.[13] Cobbett's gargantuan imagination, normally turned towards the destruction of his political opponents, reveals itself to be well suited to copy-writing.

Cobbett's public stance of disgust and distrust towards advertising was shared by more respectable authors of radical associations such as Coleridge, Hazlitt, and Leigh Hunt. There was a tradition, stretching back to the eighteenth century, that respectable journals concerned with literature and political debate did not adulterate their pages or endanger the objectivity of their copy by including advertising. Coleridge, in what is ironically a handbill advertisement for his journal *The Watchman*, was careful to place first in a list of 'its advantages' the fact that 'There being no Advertisement, a greater Quantity of original Matter must be given, and the Speeches in Parliament will be less abridged'.[14]

Leigh Hunt wrote the most detailed analyses of advertising by an intellectual radical. The 1808 publisher's prospectus for *The Examiner* stated:

No Advertisements will be admitted ... They shall neither come staring in the first page at the breakfast table to deprive the reader of a whole page of entertainment, nor shall they win their silent way into the recesses of the paper under the mask of general paragraphs to filch even a few lines; the public shall neither be tempted to listen to someone in the shape of a Wit who turns out to be a lottery keeper, nor seduced to hear a magnificent oration which finishes by retreating into a peruke or rolling off into a blacking ball ... Above all the New Paper shall not be disgraced by those abandoned hypocrites, whose greatest quackery is their denial of being quacks.[15]

Hunt, in describing the protean nature of advertising copy—the way, for example, it can adopt the style of a contemporary society columnist in order to advertise a lottery, or of political oratory to advertise a shoe polish—lays bare the versatility which was to make it so potent a vehicle for popular satire. Hunt was almost prophetic in his analysis of the powers which advertising was assuming in the media in the nineteenth century. In the articles entitled 'Newspaper

---

[13] Quoted ibid. 436.
[14] Samuel Taylor Coleridge, *The Watchman* (London, 1796), repr. in *Collected Works*, ed. Lewis Patton (London, 1970), 380.
[15] Quoted in Elliott, 155.

Principle'[16] he analysed journalism in the context of political corruption. He dismissed daily papers in the latter half of the eighteenth century as the tools of groups of patrons. Journalists have merely 'the power of uttering falsehoods under authority'. He then sets up a comparison with the papers of his own day, complaining that the new journalism had substituted the old patron system with advertising:

> the display of politics is nothing but an advantage taken off the sale of these advertisements ... one or two of the principal daily papers would not be able to proceed at all, but for these public spirited paragraphs. It is the eloquence, not of the politician, but of the perruquier, the *Money Lender* and the Quack-doctor, which keeps their patriotic energies in motion ... at the back of a bitter invective against those who 'palsy the country's energies', you shall find all sorts of diseases fixed upon you between the hours of 12 and one ... In fine there is scarcely a daily paper, which if stripped of its advertisements, would be able to keep itself alive on the strength of its present style.[17]

Hunt's argument is flawed in terms of his grasp of the economics of early nineteenth-century journalism. He overlooks the effects of the paper and advertisement taxes. He also fails to make the crucial distinction between daily newspapers and periodicals like *The Examiner*—the latter were economically far less dependent on advertising revenue.[18] Hunt's argument is essentially one of class distinction. He sets up quality journalism at one end of the scale, 'identifiable on the strength of its present style', and all advertisement on the other. What horrifies him is exactly what Hone found so useful—the capacity of advertising to break down this theoretical linguistic construct and to imitate and infiltrate what are conventionally regarded as the preserves, both in terms of language and subject, of literary language and quality journalism.

Despite the attitudes of Hunt, Coleridge, and even Cobbett, many of the extremist radicals made use of the resources of popular communication which advertising had opened up. It was mainly the anonymous authors of broadsides and handbills, and gutter pressmen who used similar material and methods to Hone's. Many of Hone's most successful parodies brought out in connection with the Queen Caroline affair were immediately published in cheap, bowdlerized versions by Catnach. Indeed he claimed in later life

---

[16] Repr. in Houtchens, 80–9.   [17] Ibid. 81–2.
[18] *The History of* The Times (London, 1935), i. 16.

that it was these productions which first gave him prominence in the competitive and often brutal street publisher's market.[19] Among the bona fide radicals of the early 1820s it is noticeable that the figures who were most directly influenced by Hone were extremists from poor backgrounds, such as Thomas Wooler and Thomas Dolby, whose commitment, sense of humour, and lack of literary pretension allowed them to engage with the forms of advertising.[20]

There was also a sensationalist ultra-radical element which came to the fore when the Queen Caroline affair was at its height, and this group embraced advertising methods with ebullient energy. The Queen was fused with the idea of the freedom of the press and marketed as a radical heroine. Every area of the gutter press was used. McCalman has drawn attention to the scurrility of William Benbow and to the antics of the radical dwarf Samuel Waddington. Benbow specialized in crude prints and posters, many of which attacked the Regent with great lewdness. He used headlines with imagination, often titling his posters with shocking announcements such as 'BRUTAL ABUSE OF THE QUEEN!!' or 'PROPOSAL TO MURDER THE QUEEN!!, which were adapted from catchpenny prints dealing with murders and rapes. Waddington was even more exotic. He styled himself 'the Queen's Champion' and composed satiric broadsides and placards. He turned *himself* into an advertisement and 'paraded through Spitalfields in boards blowing a horn to proclaim an ultra-radical meeting'. McCalman also makes the crucial point that his behaviour related to the eighteenth-century tradition of mock elections of dwarfs in Garret.[21]

A connection can be made here with that outwardly most scrupulous and respectable of radicals Francis Place. He also became an expert advertiser in his capacity as publicist for the Westminster Committee during the notoriously disputed 1807 Westminster election. He established a propaganda machine that used many different forms of publicity including advertisement parody. Yet Place's low, indeed almost invisible, public profile, and his concern to manipu-

---

[19] L. Shepard, *John Pitts, Ballad Printer* (Pinner, 1969), 35, 37, 60.

[20] Wooler's *Black Dwarf*, which had a circulation of 12,000, changed its contents and form substantially as a result of Hone's publications. See the editions for 12, 19, and 26 Jan. 1819. He not only quoted enthusiastically from Hone's satires but began to include parodies based on advertising forms and children's literature.

[21] See McCalman, *Radical Underworld*, 149–50, 163–4, 168–73. For Hone's interest in the Garret elections, see Hone's 1843 book sale catalogue, item 313. This entry reads 'Three large oblong Drawings, by Green, representing the Mock Election for Garret'.

late an electorate through mass publicity directed from a campaign headquarters, appeared loathsome and over-secretive even to other radicals. Cobbett was particularly virulent in his criticisms of the methods of the Westminster Committee.[22]

Elections, particularly those in Westminster, had always been great spawning-grounds for experiments in popular satire. Hone's substantial collection of propaganda, relating to elections and to the 1784 Westminster campaign in particular, testifies to his intimate knowledge of this area.[23] The struggle between Fox and the Pittite candidates in 1784 was exceptional for its violence and bitterness and generated a mass of exuberant satire. The most popular pieces were published in separate collections and included numerous examples of parodies using such forms as nursery rhymes and biblical texts. The introduction to *The Wit of the Day; or, The Humours of Westminster* discusses the satires:

in the discussion of the most important national questions ... an infinite number of advertisements, sanctified by the signatures of the several candidates themselves, and their active friends and adherents, as well as fatherless and anonymous publications ... have appeared not only in all the different newspapers, but in the various detached forms of hand-bills, ballads, and poetical squibs; many of which are replete with wit, humour and sentiment; and almost all of them, in some measure, deserving to be rescued from oblivion.[24]

It was the cross-fertilization between press advertising and the 'various detached forms' of advertisement which Hone and Cruikshank were to take particular advantage of in their advertising parodies. The Westminster publication contains many parodies which anticipate the forms which Hone and Cruikshank were to adopt.[25]

[22] M. S. Prochaska, 'Westminster Radicalism 1807–1832', M.Phil. diss., Oxford University, 1975, 58–62. For Cobbett, see Prochaska, 82.

[23] Hone's 1822 book sale catalogue, item 241; 1827 catalogue, items 438, 441, 446, 450; the 1843 catalogue, item 223 is described as 'Hone's Shop Bills, Placards, Broadsides, Political Pieces, on the Election of Common Councilmen for Farringdon', apparently a whole body of ephemeral works by Hone which have disappeared. The list indicates the extent and diversity of his experimentation with printed advertisement outside the press.

[24] *The Wit of the Day*, p. iii.

[25] There are handbills in the form of announcements for beast menageries and wonderful apparitions. Fox's opponent Wray is 'A LIVING MONSTER TO BE SEEN during the poll upon the hustings at Covent Garden GIVING A GHASTLY SMILE' (ibid. 51). Hone constructed *The Political Showman—at Home!* around freak-show advertising. *The Wit of the Day* (p. 87) also contains parodies of mountebank's handbills, one of Hone's favourite forms. There are mock announcements for auctions. Wray is presented as

Hone and Cruikshank were well qualified to parody advertisements because of their practical involvement with various types of 'legitimate' advertising. At the age of 9 Cruikshank was designing 'twelfth night characters' for illustrated lottery puffs. Lottery advertising constituted one of the most dynamic areas of the advertising trade and he continued to work for Bish, the largest of the lottery companies, into his maturity.[26] He also produced notices for travelling showmen and numerous product advertisements, and his work in advertising fed directly into his political satire. The process is exemplified in his work for Warren's Blacking which resulted in the creation of the most famous illustrated advertisement of the first quarter of the nineteenth century (Fig. 20). The woodcut of a cat jumping back, spitting at its reflection in a polished boot, was a breakthrough in advertising concept and design. Warren used it to spearhead what was one of the first national marketing campaigns for a household article. Cruikshank's design appeared on handbills and in journals in the provinces, and variations on the theme continued to appear in Victorian newspapers until late in the century.[27]

Cruikshank exploited the notoriety of his original design by using it as the basis for a caricature on the front page of *A Slap at Slop*. He substituted a rat for a cat and presented it admiring its own reflection in a judge's wig (Fig. 21). Hone provided prose copy to accompany the cut. This ridiculed Charles Warren for his desire to become a Justice. The piece carries a headline bristling with dismissive assonance 'WARREN'S BLACK-RAT BLACKING'. The devices of product-naming constitute some of the most important weapons in the copy-writer's armoury and among the most effective devices is the formation of a name out of a group compound. The compound phrase fascinates because it involves a paradox—a group of words is

---

Judas Iscariot, who offers 'for sale ... a large quantity of Patent Dark-lanthorns' (p. 83). An anti-Fox broadside purports to be offering for sale 'the Hopes and Interest of that unfortunate candidate Carlo Khan', a popular nickname for Fox. There is another advertisement specifically addressed to 'all the Duchesses and Ladies' which concerns 'That infamous stallion called CARLO KHAN' and speaks of him as a 'strained broken down animal'. Fox is even provided with a mock genealogy, which alludes to his history as a debtor and gambler: 'Carlo Khan was got by Public Defaulter out of Unaccounted Millions' (p. 50). This advertisement closely anticipates an attack of Hone's on the ageing Lord Liverpool in *Non Mi Ricordo!* (B3^v).

[26] Examples of this work are reproduced in Richard A. Vogler, *The Graphic Works of George Cruikshank* (New York, 1979), 26–9. The works he did as a child are to be found in V & A Cruikshank Bequest, box I 92A, folder 9700D.

[27] For the extent and originality of Warren's advertising campaigns, see Presbrey, 85–8; Turner, 54–7, 59.

THE CAT AND THE BOOT;

FIG. 20. George Cruikshank. Wood engraving. THE CAT AND THE BOOT.
Advertisement for Warren's Blacking. n.d.

WARREN's BLACK-RAT BLACKING.

CHARLES WARREN, of CHESTER-PLACE, with the
utmost diffidence, publicly announces his successful *discovery*. By
the *first* application of his *varnish* to
BOOTS, he saw his own face in them,
with a *Judge*'s wig on his head; and he
assures his OLD FRIENDS, who he knows
will take his word for it, that the *reflection*
was so strong, it almost knocked him *back*.
He earnestly desires their approbation,
and solicits their favour in his new *shop*.
He humbly begs they will support him as
much as they can. His *going round* among
strangers is insupportable to him, unless
he can get a few of his former friends to
accompany him.

FIG. 21. George Cruikshank. Wood engraving. WARREN'S BLACK-RAT
BLACKING. Mock advertisement for *A Slap at Slop*. 1821.

perceived as a single word. The most popular form of compound
formation in modern advertising is through extension of the noun
group. Hone's caption is a fine early example of the form.[28]

Hone was also extensively involved with lottery advertising. He
produced what remains the only attempt at a comprehensive history
of lotteries. This included extensive analysis of different styles of lottery advertising from the seventeenth to the nineteenth centuries.[29]

[28] The parody appeared in *A Slap at Slop*, 1[r], preliminary sketches in BM
Cruikshank Bequest, Box 22C, folder I B 4, sheet 1974 u 587. For compound nouns
in advertising, see G. N. Leech, *English in Advertising* (London, 1966), 130–2.
[29] William Hone, *The Every-Day Book*, ii. 702–67.

The lottery advertisements were important for the way they inte-
grated copy and illustration during a period when illustrated
advertisements were a rarity. The lottery puffs had further relevance
for Hone and Cruikshank's publications in the way they used the
new display faces which suddenly appeared in the early nineteenth
century. The Bish advertising campaigns were one of the first mass
applications of the new types.[30]

The phenomenon of the fat-faced and Egyptian types has consistently troubled historians of typography. Exactly where they came
from is something of a mystery. There is general agreement, however, that they led to a revolution in type design and in printing
itself. Until the end of the eighteenth century the printing industry
was centred on the production of books. Any associated printing
used conventions of layout and typography that had developed from
book production. The development of mass advertising in the first
half of the nineteenth century saw the expansion of new areas of the
print trade. Decorated paper bags, handbills, posters, broadsides,
placards, and murals were produced on a scale and decorated in
ways that were new. Loud bold type-faces were developed in an
environment where visual impact was a priority. The fat-faces and
Egyptians suddenly became widely successful because they had the
capacity to catch the eye from a distance and impart information
rapidly. Elegant eighteenth-century book types were quietly inade-
quate in this new market-place. By 1820 the variety and sheer
volume of advertisements in London was phenomenal. Print satires
show posters papering the walls and fences, and the detailed studies
which George Sharfe made in the 1820s show the streets teeming
with sandwichmen and spectacularly decorated trade vehicles.[31]

The reaction of conventional typographers to the new designs was
often one of outrage. Hansard in his *Typographia* refers to 'the folly of
fat faced monstrous disproportions' and he introduces the examples
he prints as 'typographical monstrosities'. All the fat-face experiments that appeared in the first three decades of the nineteenth
century were created out of the exaggeration of existing type designs

---

[30] A. F. Johnson, *Type Designs*, 201–7.
[31] Savage, 21; G. Dowding, *An Introduction to the History of Printing Types* (London,
1961), 161–75; Figgins, *Type Specimens 1801–1815*, 9–18; Morison, *Politics and Script*,
324–37; Nicolette Gray, *Nineteenth Century Ornamented Types and Title Pages* (London,
1976), 9, 11–34; Gray, 'Slab Serif Type Design in England 1815–1845', *Journal of the
Printing Historical Society*, 15 (1981), 1–36; Peter Jackson, *George Scharf's London* (London, 1987), 34–43.

and it was this mutation, transplantation, and desecration of elegant eighteenth-century book types which Hansard found particularly unsettling: 'The emulation to excel in cutting a new type of any peculiar feature, and the various fashions which unfortunately for the printers, have been started and patronised, have left the specimen of a British letter founder a heterogeneous compound made up of fat-faces and lean-faces, wide-set and close-set, proportioned and disproportioned, all at once crying "Quousque tandem abutere patientia nostra".'

The basic techniques of thinning, thickening, and enlargement could be applied to any existing type. Sometimes the distortions are so extreme that the letters threaten to engulf themselves. Frequently they fight to maintain their meaning as they are virtually smothered by shadow effects, great slab serifs, pearls, or floriations.[32] In the sense that they referred to existing type forms, advertising display faces in the early nineteenth century had a parodic tendency. They were a natural extension of the advertiser's ability to take established forms and to remould them to his or her own ends, namely those of publicity. They were novel, but their novelty was all the more emphatic because it stressed its origins in traditional forms.

Hone and Cruikshank's satiric method in their pamphlets was essentially parodic and it is not surprising to see them taking advantage of contemporary typographic experiments in advertising. The widespread use of the fat-faces in radical publications during the Queen Caroline affair first demonstrated their domination of ephemeral printing. Hone used the new jobbing types with panache in the broadsides which he brought out to advertise his pamphlets throughout 1820 and 1821, and he used Egyptian type-faces in the headlines for *A Slap at Slop*.[33]

Hone's expertise with advertisement should be seen in the context of his general apprenticeship to the gutter press. From 1816 he was continuously involved with the sensational methods of the lowest forms of publishing. He was a committed plagiarist and pirate. He brought out a number of opportunistic editions of Byron's poems including a forgery of the third canto of *Don Juan*. Hone also published a number of broadsides and pamphlets dealing with such

[32] This passage is quoted and discussed in Figgins, *Type Specimens 1801–1815*, 20.

[33] For Hone's interest in typography, see 1843 book sale catalogue, item 237. The only known copy of *The Printer's Address to the Queen* is discussed in *BMC*, no. 13947; Johnson, *Type Designs*, 204. For Hone's Queen Caroline placards, see *BL* Francis Place Collection, vol. 18, Queen Caroline Papers.

subjects as prize-fights, murders, trials, lunacy, slavery, and sex scandals. By 1817 he had mastered the explosive typographical conventions and the ebullient and disjunctive language used in the title-pages of such productions. Many of his title-pages deserve attention for their innovatory advertising copy. They make use of headlinese and anticipate the type of block language that was to be taken up in the press much later in the century after the abolition of the stamp and advertisement taxes had led to the development of headlines in newspapers. Broadside and handbill literature had developed the methods of headlinese to a high level long before its incorporation into the press, and Hone realized at an early stage the communicative power of this language.[34]

Headlinese constitutes an area of print culture which from an early date had the potential to communicate with a large readership of low levels of literacy. It was consequently a powerful tool in the hands of propagandists. There are several points which can be made about Hone and Cruikshank's work which have far wider implications for the history of the form. Heinrich Straumann's *Newspaper Headlines: A Study in Linguistic Method* remains the only detailed study of the subject. He states that the headline was first widely developed in the broadsheets of the ballad news-sellers of the sixteenth century. The headline was used very infrequently in British daily newspapers from the last half of the eighteenth century until the second half of the nineteenth. Straumann argues that the reluctance of the early newspapers to use headlines grew from the fact that 'the quality press would be reluctant to associate itself with anything smacking of yellow journalism. It therefore avoided anything of the slightest mountebank nature.'[35] Straumann does not, however, follow up the implications of this insight; namely that a mature headlinese or block language had been developed in advertising outside the press. The stamp and advertisement taxes had a prohibitive effect on the use of headlines in the newspapers of this period, but headlines flourished and evolved in areas of printing connected with advertising, the ballad, and the political print. Because the majority of Hone's

---

[34] Hone and Byron, see Samuel Clagett Chew, *Byron in England: His Fame and after Fame* (London, 1924), 32–3, 184–5; Bowden, 223–8. For Hone's sensational street publications of 1815–16, see Bowden, 29–75. Bowden overestimates Hone's philanthropic motivation for producing most of these pieces. For the development of the headline, see Straumann, 82–5.

[35] Quoted in Straumann, 96.

satires came out in these forms he used headlines and headlinese consistently and with great inventiveness.

Headlines are most commonly used in the Hone–Cruikshank pamphlets in combination with the half-page illustrations. This feature was novel in political journalism and was immediately and widely imitated. Given the sudden prominence of the captioned illustrations in these publications it is worth considering how the use of the headline in political etchings fed into them.

By the 1790s the captions for single-sheet satiric prints had to be striking and precise. A short phrase or compound had to embody the message of a print, which might contain involved political allegory, a narrative operating on several levels, or a set of complicated metaphors. The necessity for economic yet sensational print captions led to the development of a highly sophisticated branch of headlinese. Gillray, pre-eminent as a satiric draughtsman, is not usually thought of as an innovative verbal satirist, yet he was particularly skilful in the creation of the titles for his prints. Sheets of his sketches exist which are peppered with drafts of possible titles. Many of the titles use devices typical of headlinese including group compounding, verbal nexus, and the excision of parts of speech, especially articles, which are required in normal grammatical circumstances. The following selection gives some idea of the proximity of Gillray's captions to the style of the newspaper headline: *Phaeton Alarmed!*, *Light Expelling Darkness*, *State Jugglers*, *Weird Sisters: Ministers of Darkness: Minions of the Moon*, *Anti-Sacharites*, *Flannel-Armour-Female-Patriotism!*, *French Telegraph Making Signals in the Dark!*, *Lady Godiva's Rout—Peeping-Tom Spying out Pope-John*, *Allied Powers Unbooting Egalité!* Several prints testify to his interest in the use of headlines in advertising sheets. The most spectacular example is *The Daily Advertiser*, which shows Fox as a newsman with a trumpet and a roll of advertisement sheets. He shouts a monologue, constructed entirely out of headline announcements, at Pitt:[36] 'Bloody News! Bloody News! Bloody News!!! glorious bloody News for old England!——Bloody News!—Traitorous Taxes!—Swindling Loans!—Murdering Militias!—Ministerial Invasions!—Ruin to all Europe!—Alarming Bloody News!' (*BMC*, no. 8981). Cruikshank not only inherited Gillray's position as the

---

[36] For the detailed reworking of titles in preliminary sketches, see Draper Hill, *Fashionable Contrasts* (London, 1966), 146; 161, fig. 7; 162, fig. 9. For Gillray's increasing interest in elaborate monologues in his prints, see Hill, *Mr. Gillray the Caricaturist*, 40.

leading graphic satirist in London but also his inventive use of block language in his titles. As early as 1805 he produced *Boney Beating Mack —Nelson Giving him a Whack! (BMC*, no. 10439) where use of colloquial abbreviations for the names of the great, the internal rhyme, and the excision of articles give a very Gillrayesque effect. Other Cruikshank titles string compound nouns together and some include foreign tags. The following is a good example: *A Lollipop—Ally-Campagne—A Bull's Eye—and Brandy-Ball (BMC*, no. 14444), a print which shows four types of prostitute. The style could be adapted to political satires which ironically describe horrific events. Cruikshank's famous print brought out in protest after the Peterloo massacre carried the stark title *Massacre at St. Peter's Fields—Britons Strike Home! (BMC*, no. 13258) below a depiction of the butchery of women and children.[37]

Cruikshank put his apprenticeship with print captions to good use when he came to work with Hone. Every major pamphlet which they produced used techniques of headlinese in one way or another. In *The Political House that Jack Built* the key word or phrase in each section is printed in large capitals below the illustration. In this way the military, clergy, and tax officials are labelled 'THE VERMIN', the printing press 'THE THING', the Prince Regent 'THE DANDY OF SIXTY', and so on. Their next pamphlet, *The Man in the Moon*, is more adventurous, and instead of picking out formal titles beginning with the indefinite article it is so set up that the key phrases in the text are capitalized below each plate so that they spring out as captions. A woodcut of soldiers ramming bayonets and swords into the mouths and down the throats of supplicant, kneeling people has 'STEEL LOZENGES' printed on a single line beneath it in heavy capitals. This phrase, however, runs into the lines 'And though the radicals may still want food, / A few / STEEL LOZENGES / Will stop their pain', which are supposedly spoken by the Regent in an address to Parliament. Similarly, a print of the Regent, Lord Liverpool, the Pope, and the crowned heads of Europe dancing round a burning press with the figure of Britannia bound upon it carries the headline 'HOLY COMPACT AND ALLIANCE'. This again runs on from the following lines from the Regent's speech: 'The foreign powers / Write me word frequently / That they are ours, / Most truly and sincerely, in compliance / With our most / HOLY COMPACT AND ALLIANCE'.

In *The Queen's Matrimonial Ladder* another approach is adopted.

---

[37] For Cruikshank's skill with the contracted forms of language used in the speech bubble, see Patten, *George Cruikshank's Life*, 110–11.

Here each step scene of the ladder is inscribed with a noun of action using the -ation suffix. The first seven which ascend the left hand of the ladder are as follows: 'QUALIFICATION', 'DECLARATION' 'ACCEPTATION', 'ALTERATION' 'IMPUTATION', EXCULPATION', and 'EMIGRATION'.[38] In the pamphlet accompanying the toy ladder each of the title words is set out as a caption below a half-page illustration. The pamphlet was soon imitated in a loyalist reply, *The Radical Ladder*, which did not carry illustrations, but it imitated the use of headlines rather clumsily.

The mock newspaper *A Slap at Slop* provided Hone and Cruikshank with yet another opportunity to experiment with headlines. The front page of this was entirely composed of advertisements, and in this followed the form of contemporary leading dailies, but it combined headlines with illustrations in the manner of advertising broadsides and handbills. It is peppered with such phrases as: 'ROYAL CUCKOO CLOCK', 'CONVULSIONS ET.C.—A REAL BLESSING', 'A NONDESCRIPT'.

For David Ogilvy the headline is the crucial element in all printed advertising. He maintains that 'the importance of headlines cannot be exaggerated' and states 'the headline is the ticket that sells the meat'.[39] Headlines have particular advantages in political satire as sophisticated as Hone and Cruikshank's. The reduction of complex issues to captions or even to single words can lead to effects of stark condensation. The curt irony of the headline 'VICTORY OF PETERLOO' beneath a cut of a mock monument showing the slaughter of unarmed civilians by the cavalry or the allusion to quack advertising which underlies the caption 'STEEL LOZENGES', which again accompanies a depiction of physical outrage, have a power which tempts comparison with Cruikshank's contemporary Goya. Goya's captions to *The Disasters of War* have the terse exclamatory quality of headlines: 'A Cruel Shame!', 'Strange Devotion!', 'Barbarians!', 'On Account of a Knife', 'What Courage'. Some of them slip into a humour of savage despair—he titles a print which shows the rape and murder of Spanish peasants by the forces of Napoleon 'It serves you right' and another showing a man vomiting over a pile of corpses 'This is what you were born for'. Many other titles appear

---

[38] Patten, *George Cruikshank's Life*, 180, discusses drafts for *The Queen's Matrimonial Ladder* which show Hone and Cruikshank trying out multiple versions of the caption words.

[39] David Ogilvy, 'A New Deal for your Clients', *Journal of Advertising History*, 3 (1980), 7.

wholly undramatic throw-away comments, casual with hopelessness: 'The same thing', 'They don't want to', 'Nor these', 'Nor do these', 'They do not agree', 'It will be the same', 'All this and more', 'The same thing elsewhere!', 'Why?' The controlled irony of the captions is set off against the frenzied atrocity in the prints. Hone and Cruikshank, in the most effective of their satires, use the tension between illustration and caption to set up their own furious ironies.

Hone and Cruikshank produced several of their most elaborate advertisement parodies using forms drawn from outside the press and in this they set new fashions. A close examination of two or their most complicated and influential satires *The Queen's Matrimonial Ladder* and *The Political Showman—at Home!* reveals the cultural and semiotic heterogeneity of the work.

The Queen's Matrimonial Ladder was the most successful of Hone's pamphlet satires after *The Political House*. It ran through forty-four editions in the four months after its release in 1820 and came out in two French editions. Like *The Political House* it led to numerous loyalist imitations.[40] It comprised an illustrated pamphlet in fourteen sections which was accompanied by a free pasteboard toy, the matrimonial ladder itself. The production is a typically complicated hybrid.

Hone advertised his pamphlet as 'A National Toy, WITH FOUR-TEEN STEP SCENES; AND ILLUSTRATIONS IN VERSE', announcing 'This Pamphlet and the toy together ONE SHILLING' (Fig. 22). One shilling was the standard price for all his pamphlets, so the toy was a free handout. The idea of a free gift to encourage sales was still a relative novelty at this date and the fact that Hone thought of it in the context of a children's toy is significant, for the children's publishing market had been particularly innovative in this area.[41]

Hone's reworked account of the genesis of *The Queen's Matrimonial Ladder* states that the inspiration came directly from a real children's toy:

I was reading in the British Museum ... that was the time of the Queen's business and some of her chief partisans came to me. They urged me to write something for her. Instead of going straight home, I wandered off towards Pentonville, and stopped and looked absently into the win-

---

[40] Bowden, 320–2.

[41] D. and G. Hindley, *Advertising in Victorian England*, 47–53. John Newberry, who ran the most successful book-publishing firm in the latter half of the 18th cent., used many advanced advertising techniques. He included advertisements for his patent

THE QUEEN'S
MATRIMONIAL LADDER,

𝔄 𝔑ational 𝔗oy,

WITH FOURTEEN STEP SCENES;

AND

ILLUSTRATIONS IN VERSE,

WITH EIGHTEEN OTHER CUTS.

BY THE AUTHOR OF " THE POLITICAL HOUSE THAT JACK BUILT."

" The question is not merely whether the Queen shall have her rights, but whether the rights of any individual in the kingdom shall be free from violation."

Her Majesty's Answer to the Norwich Address.

" Here is a Gentleman, and a friend of mine!"
Measure for Measure.

𝔗wenty-first 𝔈dition.

LONDON:
PRINTED BY AND FOR WILLIAM HONE, LUDGATE-HILL.

1820.

Fig. 22. George Cruikshank. Wood engraving. Frontispiece to *The Queen's Matrimonial Ladder.* 1820.

dow of a little fancy shop—there was a toy, 'The Matrimonial Ladder.' I saw at once what I could do with that, and went home and wrote 'The Queen's Matrimonial Ladder'.[42]

A toy did exist called the Ladder of Matrimony, a folding pasteboard ladder which carried a series of step scenes telling the story of a discordant marriage. Each scene was accompanied by a single-word inscription.[43] While there is then some truth in Hone's account it is strange that he does not allude to Cruikshank's contribution to the satire. He had produced a number of pieces of work for lottery contractors based on parodic versions of children's ladder toys long before his collaboration with Hone, and one of these is clearly a source for the later satire. *Fortune's Ladder* was a puff produced for the lottery contractor Bish, consisting of a black ladder of ten rungs with a step scene between each rung (Fig. 23). The scenes tell the story of the rise from poverty to wealth and happiness of a man and his wife who buy a lottery ticket. Each rung of the ladder carries a caption in the form of a single word using the -ation suffix, a device which Cruikshank took up in the later piece, and he even repeated the caption word 'Alteration'.

There is also a pronounced similarity between the illustrational vignettes which accompany the satires in the two pieces. They are the same size and the pantomimic gestures of the characters and the backdrops, composed of simple domestic interiors, are also repeated. The figures are, however, printed white on black in *The Queen's Matrimonial Ladder*, which gives a far more dynamic emphasis to the action.[44] Each section of *Fortune's Ladder* is accompanied by a short verse explanation of the illustration, and this may well have provided the basis for the expansion of the narrative on the ladder into an extended pamphlet commentary in *The Queen's Matrimonial Ladder*. An analogy can be drawn between the poverty-stricken man in the

medicines in the text of his children's books, he invented letters from grateful parents commending his books and then had these published in the newspapers, and he frequently included free gifts, such as pincushions and balls, with his books.

[42] Rolleston, *Some Account of the Conversion of the Late William Hone*, 41–2.

[43] The item is repr. in J. Krill, *English Artist's Paper* (London, 1987), 112–13, 150.

[44] Patten, *George Cruikshank's Life*, 178, sees in the use of white on black an imitation of Bewick's 'white line style'. This is misleading, for the cuts in the Hone and Cruikshank satire are deliberately crude and technically bear no relation to Bewick. The fine pattern-making and shifting tonalities which typify Bewick's little gems would have been inappropriate to the stark clarity of the step scenes for *The Queen's Matrimonial Ladder*.

FIG. 23. George Cruikshank. Wood engraving. *Fortune's Ladder*. Lottery advertisement for Bish. n.d.

advertisement and George IV. The opening of *Fortune's Ladder*, 'A wight by poverty oppressed, / By duns and creditors distressed' is elaborated into the opening couplet of the pamphlet commentary, 'In love and in drink and o'ertoppled by debt; / With women, with wine, and with duns on the fret'.

While it related both to lottery advertising and to children's toys, *The Queen's Matrimonial Ladder* also took up and developed central icons of European graphic culture. The ladder was established as a metaphor in seventeenth- and eighteenth-century prints in a variety of contexts. The image of Jacob's ladder, and more basically the relation of ideas of ascent and descent to the Christian doctrines of salvation and damnation, had made the ladder a familiar feature of print iconography since the Middle Ages.[45] One of the most popular European prints of the seventeenth and eighteenth centuries showed human life as an ascent and descent of a flight of inscribed steps, and less commonly a ladder. A couple were shown going up and then down the steps, each one representing ten years in the passage from the cradle to the grave. In the second decade of the nineteenth century Jemmy Catnach was still producing a print on this theme.[46] Climbing up and down the ladder and more frequently the disastrous fall from it were standard ways of describing political careers in eighteenth-century political satire. The ladder metaphor in Hone and Cruikshank's pamphlet grows out of prints such as *Popular Frenzys; or The Demolition of St. Stephen's Chapel, The Treasury Ladders; or, Political Capers, A Somerset by a Celebrated Performer on the Pillar of Popularity*.[47]

Much of the impact of *The Queen's Matrimonial Ladder* comes out of the graphic dialogue which is set up between the naïvely drawn vignettes, set within the ladder, and the more refined illustrational treatment of each section in the main body of the pamphlet. The chapbook charm of the ladder is set off against the bitter refinements of political caricature in the larger-format wood engravings. The contrast is exemplified in the 'Qualification' illustrations.

The work which Cruikshank did for Hone demonstrated the refinement of which the mass-produced wood engraving was capable and the richness with which it could take up the tradition of the

---

[45] Coupe, *The German Illustrated Broadsheet*, i. 170–1; ii. 95–6.

[46] Repr. in James, *English Popular Literature*, 156.

[47] *BMC*, nos. 6248, 6438, 11385. Patten, *George Cruikshank's Life*, 178, makes an interesting connection with Cruikshank's allegorical use of the ladder in his earlier illustrations for Combe's *Life of Napoleon*.

satiric etching. Despite Bewick's achievements with wood-engraving in Newcastle its use as a commercial print form in London was still relatively unrefined by 1820. Cruikshank's 'Qualification' vignette at the bottom of the ladder shows an unrepentant if somewhat desperate libertine with arms flung wide into the black space surrounding him. Heavily delineated, his features are reduced to blots of ink. The illustration to the same scene in the pamphlet has moved on in time to present the Regent in an overblown state of inebriety slumped, squinting to focus on his audience.

This plate, and the pamphlet illustrations as a whole, exhibit a technical mastery of the wood engraving that is exceptional in popular pamphlet illustration of this period (Fig. 24). The delicate lines of Cruikshank's original tracing have been maintained through the process of engraving the block in a manner that is not merely reproductive but interpretative. The Regent's descent into a state of sodden degeneracy is partially described through technique, the shaky tracery of the Bacchanalian scenes on the background screen move into the lines of the disintegrating face, then down through thicker and thicker lines into shadows as the eye descends to the bottles under the table. The quality of the impression is all the more remarkable when it is remembered that the wood-block would have been set with the type in a single form.

The print is developed with precision out of two of Gillray's great etchings. It shows the Regent thirty years on from the way Gillray had shown him as a young debauchee in the famous *A VOLUPTUARY under the horrors of Digestion*. (Fig. 25). With even deeper irony, however, most of Cruikshank's details are taken from the figure of the comte de Barras in the left-hand side of the print *ci-devant Occupations—or—Madame Talian and the Empress Josephine dancing Naked before Barrass in the Winter of 1797.—A Fact!* (Fig. 26). This vicious print explained the origins of Napoleon's attachment to Josephine in the fact that Barras needed his second-best mistress taken off his hands. That a small-scale wood engraving produced in hundreds of thousands of copies could find accurate technical equivalents for the copperplate wizardry of the mature Gillray is a final testament to the ambition and quality of Cruikshank's work for Hone.

Hone and Cruikshank's final pamphlet satire *The Political Showman—at Home!* went through twenty-seven editions. It contained a text based on far more erudite sources than the previous pamphlets, and

Give not thy strength unto women, nor thy ways to that which destroyeth kings.

Solomon.

QUALIFICATION.

FIG. 24. George Cruikshank. Wood engraving. Plate 'QUALIFICATION' for
The Queen's Matrimonial Ladder. 1820.

Fig. 25. James Gillray. *A Voluptuary under the Horrors of Digestion*. Coloured etching. 1792.

Fig. 26. James Gillray. Coloured etching, detail.—*ci devant Occupations—or —Madame Talian and the Empress Josephine dancing Naked before Barrass*. 1805.

the number of illustrations was also far larger. It was the culmination of their collaboration and Hone's personal favourite of their satires.[48]

The satire grows out of various applications of monster lore to political satire. The pamphlet consequently relates to traditions of religious satire that first became widely popular in the Reformation and which survived in England into the late eighteenth and early nineteenth centuries, particularly in the context of the millennialist revival. The pamphlet uses material relating to monster-shows and the advertising surrounding them and also uses language and imagery which derive from late eighteenth-century natural histories. It is located in various areas of late eighteenth-century satire which had already drawn on such material, and in its turn was used as a model for radical satire in the early 1830s.[49]

The main text of *The Political Showman* is sandwiched between an elaborate illustrated frontispiece and a three-page epilogue. Both of these are centred upon the imagery of the beasts in Revelation. The beast was identified with the Pope in woodcuts and illustrated broadsheets from an early stage of the Reformation. Luther developed his terrifying thesis whereby the last three centuries of papal authority could be identified with the reign of Antichrist, and the identification of the Pope with the beast from Revelation appears to have developed out of this theory.[50] The beast came to be a staple in English print satires during the seventeenth century. There was also a mass of print and pamphlet material during the Napoleonic wars which presented Bonaparte in the same guise.[51] The frontispiece to *The Political Showman* develops the propagandistic applications of the Beast. A seven-headed monster represents the newly formed Holy Alliance. The union of the Pope and the sovereigns of Prussia, Austria, and Russia under the banner of 'legitimate monarchy', dismissed by Castlereagh as a 'piece of sublime mysticism and nonsense', was seen by the English radicals as the reimposition of a decayed and despotic monarchism on post-Napoleonic Europe. The Holy Alliance and the concept of the Divine Right of Kings were widely attacked by the English radicals and form the focal point of Hone's satire.

There are three beasts which appear to John in Revelation. The

---

[48] Bowden, 379–80, 388–90.

[49] See *Asmodeus; or, The Devil in London*, 18 (June 1832), 70–2; 28 (Sept. 1832), 111; 35 (Oct. 1832), 139.

[50] F. S. Saxl, 'Illustrated Pamphlets of the Reformation', in *Lectures*, 2 vols. (London, 1957), i. 262–6.

[51] Ashton, *English Caricature and Satire on Napoleon I*, 7–11; Garrett, 165–6.

first is described as 'a great red dragon, having seven heads and ten horns and seven crowns upon his heads' (12: 3). Cruikshank's title-page shows the European monarchies as this first beast. In Revelation the first beast then gives way to a beast from the sea and a beast from the earth. These are taken up in the epilogue to *The Political Showman*. This three-page finale describes a monster termed the 'Boa-desolator or Legitimate Vampire'. This is identified with the beast from the sea. He 'lives in defiance and scorn of Providence, and in hatred to the happiness of man. When distended with human carnage, and wet with the gore of the innocent and helpless, he lifts up an impious *form* to heaven in solemn mockery. He was predicted by the Seer of old, as the BEAST with many heads and crowns, bearing the name of BLASPHEMY' (*The Political Showman*, D2ᵛ). In Revelation the prophet sees 'a beast rise up out of the sea, having seven heads and ten horns, and upon his horns ten crowns, and upon his heads the name of blasphemy ... and the dragon gave him his power and his seat and great authority ... and there was given unto him a mouth speaking great things and blasphemies' (13: 1–5). Satan's transference of authority to the beast from the sea which reigns upon earth amidst blasphemy is developed by Hone into a metaphor for the establishment of legitimate monarchy.

The creation of an apocalyptic framework for *The Political Showman* was both a parody of, and a contribution to, the literature of popular millennialism. The late eighteenth and early nineteenth centuries saw the appearance of many millennial movements in England. Self-appointed prophets flourished in the period 1780–1830, the most notorious being John Wroe, Richard Brothers, Zion Ward, Sir William Courtenay, and Joanna Southcott.[52] Popular millennialism had frequently been linked with political agitation and during this period it had specific links with radicalism. Hone and Cruikshank's use of Revelation to provide a framework for their satire places it among a host of print and pamphlet satires from the 1780s onwards which used similar models. Apocalyptic scenes also form the basis of many of Gillray's mature prints and occur in other satiric prints of the day. In 1821 Cruikshank's brother Robert produced a series of woodcut illustrations for a satiric almanac, *The Total Eclipse: A Grand Historical Politico Astrological Phenomenon*, which used conventions of millennialist publications to attack the Regent and government.

[52] Harrison, *The Second Coming*, 60–78, 86–134, 138–52, 153–60, 213–15.

The central section of *The Political House* takes the form of a mon-ster-show in which the bishops, the Duke of Clarence, and each significant member of the Liverpool administration are presented as monstrous freaks. The presentation of politicians as natural curiosities is given a special twist by the apocalyptic framework, for such aberrant forms had featured in political propaganda since the Reformation. Freaks such as the 'Monkish Calf' and 'Pope's Ass' were interpreted in Lutheran pamphlets as God's personal pro-nouncements on the Pope, and every detail of their appearance and discovery had significance. In the late sixteenth and early seven-teenth centuries the illustrated pamphlet using monster lore became generally popular.[53] This tradition was still very much alive, admittedly in a devolved and simplified form, in the ballads and chapbooks of early nineteenth-century England.[54]

It is in this context that Hone and Cruikshank's creation of a political cabinet of monstrosities touched upon ideas deeply rooted in the popular imagination. In the early nineteenth century there was also still no clear division between the scientific study of natural history and the sheer thrill of encountering natural aberrations, while superstitions still connected unnatural forms with religious prophecy.[55] In this pre-Darwinian environment standard works of natural history concerned themselves with nondescripts as peculiarly revealing and vital areas of natural creation. Distorted animal, and particularly human, forms inhabited a fascinating area where species overlapped and status was suspended. Both the texts which Hone primarily drew upon for his descriptions of the monsters in *The Politi-cal Showman*—Buffon's *Histoire naturelle du l'homme* and Goldsmith's *Animated Nature*—have extensive sections dealing with monsters and monstrous humans in terms of their relation to man's place in the created order of things. Hone exploited this continuing fascination with the human monster. Each politician is turned into an aberrant

[53] James, *English Popular Literature*, 54, 56; Garrett, 162–3; Jonathan Anson Mee, 'The Political Rhetoric of William Blake's Early Prophecies', Ph.D. diss., Cambridge University, 1989, 10–11, 134. For the government's prosecution of dissenting ministers preaching millennialism, see Harrison, *The Second Coming*, 73–80.

[54] For Gillray's prints on apocalyptic themes, see *BMC*, nos. 8644, 8655, 10719, 10972, 11031. For other print satires, see R. Godfrey, *English Caricature 1620 to the Present*, exhibition cat. (London, 1984), 52, 93–4); also *The Political Eclipse: A Grand Politico-Astronomical Phenomenon*, illus. I. Cruikshank (London, 1820).

[55] Garrett, 145–78; Shepard, *John Pitts*, 16–18; also L. Shepard, *The History of Street Literature* (Newton Abbot, 1973), 17; R. Collison, *The Story of Street Literature, Forerunner of the Press* (London, 1973), 147–9; Altick, *The Shows of London*, 253–68, 302–20.

form which exists outside the natural order. Fascinating, but loathsome and infertile, his creatures are symbolic manifestations of
political corruption.

The satire relates to several models including the bestiary and
natural history, but the dominant form is that of the showman's
notice. The presentation of political enemies as natural curiosities in
a show was widespread in political print satires by the 1820s. Group
animalizaton was a dominant trope in Gillray's prints. From 1790 to
1810 he produced a series of compositions based on the mass conversion of the Whig hierarchy into various animal forms. In 1797 he
produced *The Learned Pig*, which employed a realistic parody of a
showman's rhetoric to ridicule a recent political speech: 'Walk in!
Walk in! Gentleman. How to save your bacon. Great and Extraordinary News. Lately arrived in Leeds ... Billy Pitt's Company of
Puppets' (*BMC*, no. 9056). *The British Menagerie* (*BMC*, no. 8821), a
print by George Cruikshank's father Isaac of 1795, had featured an
equally realistic parody of the showman's style. The showman,
Henry Dundas, carrying a long pole, announces: 'Walk in ladies and
gentlemen and see the Collection of Curiosities. The only complete
collection in Europe'. The King and Queen are shown gazing at
various caged animals representing the sovereigns of Europe, the
Russian Bear, the Austrian Leopard, the double-headed Habsburg
Eagle; only the Pope is shown caged in human form. The frontispiece to *The Political Showman* is constructed around a similar
animalistic assault on the sovereigns of Europe, this time from a
radical rather than a loyalist perspective. Elaborate print satires
using the idea of the beast menagerie continued to be used in the
period leading up to *The Political Showman*.[56]

Hone and Cruikshank were developing a model which had been
extensively reworked in print satires, yet their transference of the
forms of showman's advertising into a pamphlet provided a rich new
environment. I stress, in my discussion of their earlier pamphlet *The
Political House that Jack Built*, the way Hone and Cruikshank set up
narrative interrelations and tensions between facing pages.[57] *The
Political Showman* again uses such techniques with great subtlety. Each
victim is attacked on a double-page spread. The left-hand page
presents a curiosity or *lusus naturae* in the form of a composite emblem, the right-hand page an animal which symbolizes the same
subject. Lord Liverpool is shown as 'A prime crutch', and as 'An

---

[56] *BMC*, nos. 11549, 12267.   [57] See pp. 241–4 below.

BAGS.—*(a Scruple Balance.)*

A CROCODILE.

FIG. 27. George Cruikshank. Wood engraving. Plates 'BAGS.—*(a Scruple Balance)*' (A4^v) and 'A CROCODILE' (B1^r). For *The Political Showman at Home.* 1821.

Opossum'; the Duke of Clarence is 'A Cadge Anchor' and 'A Water Scorpion'. The effect is a bizarre double-barrelled combination of political emblem book and freak-show menagerie. The pages attacking Eldon exemplify the technique (Fig. 27).

Lord Eldon is presented on the left-hand page as 'BAGS.—*(a Scruple Balance)*'; on the right-hand page he is shown as 'A CROCODILE'. The left-hand design combines the ancient methods of eblematization with the more recent art of caricature. Eldon's face, caricatured in a square, is flanked by two hanging bags. His owl-like body is formed out of the purse of the great seal and the whole assemblage is propped up by a hammer. Hone's text is a similarly composite product formed out of six fragments of varying lengths by different authors pasted together. They range in length from a two-word Latin tag, 'Juglator Regis', taken from Strutt's *Sports and Pastimes*, to a ten-line quotation from *The Task*. The graphic and literary techniques compliment each other. Cruikshank builds his attack out of various images and symbols which relate to the political background and to Eldon's family history. The bags of the caption, for example, refer to the fact that his family's wealth was founded on coal and to the royal family's consequent coining of the nickname 'Bags' for him. At the same time the bags are hung on his head in semblance of a wig in reference to his judicial position. His body is formed out of yet another bag—the purse of the great seal. The creature is made up of cumbrous and heavy parts which are at the same time insubstantially thrown together and precariously propped up.

In a similar way the disparate materials of the text, which range in length, type, and period to an astonishing degree, form the portrait of a man whose cunningness and insubstantiality is disguised behind a façade of grave portentousness. Some of the lines work as elaborations of elements in the plate, as in the quotation from Bishop Corbet for 'A most officious Drudge, / His face and gown drawn out with the same budge, / His pendant pouch, which is both large and wide, / Looks like a letters-patent'. Hone wrote 'I took a pair of scissors and some paste, for such is my way of composing books'.[58] His ability to create a single text out of a gallimaufry of quotations was perhaps partly the result of his early experience as a plagiarist and pirate publisher, while he may also have been influenced by Spence's creative anthologies in his journal *Pig's Meat*. The technique offered great advantages. It challenged the idea of the primacy of one text over another and forced different styles and linguistic registers up against one another.

The right-hand page is very different. It strikes the eye with the conventionality and comparative calm of its layout. The crocodile is given to Eldon as an emblem but is drawn quite naturalistically. Only the addition of tears and a judge's wig locate it satirically. The image is adapted with some precision from the plate illustrating the crocodile in the eight-volume edition of Goldsmith's *A History of the Earth and Animated Nature*. Hone's text again methodologically complements the illustration. Apart from two short prefatory quotations,

[58] Hone, *Aspersions Answered*, 54–7; Hone gives an account of the composition of his *Apocryphal New Testament*.

Hone provides a consecutive description in the style of a natural history. Hone's text also draws largely on the *Animated Nature* and is a closely worked parody of Goldsmith's description.[59] Hone italicizes and embellishes the original to introduce satiric *double entendre*. Many of the phrases that appear particularly clever, such as the reference to the crocodile's '*facility of creeping through narrow and intricate ways*', and the fact that he is 'so *pliable* that he can *wheel* round with the utmost facility', are direct quotations. The attacks on the bishops as 'locusts', Liverpool as an 'opossum', Castlereagh as a 'bloodhound', and Sidmouth as a 'booby', follow much the same formula. *The Political Showman* is a fitting finale to Hone and Cruikshank's collaboration. The effect of the double-page spreads is quickfire. An exuberant display bombards the reader with information and imagery. It is a satire of aggregation formally innovative yet rooted in tradition.

Hone, Cruikshank, and Newspaper Parody

In 1821 Hone and Cruikshank brought out *A Slap at Slop*, an elaborate parody of a four-page folio daily newspaper. It developed a well-established satiric form—the parodic newspaper—which had become increasingly popular during the first two decades of the nineteenth century. Hone had experimented with this form as early as 1815 in a mock broadside edition of *The Times* called *Buonapartephobia*. This in its turn related closely to the notorious parody which *The Times* made of itself in 1794 as a contribution to anti-French propaganda. By 1819 parodic newspapers were appearing as both social and political satire. The advertisement parody in *A Slap at Slop* is prefigured in the social satires of such publications as *The Quizzical Gazette* and *The Rump Chronicle*. Radical appropriation of the press assumed a chameleon complexity.

Hone's parodies of press advertising reflected the pressures exerted by the stamp and advertisement taxes. The typography, style, and content of the early nineteenth-century newspaper were dominated by the pressures which the stamp tax exerted on space and by the consequent desire to include as large an amount of advertising as possible. The first 'tax on knowledge' was imposed in 1712. The rate of the paper tax was fixed at 1*d.* for a printed sheet and $\frac{1}{2}d.$ for a half sheet or less with a further charge of 1*s.* for each advertisement.

---

[59] Oliver Goldsmith, *A History of the Earth and Animated Nature*, 8 vols. (London, 1774), vii, pl. facing p. 118.

It applied to 'any printed paper made public weekly or oftener'. It was not, however, the stamp tax but the tax on advertisements that struck the real economic blow against the papers. By 1820 advertisements, not subscription sales, furnished the largest part of the revenue of daily papers.[60] The taxes increased steadily from 1714 until 1837 and were only finally abolished in 1854. They were manipulated by successive governments to enforce censorship of the press, and the raising of taxes often coincided with periods of national unrest.[61]

Hone's exclusive use of parodic advertising for the front page of *A Slap at Slop* resulted from the fact that those newspapers which were surviving and making a profit despite the taxes had come to rely almost entirely on the revenue from advertisements. Their increasing dominance of front pages testifies to their economic importance.[62]

Hone and his radical imitators experimented with parodic press advertisement during a period of general change for this form of publicity. When *A Slap at Slop* came out in 1821 advertisements held a position of dominance in the quality press that was quite new. In many respectable papers the position had been reached where news and editorial matter were fighting for space with advertisements, and the situation was complicated even more by the fact that many advertisements were disguised in the forms of news announcements. The problem of how to maximize profits without seriously jeopardizing the amount of space given over to important political matter and legitimate journalism was a continual and complicated one for both the leading dailies *The Times* and *The Morning Chronicle*. Both papers had to juggle the various possibilities for getting more printed matter into the same space.[63]

In 1818 *The Times* was forced to bring out a supplement devoted to

[60] See Lawrence Lewis, *The Advertisements of the Spectator* (London, 1909), 62–76; Morison, *The English Newspaper*, 144; Oscar Hersberg, 'The Evolution of Newspaper Advertising', *Lippincott's Magazine*, 60 (1897), 107–12.

[61] Stephen Koss, *The Rise and Fall of the Political Press in Britain*, 2 vols. (London, 1981), i. 31–2, 143; Presbrey, 74–6; *History of* The Times, i. 17–21; Munter, *The History of the Irish Newspaper*, 57–8; A. Aspinall, *Politics and the Press* c. 1780–1850 (London, 1949), 128–33.

[62] *History of* The Times, i. 25–6; also Morison, *The English Newspaper*, 161–3; Presbrey, 77; Ivon Asquith, 'Advertising and the Press in the Late Eighteenth and Early Nineteenth Centuries', *Historical Journal*, 18 (1975), 703–24.

[63] Wood, 114; Asquith, 'Advertising and the Press', 711–12; Lucy Brown, *Victorian News and Newspapers* (Oxford, 1985), 14–16; *History of* The Times, i. 20.

clearing its backlog of advertisements, and the editor's uneasiness about the situation came out clearly in an accompanying statement in which he stressed, rather unconvincingly, the independence of his copy from advertising texts. He also attempted to argue that his paper maintained its appeal to advertisers on account of the quality of its journalism.[64] Contemporary reactions indicate that things were not quite that straightforward and that the advertisements which covered the 'black paper' front pages of the major dailies were read with great care and constituted one of the major attractions of the early nineteenth-century newspaper. Lord Milton wrote from Naples in 1818:

> we laugh at all the tittle tattle of the newspapers, at the advertisements for the lottery, patent blacking ... dinners &c; but if the newspapers were deprived of all this nonsense & reduced to the paragraphs w[hi]ch announce great public events, they w[oul]d go a very little way towards presenting their readers with an idea of the English world, & the incessant motion & activity by which it is distinguished from others.[65]

Lord Milton expresses pride in the way the form and content of the newspaper reflects the energy and industry of the English way of life. Cowper anticipated this attitude at the opening of the fourth book of *The Task* in a lengthy consideration of the effect of reading a newspaper. This passage analyses the power which advertising exerted over the reader and is of particular interest for this study because of Hone's involvement with it. Hone singled out the passage for discussion and lengthy quotation in an article in his *Table Book*. The article in question, titled 'The Newsman', opens with a general discussion of the working conditions and function of the newsman in the early nineteenth century. Hone then goes on to describe the effect of reading a newspaper and prints a conflated and rearranged version of Cowper's description.

> This folio of four pages, happy work!
> Which not ev'n critics criticise; that holds
> Inquisitive Attention, while I read,
> Fast bound in chains of silence, which the fair,
> Though eloquent themselves, yet fear to break,
> What is it but a map of busy life,
> Its fluctuations, and its vast concerns?
> Houses in ashes, and the fall of stocks,
> Births, deaths, and marriages ————

---

[64] *The Times* (23 May 1818), 1ʳ.
[65] Quoted in Asquith 'Advertising and the Press', 718.

——————————— The grand debate,
The popular harangue, the tart reply,
The logic, and the wisdom, and the wit,
And the loud laugh ————————————
Cat'racts of declamation thunder here;
There forests of no meaning spread the page,
In which all comprehension wanders lost;
While fields of pleasantry amuse us there,
With merry descants on a nation's woes.
The rest appears a wilderness of strange
But gay confusion; roses for the cheeks,
And lilies for the brows of faded age,
Teeth for the toothless, ringlets for the bald,
Heav'n, earth, and ocean, plunder'd of their sweets,
Nectarous essences, Olympian dews,
Sermons, and city feasts, and fav'rite airs,
Aethereal journeys, submarine exploits,
And Katerfalto, with his hair on end
At his own wonders, wand'ring for his bread.
'Tis pleasant through the loopholes of retreat,
To peep at such a world; to see the stir
Of the great Babel, and not feel the crowd.[66]

Hone had a special regard for Cowper's poetry. He had published a long extract from the fifth book of *The Task* on the subject of liberty in his radical periodical *Hone's Reformist's Register*.[67] *The Political House*, Hone's most successful publication, used quotations from *The Task* beneath every plate. The quotation accompanying Cruikshank's drawing of Canning in the tenth plate of *The Political House* adapts the line 'With merry descants on a nation's woes' from the passage just quoted and is a typical example of the freedom with which Hone treated Cowper's verse, plucking lines and passages from various contexts and rearranging them to his own ends. Hone continued to use quotations from Cowper to provide captions for the plates in many of his most successful pamphlets. Cowper's general, sometimes naïve, and frequently aphoristic pronouncements on such topics as the corrupting influence of power, or the sufferings of the poor, combined an accessible diction and style with literary respectability and were consequently harnessed to radical propaganda.

It is enlightening to see Hone's quotation of Cowper in *The Table*

[66] William Hone, *The Table Book*, 2 vols. (London, 1827), i. col. 65.
[67] *Hone's Reformist's Register*, i, cols. 733–6.

Book from this perspective. In this passage Hone has radically altered and rearranged the text.[68] Hone extracts all the passages which describe the contents of the newspaper and places them so as to form a consecutive inventory. In the original there are a series of interspersed passages containing Cowper's reflections on, and analysis of, his state of mind and domestic surroundings. These cushion the effect of the descriptions which present the paper itself. Cowper draws attention to the paper's existence outside the concerns of literary critics and goes on to suggest that it mimics the processes of life. 'What is it but a map of busy life, / Its fluctuations and its vast concerns?' The map metaphor is precise, suggesting that the paper is simultaneously a part of life and a representation of it. Under Hone's direction the verse then breaks from general discussion to specific description. Lines 8–29 create a poetry of mesmeric inventory. As the description develops, the heterogeneous contents of the paper are described in imagery that is increasingly violent and overwhelming. In lines 14–19 Cowper develops the map metaphor and presents the different journalistic forms of the paper as a series of landscape effects: 'cataracts of declamation', 'forests of no meaning', 'fields of pleasantry', 'The rest appears a wilderness'. The language of the press is equated with the power of natural phenomena in its ability to amaze and overwhelm the individual. Forests, cataracts, and wilderness are manifestations of the irrational, wild, and dangerous aspects of nature which had been theoretically designated by Burke as the proper subject-matter for painters of the sublime.

Cowper finally breaks into a series of details describing the items which constitute the 'wilderness of strange but gay confusion'. This sudden and climactic outpouring is entirely composed of advertisements. Cosmetics, medicines, inventions, entertainments, and all the variety of contemporary advertising are included. The passage as a whole is a celebration of the energy, and perhaps the anarchy, of the newspaper. The mixtures of style and subject, of high and low, general and specific, tragic and comic, communicate the ability of the newspaper to reduce all things to one level of seething activity. One of Cowper's imaginative achievements in *The Task* is his ability

[68] The following table describes the rearrangement, by line:

Hone's text	*The Task*, book IV
1–7	50–6
8–9	16–17
10–13	30–3
14–38	73–107

to ruminate on objects conventionally considered to be mundane—a sofa, a timepiece, a newspaper—and somehow to reveal their hidden significance through his devoted meditation. This led him to an advanced understanding of print culture and allowed him to uncover the aesthetic power underlying the hectic juxtaposition of form in a newspaper.[69]

The formal tensions and stylistic freedoms opened up by the dailies were soon capitalized upon by satirists. The late eighteenth century saw the appearance of the first newspaper parodies and it is probable that the most influential and elaborate model for *A Slap at Slop* was the celebrated parody which *The Times* made of itself. This came out under the title of *The New Times* on 6 November 1794. The whole of the third page of this issue of the paper was given over to an involved mock-up of the normal front page. It attacked various aspects of Jacobinism and French revolutionary theory. Beneath the title the text explained that 'At a period when Revolutions are so much the general topic of conversation, it may not be unentertaining to the reader of the *Old Times*, to take a peep into what would, most probably, be the diurnal news of a *New Times*, should such a misfortune as a *Change of Constitution* take place in this country.'

The parody was a government-backed propaganda exercise probably organized by Dundas, the Secretary of State. It was carried through to the formal minutiae of the paper. The factotum took the form of a guillotine surmounted by crossed pikes, one bearing a cap of liberty and one a dripping head. An initial announcement catches the paper's somewhat stuffy and self-congratulatory editorial style: 'letters, Advertisements and Articles of Intelligence, will be received at the office of the *New Times* . . . nothing but what accords with the true patriotic principles of this paper can be admitted'. The paper was then dated and priced 'First year of the Republic, one and indivisible, Saturday the 10 June, 1800. Price One Shilling in specie!' There was also an abundance of mock advertisements directed at the main figures of eighteenth-century radicalism, including 'Citizen Paine', and the leading lights of the London Corresponding Society.[70]

[69] Crabbe's *The Newspaper* was published in the same year as *The Task* and takes an unremittingly hostile attitude to newspapers and advertising.

[70] The *Times* parody is repr. in *History of* The Times, i. 66, and the political background discussed at p. 67 and Elliott, 147. No copy of the original appears to be extant.

Hone produced a mock news-sheet of his own in 1815 called *Buonaparte-phobia*. This attacked *The Times* for its violently pro-Bourbon and anti-Bonapartist rhetoric at the time of Waterloo and it is tempting to believe that Hone was aware of the *Times's* earlier parodic experiment. Hone's piece is composed of many elements. It adapts the headline typography and logo from the front page of *The Times*. The half-sheet format, however, and the use of illustration (a large portrait of Napoleon appears in the middle of the main text) are generally closer to broadsides and news-sheets of the day. A more specific model is the popular single-sheet satire which was printed by G. G. Shelton entitled *Memoirs of Napoleon*.[71]

The direct stimulants for the creation of *Buonaparte-phobia* were the particularly vitriolic and ultra-Tory leading articles of *The Times* composed by the editor, John Stoddart. This man was to become an inveterate enemy of Hone's and, under the nickname of Doctor Slop, which Hone first applied to him in *Buonaparte-phobia*, was to be the inspiration for and central butt in *A Slap at Slop*. In 1815 the wife of John Walter, the proprietor of *The Times*, fell ill, and Stoddart had a virtually free rein at the paper throughout the summer. With Napoleon's escape from Elba, Stoddart's writing adopted a tone of unreasoning fury. Hone's parody was directed against, and in fact largely constructed out of, the articles which Stoddart wrote at this time.[72]

The majority of *Buonaparte-phobia* consists of uninterrupted passages of abusive epithet. Stoddart in the character of Slop rails against Napoleon:

no sooner is a piece of successful villainy achieved by this *Monster*, than our print-shops exhibit the iron countenance of NAPOLEON THE GREAT!—the *portrait* of that execrable *Villain!* that *bare-faced* Villain! that *daring* Villain! that *perjured* Villain!—that *Disgrace* of the *Human Species*—the *Corsican!* the *low-minded* Corsican! the *wily* Corsican! the *vile* Corsican! the *once-insolent* Corsican! the *beaten, disgraced and perjured* Corsican! the faithless *perjured craft-loving* Corsican!—a *Fugitive!*—an *Adventurer!*—a *blustering Charlatan!* such a *Fellow!*—a *Scoundrel* with a Degraded Character!—an Imposter!—a Despicable *Imposter!*—a notorious Imposter! (*Buonaparte-phobia*, col. 1)

At the heart of the satire is the fact that every insult quoted has been

---

[71] For the complicated bibliographic background to the publication of the various edns. of *Buonaparte-phobia*, see Bowden, 45–6. *Memoirs of Napoleon* is *BMC*, no. 12204A.

[72] *History of* The Times, i. 157. See also Bowden, 42–4.

extracted from Stoddart's recent articles: he is served up with his own inarticulate poison. As the satire develops this blind abuse of language is made to appear both threatening and outrageous. The reader is constantly reminded that a civilized social norm exists beyond Stoddart's unbalanced and vain hatred. This process begins in the titling. Hone underlines the invasive nature of Stoddart's journalism by stating that it has been 'regularly served up, for some time past, in many respectable Families, with the Breakfast apparatus' and that it is 'designed FOR THE USE OF MEN WOMEN AND CHILDREN' (*Buonaparte-phobia*, col. 2).

Hone provides an overall parodic framework within that of the news-sheet by adopting ideas from Sterne's *Tristram Shandy*.[73] Book III, chapters vii–xiii of *Tristram Shandy* consist of an extended discussion of the subjects of swearing and the cursing of enemies, and Hone develops these passages in the context of contemporary political satire. When Stoddart's cursing reaches an apoplectic climax Mr Shandy and Uncle Toby have the following exchange:

'Small curses Doctor Slop, upon great occasions', quoth my Father 'are but so much waste of our strength and soul's health, to no manner of purpose.' 'I own it' replied Doctor Slop. 'They are like sparrow shot', quoth my Uncle Toby, 'fired against a bastion.' 'They serve', continued my Father, 'To stir the humours, but carry off none of their acrimony:—for my own part I seldom curse or swear at all—I hold it bad—but if I fall into it by surprise I generally retain so much presence of mind as to make it answer my purpose—that is—I swear on till I find myself easy.' (*Buonaparte-phobia*, col. 2)

This is composed of two passages from *Tristram Shandy* which are best understood from the perspective of the original. The immediate catalyst for the discussion of the curse is the fact that Doctor Slop, who has just arrived to deliver Tristram, has cut his thumb trying to undo his bag of obstetric instruments which his servant, Obadiah, had tied with a mass of knots. In exasperation Doctor Slop curses Obadiah: 'curse the fellow—I wish the scoundrel hanged—I wish he was shot—I wish all the devils in hell had him for a blockhead.' Tristram's father is devoted to Obadiah, and consequently he is 'determined to have his revenge'. The mode he adopts is firstly to

---

[73] Bowden's is the only scholarly discussion to take up Hone's use of Sterne. She states that in *Buonoparte-phobia* 'Hone does not quote at all from Sterne, but rather uses three of his characters' (p. 42). This is untrue. Hone quotes two sections of dialogue and several separate phrases from *Tristram Shandy*, book III, ch. viii.

address an abstract and highly involved discourse on cursing to
Doctor Slop. This opens with the passage quoted by Hone up to
the phrase 'find myself easy'. It then develops with Mr Shandy
presenting with high irony the thesis that he has 'the greatest ven-
eration in the world for that gentleman who ... sat down and
composed (that is at his leisure) fit forms of swearing suitable to all
cases, from the lowest to the highest provocation which could pos-
sibly happen to him'.[74] When Doctor Slop takes the bait and says
that he thinks such a thing impossible, Mr Shandy takes down *The
Curse of Excommunication* written by Bishop Ernulphus and requires
Doctor Slop to read it aloud as more befitting the doctor's sense of
just outrage. Hone develops Mr Shandy's ironic method of revenge
and ingeniously applies it to Stoddart, presenting his ravings as a
'course in: Cursing made Easy TO THE MEANEST CAPACITY ... EM-
BRACING The Times VOCABULARY of Easy EPITHETS and choice
CURSES against BUONAPARTE ... showing HOW TO NICKNAME AND
CURSE NAPOLEON to the best advantage on all occasions'.

Ernulphus's *Curse of Excommunication* is composed with great
order. It calls curses down from every heavenly body, moving
through the Father, the Son, the Holy Ghost, the Holy Virgin, and
the angels. Then every part of the victim's body and soul are cursed with an equal attention to detail and method while Mr
Shandy's and Uncle Toby's reactions are humorously interlarded:
' "May he be cursed in his reins and in his groin," (God in Heaven
forbid, quoth my uncle *Toby*) "in his thighs, in his genitals," (my
father shook his head) "and in his hips, and in his knees, his legs,
and feet, and toenails!" '[75]

While the commentary from Slop's listeners serves to deflate the
curse, its controlled hatred and malicious savagery still have the
ability to shock. The curse, given in full by Sterne in parallel Latin
and English texts, demonstrates the power and dignity of which
this ancient satiric form is capable. R. C. Elliott has written at
length of the magical origins of the curse, and of how the first
satirists brought down curses upon the heads of their enemies
which were believed to be literally fatal.[76] Ernulphus's curse was
embedded in popular culture and had been around since the 1680s

---

[74] Lawrence Sterne, *Tristram Shandy*, ed. M. and J. New, The Florida Edition of the Works of Lawrence Sterne 3 vols. (Gainsville, Fla.), 1978–84, i. 200.

[75] *Tristram Shandy*, i. 209.

[76] R. C. Elliott, *Satire and Magic* (Princeton, NJ, 1960), 3–15.

as an anti-papal broadside. Hone spotted the popular basis of Sterne's satire and reapplied it to Stoddart.[77]

Stoddart's cursing of Napoleon is an anarchic travesty of Ernulphus. His language is shown to be both degraded and ineffectual when compared with the grandeur of the earlier curse. Every new outburst begins in a semblance of order. Hone uses the repetition of certain catchwords such as 'villain' or 'Corsican' to create an appearance of development before the descent into disordered and arbitrary name-calling. Hone's transference of Sterne's text is lethal. Mr Shandy's and Uncle Toby's ironic statements upon the nature of small curses refer to Doctor Slop's initial outburst. Hone inserts this dialogue at the end of his satire, applying it to all of Stoddart's preceding speech and by implication all of his writing for *The Times*.

Stoddart's swearing is doubly ironic in the context of the radical use of cursing in tavern debating clubs and free-and-easies. Robert Wedderburn was prosecuted for blasphemy on account of the profane curses recorded by a government spy at one of his 'sermons'. For the radicals, cursing constituted a primal expression of linguistic and intellectual freedom and it must also have been a lot of fun. It is an area where the young Shelley merges in spirit with the ultra-radical activists. He performed his own variations on a papist curse:

Two or three Eton boys called another day, and begged their former schoolfellow [Shelley] to curse his father and the king, as he used occasionally to do at school ... as they continued to urge him, by reason of their opportunity he suddenly broke out, and delivered with vehemence and animation, a string of execrations, greatly resembling in its absurdity a papal anathema.[78]

Tristram Shandy offered many advantages for radical satire apart from the curse. In using Sterne Hone took up a figure of great fashionability. Peter Conrad has argued that Shandyism, in its conscious and unconscious manifestations, anticipated and influenced much Romantic thought. For him *Tristram Shandy* should be seen as 'anticipating in comedy the ethics and aesthetics of Romantic poetry'. For the late eighteenth- and early nineteenth-century reader Shandyism typically acted in less rarefied ways. Sterne's novel spawned an enormous literature of parody and commentary. The pamphlets and

[77] For the broadside history of the Curse of Ernulphus, see M. and J. New, 'Some Borrowings in *Tristram Shandy*', *SB* 29 (1976), 322–8; *Tristram Shandy*, iii. 952–7.
[78] Quoted in P. M. S. Dawson, *The Unacknowledged Legislator* (Oxford, 1980), 11.

broadsides which proliferated for the forty years following its publication were mostly popular and sometimes political. The book was widely translated and Shandyan cults and societies appeared across Europe. The first pamphlet response to *Tristram Shandy* in England, *Explanatory Remarks Upon the Life and Opinions of T. Shandy*, read Sterne's work as a political allegory. *Tristram Shandy* immediately entered popular culture in ways that shocked the delicate. Its *double entendre* appears to have been in vogue with all levels of society. The household clock became a sexually charged metaphor. *The Clockworker's Outcry* alleged that ladies were throwing out clocks by the dozen because of the unfortunate question asked by Tristram's mother. Prostitutes approached clients with the question 'Will you have your clock wound up, Sir?' There were more editions of popular anthologies and selections, some remarkably simplified, than of the original text.[79]

With the coming of the French Revolution reactionaries began to see sinister links between Sterne's Francophilia and the collapse of morality in the lower orders in Britain. The clearest expression of these feelings is to be found in the fiery 1799 pamphlet *The Fallacy of French Freedom and Dangerous Tendency of Sterne's Writings; or, An Essay Showing that Irreligion and Immorality Pave the Way for Tyranny and Anarchy: and that Sterne's Writings are both Irreligious and Immoral*. Sterne is set up as a dangerous author enamoured of disgusting French manners who has inherited the tradition of Voltaire but adapted his sophistries 'to the bulk of mankind'. Even worse, 'An oversight in the legislature' has allowed a situation where 'instead of being proscribed like the poisonous writings of Tom Paine ... they [Sterne's works] should be allowed to be an intimate of every house and used in almost every school'.

Buonaparte-phobia relates to this popular tradition: it is both a contribution to the literature of Shandyism and a practical refutation of the kind of attack launched in *The Fallacy of French Freedom*. Stoddart professed himself very much an English gentleman, and 'was at this time on terms of general intimacy with Sir Walter Scott, Charles Lamb, Wordsworth, Coleridge and particularly Southey', yet appears capable of expressing himself only in the most vulgar oaths. The climax of the parody moves beyond the framework provided by Sterne to force home the dislocation between Stoddart's social pos-

---

[79] The best account of the different manifestations of Shandyism in popular publishing is still J. C. T. Oates, *Shandyism and Sentiment* (Cambridge, 1968).

ition and the language he is in fact seen to use. Stoddart's insults move into the realm of a personal fantasy, his metaphors are drawn from the world of the fairground and the freak-show as he rails against 'the monster in human shape; . . . this *Tyger!* this *Hyena!*—this *Fiend!*—this *Bloody* Dog! . . . the *Pacha of Paris!*—the *Emperor of the Rag Fair!*—the *Tyger Tyrant!*' Yet Stoddart's only reply to Uncle Toby's assertion that 'my heart would not let me curse the devil himself with so much bitterness' is to fall back on his social position as a justification: 'when a gentleman is disposed to swear it is not for any stander-by to curtail his curses'.

This raises a central issue in Hone's work. He recognized that certain forms of language normally considered taboo were permitted when spoken by educated people in positions of power who voiced officially acceptable opinions. Hone had demonstrated this publicly when he triumphantly defended his use of biblical parody during his three state trials for blasphemous libel. He was also aware that the mass petitions of the reformers had been consistently rejected by Parliament from 1793 to 1820 on the official pretext that they were framed in language that the government did not find 'decent and respectful'.[80]

Hone's final point in *Buonaparte-phobia* is that Stoddart has abused the gift of language and as a result vitiated his position not only as a journalist but as a civilized human. This is explicitly brought out when Hone has Stoddart follow his profession that he is a gentleman with Caliban's words '*they* taught me *language*; and my profit on't is,—I *know* HOW TO CURSE'. Stoddart's education and elevated position have led him to a brutish perversion of language. The final coup is provided by a return to Stoddart's own words, only this time Hone turns the tables on him once again by ironically quoting a phrase of Stoddart's formed in a style of civilized urbanity: 'It is amusing to see the NATIVE VULGARITY of *Buonaparte's* mind and manners breaking forth in his LANGUAGE!!!—!!!—!!! THE TIMES! 6'th of May 1815'.

Buonaparte-phobia is central to Hone's development as a satirist. It was his first parody and it was a popular success which ran through at least eight editions. The ambitious attempt to fuse a popular form with more elevated and complicated satiric models anticipates the bold experiments of the late satires.

During the period between the publication of *Buonaparte-phobia* in

[80] See Smith, 30–4.

1815 and *A Slap at Slop* in 1821 newspaper parodies became increasingly popular both in social and political satire. Three parodic newspapers almost wholly devoted to mock advertisements were published in 1819. *The New Daily Advertiser* and *The Rump Chronicle* were produced as propaganda attacking the Westminster rump candidates during the election of 1819.[81] Many of the advertisement parodies in these papers establish a wider context for Hone's work and can be used as critical tools with which to uncover his working methods.

The New Daily Advertiser contains a parody of a 'wants a place' advertisement. An opposition candidate is presented as 'A Young Man at present out of employment, has no objection to work of any kind however dirty' (*NDA* 2: 1). This type of advertisement was widely used by the radicals in broadside and handbill parodies during the Queen Caroline affair. Hone was to adopt this form on several occasions. The series of 'ADVERTISEMENTS EXTRAORDINARY' which fill the final three pages of his pamphlet *Non Mi Ricordo!* include two of this type. The first attacks one of the corrupt Italian female witnesses at Queen Caroline's trial: 'TO LAUNDRESSES, WANTS A PLACE. An Old Woman, accustomed to coarse things; and work, however filthy ... '. The second is far more hard-hitting, and directed at Castlereagh, who is presented as the author of a notice running

TO MANGLERS, JUST LEAVING HIS PLACE. A STOUT ABLE-BODIED IRISHMAN, for a long time a master hand at mangling; when he begins there is no stopping him, and never tires. Can fold and smooth, and double and iron, all day. Will turn with any body. Was formerly a master in Dublin, where his mangling will never be forgotten. His Character may be had of anybody there. Is very smooth spoken, of good address, looks like an upper Valet, and is a perfect devil at his Work. May be heard of at the Triangle in Bird-cage Walk. (*Non Mi Ricordo!*, B3^v)

This makes a damning play on Castlereagh's supposed use of torture while a minister in Ireland. The final address alludes to the triangular frame on which people were suspended by the wrists to be flogged. The constant punning and innuendo are not allowed to disrupt the surface of the model. The tone of someone almost too eager to please is treacherous. The sentence 'can fold and smooth, and double and iron, all day', with its lulling rhythms and insistent

---

[81] BL Francis Place Collection, set xx, folders 96, 206–8, 212.

connectives, suggests a temperament that is insidious in its indefatigable continuity.

The first issue of *The Rump Chronicle* contains an announcement for a showman which presents the radical candidate Sir Francis Burdett as a juggler, sword-swallower, and fire-eater: 'Sir Francis Bugbear, the famous juggler, will dance a hornpipe, swallow a sword, assisted by his pupil called, "The Little Hobgoblin" ' (p. 1^{r-v}). The showman's notice was one of the oldest and most widely used forms of advertising. The theme of jugglers had become an exceptionally fashionable subset of this type of parody in the second decade of the nineteenth century. The appearance of groups of jugglers from India led to a series of print and press satires on the theme. There was a set of Indian fire-eaters and jugglers performing in London in 1819 who had become topical in literary circles as a result of Hazlitt's essay *The Indian Jugglers*. The essay had used the performance to elaborate an argument which defined skill or talent in relation to genius or greatness. Hazlitt's essay incorporated a political element. There is, for example, an aside in which 'the hearing of a speech in Parliament, drawled or stammered by the Honourable Member or the right Noble Lord' is compared unfavourably with the juggler's performance. Hone and Cruikshank used the Indian Jugglers, and the advertising surrounding them, in a more direct way as the basis for one of the most destructive items in *A Slap at Slop* (Fig. 28). The Duke of Wellington is presented as THE NEW INDIAN JUGGLER. Cruikshank's plate shows Wellington in a turban, thrusting, with both hands, a huge glave down the throat of a kneeling figure of Britannia. The copy reads:

THIS CELEBRATED PERFORMER, whose early operations in Asia, and subsequent slight-of-hand in Europe, have rendered him notorious, will perform the first opportunity. If he has the consent of his landlady's friends, he will put the sword down her throat, and keep it there as long as he pleases—the like not exhibited in England. He will then set the balls a-flying like winged messengers. These tricks, with permission, he is ready to exhibit. Further particulars in future Advertisements. (*A Slap at Slop*, 1^r)

The satire in *The Rump Chronicle* works through a ridicule of association. The dubious occupation of the performer and the ludicrous nature of his actions are supposed to make him a figure of fun. But, while Burdett performs his dangerous feats upon himself, Wellington is presented as endangering and abusing Britannia. She is not only a symbol of the nation and the people, but, most immediately in terms

Advertisements.

THE NEW INDIAN JUGGLER.

FIG. 28. George Cruikshank. Wood engraving. THE NEW INDIAN JUGGLER.
Mock showman's notice for front page of *A Slap at Slop*. 1821.

of the impact of the design, a woman. In envisioning Wellington as a
performer playing with the sword and juggling with fire, Hone and
Cruikshank deftly conjure up his military past in the most unflat-
tering terms. The transformation of military leader into dangerous
showman obliquely introduces the imputation that while war was for
him a high-risk game, and a profitable one, the people not only
suffered but were somehow tricked. Cruikshank's print could stand
as an independent political caricature. It is activated by the tensions
which pervade his larger single-sheet copperplate prints. The contrasts in the military character between violence, childishness, and
foppery, constantly apparent in his earlier Napoleonic prints, is central here.[82] Wellington's costume is curiously suspended between
showman and soldier. The composition is based on a right-angled
triangle. The hypotenuse runs up from the pointed toe of Wellington's left boot through his body and along his arms to the
pummel of his sword. The vertical descends along the hard geomet-

[82] For earlier examples, see *BMC*, nos. 12214, 122218, 122196.

rical lines of the sword-blade and then swells out into the soft curves of the buxom Britannia. The way the mouth is stretched to deformity in order to accommodate the great blade is sickening and perversely resonant.

The Rump Chronicle also has an advertisement attacking John Camb Hobhouse and presenting him as a 'Wonderful Animal ... Imported and trained by Sir Francis Fickle ... the redness of his eyes proves him to be a Hob Ferret' (2: 1ʳ). Hone and Cruikshank similarly included a beast advertisement in *A Slap at Slop*. This compared George IV with the Bonassus and the coronation in Westminster Cathedral with a grand exhibition:

ADVERTISEMENT COPIED FROM THE NEWSPAPERS; BONASSUS—The proprietor of this *interesting animal* returns his grateful thanks to his numerous patrons, who have enabled him to *divide the town* for so many days, *as it is doubtful which Exhibition has been the most admired, the exhibition in Westminster or that in the Strand.* The buildings at *Westminster* must be broken down: the *Bonassus* stands secure upon the foundation of *popular applause,* that Providence alone has the power to 'Knock *him up*', or 'break *him down*', in this world. The soldiers and sailors, heroes of Trafalgar and Waterloo, will be admitted to see the Bonassus at half price until Thursday, when the Abbey closes. (*A Slap at Slop,* 2ʳ)

The Bonassus was the name given to the American buffalo which was being shown in England for the first time in August 1821. Hone's claim that the advertisement was copied from contemporary newspapers is true. The owner of the Bonassus, which was exhibited at 287 The Strand, had decided that a comparison between the pulling power of his creature and that of the new monarch would be a daring sales gimmick. The fact that various members of the royal family had actually come to see the Bonassus only added to the potential richness of the situation. Another equally cheeky advertisement was put into the papers in October 1821 announcing:

CORONATION EXTRAORDINARY

The BONASSUS is crowned by the plaudits of universal approbation every day in the STRAND ... with his usual condescension he has prolonged his stay in town, and will be found 'AT HOME' to receive visitors at his levee every day of the ensuing week,——PATRONISED by the ROYAL FAMILY.[83]

---

[83] *Bodl.* John Johnson Collection, 'Animals on Show', box 1, Bonassus. For anti-Caroline print satire using the Bonassus, see *BMC,* no. 14192. This print predates the publication of *A Slap at Slop* and may be a source.

That Hone could transplant wholesale a genuine advertisement into *A Slap at Slop* and present it as a political parody reveals how easily and effectively the sales methods of the early nineteenth-century advertisers could be adapted into political propaganda.

The second parodic newspaper which appeared in 1819 was *The Quizzical Gazette Extraordinary!!!! and Wonderful Advertiser*. It was issued annually over a decade as a sort of April Fool's joke and consisted mainly of social satire. It indicates popular interest in advertisements as a form of humorous entertainment and suggests the degree to which advertising language had become stylistically distinct. The editor, John Fairburn, a man of fluctuating radical sympathies, drew attention to the relationship between Hone's publications and his paper: 'Mr. Hone fired off his "Slap at Slop", but not having the fear of an injunction or retaliation from our Editor, his shot were wadded with several scraps that ought to have been inserted in our gazette.'[84] There are many links between the satiric methods and models used by the two satirists, and Fairburn at one point even employed Hone as an editor.

Despite the predominant stylistic restraint and good taste of *The Quizzical Gazette*, there are several items in its pages which suggest that the apparently brutal humour of the radical pamphleteers grew naturally out of the sense of humour of the period. The following piece mocks the pitiful details which sometimes appeared in advertisements for missing persons: 'LOST, this morning a LITTLE BOY with a remarkable large head; face much seamed with the small pox, by which cruel disorder he has lost one eye the other very weak, has three sores on his neck, ... a very prominent belly, (occasioned, as it is supposed, by worms), and has joint irons on both legs' (*Quizzical Gazette*, 1: 4). This suggests a robust not to say callous attitude towards the suffering of children which would have been unlikely in a Victorian journal. This type of advertisement had long been popular in satire. Gillray had used it and it was adapted by Hone in a parody that became celebrated and widely imitated. This appeared as a whole sheet mock advertisement at the back of *Non Mi Ricordo!*.[85]

STRAYED AND MISSING. AN INFIRM AND ELDERLY GENTLEMAN in a Public Office, lately left his home, just after dreadfully ill using his wife about half a Crown and trying to beat her ... He was last seen walking swiftly towards

[84] *Quizzical Gazette Extraordinary and Wonderful Advertiser*, 4 (Apr., 1822), 45.
[85] For Gillray's use of the form, see the discussion of the attacks on Philip Thicknesse in Hill, *Mr. Gillray the Caricaturist*, 36.

the Horns without a Crown to his hat, accompanied by some evil disposed persons who tied a great green bag to his tail full of crackers, which he mistook for sweetmeats and burn't himself dreadfully ... He is very deaf and very obstinate and can not bear to be looked at or spoken to ... If this should meet his eye, it is earnestly requested that he will return to his duty, and he will be kindly received and no questions asked. (*Non Mi Ricordo!*, B4ʳ)

The advertisement concerns the plight of the Regent during the Queen Caroline affair and works into the description many of the more humiliating details connected with the trial and with the private life of the Regent. This satire is a good example of the way Hone's parodies could be taken up by different sections of the publishing market. It was brought out as a mock handbill by at least two other publishers and was also absorbed into the illustrated pamphlet *A Peep at the P–v———n; or, Boiled Mutton with Caper sauce at the Temple of Joss*. The second and third parts of this verse satire are a rewriting and commentary upon Hone's 'Strayed and Missing'. During 1820 a series of other variations loosely based on Hone's 'Strayed and Missing' began to appear. J. C. Turner brought out a set of mock advertisements supporting the Queen, which were collected in pamphlet form. The title ran 'ABSCONDED, IN A DISCONSOLATE STATE, DIVERSE PERSONS, BETTER KNOWN THAN TRUSTED. FOR FURTHER PARTICULARS ENQUIRE WITHIN'. These variations on Hone's original suggest not only the versatility of the radical publishing market but the extent to which Hone was a leader of popular taste.[86]

By far the most numerous advertisements both in the newspapers and in the parodies in *The Quizzical Gazette* are for books, patent medicines, and new inventions. Hone was to use all of these in *A Slap at Slop*. His attacks on Robert Southey exploit two of these forms. When George III died Southey wrote his memorial poem *The Vision of Judgement*. The poem was parodied by Byron under the same title. Hone also included a full-length parody on the inside pages of *A Slap at Slop* entitled *A Vision of Want of Judgement*. On the front page of *A Slap at Slop* there was a parody of Southey's original bookseller's

---

[86] The broadside versions are *£0,000,000 Reward. Strayed and Missing* (London, 1820), printed for O. Hodgson. One Penny; *£0,000,000 Reward. Strayed and Missing* (London, 1820), Whiteman and Co. Printers. Bowden has noticed a less involved verse 'translation' in the pamphlet *A Peep into W———r Castle after the lost Mutton* (London, 1820), printed by W. Benbow. Bowden has also located a broadside by Pitts using the advertisement; see Bowden, 356. For a later imitation, see Absconded in a Disconsolate State, Divers Persons Better Known than Trusted (London, 1820), printed by J. C. Turner.

advertisement which had appeared in most leading journals and newspapers early in April 1821. The original ran: 'Mr. Southey's New Poem / This day is published in thin quarto. Price 15 s. boards. / A vision of judgement. A Poem. By Robert Southey, Esq. / L.L.D. Poet Laureate; Member of the Royal Spanish Academy of History, and of the Royal Institute of the Netherlands. etc.'[87] Hone followed the format of this advertisement closely. His changes were slight but lethal. He used a number of puns to turn Southey's grandiloquent series of titles against him, the immodesty of his self-advertisement becoming his downfall: 'A Vision of Want of Judgement, by Slobbered Mouthey esq. Hell. Hell. d. Poet Sorryhead, Member of the Royal Spanish Satiety. etc. etc.' (*A Slap at Slop*, 2[r]). The other advertisement attacking Southey takes the form of a quack announcement for a magic ointment: 'GOLDEN OINTMENT FOR THE EYES. This invaluable Ointment enables the patient to see in the dark. (CASE.) DEAR SIR; Your invaluable ointment being strongly recommended to me some years ago, I was induced to try a box. Its effects were astonishing!—I immediately looked two ways at once, and saw my way clear to the Laureateship. I have seen in the dark ever since! . . . I am dear Sir, your's, R. Southey Esq. LL.D' (*A Slap at Slop*, 2[r]).

The main force of the satire comes out of the ironic conflation of two types of sales gimmick adopted by advertisers and still in use today. Geoffrey Leech has pointed out that there are two basic forms of testimonial used to sell a product. The testimony in the form of a monologue from an ordinary consumer and the monologue from a celebrity.[88] Hone has Southey appear as something of both. As a famous figure he appears to be attempting to sell the public a product which he believes in. He can, however, only believe in it from the perspective of his blindness, and as a common victim of quackery he tries to pass it on to the public. Again Hone turns the disreputable associations of patent-medicine advertising on his victim.

A Slap at Slop, although using many of the elements from earlier newspaper parody, was quite unlike any genuine newspaper that had appeared before. The diversity of forms which it incorporates is enormous and it threatens to overpower the basic framework of its model. *A Slap at Slop* carries fifteen woodcuts on its front page and in its chaotic format it is unlike any contemporary publication and

[87] *Bodl.* John Johnson Collection, box for advertisements 1766–1827, envelope, *The London Magazine*, advertisement wrapper for 1 Apr. 1821.

[88] Leech, *English in Advertising*, 52–4.

anticipates the newspaper layouts of the late nineteenth- and even early twentieth-century dailies. The only contemporary publications which approached *A Slap at Slop* in terms of their typographic anarchy were the long song sheets developed by Catnach towards the end of the second decade of the nineteenth century.[89]

Hone's satire bears little relation to Stoddart's *New Times*, its supposed model. The only resemblance is in the title which takes up the elaborate shaded capitals which Stoddart had used. The typography in other parts of *A Slap at Slop* departs radically from the conservatism of the early nineteenth-century dailies. Hone uses a great variety of classic eighteenth-century types for his headlines as well as fat-faced display faces mixing scale and weight to create effects of imbalance. Many of the illustrated advertisements on the front page of *A Slap at Slop* are complicated hybrids which incorporate material from the woodcuts in contemporary handbills, broadsides, lottery puffs, and imagery from copperplate print satires. They also draw on diverse sources outside the environment of the jobbing printer including book illustration and official state-backed art connected with funerary monuments and numismatic design. Two of the most powerful parodies in *A Slap at Slop* concern the Peterloo massacre, and this chapter concludes with a detailed analysis of them. They take the form of mock subscription announcements for a medal and a public monument. Both of them are designed to commemorate the activity of the cavalry during the massacre.

The 'Peterloo Monument' is suggested as a design for an equestrian statue (Fig. 29). It stands out against a white tombstone enclosed by a black border. A Manchester Yeomanry cavalryman with the initials of his regiment and of the King conspicuous on his saddle is shown slashing down at a prostrate woman. She clasps an infant in one arm and raises the other to ward off the blow. Her figure and gestures are counterbalanced by a ragged man who lies back and clasps his head in horror. The base of the monument is decorated on the top and sides with a border of skulls on a black ground. Bulky manacles hang from each side. The centre of the base shows a crown with irradiating lines composed of bayonets, swords, and daggers. Hone's text is carefully composed in the style of a subscription notice for a public monument and carries the headline 'VICTORY OF PETERLOO'.

The intense irony of this satire would have been heightened by the

[89] See Morison, *The English Newspaper*, 255–9, 305–15; Marshall McLuhan, *The Mechanical Bride: Folklore of Industrial Man* (London, 1967), 1–4.

FIG. 29. George Cruikshank. Wood engraving. VICTORY OF PETERLOO.
Mock monument for front page of *A Slap at Slop*. 1821.

well-publicized and unprecedented boom in public monuments which occurred in the first two decades of the nineteenth century. B. R. Haydon complained in 1812: 'You ... lavish thousands upon thousands on sculpture without effect. In no country under heaven has such patronage been met by such shameful, disgraceful indolence as in this. Masses of marble scarcely shaped into intelligibility; boots, spurs, epaulettes, sashes, hats and belts huddled on to cover ignorance and to hide defects.' A Committee of National Monuments was established in 1802 to supervise the construction of a series of sculptured tombs in St Paul's Cathedral. This marked a new era in English public sculpture. The government's policy was supported by wealthy companies such as Lloyds and the West India Association. The demand for public monuments became widespread. The death of Nelson in 1805, and of Pitt in 1806, led to the collection of large amounts of money through advertising for subscriptions. A radically new development for public patronage of this kind was most uncommon in the eighteenth century. Several satiric prints came out concerning Nelson's monument, some in the form of mock monuments.[90]

In advertising for a statue that would be an expression of public mourning, Hone and Cruikshank questioned the assumptions which led the government to commission public sculpture. Arthur Danto has considered the national motivations which lie behind the construction of monuments and memorials: 'We erect monuments so that we shall always remember, and build memorials so that we shall never forget. Very few Nations erect monuments to their defeats, but many set up memorials to the defeated dead.'[91] Public monuments traditionally celebrated rich and powerful figures and used grandiose iconography drawn from classical and heraldic sources. Hone and Cruikshank recorded the mass suffering of the anonymous victims of Peterloo by travestying the elaborate and frequently ungainly effects of contemporary monumental sculpture.

Cruikshank must have been aware of the numerous copperplate prints produced from the 1790s onwards which used ideas connected with funerary and monumental sculpture. Equestrian

---

[90] Haydon is quoted in Margaret Whinney, *Sculpture in Britain 1530–1830* (Harmondsworth, 1964), 197, and she discusses the Committee, pp. 197–209. For satires on Nelson's monument, see *BMC*, no. 10445; also Mary Dorothy George, *English Political Caricature 1793–1832: A Study of Opinion and Propaganda* (Oxford, 1959), 86.

[91] Arthur C. Danto, *The State of the Art* (New York, 1987), 112.

monuments had been frequently parodied in print satires. Gillray's
PATER URBUM Subscribi Statuis (*BMC*, no. 8800) of 1796 was an in-
scribed mock monument showing an obese and docile Prince
Regent on an elegant charger. In 1805 Gillray followed up with *St
GEORGE and the DRAGON* (*BMC*, no. 10424) (Fig. 30) subtitled 'A Design for an Equestrian Statue, from the Original in Windsor-Castle'.
This print shows George III as St George dealing a fatal blow to a
dragon with the head of Napoleon. The print *appears* to have its basis
in patriotic feeling, presenting the King as the patron saint of
England slaying the national foe. Things are not, however, this
straightforward. The presentation of heroic royal endeavour is
undercut through the depiction of George III in caricature. His
determined frown and bulging eye are rendered all the more ridiculous by the awkward and unconvincing gesture with which his sword
is raised and gripped. If he manages to continue holding the weapon
at all then the decapitation of his horse appears the only likely result
of any attempt to strike the dragon. Gillray, with typical ambivalence, ridicules what he is supposed to be celebrating. Both in
tone and composition this print relates closely to the design for the
'Peterloo Monument'. Cruikshank's print differs stylistically from
Gillray's in that the figures of the horseman and his victims are drawn
naturalistically, avoiding the distortions and exaggerations typical of
caricature. Cruikshank's portrayal of the horseman's sword arm, in
particular, is far more competent than Gillray's. Certain elements
such as the posture of the woman have been directly absorbed from
the earlier print.

Much of the power of Cruikshank's woodcut comes from the
stylistic contrasts within it: there is a tension between symbolism and
realism. The theme of St George and the dragon is taken up with
furious irony. It had long been used as a stock political metaphor for
the triumph of good over evil. As early as 1577 M. Gheerardts produced a print *William of Orange as St George* (Fig. 31).[92] This was an
engraved representation of a monument in which a detailed key
describes how each part of the writhing dragon represents an aspect
of evil. The coils of the dragon are used to set off the elegant poise
and heroic purpose of St George. Cruikshank substitutes the suffering mass of bodies at Peterloo for the dying dragon. The

---

[92] See E. H. Gombrich, 'The Cartoonist's Armoury', in *Meditations on a Hobby Horse* (Oxford, 1963), 133–4. Gombrich singles out the print as an example of efficient symbolic propaganda.

FIG. 30. James Gillray. Etching. *St GEORGE and the DRAGON*. 1805.

FIG. 31. M. Gheerardts. Etching. *William of Orange as St George*. 1577.

nationalistic mythology underlying the design is overturned and used to explode the pretended motives of the soldiers. They see themselves as national heroes fighting the monster Reform while we are shown a butcher riding down and sabring a mother and child. Their fantasy is simultaneously presented and exposed.

The print is starkly divided stylistically. The delicate and sophisticated technique used to portray the figures aspires to documentary realism. The base of the monument is conversely drawn in harsh, crude outlines; images of bayonets, skulls, daggers, and manacles stand out as funereal emblems in hard white on black. This absolute tonal division is taken up into the figure group in one detail; the face of the cavalryman has been completely blackened out. The effect of this device is complicated. It conveys the sense of impersonality which a uniform can provide: the soldier is literally faceless. The defacement is also, however, the graphic satirist's primitive revenge on his victim.

As a supplement to the Peterloo monument Hone and Cruikshank also advertised the 'Peterloo Medal'. The print and accompanying text are anticipated by a handbill produced during the OP (Old Price) theatre riots at Covent Garden during 1807.[93] This advertised a 'Good Theatrical Medal' which is carefully described in the style of a coin-collector's catalogue; yet the Hone and Cruikshank piece is enmeshed in medallic history in a far more central and complicated way.[94]

Cruikshank's illustration (Fig. 32) consists of a decorative border with detached skulls and crossbones repeated on a black background. The central design shows a soldier, with face again blacked out, raising a dripping axe over a kneeling man with outstretched arms. The supine corpse of a woman lies across the background. The subscription consists of two lines of dialogue. The poor man asks, 'Am I not a Man and a Brother?', the soldier replies, 'No you are a poor Weaver'. Hone provided a clever parody of the type of patriotic press announcement which had appeared in the papers to advertise medals privately struck to celebrate battles during the Napoleonic wars. In 1813, for example, *The Gentleman's Magazine* contained an advertisement for 'A MEDALLION, / WITH A PORTRAIT OF / THE EMPEROR ALEXANDER / AND ON THE REVERSE, / AN EM-

---

[93] See p. 231.
[94] The parody is pasted into an uncatalogued interleaved copy of James Boaden, *The Life of John Philip Kemble* (London, 1825) in *Bodl.* John Johnson Collection.

BLEMATICAL FIGURE OF RUSSIA, / Treading underfoot the French Eagle, and inflicting punishment on the guilty blood of the enemy'.[95] Hone carefully re-creates such tones in his parody, but all the details are barbed: 'ADVERTISEMENTS. It is further proposed that MEAGHER'S TRUMPET shall be melted down, and that the brass shall be carefully applied to the purpose of multiplying an appropriate design to be distributed among the warriors who distinguished themselves on the occasion, and to be worn by each as a PETERLOO MEDAL; (*A Slap at Slop*, 1ᵛ). Edward Meagher was the trumpeter who led the troop of Manchester Yeomanry cavalry into the massacre. He was among the most hated of any connected with the affair having led a vindictive personal charge on civilians in Lloyd Street well after the meeting had been cleared.[96]

The last part of Hone's announcement shows that the parody was referring specifically to a campaign medal to be distributed to every man. Hone and Cruikshank exploit the Waterloo–Peterloo conflation by taking up the unique position of the genuine Waterloo medal in the history of English campaign medals. These were very rare in England before the middle of the nineteenth century. An unofficial medal had been struck by Mr Davison, Nelson's prize agent after the Battle of the Nile. This was a sales gimmick which maximized profits from the publicity of the battle. The Waterloo medal was produced in an altogether different manner and was the most renowned and important military medal that had been struck in England up to that point. It celebrated national pride in a great victory and was given to every soldier engaged in the battle. It also indicated respect and concern for the bereaved, for it was the first medal to be awarded to the next of kin of men killed in action.[97]

The Peterloo medal exploited the emotional force of a newly developed aspect of state-backed military iconography in the context of a pacifist satire. Cruikshank's design was again adapted from a specific source which would have charged it with an irony particularly embarrassing to the state. The most widely reproduced and influential image connected with the abolition movement was the

[95] *The Gentleman's Magazine*, 377 (May 1813), advertisement.

[96] Marlow, 142, 145–6, 154–5, 180.

[97] Accounts of the importance of the Waterloo medal in the history of the campaign medal are: Taprell Dorking, *Ribbons and Medals: The World's Civil and Military Awards* (London, 1974), 38–40, 91–2; L. L. Gordon, *British Battle and Campaign Medals* (London, 1979), 49, 55; John Laffin, *British Campaign Medals* (London, 1964), 13–24, 69; Marlow, 29–30, 31, 55, 62, 119, 124, 170–6.

FIG. 32. George Cruikshank. Wood engraving. PETERLOO MEDAL. Mock medal for front page of *A Slap at Slop*. 1821.

FIG. 33. Josiah Wedgwood. Anti-slavery medallion in black jasper on white jasper. 'AM I NOT A MAN AND A BROTHER?' 1787.

seal of the Anti-slavery Society also produced as a print and a medallion. It showed a kneeling slave in chains. The surrounding inscription again read 'AM I NOT A MAN AND A BROTHER?' (Fig. 33).[98] The image was produced in cheap form as tokens in the 1790s, including one by Thomas Spence, and continued to be reproduced in a great variety of forms well into the nineteenth century. The Peterloo medal parodied both the original inscription and the figure of the supplicant—the figure of a ragged English weaver was substituted for the slave. The implied accusation is that the poor in England share the same lack of basic human rights and the same poverty as black Africans before the abolition of the slave trade in 1807. This was a common charge levelled at Wilberforce and one which found its most furious advocate in Cobbett.

There may have been yet another irony in the unencumbered simplicity of the design. It was well known in artistic circles that the famous gem- and medal-engraver Benedetto Pistrucci had come to London in 1814 and in 1816 had been working on designs of George III and George and the dragon for the new national coinage. He worked on official state medals and was to design the coronation medal for George IV. Since 1819 he had been working on a special privately commissioned Waterloo medal. It was to have been a big chunk of metal measuring nine centimetres in diameter. Pistrucci's design consisted of a mass of confused imagery supposedly connected with victory which incorporated tritons, horsemen, chariots, angels, and liberty trees, with portraits of the victorious allied monarchs in the centre.[99] This white elephant was never struck and only a few electrotype copies survive. Whether Hone or Cruikshank had come across the abandoned scheme or not, the projected medal is a good example of the type of state propaganda which their parodic medal deflated.

The radical reaction to the Peterloo massacre was massive and prolonged and generated much satire aimed ironically at the military. E. P. Thompson has argued that it was the tone of jeering disgust which the radical propagandists adopted which was most difficult for the government to counter and indeed endure.[100] Hone and Cruikshank both contributed to the publicity. Hone took account of the fact that there were many Waterloo veterans present

[98] Thomas Clarkson, *A History of the Abolition of the Slave Trade*, 2 vols. (London, 1808), 450–6.
[99] See Mark Jones, *The Art of the Medal* (London, 1979), 102–7.
[100] Thompson, 688–9, 702–3.

in the crowd during the Peterloo massacre. One of these, John Lees, who died agonizingly of his wounds, became the subject of a show inquest in which the identification of his killers was attempted. In 1820 Hone published a 700-page account of this inquest.[101] Cruikshank produced *Massacre at St. Peter's* (*BMC*, no. 13258), which appeared in August 1819, just days after news of the massacre had reached London. This was the most elaborate and notorious print satire on Peterloo. It is a melodramatic scene of orgiastic violence presenting soldiers with butcher's axes hacking up a prostrate crowd consisting mainly of women and children. The two Peterloo satires in *A Slap at Slop* are more controlled and distilled than these earlier reactions. The outrage is expressed through an involved set of ironies. The conventions of an art which celebrates war and condones murder through a rhetoric of patriotism are ridiculed, while at the same time the victims of Peterloo are commemorated.

[101] William Hone, *The Whole Proceedings Before the Coroner's Inquest at Oldham, &c. on the Body of John Lees, who Died of Sabre Wounds at Manchester, August the 16, 1819* (London, 1820).

5

The Political House that Jack Built: Children's Publishing and Political Satire

IN December 1819, when public outrage at the Peterloo Massacre was still strong, Hone published *The Political House that Jack Built*. The pamphlet, set in the form of an early nineteenth-century children's nursery rhyme book, sold over 100,000 copies within the first few months of publication. It was the most notorious popular satiric re-action to the Peterloo massacre. The satire's focal point was the massacre, yet it used this as a platform from which to treat more general problems relating to reform.[1]

The Political House was one of the most influential satires to appear in the first three decades of the nineteenth century. It established the basic form in which the majority of Hone and Cruikshank's other satiric pamphlets were to be produced. It also led to a host of imit-ations and counter-imitations by both the radical and loyalist press. Radical publishers including William Benbow, Thomas Dolby, John Fairburn, and John Cahuac brought out satires based on the forms of nursery rhyme books, and nursery rhyme parody became part of the currency of popular satire. Jemmy Catnach, the broadside entre-preneur, brought out cheap bowdlerized editions of all Hone's most successful pamphlets. The influence of the Hone and Cruikshank pamphlets extended well into the nineteenth century. Much of the illustrated satire produced from 1830 to 1832, as part of the agitation

---

[1] The most authoritative account of the probable sales of *The Political House* is Bowden, 243–4, 287. Estimates are also provided in Thompson, 719; Edgell Rickword, *Radical Squibs and Loyal Ripostes: Satirical Pamphlets of the Regency Period 1819–1821* (Bath, 1971), 24. Patricia Anderson, *The Printed Image and the Transforma-tion of Popular Culture* (Oxford, 1990), 36, argues that the price of 1s. would have put the pamphlet out of the reach of the majority of working people.

for the First Reform Bill, drew directly on the earlier Hone and Cruikshank publications.[2]

Hone described the genesis of *The Political House* twenty years after its appearance:

One day, when I had been exasperated beyond bearing, one of my children, a little girl of four years old, was sitting on my knee, very busy looking at the pictures of a child's book, 'What have you got there?' said I,—'the House that dack Built'—an idea flashed through my mind; I took it away from her ... I sat up all night and wrote—'The House that Jack Built'. In the morning I sent for Cruikshank, read it to him, and put myself into the attitudes of the figures I wanted drawn.[3]

Hone claims to have seen a child's book, and then to have collaborated with Cruikshank to produce the illustrations: two newly developed areas of the publishing industry, the children's book and the political print, are fused. In 1842 Thackeray thought of the print-shops of his youth, and his reminiscences highlight the strangely suspended status of Hone's nursery rhyme parody: 'Knight's in Sweeting's Alley; Fairburn's in a court off Ludgate Hill; Hone's in Fleet Street—Bright, enchanted palaces, which George Cruikshank used to people with grinning fantastical imps and merry harmless sprites,—where are they? ... the atrocious Castlereagh, ... the "Dandy of Sixty", who used to glance at us from Hone's friendly windows—where are they?'[4] Thackeray nostalgically remembers looking at the satire when a boy of 9 or 10 as if it really were a

---

[2] Bowden, 260–77, 323–4, 379. For the imitations, see Rickword, *Radical Squibs*, M. D. George's notes to *BMC*, nos. 13318–45, 13522–30, 13564–87, 13640–7, 13672–80. For the gutter press bowdlerizations of Hone, see Charles Hindley, *The Life and Times of Jemmy Catnach* (London, 1878), 94–105; Hackwood, 224; Shepard, *John Pitts*, 37, 63–4. For Hone's influence on 1830s reform agitation, see *A Political Alphabet* (London, 1830). The illustrations are a mixture of Cruikshank blocks from the Hone pamphlets of 1819–21. See also the reform journal *Asmodeus; or, The Devil in London*, 1, 4, 11, 13, 18, 28, 35, 26. Also the journal *A Slap at the Church* which ran from Jan. to May 1832. It adapted its title from Hone and Cruikshank's *A Slap at Slop* and contains many Cruikshank plates for the earlier Hone publications.

[3] Rolleston, *Some Account of the Conversion of the late William Hone*, 41. Hone's account should not be taken too literally. Bowden, 240, has discovered a draft sheet which, she argues, suggests that Cruikshank may have arrived at the basic structure for the rhyme independently. Patten, *George Cruikshank's Life*, 158, also argues for caution in accepting Hone's account, and quotes Charles Knight's eyewitness account of Hone and Cruikshank at work on the satire. Knight describes Cruikshank as the dominant and inspirational force in the collaboration. For a more detailed account of the role of Cruikshank and of his familiarity with the history of print satires based on the rhyme, see below, pp. 233.

[4] W. M. Thackeray, 'George Cruikshank', *Westminster Review*, 66 (1840), 6.

FIG. 34. George Cruikshank. Woodcut. Plate 'THE MAN—all shaven and shorn' (B3ᵛ) for *The Political House.* 1819.

children's book. The 'atrocious Castlereagh', who appears in the tenth plate of *The Political House*, and 'the Dandy of Sixty', who first appeared in the notorious eighth plate (Fig. 34), are seen not as devastating political satire but as 'grinning fantastical imps' and 'merry harmless sprights'. In 1819 the Prince Regent and the Cabinet viewed these pictures very differently; they were a manifestation of the challenging and seditious powers of the radical free press.[5] The interpretative divergence is not simply the result of the different political perspectives of 1819 and 1842 but grows out of the complicated relationship which existed between adult satire and

[5] John Wardroper, *The Caricatures of George Cruikshank* (London, 1977), 17, 92, 98–9.

children's publications in the first two decades of the nineteenth century. It also indicates the successful exploitation of this situation by Hone and Cruikshank.

The use of children's literature as a vehicle for satire was made possible by the recent increase in the juvenile market. J. H. Plumb places the commercialization of children in the eighteenth century in a context of generally expanding leisure industries that included music, dancing, food, sport, the theatre, and political print. During the latter half of the eighteenth century toys were mass-produced for the first time and children's books developed as an important part of the publishing industry.[6]

William Dicey's newly designed chapbooks and nursery books in the 1730s applied higher standards of printing and illustration to the child's book and the improvement and mass publishing of nursery books by John Newberry and his imitators meant that children's rhymes and tales were increasingly popularized from the 1740s onwards. They became embedded in the national consciousness as part of the aural and visual tradition, Newberry's books were quite startling. Although they were tiny, he bound them in boards and they were covered with the brightly coloured and gilded Dutch papers which became his hallmark. He also included numerous half-page wood-block or whole-page copperplate illustrations. Often these had only a caption for the text.[7]

These children's books were a new and popularly accessible area of the book trade. Their potential as vehicles for political satire was quite quickly explored. In 1757 Newberry brought out *A Collection of Pretty Poems for the Amusement of Children Six Feet High*, an adult satire

[6] J. H. Plumb, 'The Commercialization of Leisure in Eighteenth-Century England', Stenton Lecture, Reading, 1972. Plumb, 'The First Flourishing of Children's Books', in G. Gottlieb (ed.), *Early Children's Books and their Illustration* in McKendrick *et al.* (eds.), (London, 1975); Plumb, 'The New World of Children', *The Birth of a Consumer Society*, 286–316. For an account of the political implications of the developments of children's toys and fashions, see Elizabeth Ewing, *A History of Children's Costumes* (London, 1977), 45–79; Phillis Cunnington and Ann Buck, *Children's Costume in England* (London, 1965), 49, 52.

[7] A. W. Tuer, *Pages from Forgotten Children's Books* (London, 1898), 17, 19, 22, 28; *ODN* 4–5, 30–7; Charles Ryskamp, preface, in G. Gottlieb (ed.), *Early Children's Books and their Illustration* (London, 1975), pp. viii–ix; Percy Muir, *English Children's Books 1744–1945* (London, 1954), 58–68; Ann Thaxter Eaton, 'Illustrated Books for Children Before 1800', in *Illustrators of Children's Books 1744–1945*, comp. Bertha E. Mahony, Louise Payson Latimer, and Beulah Folmsbee (London, 1961), 3–25; Jacob Blanck, 'A Twentieth Century Look at Nineteenth Century Children's Books', lecture, Simmons College, Boston, 27 Apr. 1954. For John Newberry, see Welsh, *John Newberry*, 91–2.

mimicking the form of his own children's books. This anticipates several aspects of *The Political House*. It was probably known to Hone, for he quotes from its title in his dedication of his own parody to 'the nursery of children six feet high'.

In size and format *A Collection* was identical to Newberry's genuine children's books.[8] Its title is adapted from Newberry's volume which came out the year before, *A Collection of Pretty Poems for the Amusement of Children Three Feet High*. The probable editor, Christopher Smart, used the title-page and physical make-up as a disguise for his satire, announcing in the preface that as 'these poems are professedly published for the use of children six feet high, none else have any business to buy them ... which consideration alone will prevent any application being made to those of a more elevated rank and situation'.[9] Smart feigns innocence and simultaneously exploits the advantage offered him by his disguise. Hone was to adopt a similar method in *The Political House*. Unlike Hone's publication, however, the mimicry is not carried over into the illustrations, which are crudely adapted from the style of the mid-eighteenth-century satiric etching. At this time small-format anthologies of the most popular single-sheet print caricatures were common and Newberry's book appears to have been modelled on these.

Thomas Spence, who anticipated Hone's parodic use of advertising forms, was also quick to see the potential of children's literature. Hone was clearly influenced by Spence's experiments with the structural aspects of children's books and owned a copy of Spence's chapbook parody of *Robinson Crusoe*. Spence brought out a series of chapbooks which expressed his theories of land and language reform and attacked his political opponents. In 1782 he produced *A Supplement to the history of Robinson Crusoe*, 'Published for the agreeable perusal of Robinson Crusoe's friends of all sizes'. This utopian vision is set in a country which has carried out Spence's theories of land reform. The volume also included three other works in the style of children's chapbooks. These were *A History of the Progress of Learning in Lilliput*, *A History of the Mercolions by Master Brolio of*

---

[8] The Bodleian copy, still in its original binding, measures 8 cm by 12 cm. It is bound in a patterned brightly coloured Dutch paper and carries several single-page copperplate illustrations.

[9] For the attribution to Smart, see Arthur Sherbo, 'Survival in Grub Street: Another Essay in Attribution', *Bulletin of the New York Public Library*, 64 (1975), 147–58; also Robert Mahony and Betty Rizzo, *Christopher Smart: An Annotated Bibliography 1743–1983* (New York, 1984), 35–6, 213–14, 234–5, 247, 264.

Lilliput and *What Happened on a Journey with Old Zigzag*. The last of
these was illustrated by Bewick and teaches basic levelling principles
through beast allegories. Spence continued to produce parodic
children's books after his move to London in the early 1790s. His
Description of Spensonia takes plot elements from both *A Tale of a Tub*
and *Robinson Crusoe*.

When Hone and Cruikshank took up the nursery rhyme book in
1819 it was not only the involvement of children's books in political
satire that made it an apt model: the children's book had become
intensely politicized in its own right. The upheavals of 1789–1815
had greatly intensified state interest in the political and religious
education of the young and the poor.[10] One practical result of this
had been the organized production of morally hidebound but often
entertainingly written tracts and chapbooks. The early 1790s saw
the endeavours of the Clapham Sect begin the flood of publications
encouraging obedience to Church, King, and country. In 1792
Hannah More wrote *Village Politics*, a widely sold rebuttal of *The
Rights of Man* designed for 'lowly' adults and children. She refused
official requests to write a similar popular attack on *The Age of Reason*
and switched her attention to the composition and organization of a
major propaganda offensive, the *Cheap Repository Tracts*. More intended to reach a popular readership and shrewdly set about the
infiltration of the ballad and chapbook market. The *Cheap Repository
Tracts* used the typography and illustrational methods of the
chapbook and ballad sheet. At the official ceremony to launch the
tracts More and her co-organizers went so far as to invite street-
hawkers, to whom they gave free samples of the tracts for distribution. With a well-organized central committee behind them, and
efficient publishing and distribution networks, the tracts soon
became a self-supporting endeavour and had sold 2 million copies by
mid-1796.[11]

The tracts started a publishing trend which targeted the poor and
their children. From 1795 to 1815 Hannah More, Sarah Trimmer,
and a host of less celebrated followers wrote for the popular publishing market. They produced chapbooks, ballads, and popular
didactic religious forms such as catechisms and creeds. They
preached a patriotic evangelicalism encouraging humility, servitude,
gratitude, industry, and patience in the face of hardship. Martha

[10] See pp. 107–10 above.
[11] M. G. Jones, *Hannah More* (London, 1952), 139–49. Jackson, 169–223.

Sherwood's *History of the Fairchild Family* is full of scenes where implacably calm and ruthlessly benign parents inflict physical punishment and terrible psychological cruelty on children who accept whatever these authority figures throw at them as inevitably improving. The remarkable list that concludes More's ballad *The Ploughman's Ditty* gives the essence of the values promoted and the confusions compounded in Church and state popular literature. The ploughman rejects the argument that insurrection is justified on the ground he has nothing to lose with the triumphant chorus: 'King, Church, Babes and Wife, Laws, Liberty, and Life, Now tell me I've nothing to lose sir.' Authority, family, religion, monarchy, freedom, and the law form a single sinister inventory of the poor man's privileges.

The production of propaganda was only one side of the coin, censorship was the other. Many chapbook classics were considered to support subversive ideas and were condemned. The pages of Sarah Trimmer's aptly titled periodical *The Guardian of Education* fulminated against the continuing existence of such titles as *Goody Two Shoes* and *Primrose Pretty Face*. They were seen to encourage the young and uneducated to consider marriage outside their social sphere a possibility, and they supported irresponsible notions of enjoyment. The presentation of the local squire and farmer as grasping and exploitative in *Goody Two Shoes* was seen as a particularly dangerous attack on the ruling classes.[12] *The Guardian of Education* was highly polemical and carried an enormous review section which screened new children's publications and ruthlessly hunted down frivolity and fantasy.

These developments did not go unchallenged. It was the books which resulted from the counter-offensive which were to provide Hone and Cruikshank with the models for their satires. Charles Lamb publicly expressed disgust at the productions of Hannah More and Mrs Barbauld.[13] The Romantic revival of interest in folklore, the ballad, and the psychological state of children had a practical

[12] Sarah Trimmer, *The Guardian of Education 1802–1806*, i. 430–1, 436; Jackson, 179–80, 185–6.

[13] Anna Letitia Barbauld (1743–1793) was a friend of Hannah More and became identified by Lamb's circle with the drive to excise frivolity from children's books and to base juvenile instruction in the Scriptures. Her popular reputation has, however, not served her well for she was a deeply erudite and creative figure. Her most enduring children's publication, *Hymns in Prose for Children* (1781), is a complicated and beautiful text which contains descriptions of nature which are reminiscent of Traherne's *Centuries of Meditations*.

effect on children's book publishing. William Godwin set up his own children's book publishing company and attempted to enlist the talents of his various literary friends including Wordsworth, Coleridge, Hazlitt, and Lamb; only the latter two eventually contributed. Godwin hoped to make money out of the enterprise but also saw his books as an assault on More and Trimmer. His preface to *Bible Stories: Memorable Acts of the Ancient Patriarchs* of 1802 complains that 'these modern improvers have left out of their system that most essential branch of human nature, the imagination'.[14]

In fact imagination had never been entirely absent from children's publishing. Enlightened antiquarianism had kept the ballad and popular rhyme alive and Joseph Ritson's 1784 publication of *Gammar Gurton's Needle* maintained intellectual interest in the chapbook. In the first decade of the nineteenth century small-format brightly illustrated children's books began to appear in large numbers. Some of these had a political edge. Ann Taylor's 1807 *Signior Topsy Turvey's Magic Lantern* was a reworking of the popular compartmentalized prints showing the world turned upside-down. It included such un-Trimmer-like sentiments as: 'A hare who long had hung for dead, But really brewed sedition'.

In the second decade of the nineteenth century the publisher Marshal brought out several books illustrated by George Cruikshank's brother Robert which consisted of nonsense and weird word-play. *The Gaping Wide Mouthed Waddling Frog*, *The Frisking Barking Lady's Lapdog*, and *The Hopping Chattering Prating Magpie* were destitute of moral instruction and treated language with an anarchic delight in travesty. The publications of Marshal, Benjamin Tabart, and Dean and Monday took elements from the popular chapbook but were up-market compared to the genuine article, which was still being produced by popular printers such as John Pitts. The greatest exponent of the new type of children's book was John Harris. The books which he published between 1816 and 1820 provided the specific models for a host of subsequent children's books and for the pamphlet satires of Hone, Cruikshank, and their radical and loyalist imitators.

By the beginning of the nineteenth century Harris had gained control of the most famous and prolific children's book publishing company of the eighteenth century, that of the Newberry family. In

[14] William St Clair, 'William Godwin as Children's Bookseller', in Gillian Avery and Julia Briggs (eds.), *Children and their Books* (Oxford, 1989), 165–77.

1805 Harris enjoyed a tremendous vogue with his booklet *The Comic Adventures of Old Mother Hubbard*, which went through twenty editions within a year.[15] Much of the book's success lay in the way it bridged the gap between the adult and juvenile market. It became a bestseller in high society as well as in the nursery. Printed on fine paper, with an engraved illustration on each page, it was more lavish than the chapbooks which were still the principal form of children's publication. Its success with adult readers resulted from its being mistaken for a lampoon concerning a politician. This assumption sprung from a mysterious dedication by the authoress, Sarah Martin, to a Member of Parliament, 'at whose suggestion and at whose house these notable sketches were designed'.[16]

That the adult world show an interest in nursery rhyme literature, and that it should assume that such literature could house political satire, is yet another indication of the ripeness of the market for nursery rhyme parody. The book was a breakthrough for the anti-Trimmer publishers. By 1812 it was in its twelfth edition and had opened up the market for entertaining and imaginative children's poetry books.

Harris followed up his success with a number of sequels including *The Butterfly's Ball*, which set a vogue for the papillionade which carried through the nineteenth century. In 1819, the same year in which *The Political House* came out, Harris radically altered the style of his children's books once again. He enlarged the size from the smaller square formats, which he had been using, to a rectangle of about seven inches by four. In this new space the text and illustration could comfortably work together on a single page. The text was typeset and no longer etched on to the plate with the illustration. The style of illustration facilitated the production of coloured editions. The pictures were drawn with simple heavy outlines; the resulting clearly defined areas could then be filled quickly with water-colour washes. The Harris books were open to a readership of all ages and both sexes. They employed language that was deeply rooted in the popular imagination and unconstricted by conventional notions of style. These qualities made them an ideal vehicle for popular illustrated satire.

Hone and Cruikshank adapted all the characteristics of the new-

---

[15] S. Roscoe, *John Newberry and his Successors* (Wormley, 1973), 3–33; *ODN* 316–22; also Iona and Peter Opie, *A Nursery Companion* (Oxford, 1980), 5–6; *John Harris's Books for Youth 1801–1843*, comp. Marjorie Moon (Folkestone, 1992).

[16] Quoted in *ODN* 319. Jackson, 199–200.

style Harris books to their pamphlets. *The Political House, The Man in the Moon, The Queen's Matrimonial Ladder, Non Mi Ricordo!*, and most explicitly of all *The Political A Apple Pie* (illustrated by Cruikshank, but not written by Hone) are very closely modelled on Harris. They echo the size and take up the novel feature of combining text and illustration on a single page. Cruikshank's illustrations, unlike Harris's copper engravings, are wood engravings and draw on a variety of graphic traditions. Many plates, however, employ the Harris 'house style', using thick outlines, simplified forms, and barely suggested or even blank backgrounds. The proximity between the two styles of engraving is further emphasized by the fact that Hone produced deluxe coloured editions of his most successful pamphlets, the plates appearing naturally suited to the process.[17]

Recent critical interpretations of *The Political House* have over-emphasized Hone's unconventionality in using a nursery rhyme as the vehicle for his satire. The form was highly conventional when viewed from the perspective of political print satire. The novelty of *The Political House* lay in the way Hone and Cruikshank took up a nursery rhyme that had been commonly used in political prints for thirty years and developed it in the context of the contemporary children's book market.

Critical responses have concentrated on the text of *The Political House* rather at the expense of the illustrations and consequently exaggerate Hone's role as the creator.[18] Hone's self-aggrandizing account of the pamphlet's genesis has been too readily accepted. George Cruikshank and his father Isaac experimented widely with nursery rhymes in prints before Cruikshank's collaboration with

---

[17] This is shown in the advertisements at the back of many pamphlets. The advertisements printed on the final page of Hone's pamphlet *The Man in the Moon* include 'A SUPERIOR EDITION OF THE POLITICAL HOUSE THAT JACK BUILT, is now published printed on fine Vellum Drawing Paper, with Cuts handsomely COLOURED, Price 3s.'

[18] Hackwood, 219–20; Bowden, 236–7, 241–2; Smith, 166, 168–70; James, *English Popular Literature*, 72; James observes that Hone's 'nursery rhyme parody may have been suggested by the Manchester Observer of August 28, which included the lines: "these are the public informers who met, / On the state of affairs to debate, / At the field of Peterloo"'. Smith draws attention to a reference to the original rhyme by the defending council during Thomas Hardy's trial for high treason in 1794. This is not, however, a parody, and has no bearing on the form of Hone's pamphlet. Patten (*George Cruikshank's Life*, 66–7, 157) has begun the process of redressing the balance and considers some of the plates to *The Political House* in detail. He also notes the existence of print parodies of *The House that Jack Built* during the Old Price riots.

Hone. A consideration of the tradition of print satire using nursery rhymes provides a clearer picture of the collaboration.

The increasing popularity of children's books generated a widespread use of nursery rhymes as both texts and sources for illustrations in political satire. Political satires using the forms of children's books became common from the 1780s. During the four decades before the publication of *The Political House* the interrelationship between satire and children's literature had become complex. Nursery rhyme parody became an element in satiric prints by the end of the eighteenth century. Both *Gulliver's Travels* and *Robinson Crusoe* exemplify a complementary process: the absorption of adult political satire into the children's book market. *Gulliver's Travels* was produced as a children's book in many versions before 1819 and it also consistently provided themes, situations, and captions for political prints. Chapbook editions giving illustrated simplified versions of the first two books of *Gulliver's Travels* had appeared certainly by the early 1770s. By the 1780s Swift's original had become converted into a children's classic. It remained constantly in print in a variety of children's versions between 1780 and 1820.[19]

The themes and images used in children's versions of *Gulliver's Travels* were also incorporated into print satires from the 1790s onwards. These include work by every major caricaturist during the period commonly termed the 'golden age' of print satire. Almost all the prints were developed from images and themes concerning Brobdingnagians and Lilliputians.[20]

Some of the prints go no further than using the basic satiric device of reduction: the political enemy is turned into a lilliputian midget. Of those that produce a variation on a theme from *Gulliver's Travels* it is noticeable that the episodes are nearly always those where Gulliver's activities mimic children's games. John Traugott has argued that children's games are central to Swift's satiric method in the first two books of *Gulliver's Travels*.[21] In the first book Gulliver is the child giant and Lilliput is his world of playthings. The political life and social hierarchy of Lilliput are decided by a series of court games

[19] A. H. Scouten (ed.), *A Bibliography of the Writings of Jonathan Swift*, rev. edn. H. Teerink (Pennsylvania, 1963), 213–22, items 310, 323, 329B, 329C, 332, 332A, 338, 340, 342.
[20] *BMC*, nos. 6919, 6929, 9088, 9392, 9507, 10034, 10111, 10112, 11581, 11582. For the continuity of Swiftian themes in print satire from the 18th to the 20th cents., see Philippe, *Political Graphics*, 20–1.
[21] J. Traugott, 'The Yahoo in the Doll's House', 127–51.

which fill the bulk of the third chapter. The houses are like doll's houses and Gulliver's naval battle is reminiscent of a child's maritime fantasy with toy boats. Similarly, Gulliver urinating into the royal palace suggests a child's excretion game. In the second book Gulliver himself becomes a plaything. At first the King thinks that Gulliver must be a clockwork toy. He is built a little house to live in and cutlery 'not much bigger than what I have seen in a London toy shop, for the furniture of a baby house'.[22] It was primarily the imagery connected with infantile ludic behaviour which Gillray developed in his devastating attacks on Napoleon–Gulliver performing before George III–King of Brobdingnag. The same material underpins the caricatures using Swiftian themes to attack the Pitt and Liverpool administrations.

The use of children's literature in print satire during this period had become general. By the mid-eighteenth century prints frequently drew on children's literature and on images taken from children's games and entertainments. In 1743 the print *A New Court Lesson* (*BMC*, no. 2588) attacked the Secretary of State in the form of an alphabet rhyme. ABC rhymes were more commonly used in political parody in the first three decades of the nineteenth century than any other nursery rhyme, with the exception of *The House that Jack Built*, and by 1820 had their own tradition of parody.[23] As the conventions for satire using material connected with children became more firmly established, certain political figures were singled out for presentation in nursery environments. Because of his youth when he became Prime Minister William Pitt was often shown as an infant or juvenile in print satires of the 1780s and 1790s. A number of prints exploit the theme of the clever child playing dirty tricks on his friends and they often use props such as children's toys, books, and rhymes.[24] Child imagery was also prominent in the propaganda aimed at Napoleon, which made great play out of his smallness. Cruikshank produced several prints immediately after

[22] Jonathan Swift, *Gulliver's Travels* (1726), ed. Harold Williams (Oxford, 1941), 89–90.

[23] *BMC*, nos. 10228, 10276, 13588–610; also Robinson, no. 1216, and the pamphlets *John Bull's Constitutional Apple Pie* (London, 1820), *The Constitutional Apple Pie; or, Rhythmical Red Book* (London, 1820), Peter Pangloss, pseud., *A New Favourite Royal Alphabet* (London, 1821).

[24] *BMC*, nos. 6425, 7856, 8812, 8829; Ashton, *English Caricature and Satire on Napoleon I*, 16–17, 240, 322, 372; Catherine Clerk, *Le Caricature contre Napoleon* ([Paris,] 1985), 158, 159, 164, 166, 235, 239, 247, 255, 275.

Waterloo which show Napoleon as a child and as various sorts of toy with which the victorious allied leaders play.[25]

George Cruikshank was active in his father Isaac's workshop from the age of 7.[26] Isaac was a leading political caricaturist in the late eighteenth and early nineteenth centuries. He produced many prints based on nursery rhymes. In September 1808 he brought out *The Spanish Pie; or, A Ditty for Young Patriots*, which concerned the defeat of Joseph Bonaparte and the French by the Spanish Patriots. The print is both a visual and verbal parody of the rhyme *Sing a Song of Sixpence*. The Cruikshank version shows Joseph Bonaparte leaping back from a table in horror, his knife raised and mouth open. An army of tiny patriots burst out from the crust of an enormous pie. The text above reads:

> Sing a song of sixpence—a bag full of rye,
> Four and twenty patriots baked in a pye,
> When the pye was opened the boys began to sing
> Now was not that a dainty dish to set before a King.[27]

FIG. 35. Isaac and George Cruikshank. Etching, detail. RHYMS for GROWN BABIES in the MINISTERIAL NURSERY. 1809

[25] *BMC*, nos. 12196, 12214, 12218.   [26] Hamilton, 25–6.
[27] E. B. Krumbhaar, *Isaac Cruikshank: A Catalogue Raisonné* (Philadelphia, 1966), items 1132–4.

In October 1809 the Cruikshank workshop brought out a more
elaborate print based upon a series of nursery rhyme parodies,
RHYMS for GROWN BABIES in the MINISTERIAL NURSERY.[28] The print consists
of six compartments, each of which contains a parody of a nursery
rhyme all attacking the person caricatured in the accompanying
illustration. The rhymes parodied are Ride a Cock-Horse, See-Saw Marjory Daw, Mary Mary Quite Contrary, Girls and Boys Come out to Play, and
Sing a Song of Sixpence.

The only section which attempts a graphic interpretation of the
verse is that accompanying Sing a Song of Sixpence (Fig. 35). George III
examines   the   baronets–blackbirds   through   an   opera-glass.
Baudelaire particularly admired the grotesque extremities of distortion in Cruikshank's physiognomies: 'I should say that the essence of
Cruikshank's grotesque is an extravagant violence of gesture and
movement, and a kind of explosion, so to speak, within the expression.'[29] This quality is already apparent in the way the tiny faces
dissolve into beaks. This section of the print establishes that
Cruikshank was interested in the integration of text and illustration
in nursery rhyme parody, and his style here looks forward to some of
the plates in The Political House. He does not yet, however, exploit the
styles of children's chapbook illustration. The graphic mode is still
that of the eighteenth-century satiric etching. The composition and
the treatment of the figure of George III are adapted from Gillray's
The King of Brobdingnag, which shows George III examining a tiny
Napoleon–Gulliver through an opera-glass. Cruikshank reveals, ten
years before the first Hone pamphlet, his ability to empathize with
the elements of extravagant fantasy at the heart of this rhyme. He
fuses the sophisticated techniques of the satiric etching with the bizarre elements present in nursery rhymes.

The involvement of the Cruikshank workshop with The House that
Jack Built can be traced back to the occasion when it first became
embedded in popular parody in the early 1790s. A Miss Gunning

---

[28] The print is of historic importance on two counts. First, because the title
anticipates the earliest recorded use of the compound 'nursery rhyme' in the OED,
which is for 1854. Barbara Garlitz has traced the term back to 1815 where it is
insultingly applied to Wordsworth in a review of The Excursion (British Review and
London Critical Journal, 6 (Aug. 1815), 55); quoted in Barbara Garlitz, unpub. letter to
Iona Opie (1 Jan. 1959). Secondly, because the ODN does not record any parodies
for Ride a Cock-Horse, See-Saw Marjory Daw, or Mary Mary Quite Contrary, and only one
in 1954 for Sing a Song of Sixpence.

[29] Charles Baudelaire, 'Some Foreign Caricaturists', in Selected Writings on Art
(Cambridge, 1981), 234.

was believed to have fabricated evidence of her courtship with the Marquis of Blandford. This included a forged letter from the Duke of York consenting to the marriage, which was popularly known as 'the note which nobody wrote'. A parody focusing on the letter and based on the nursery rhyme resulted. It enjoyed great popular success in high and low society. In 1792 Isaac Cruikshank brought out a satiric etching based on the parody entitled *The House that Jack Built*.[30] The print is divided into eight sections, of which all except the opening one, which shows 'the note that nobody wrote', take the form of crudely drawn character heads of the people involved in the scandal. The print used compartmentalized sequential format and each section contains a single illustration. The satire unfolds in a narrative manner somewhat analogous to a comic strip and established a format followed by other single-print parodies of the rhyme. This format was consequently absorbed into the pamphlet productions of Hone and Cruikshank.

The rhyme was soon taken up in a number of contexts. George Packwood, 'the celebrated razor strop maker and author of *The Gold-finch's Nest*', was a remarkable self-publicist who throughout 1795–6 masterminded a one-man advertising campaign promoting his razor strops. His advertisements appeared in every leading newspaper and in their number, variety, and inventiveness were unprecedented. They were almost all parodic, appearing as mock articles, songs, tales, plays, poems, fables, dialogues, letters to the editor, and nursery rhymes. He collected every piece he had produced, and published them as *Packwood's Whim. The Goldfinch's Nest*. A parody of *The House that Jack Built* was printed under the title *Small Children's Amusement; and a Comfort to those of Larger Growth*.[31] This conflates 'the man all tattered and torn' and 'the priest all shaven and shorn' of the original and makes clever play out of this imagery and the kissing of the maiden which occurs at the end of the original rhyme:

> This is the fair Damsel—see her pleasures increase;
> The rough beard is remov'd, left like down in its place;
> Great enjoyment she takes in her lover's smooth face.
> that was kissed by the man [*sic*], that was shaved by the

[30] Horace Walpole, *Horace Walpole's Correspondence*, ed. W. S. Lewis, 48 vols. (Oxford, 1944), xi. 279–80; John Nichols, *Illustrations of the Literary History of the Eighteenth Century*, 8 vols. (London, 1817–58), vii. 716; *Scots Magazine*, 53 (Oct. 1791), 505. The Cruikshank print is *BMC*, no. 8163.

[31] Packwood, *Packwood's Whim*, 29. For a detailed discussion of Packwood's advertising methods, see McKendrick *et al.* (eds.), *The Birth of a Consumer Society*, 146–97.

barber, that removed the notches from the Razor, by whetting it
on the Paste, that is spread on the Strop, that Packwood made

(*Packwood's Whim*, 29)

In December 1797 the rhyme resurfaced again in a political print,
This is the House for Cash Built (*BMC*, no. 9044), the 'house' in question
being the Treasury. The piece is a generalized attack on Whig economic policy, and supportively presents Pitt as the 'Youth who to speak
truth, / Looked after the coal that lay in the hole, / In the midst of the
house for cash built'. The first image gives a view through a simple
Roman arch representing the Treasury. The second presents a circle
of sacks full of coins, with more money scattered about on the floor.
Both images stand out boldly with no background. They relate closely
to the first two lines of the original rhyme, 'This is the House that Jack
built, / This is the wealth that lay in the House that Jack built'.

The first two illustrations probably influenced the style of the
opening of Hone and Cruikshank's *The Political House*. Hone
maintained the first two lines of the nursery rhyme unchanged.
Cruikshank's illustrations present the 'house' as a symbolic temple. Its
outline forms a simple arch, while the wealth is shown as a treasure
chest with sacks of coins leaning against it, and a pile of coins scattered
about. The chest is filled with documents inscribed 'Bill of Rights',
'Magna Carta', and 'Habeas Corpus'. Cruikshank adapted the earlier
print imagery to fuse conventional images of wealth with the idea of
liberty.

The rhyme was again put to use in connection with the public
outcry surrounding the Convention of Cintra. On 3 February 1809 a
Williams print came out—*The Convention of Cintra, A Portuguese Gambol
for the Amusement of Iohn Bull* (*BMC*, no. 11215) with the following final
accumulation:

> This is John Bull, in great dismay, at the sight
> of the Ships, which carried away the gold and
> silver and all the spoil, the French had plundered
> with so much toil, after the convention which nobody
> owns, which saved old Junois Baggage and Bones
> altho Sir Arthur (whose Valour and Skill, began
> so well but ended so ill) had beaten the French
> who took the Gold, that lay in the City of Lisbon.

The apparently logical progression of the rhyme's sequences is
skilfully used. A set of international political events and diplomatic
manœuvrings is compressed into a striking and available narrative.

The simple message—that the French have got away with murder and that John Bull has been cheated of his just deserts—comes over powerfully. It is a distortion of the historical circumstances surrounding the Convention, and exemplifies the potential of this nursery rhyme as an instrument for political propaganda.[32]

Before *The Political House* the most sophisticated use of the rhyme occurred in the context of the propaganda war launched against the actor John Kemble during the OP (Old Price) riots. These riots manifested popular disgust with many of Kemble's policies when he reopened Covent Garden after rebuilding it. The chief objections concerned ticket prices, the number of private boxes, and the fees of the foreign stars—although there is evidence that the riots were motivated by a response to wider political issues and that the Westminster radicals had a hand in their organization.[33] A proliferation of satirical placards, banners, prints, and pamphlets accompanied the riots. Leigh Hunt's *Examiner* gave an eyewitness account emphasizing the role of graphic satire in the riots: 'each succeeding evening increased in noise; to catcalls were added horns and trumpets; and to a placard or two, banners all over the house covered with proverbs, lampoons and encouragements to unanimity'.[34]

Among the most popular of these lampoons was one based on *The House that Jack Built*. *The Examiner* reprinted the parody and it came out in at least four versions in political etchings.[35] By far the most effective was Rowlandson's THIS IS THE HOUSE THAT JACK BUILT (Fig. 36). The print dwells in a hinterland between documentary realism and satiric fantasy. The startling view of the empty theatre in the opening section has a diagrammatic aridity enforced by satiric labels. Some of these are politically charged, as in 'Pigeon holes for the swinish multitude' with its quotation of Burke's notorious phrase describing the common people. The second section zooms in to give

---

[32] See George, discussion of *BMC*, no. 11215.

[33] Marc Baer, *Theatre and Disorder in Late Georgian London* (Oxford, 1992), 86–7, 115–32, provides a full discussion of the complicated relations between the riots and popular politics.

[34] *Examiner*, 91 (24 Sept. 1809), 619. For the background to the riots and their political implications, see *The Political Register*, 16 (Sept. 1809), 890–2, 911; *Examiner*, 91 (24 Sept. 1809), 617–20; Thompson, 735; also Arnott and Robinson, nos 1202–93. Arnott and Robinson, nos. 1208, 1216, 1223, 1226, 1237, and 1290 are relevant in establishing the popularity of parodies concerning nursery rhymes and themes connected with children's amusements.

[35] *BMC*, nos. 11414–17. The text is printed in *The Examiner*, 91 (24 Sept. 1809), 617.

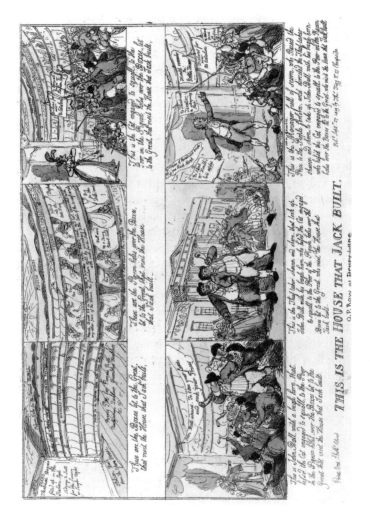

Fig. 36. Thomas Rowlandson. Etching. *THIS IS THE HOUSE THAT JACK BUILT.* 1809.

a sudden enlargement of an area of the private boxes. The owners are glimpsed as absurd forms engaged in ludicrous amatory frolics. Their licentiousness is suddenly forced home in the view of a pair of tiny, parted, up-ended legs sticking over a balcony. The mob dominates the next four scenes and is presented through a variety of viewpoints ranging from eye-level views of the proscenium to the external space of the fifth scene with its uncluttered foreground.

Compared to the Rowlandson, the other OP parodies of the print are weak. Two of them, however, are by the Cruikshank workshop.[36] Both are divided into two tiers: the crowd scenes in the top half are by George and the crude caricatures below by Isaac. These prints show that George Cruikshank had worked on parodic versions of *The House that Jack Built* long before his collaboration with Hone.[37]

The rhyme continued to feature in prints. In April 1810 William Heath produced *The Progress of the Warrant* (*BMC*, no. 11552) concerning the arrest and subsequent release of the Whig member of Parliament Sir Francis Burdett. The print adopts a popular radical stance and in tone and satiric method is quite close to Hone's pamphlet. Some details of the text may even have been directly adapted. The terming of the warrant as 'the thing' in the first six verses is a probable source for Hone's denomination of the printing-press as 'the thing' in the fifth plate of *The Political House*. Earlier in 1810 Williams produced a print parody of *The House that Jack Built* ridiculing the amorous scandal between the Duke of York and Mrs Clarke (*BMC*, no. 11526). The print was then adapted into a pamphlet printed by Watts & Co. also in 1810 and entitled *The Magical Note*.[38] The title-page indicates that the book was designed to suggest children's literature. It states that the note has 'placed many little ones on the stool of repentance'. The pamphlet adopts the format of the early publications of John Harris which followed on the publication of his *Old Mother Hubbard*, before he switched to the larger formats which would influence Hone and Cruikshank. It demon-

---

[36] Cohn, 168, states, 'the Bruton copy [of *The House that Jack Built*] was autographed in the first section "this by me, the others chiefly by my father"'.

[37] Baer, 230, 256, notices the formal connection between Rowlandson's *The House that Jack Built* and Hone's *The Political House*. He is not familiar with the varied history of the rhyme in print satire and consequently over-emphasizes the influence of the OP print, seeing it as evidence that 'new codes' were developed for propaganda by the riots.

[38] *The Magical Note and its Consequences* (London, 1810). The copy in the library of the V & A appears to be unique.

strates how closely children's book parody and the satiric etching were becoming interlinked in the years leading up to Hone's pamphlets.

The House that Jack Built was also taken up in the radical periodical press in the months before Hone's pamphlet came out. In January 1818 a parody version appeared in *The Black Dwarf* as part of the celebrations for Hone's trials and acquittal. It presented the forces that had led to the trial with some accuracy:

> This is the verdict recorded and found,
> By the Jury unbiass'd, unpack'd and *unfrown'd*
> That frighten'd the Judge so choleric and old,
> Who swore 'by the oath of his office' so bold,
> 'Twas an impious, blasphemous libel, and so,
> The man should be ruined ex-officio,
> By the servant of servants who bluster'd so big,
> With his ears in his hand and his wits in his wig;
> To please the Ministers
> Who hated the truth
> That was told by the man [Hone]
> Who published the parodies.[39]

A parody of the rhyme with an even more direct bearing on Hone's pamphlet appeared in Hunt's *Examiner* for 19 October 1819. This dealt with the political background to the Peterloo outrage and was titled *A New House that Jack Built*. It was to be 'Set to the tune of the old Words, and adapted to the understanding of the Children of Reformers, and the Fathers of Corruptionists'.[40] There is also a statement that the parody was originally supposed to be accompanied by illustrations. The final accumulation which was to be accompanied by a picture of 'The Bank Bubble Exploding' ran:

This is the shock that rose in the morn, and wakened the beast all Scraping and Scorn (a rich Placeman), that badgered the Man all tattered and torn (a poor Englishman), that Hissed the Paid'un, all for lawn (a reverend Manchester Magistrate), that willed the row with the Trump and all (the Manchester Outrage), that crossed the Log (a Boroughmonger), that governed the Band that pinned the Hand (Ministers and other Anti-reformers), that met the fault (rotten seats marked with prices), that lay in the house that Jack built (a house in Westminster).

The parody is much shorter than Hone's and does not contain the mixture of personal attack and general political discussion which makes *The Political House* such a telling exposé of the pressures leading

[39] *BD* 3, (1818), 45.   [40] *Examiner*, 74 (10 Oct. 1819), 652.

to the massacre. The popular appeal of *The Political House* resulted to a large extent from the way in which it amalgamated visual and linguistic satire. Imagery and text had become closely linked in the print parodies of the rhyme, but the special nature of the Hone and Cruikshank collaboration led to satire of a wholly new complexity and intensity.

Recent discussions of *The Political House* have paid scant attention to the nature of the collaboration and tend to foreground Hone's text. Nineteenth-century critics, beginning with Hone's loyalist enemies, conversely expressed their belief that Hone's text was completely dependent on Cruikshank's cuts. The earliest and most elaborate development of this theme appeared in John Stoddart's verse satire *Slop's Shave at a Broken Hone*:

> For instance such dull boggling slang as you [Hone] sell,
> However coarse, attention would not stir,
> Nor barrow women of their pence bamboozle,
> Without a woodcut to explain the sense,
> And help along its lame incompetence.
> Therefore the wisest job that ever you did,
> (Next to your well known trial and subscription)
> Was your flash bargain with a wag concluded
> To aid your threadbare talent for description;
> For who, in fits at Cruiky's droll designs,
> Can stay to criticise lop sided lines?[41]

Other loyalist pamphlets were even more violent in their criticisms of Hone. Although not motivated by the personal animosity of Hone's political enemies, Cruikshank's late nineteenth-century biographers reiterate the charges against Hone regarding the inadequacy of his text and its dependence on the illustrations. They add the unfounded accusation that Hone treated Cruikshank shabbily in financial terms.[42]

---

[41] John Stoddart, *Slop's Shave at a Broken Hone* (London, 1820), 11.

[42] *The Radical Chiefs*, 12–13; Hamilton, 30; Jerrold, 58, 70. Hone and Cruikshank's financial relationship during this period, from which Hone emerges honourably, is recorded in detail in the letters of George T. Lawley, New York Public Library, Berg Collection, albums 1 and 2; and Patten, *George Cruikshank's Life*, 110–11, 117, 127, 147–58. Patten, Cruikshank's most recent biographer, has gone a long way towards providing a clear picture of Hone's influence over Cruikshank's political thought and social behaviour during the period of the collaboration. He does not, however, go into the interaction of text and illustration in any detail (which, given his focus on Cruikshank, is not that surprising) or attempt to trace the rich visual analogues for the illustrations in earlier print satire (which is). As a connoisseur and a biographer of

The recent resurgence of interest in the work of William Hone has produced two discussions of *The Political House* which perform the necessary function of considering Hone's text seriously for the first time. Ann Bowden has also discovered sketches which show Cruikshank playing with various plans for the parody, and these suggest that he was responsible for the conception of its overall structure.[43]

Olivia Smith's discussion in *The Politics of Language* almost completely ignores Cruikshank's role in the creation of *The Political House*. Smith's only major discussion of the illustrations does not mention Cruikshank at all and contains basic errors. She states: '*The Political House* contained illustrations printed on a type of wood block that had long been out of use and that had previously appeared only in chap books and broad sheets. Hone adapted the old form of illustrations to provide inexpensive prints that were first used in *The Political House*. Hone controlled and to some extent designed the illustrations, he wrote the text, he printed, published and sold it . . .'[44]

No evidence is provided for any of these assertions, several of which are inaccurate. In fact wood-block illustration similar to that used by Hone and Cruikshank was not uncommon in the early nineteenth century. The cuts that appeared in the headpieces and factotums of newspapers, on trade cards, in the new children's books, on lottery puffs and other advertisement hand-outs, and on the headpieces of the broadsides of Pitts and Catnach were produced on similar blocks to those used for the Cruikshank plates for *The Political House*. The styles of commercial wood-block engraving also have strong similarities with the later plates.[45] Cruikshank's

Cruikshank he is apt to see Hone as an intrusive political force, and he argues that all Cruikshank's work for Hone 'belongs less to the history of art than to the history of propaganda'.

[43] Bowden, 236–78.   [44] Smith, 170.

[45] For Cruikshank's wood engravings before 1819, see Cohn, 160, 172, 454, 784, 796. He produced a number of wood engravings for Hone publications before those for *The Political House that Jack Built*; see Cohn, 105, 526, 614. For similar wood engravings in the children's books of Newberry and his successors, see Rosco, *John Newberry and his Successors*, J 217, J 233, J 253(13), 267(4), J 269(5); also A. W. Tuer, *1,000 Quaint Cuts from Books of Other Days* (London [, 1886]), 28, 29, 30, 97. For the continued popularity of wood engraving in the late 18th and early 19th cents., see Simon Houfe, *A Dictionary of British Book Illustrators and Caricaturists 1800–1914* (Woodbridge, 1978), 26–7, 174–5; Sinclair Hamilton, *Early American Book Illustrators and Wood Engravers*, 2 vols. (Princeton, NJ, 1968), 32–56; R. K. Eagen, *A Dictionary of Victorian Wood Engravers* (Cambridge, 1985), 59–60; R. N. Essick, *William Blake, Printmaker* (Princeton, NJ, 1980), 224–7.

lottery puff advertisements, some of which he is known to have produced as a boy long before he knew Hone, have very strong affinities with the later illustrations.[46] That Hone was responsible either for the adaptation of the illustrations or that he had any part in their design appears unlikely. When Cruikshank collaborated with Hone he was already the leading caricaturist of the day and his experience in commercial graphic art was enormous.[47]

Smith's study also suffers from her lack of familiarity with the history of print satires which lie behind *The Political House*.[48] Much of the strength of Hone's satire stems from its roots in a popular tradition rather than from its individual novelty. The same argument can be put forward for Cruikshank's illustrations. *The Political House* was lavishly illustrated with numerous half- and full-page woodcuts. These prints were the most striking aspect of the publication and, as contemporary reactions suggest, were largely responsible for the pamphlet's whirlwind success.[49] Their appeal grew out of the way they combined a variety of styles including the caricature etching, the children's chapbook woodcut, and more naturalistic styles of book illustration. The satire was sophisticated, yet immediately accessible to a large public varying in levels of literacy. In many of the plates the fantastic elements of the nursery rhyme were fused with tropes from graphic political satire. Cruikshank, whom Ruskin was to consider the greatest children's book illustrator of the nineteenth century, was uniquely qualified to combine the styles of the children's book wood engraving and the political etching.[50]

The frontispiece to *The Political House* (Fig. 37) shows the Duke of

[46] Cohn lists more than 360 woodcut designs which Cruikshank made for lottery puffs. Many of these pre-date *The Political House*. See Cohn, 1564–74, 1585–1606.

[47] The richest holdings of very early Cruikshank material, much of which he autographed in old age, are in the Widener Collection, in the Houghton Library, Harvard University. Also see Vogler, *Graphic Works of George Cruikshank*, 26–9.

[48] Smith describes Hone's nursery rhyme model as 'unconventional', and presents the pamphlet as a personal triumph for Hone in which he consciously forged a distinctive style: 'with the writing of *The Political House*, Hone reached his mature style and developed the genre for which he was most famous, a mock innocence which is reminiscent of Blake' (Smith, 165). As I have shown, the model was highly conventional. It is misleading to analyse Hone's satires in terms of the development of a mature style. Hone did not develop in this way. His appeal to popular taste is largely dependent on his ability to allow his parody to disappear into its models.

[49] Stoddart, *Slop's Shave at a Broken Hone*, 11, 20–6; *The Radical Chiefs*, 12–13; Hamilton, 58–70.

[50] John Ruskin, *Works*, ed. E. T. Cook and A. Wedderburn, 39 vols. (London, 1903–12), xv. 204, 222–3.

THE POLITICAL

HOUSE

THAT

JACK BUILT.

" A straw—thrown up to show which way the wind blows."

WITH THIRTEEN CUTS.

The Pen and the Sword.

FIG. 37.   George Cruikshank. Wood engraving. Frontispiece for *The Political House.* 1819.

Wellington in profile tossing his sword into one side of a huge pair of scales. Three documents bearing the names of recent pieces of repressive government legislation already fill this side of the balance. The combined mass of these is still less than that of a large quill, representing freedom of expression, which lies in the other side of the balance.

The overall style of the frontispiece with its thick, simple outlines, lack of background, and dramatic presentation of Wellington's gesture is adapted from the figures in the Harris booklets. The scales, however, have a complicated history in print satire. They were commonly used in Lutheran political prints and are one of the most frequent images in English print satire from the eighteenth century. The image of the scales defying the laws of gravity to describe good overpowering evil, and the image of documents weighed in the scales, were very frequent in Reformation satire. The two ideas were wittily combined in the title-page of *Ein schöns tractetlein von dem Götlichen und romischen Ablas* as early as 1525. In this print the figure of Christ holds a piece of paper representing the true remission of sin. He outweighs the combined mass of the Pope and a cardinal, who fly into the air. They clutch a bull of indulgence signed with the papal seal.[51] Cruikshank similarly includes labelled documents in his scales. The scales, as in the earlier print, are suspended mysteriously from above, a convention used to indicate that they are held by the hand of God.

Cruikshank's drawing of Wellington combines old graphic conventions, which present abstract ideas as concrete images, with the newer techniques of personal caricature. The cut is a simple graphic rendering of the old proverb 'The pen is mightier that the sword', which is given in abbreviated form below the picture. But by making the sword Wellington's and by having the pen stand for freedom of expression, the proverb is located in the political present. Wellington had been recently appointed to the Cabinet with a special responsibility to advise the government on the treatment of mobs.[52]

It is noticeable how many of the plates for *The Political House* dispense with caricature and consist of large drawings of one symbolic object. Many of the plates operate through a simple, old-fashioned didacticism. The eleventh plate consists of a large banner (Fig. 38), surrounded by a laurel wreath, with the word 'REFORM' inscribed on it in large capitals. The image invokes the great embroidered banners, carrying slogans such as 'Reform' and 'Universal Suffrage' which were carried to the mass reform meetings including Peterloo.[53] There is a similar didactic power in the first plate (Fig. 39) which shows a classical temple and three columns inscribed 'KINGS', 'LORDS', 'COMMONS', the three pillars of the state. The plate is a conventional embodiment of constitutional monarchy. The representation of the state as a symbolic structure was a commonplace in political prints going back as far as the 1750s. It is only a single detail which shifts the illustration into the realm of political satire— the portrait of Britannia on top of the temple has a liberty cap on her staff.[54]

The fifth plate shows a printing-press (Fig. 40). The press is drawn with great technical accuracy and attention to detail. It stands out

---

[51] The title-page is repr. and discussed in Scribner, 116.

[52] *DNB*, 'Wellesley'.

[53] Samuel Bamford, *Passages in the Life of a Radical* (Oxford, 1984), 146; Thompson, 679–80.

[54] For the use of the temple of state in political prints in England, see *BMC*, 3333, 4192, 5984, 6485, 8424, 9002, 12037, 13287. Patten, *George Cruikshank's Life*, 159, argues that the use of the Palladian temple and the Phrygian cap are to be interpreted as implying a specifically Whig theory of government.

FIG. 38. George Cruikshank. Wood engraving. Plate 'This WORD is the Watchword—' (D1ᵛ) for *The Political House.* 1819.

" A distant age asks where the fabric stood."
THIS IS THE HOUSE THAT JACK BUILT.

FIG. 39. George Cruikshank. Wood engraving. Plate 'THIS IS THE HOUSE THAT JACK BUILT' (A2ᵛ) for *The Political House.* 1819.

" Once enslaved, farewell!

. . .

Do I forebode impossible events,
And tremble at vain dreams? Heav'n grant I may!"

THIS IS

THE THING,

that, in spite of new Acts,
by Soldiers or Tax,
And attempts to restrain it,
Will *poison* the Vermin,
That plunder the Wealth,
That lay in the House,
That Jack built.

" A race obscene,
Spawn'd in the muddy beds of Nile, came forth,
Polluting Egypt : gardens, fields, and plains,
Were cover'd with the pest ;
The croaking nuisance lurk'd in every nook ;
Nor palaces, nor even chambers, 'scap'd ;
And the land stank—so num'rous was the fry.

THESE ARE

THE VERMIN

That Plunder the Wealth,
That lay in the House,
That Jack built.

FIG. 40. George Cruikshank. Wood engraving. Plates 'THE VERMIN' (B1ᵛ) and 'THE THING' (B2ʳ) for *The Political House*. 1819.

through its rigid impersonality and looks as if it had been transplanted from a technical manual on printing. The image had been used on the title-pages of sixteenth- and seventeenth-century books as a manifestation of the enlightening capacity of a free press. Perhaps the most spectacular example is the frontispiece to Prosper Marchand's *Histoire de l'origine et des premiers progrès de l'imprimerie*. The press is shown descending from the heavens in baroque splendour in a full-blown parody of the conventions of an assumption.[55]

Cruikshank creates a strikingly different effect. His draftsmanship concentrates on the functional beauty of the machine and forms a graphic contrast of great power with the plate on the facing page. This shows 'the vermin that plunder the wealth that lay in the house that Jack built'. It presents a series of stereotypical caricature drawings of state functionaries: soldiers, an aristocrat, a tax-gatherer, a lawyer, and a clerical magistrate. Their faces are debauched or cynical. They strike a series of poses. The short curving lines with which the forms and elaborate head-dresses of the figures are drawn contrast with the straight lines and rigid geometry of the press, which dwarfs them.

Cruikshank's ability to use the narrative potential of facing pages is also exhibited in the eighth and ninth plates (Fig. 41). The figure of the 'PUBLIC INFORMER' is a personal caricature of Robert Gifford. He was Attorney-General and widely disliked for his abuse of the power of *ex-officio* arrest in the context of seditious publishing. He is presented in strict profile. The heavy cross-hatching in this plate is technically close to that of chapbooks, and its coarseness provides a graphic expression of the nature of Gifford's fury. He stares straight out across the page at 'THE *REASONS* OF LAWLESS POWER, / That back the Public Informer' in the opposite plate. A group of four figures half Gifford's size stand round a cannon, which points out of the picture to the right of the reader. Three of these are soldiers, who have expressions of dismay or uncertainty. They are presented as unwilling accomplices of the state. The fourth figure is a caricature representation of Nadin of Manchester, a much-hated police official who is an embodiment of thick-skulled amenability.[56] Hone used noticeably short quotations from Cowper to accompany these plates. The two phrases relating to the plate 'THE *REASONS* OF LAWLESS

[55] This is discussed and the title-page repr. in E. L. Eisenstein, *The Printing Revolution in Early Modern Europe* (Cambridge, 1983), 216–19 and frontispiece.
[56] For these identifications, see Bowden, 252.

"Ruffians are abroad——"

"Leviathan is not so tamed."

THESE ARE

THE *REASONS* OF LAWLESS POWER

That back the Public Informer,

who

Would put down the *Thing*,

that, in spite of new Acts,

And attempts to restrain it,

by Soldiers or Tax,

Will *poison* the Vermin,

That plunder the Wealth,

That lay in the House,

That Jack built.

"The seals of office glitter in his eyes ;
He climbs, he pants, he grasps them——
To be a pest where he was useful once."

THIS IS

THE PUBLIC INFORMER,

who

Would put down the *Thing*,

that, in spite of new Acts,

And attempts to restrain it,

by Soldiers or Tax,

Will *poison* the Vermin, that plunder the Wealth,

That lay in the House, that Jack built.

FIG. 41. George Cruikshank. Wood engraving. Plates 'THE PUBLIC INFORMER'. (B2ᵛ) and 'THE *REASONS* OF LAWLESS POWER' (B3ᵛ) for *The Political House.* 1819.

POWER' have an aphoristic intensity: 'Ruffians are abroad—/ Leviathan is not so tamed'. Leviathan, Hobbes's metaphor for the organism of political society, is presented as something powerfully alive outside government control.

Part of the effectiveness of Hone and Cruikshank's parody lies in the way text and illustrations constantly enforce and develop each other while never moving too far away from the conventions of the nursery rhyme book. The parodic version of the rhyme is considerably longer than the original, running to forty-four lines instead of eleven. The opening six sections, however, are closely modelled on both the rhyme and the format of Harris's book. Harris's edition of *The House that Jack Built* had one illustration for each new line in the verse. Hone follows this convention for the first six plates, and for the first four plates the rhyme parody also follows the original closely in both length and metre.

It is only with the introduction of the Prince Regent in the fifth plate that the verse departs radically from the structure of the source. Hone did, however, retain two important line-endings from his model. They are ironically transformed in the first couplet. 'This is THE MAN all shaven and shorn, / All cover'd with Orders—and all forlorn'. 'Shaven and shorn' in the original refers to the humility of 'the priest all shaven and shorn'. Hone applies it to the notorious vanity of the Prince Regent, who by this time sported huge sideburns, perukes, and false curls. The next couplet takes up the theme, 'THE DANDY OF SIXTY, who bows with a grace / And has *taste* in wigs, collars, cuirasses and lace'. The other line-ending, 'all forlorn', has the Regent take the place of 'the maiden all forlorn' of the original. Cruikshank faithfully presents the details of Hone's text. The Regent is 'all covered with orders' and wearing a huge collar, an ornamental cuirass, and a wig. The whole paraphernalia of royal regalia and heraldic device is sent up. Slipped in among the orders hanging from the enormous royal girth is a corkscrew. The fleur-de-lis, traditional emblem of the Prince of Wales, is changed into three enormous peacock's feathers symbolizing pride. The elaborate uniform is a swipe at the Regent's well-known delight in designing preposterous military outfits for himself and his guards. His hopeless vanity is taken up in the details—the gloves and breeches that cover the fat hands and legs are skin-tight.[57]

The seventh plate, which follows directly on from the Prince

[57] Hibbert, *George IV*, 233–4; Bryant, *The Age of Elegance*, 126.

Regent, uses another of the memorable catch-phrases from the original rhyme but reincorporates it to devastating effect. The 'man all tattered and torn' becomes 'the people all tattered and torn'. The open vowel of the end rhyme is taken up in the succeeding lines to create an effect of percussive repetition:

> These are
> THE PEOPLE
> all tatter'd and torn,
> Who curse the day
> wherein they were born,
> On account of Taxation
> too great to be borne,
> And pray for relief,
> from night to morn;
> Who, in vain, Petition
> in every form,
> Who, peaceably Meeting
> to ask for Reform
> Were sabred by Yeomanry Cavalry
> who,
> Were thank'd by THE MAN,
> all shaven and shorn
>
> (*The Political House*, B2^v–B3^r)

The lines referring to the Regent have their irony resharpened as they now run into this articulation of mass suffering. Most damning of all is the reference to the King's letter of thanks to the cavalry after the Peterloo massacre. The general social sufferings of the poor are suddenly lodged in a precise political present. This is the only specific reference to the massacre in the poem. Cruikshank graphically complements the bleak message of the verse by drawing 'the people all tattered and torn' in a style approaching documentary realism. The gestures of the hands of the three adults are emphatically undemonstrative. They appear wrapped in an intense static misery and are oblivious to the scene of carnage behind them.

The eighth plate makes yet another sudden stylistic break from its predecessor (Fig. 42). It shows three members of the Cabinet, Sidmouth, Canning, and Castlereagh. The elements of exaggeration in the faces of Canning and Castlereagh are very slight. Castlereagh grins and gestures jauntily to Canning. He holds a scourge lightly in his other hand, which is reversed and placed with affected delicacy

FIG. 42.   George Cruikshank. Wood engraving. Plate 'This is THE DOCTOR'
(C1ᵛ) for *The Political House.* 1819.

on his hip. His sense of well-being and of urbane disconcern is damning, coming after the representation of suffering in the last plate.
He is dressed in the height of fashion, wearing the loose high-
waisted trousers, the tight-waisted velvet jacket, and the excessively
pointed shoes of the Regency dandy. Canning is shown striking an
arrogant and assertive pose and his face is not caricatured at all.
Sidmouth on the far left is presented in full-blown caricature. He is
drawn with much coarser lines and his face is contorted in an expression of senile concentration.

The text complements the drawings. The quotations from
Cowper are again very terse but are prefixed by the names which
Hone had previously applied to his enemies in *The Reformist's Register*:

THE DOCTOR 'At his last gasp—as if with opium drugged.'
DERRY—DOWN TRIANGLE 'He that sold his country.'
THE SPOUTER OF FROTH 'With merry descants on a nations woes—There is
a public mischief in his mirth.'

From the concentrated statement of the condition of the people which formed the subject of the previous accumulation, Hone has moved into a mode of open name-calling, which continues with almost uncontrolled fury:

> This is THE DOCTOR
>> of *Circular* fame,
> A Driv'ller, a Bigot, a Knave
>> without shame:
> And *that's* DERRY DOWN TRIANGLE
>> by name
> From the Land of mis-rule
>> and half-hanging, and flame:
> And *that* is THE SPOUTER OF FROTH
>> BY THE HOUR,
> The worthless colleague
>> of their infamous power;
> Who dubb'd *him* 'the Doctor'
>> whom now he calls 'brother',
> And, to get at his Place,
>> took a shot at the other;
>
> (*The Political House*, B3ᵛ–B4ʳ)

It is as if Hone is not only writing a children's rhyme but writing as a child himself. The taunting, jeering tone and the simple rudeness are reminiscent of the language of the playground. The verse shows Hone's ability to exploit the advantages which the nursery rhyme model provides. The tone of committed but somehow trivial hatred which he adopts here could not function in a context of conventional adult satire. As part of a children's rhyme it is both funny and formally appropriate. Name-calling is one of the oldest and purest forms of satire. Name magic is a common way of attacking an enemy in primitive societies. R. C. Elliott, talking of primitive satiric devices, states that 'the name is the man, and when it is entrapped in the mysterious bonds of a magical verse, the man himself is entrapped'. The creation of secret names for an enemy is another ancient form of satire, which gives the writer power over his victim.[58]

Despite the fact that by the beginning of the nineteenth century the primitive echoes of such name magic would have been remote there was, and is, one area where these primitive and violent forms of satire survived. Douglas Newton states that 'the world fraternity

---

[58] Elliott, *Satire and Magic*, 39.

of children is the greatest of savage tribes, and the only one which shows no signs of dying out'. The Opies' study of child culture reveals that nicknaming is still a central and complicated part of children's rituals and one of the central devices for shaming or ostracizing someone who is either feared or disliked.[59] The nursery rhyme model legitimizes Hone's use of what is, quite literally, childish abuse. Hone's armoury of frivolous and exuberant nicknames was widely effective. Most of the names he used, and many of them he invented as well as popularized, stuck to their targets. They were commonly used in prints and were taken up in Thomas Wooler and Richard Carlile's publications, and in the ultra-radical journals such as *The Gorgon* and *The Medusa*.

Name-calling was something of a stylistic stronghold for the radicals. Hazlitt speaks of Cobbett's genius for inventing insulting nicknames as one of the central features of his prose: 'if anything is ever quoted from him, it is an epithet of abuse or a nickname. He is an excellent hand at invention in that way, and has "damnable iteration in him".'[60] Nicknaming was also a central element in the ribald satiric world of the ultra-radical tavern debating societies. The Spenceans not only attacked authority figures through the use of stock nicknames but ridiculed their political enemies by giving each other nicknames charged with sarcasm. The blaspheming mulatto preacher and brothel-keeper Robert Wedderburn was called 'Black Prince', Thomas Preston 'Bishop', John Cannon 'Brown Friar', and so on.[61]

Hone's attack combines an apparently simple savagery of expression with telling details relating to the pasts of the politicians. 'Derry-Down Triangle' refers to Castlereagh's Irish background and to his rumoured sanction of torture while he was Foreign Minister. The claim that Canning first gave Sidmouth the nickname 'the Doctor' is true. Canning, who in his early years had been a very active and clever political parodist, had written a cruel satire at the expense of Sidmouth ridiculing his father's humble past as a country doctor, and insulting him quite outrageously. Lord Folkestone quoted the parody to the House of Commons after Canning had, on a later occasion, eulogized the talents of Sidmouth to the House. Hone took

[59] Quoted in Iona and Peter Opie, *The Lore and Language of Schoolchildren* (Oxford, 1959), 2.

[60] William Hazlitt, *The Complete Works of William Hazlitt*, 21 vols. Bungay, 1930–4, viii. 51.

[61] McCalman, *Radical Underworld*, 150.

up the episode and quoted the parody in full, accompanied by a Cruikshank woodcut, at the end of his pamphlet *The Man in the Moon*. The reference to the 'shot' is also based on fact, for Canning and Castlereagh had previously fought a duel.[62]

The Political House ends with a four-page section which stands as a separate poem. Still written in the metre of the nursery rhyme it does not incorporate any of the earlier accumulations. It attacks the practice of clergymen becoming magistrates. In the title woodcut (Fig. 43) Cruikshank again takes up an image with a complicated history in satiric iconography. The 'Janus head' can be traced back in political prints to Lutheran satires. It remained popular in eighteenth-century print satire and there are many prints satirizing the Fox–North coalition of 1783 which use devices of facial conjunction.[63]

There are also many eighteenth-century prints which present the clergy as double-headed or two-faced. One of these is a source for Cruikshank's cut. *The British Janus* (Fig. 44) shows a figure which is half bishop and half Puritan in a pulpit. It is an attack on Low-Churchmen and ridicules their professed disinterest in worldly matters. The box in which the figure is placed, the half-length fusion of the bodies, and the use of the full profile are all taken up in the Cruikshank print.

The proximity of the two prints is surprising when the genesis of Cruikshank's cut is considered. Early in December 1818 he produced a working drawing and a print from this drawing which deal with the same subject-matter as the later woodcut. The transformation of print to woodcut provides an unusual opportunity to see the processes of simplification and intensification which Cruikshank's style underwent as he shifted from the mode of the political etching to the woodcuts for *The Political House*.

The etching *Preachee and Floggy too!* (Fig. 45) shows two versions of the same figure standing back to back. One represents a magistrate and the other a clergyman. Both figures are surrounded by a wealth of local detail, including two crowd scenes representing a church

---

[62] For Castlereagh and torture, see *Hone's Reformist's Register and Weekly Commentary*, 26 (July 1817), 814–18. For Lord Folkestone's reading of the Canning parody and a detailed account of the complicated bibliographic background to Hone's quotation of it, see Bowden, 304, 348–9. For other radical treatments of the Canning–Castlereagh duel, see *BMC*, nos. 11370, 11371, and 13520, and *The Constitutional Apple Pie*, pl. 3.

[63] See above, p. 80.

THE CLERICAL MAGISTRATE.

FIG. 43. George Cruikshank. Wood engraving. Plate 'THE CLERICAL MAGISTRATE' (D3ʳ) for *The Political House.* 1819.

FIG. 44. Anon. Engraving. *The British Janus.* 1709.

FIG. 45. George Cruikshank. Coloured etching. *Preachee and Floggy too!* 1819.

congregation and prisoners standing in the dock. The woodcut is simply drawn and fuses the two figures into a single monster, the heads seamlessly conjoined much in the manner of Goya's *Disparate Desorendo*. The two-headed human was still a common feature in the freak-shows of the Regency and this print carries the association. The delicate curves of the etching disappear and the profiles are given in small, chunky lines. The two halves perform in rigorous symmetry. The gestures emphasize the surrounding symbols. A single box encloses both halves of the figure, and this containment makes the figure more monstrous.

Although the satire is general, it also has a specific application. The cleric's words, 'Some of you Reformers ought to be hanged, and some of you are sure to be hanged, the rope is already around your necks', are derived from a notorious address by Ethelstone, the magistrate who read the Riot Act at the Peterloo massacre.[64] Hone takes up the theme of Ethelstone's part in the massacre in the lines: 'If the People were legally Meeting / in quiet, / Would pronounce it decidedly—*sec. Stat.*—/ a Riot, / And order the Soldiers / "to aid and assist", / That is—Kill the helpless, / Who cannot resist' (*The Political House*, 4D^r).

Taken as a whole the plates for *The Political House* exhibit stylistic diversity. Their mass appeal was based as much upon their graphic traditionalism as their novelty. Many of the plates are much closer to the popular traditions of emblem literature than they are to the more naturalistically inclined conventions of the political etching. Even those which use individual caricature frequently include emblematic elements. By the end of the eighteenth century emblem books still flourished but in simplified popular forms with a special emphasis on the children's book market. As early as the end of the seventeenth century the emblem tradition had shifted from high to low areas of the publishing market. Rosemary Freeman summarizes the situation at this time, stating 'there was, in fact, still scope for devotional emblems, for nursery emblems and for emblems as the lightest of entertainments; but there was no longer any place for emblems in the main course of literature.[65] However, when considering the use of emblems in political print satires, the situation is greatly complicated by the fact that ancient emblematic devices had survived in prints in quite pure forms at the same time that the new styles of personal caricature were being developed.

[64] Donald Read, *Peterloo: The Massacre and its Background* (Manchester, 1958), 77.
[65] Rosemary Freeman, *English Emblem Books* (London, 1948), 206.

By the early nineteenth century the publishing environment which existed for prints and illustrated pamphlets possessed a rich potential for the combination of new and old styles of graphic satire, and many of the satires which Gillray and Cruikshank produced are capable of amalgamating caricature and symbolism with great sophistication. E. H. Gombrich has described the complicated tensions which could be created by the fusion of styles. He argues that the shift from the Middle Ages, 'when artistic conventions were entirely based on the symbolic use of images', to 'the victory of a realistic conception of art' from the fifteenth to eighteenth centuries did not occur in the area of popular visual satire. He concludes:

To a public accustomed to see images as representations of a visual reality, the mere juxtaposition of disconnected symbols [in satirical prints] produces a disquieting paradox, in need of resolution. Thus, while the medieval idiom and medieval motifs lived on in satirical broadsheets and prints with remarkable tenacity, we also witness continual efforts to rationalize and justify this antiquated language and to reconcile it with realistic conventions.[66]

Gombrich perhaps underestimates the late eighteenth- and early nineteenth-century capacity to read parallel visual conventions simultaneously yet separately. In the prints of Cruikshank the complicated mixtures of style and convention create effects of layering. These different levels do not confuse or negate each other; the effect is rather one of enrichment and dynamic tension. Caricature is constantly take into a wider iconographic environment. The pamphlet form allowed for extended commentary on the illustrations in a way that was not possible in single-sheet print satire. This frequently allowed Hone and Cruikshank to reapply the didactic tradition of the emblem books to political caricature. This process, which began in *The Political House*, was taken much further in later pamphlets. The 'PUBLICATION' plate and its commentary in *The Queen's Matrimonial Ladder* (Fig. 46), for example, fuse three distinct graphic traditions: the seventeenth-century emblem book, seventeenth-century anti-papist propaganda based on the Gunpowder Plot, and the eighteenth-century print satires which grew out of the earlier propaganda.

In 1621 Samuel Ward produced his influential anti-Spanish and anti-papist satire *The Double Deliveraunce* (*BMC*, no. 41) showing, side

---

[66] E. H. Gombrich, 'Imagery and Art in the Romantic Period', in *Meditations on a Hobby Horse*, 122.

FIG. 46.　George Cruikshank. Wood engraving. Plate 'PUBLICATION' (C1ᵛ)
for *The Queen's Matrimonial Ladder*. 1820.

by side, the destruction of the Armada by storm in 1588 and Guy
Fawkes entering the cellars of the Houses of Parliament. He wears a
steeple hat, carries a dark lanthorn, and is detected by the irradiated
eye of God. This image of Fawkes was immediately taken up in
countless seventeenth-century print versions and was a standard element in the anti-papist medley prints showing *Popish Plots and Treasons
from the Beginning of the Reign of Queen Elizabeth* (*BMC*, no. 13). It was then
absorbed into numerous satiric prints in the eighteenth century which
showed various politicians, Fox's name making him a favourite, in the

F<small>IG</small>. 47. Samuel Ward. Engraving, detail. *The Double Deliveraunce.* 1621.

guise of Fawkes, and which take up the major narrative and compositional details of Ward's original.[67]

The most elaborate of these was a late Gillray of 1807, *The PILLAR of THE CONSTITUTION* (*BMC*, no. 10738) which showed the entire Opposition converted into Fawkes and which substituted the face of George III for the eye of God. Cruikshank's woodcut takes up the tradition with outrageous boldness. Queen Caroline is substituted for the King, her house, inscribed 'Albion Life Assurance', replaces the Houses of Parliament. The gunpowder barrels make way for an enormous sack—the notorious green bag supposed to contain evidence of the Queen's infidelities—and the eye of God frames an image of a printing-press. Most damning of all, the Regent, typically caricatured, is turned into a ludicrous Guy Fawkes accompanied by a blind, lame, poxed Cupid. The future King is converted into the most notorious icon of papist anti-constitutionalism, but even in this guise his celebrated vanity is cruelly brought out: his high-heeled cavalier boots have enormous turndowns and he sports a ruff and dainty short cloak.

Hone's text, written in the couplet style of the popular seventeenth-century emblem books, carefully explains the iconography:

> As yon bright orb, that vivifies our ball,
> Sees through our system, and illumines all;
> So, sees and shines, our MORAL SUN, THE PRESS,
> Alike to vivify the mind, and bless . . .
> Sees Him, for whom they work the treacherous task . . .
> Fat, fifty-eight, and frisky, still a beau,
> Grasping a half-made match, by *Leech*-light go;
> Led by a passion, prurient, blind and batter'd,
> Lame, bloated, pointless, flameless, age'd and shatter'd,
> Creeping, like Guy Fawkes, to blow up his wife,
> Whom, spurn'd in youth, he dogs in after-life.

The verse deftly moves from an assumed dignity and latinate archaism—'yon bright orb', 'vivifies', 'illumines'—which describe the press, to the blunt piling-up of adjectives—'Lame, bloated, pointless, flameless, age'd and shatter'd'—used to describe Cupid,

[67] See *BMC*, no. 10739, *Guy Faux and His Treason*: no. 6389, *Guy Vaux or F——Blowing up the P——t House*. For other treatments of the Guy Fawkes theme, see *BMC*, nos. 7862, 8424, 10738, 10739, 12103.

FIG. 48. James Gillray. Etching. *The PILLAR of THE CONSTITUTION*. 1807.

the personification of the King's moral decrepitude.[68] *The Queen's Matrimonial Ladder* was a triumphant refinement of the stylistic and semiotic resources which *The Political House* had opened up.

The Political House changed the face of popular pamphlet satire. Its format and style of illustration were quickly and generally adopted. It led to a string of direct imitations from 1819 to 1820 and a further spate followed from 1830 to 1832.[69] The loyalist press, dismayed at the sudden success of Hone's pamphlets, promptly brought out several imitations. None of these were popular and an analysis of the reasons behind their failure explains the success of the radical satire that inspired them. *The Political House* was immune against loyalist satiric appropriation. A children's rhyme provides the framework for a satire which incorporates primitive taunts and a style of illustration associated with the rude humour and didacticism of children's books. It attacks figures who were both powerful and famous, or, in 1819, infamous. It purports to give an antidote to the official version of what the King and his Cabinet constitute, to present the shabby reality behind the façade of constitutional monarchy. It is a satire of reduction which is dependent for its success on the elevated social and political status of its targets.

Hone's pamphlets showed the Regent as a fat, overgrown child guided by his sensual appetites and a Cabinet of corrupt and hypocritical self-seekers. The personal caricature in *The Political House* is exclusively devoted to the Regent, the Cabinet, and official functionaries. Cruikshank's images of these figures fed off the various interpretations and graphic formulas which caricaturists had applied to them over the preceding two decades. Cruikshank inherited the Regent as an entity in caricature in much the same way that he inherited Gillray's Napoleon with his huge boots and hat, dwarfish proportions, and perpetual frenzies. Cruikshank blew up, aged, and decked out the decaying Regent as he saw fit. The great mutton chop sideboards, the belly, and the elaborate thigh-length boots had become as much part of his personal iconography as the fleur-de-lis.

Conversely, when it came to portraying radicalism in *The Political*

---

[68] The metric variation and skill of Hone's text to *The Queen's Matrimonial Ladder* continues to be misrepresented. Patten, *George Cruikshank's Life*, 178, states 'Hone's verses, while sometimes imitating the scansion of *The Political House*, are original, though of no distinction.'

[69] The complicated bibliography of the pamphlet imitations of *The Political House* and of all Hone's major pamphlets is fully dealt with in Bowden, 257–76, 451–73, 540–55.

House it is done, almost exclusively, through symbolism. The aims and ideals of the radicals are consequently abstracted. The freedom of the press is shown as an enormous printing-press, constitutional reform as a temple surmounted by a cap of liberty, and the right to trial by jury as a box containing the Bill of Rights. The only illustration of humans sympathetic to the radical cause is the anonymous group 'the people all tattered and torn' of the seventh plate. The radical leaders are conspicuously absent.

When they attempted to appropriate the form the loyalists were hamstrung. They were left with two options: to attempt to change the image of the Regent and Cabinet and to try to ridicule the radical leaders by using caricature and lampoon. The first option failed because the form of both the verse and the illustration for *The Political House* were inappropriate as a framework for aggrandizement. The loyalists had to try to present the Regent and Cabinet as astute and benevolent leaders guiding the ship of state and looking after the interests of the nation. They inherited a satiric vehicle which they attempted, inappropriately, to use as a basis for unironic eulogy. The second option failed because it placed the radical leaders in the position occupied in Hone's satire by the loyalist leaders, the substitution having the effect of elevation. The radical leaders, with the exception of gentlemen radicals such as Burdette and Brougham, were nothing like as well known in caricature as the loyalists.

Loyalist propaganda also suffered from its inability to find an equivalent partnership to that of Hone and Cruikshank. The level of skill in the loyalist pamphlets was generally very low, the interaction of text and illustration minimal. It was only in pamphlets such as *The Radical Ladder* or *The Men in the Moon; or, The Devil to Pay*, which Cruikshank illustrated himself for the loyalist camp, that the caricatures of radicals, including on several occasions Hone himself, are recognizable. Cruikshank, throughout the period of his collaboration with Hone, would occasionally produce work for the loyalist press. Cruikshank's motives for doing this have never been satisfactorily explained. He received payment from representatives of the Regent and Cabinet, but there is no evidence that he ever went as far as accepting a government pension, as Gillray had before him. Maybe the explanation for Cruikshank's ambivalence lay in a desire to keep his satiric options open, or in a healthy belief that both sides had their faults and their villains. The majority of the satire he produced from 1816 to 1822 *was* for the radical cause, but Cruikshank undoubtedly enjoyed the creative process of playing the radicals and loyalists off against each other. Some of the work he produced during the Caroline affair attacking the radicals and celebrating the Regent is of undisputed force and quality, and the best of it invariably singles out Hone himself. The 1820 print *CORIOLANUS addressing the PLEBEIANS* (Fig. 49) places Hone at the front of the crowd of radicals who confront the heroically defiant Regent. Hone is identified through accurate caricature and beyond this by the two clubs he bears inscribed 'Parody' and 'Man in the Moon—House that Jack Built'. He is alone among the radicals in adopting a stance of dignified assertiveness.

On other occasions Cruikshank was not so generous to his parodic mentor. The frontispiece to the otherwise tedious pamphlet published by the loyalist Association *The radical ladder; or, Hone's political ladder and his Non Me Ricordo explained and applied* (Fig. 50) took the form of a superb variation on Cruikshank's earlier design for the frontispiece to Hone's *The Queen's Matrimonial Ladder*. The matrimonial ladder is now loaded on each rung with bloodthirsty radicals. Sporting the *bonnet rouge* they creep up, hidden beneath Caroline's flowing cloak. This image plays on the time-honoured graphic metaphor of 'petticoat government'. Hone, again bearing a club, is shown mounting the second rung. The Queen, precariously perched atop the ladder, and about to fall to her ruin past rungs marked 'revolution', 'anarchy', and 'ruin', bears a flaming torch and attempts to fire a Bible and emblazoned crown which rest on top of a pillar marked 'king', 'lords', and 'commons'. Perhaps the ultimate challenge and pleasure for the graphic parodist was to be found in parodying his own parody.

When unable to command the talents of Cruikshank as an illustrator for their publications the loyalists were hamstrung. The attribution of characters in publications such as *The Real or Constitutional House that Jack Built* or *The Loyal Man in the Moon* is done laboriously through labelling or through crude graphic signification. Thomas Wooler, for example, nicknamed after his periodical *The Black Dwarf*, is invariably shown as a tiny figure with blacked-out face.

The illustrations in *The Constitutional House that Jack Built* are stiff and clumsy. The plates are frequently overcrowded and their symbolism overdeveloped. The depiction of Cobbett in the eighth plate

FIG. 49. George Cruikshank. Coloured etching. *CORIOLANUS addressing the PLEBEIANS.* 1820.

The RADICAL LADDER

Fig 50. George Cruikshank. Wood engraving. Plate 'The RADICAL LADDER', frontispiece for *The Radical Ladder; or, Hone's Non Mi Ricordo Explained and Applied.* 1820.

appears no closer to caricature than those of the Prince Regent or Pitt. Hone's economic verse is replaced by over-excited and rambling accounts which attempt to trace the origins of radicalism in Whig support for the French Revolution. In place of Hone's sharp quotations from *The Task*, *The Constitutional House* uses long and confused quotations from a variety of sources. In its grim self-righteousness the publication is almost completely humourless. This is a common failing in the loyalist imitations of the Hone pamphlets. They do not capture the combination of fantasy, frivolity, and rage which underpins the originals. This is hardly surprising given that the didactic impulse behind loyalist propaganda was one of reassurance. It is hard to work up a tone of savage indignation when one's basic message is to tell the people that, despite appearances, they are really living in an ideal state.

The failure of the imitations is also a result of their stylistic and emotional rigidity. It was the diversity of both Hone and Cruikshank as parodists which gave their pamphlets such protean power. They took up the ebullience and simple energy of their nursery rhyme models and never lost sight of the primitive savagery of children's own modes of satire. I said earlier that Hone sometimes wrote as if he were himself a child and the same may be said of Cruikshank as a draughtsman. He is capable of assuming a coarse and clumsy style. In political caricature 'bad' drawing can be used as part of the satiric armoury. Primitive humour, or the reduction of adults to children, can be graphically complemented by the adoption of an appropriately reduced style. Sometimes utter crudity in form and content is the only appropriate response: Max Lieberman reacted to a pompous man with the aside—'a face like his I can piss into snow'. It is only the great draughtsmen who attain a level of mastery which allows for internal stylistic parody: Gillray offers the only other example in Regency caricature.[70] In the work which Cruikshank did for Hone the movement between different styles of representation is part and parcel of the satiric method.

---

[70] Lieberman, quoted in Kris, *Psychoanalytic Explorations in Art*, 192. Gillray could adopt a crude, consciously juvenile style at will. The print of June 1706 *Billy Playing Johnny a Dirty Trick* (*BMC*, no. 8812) is a good example.

CONCLUSION
Satire, Radicalism, and Radical Romanticism

What makes a Libel?
A Fable.
In *Aesop's* new made World of Wit,
Where Beasts could talk, and read, and write,
And say and do as he thought fit;
A certain fellow thought himself abus'd,
And represented by an *Ass*
And *Aesop* to the Judge Accus'd
That he defamed was.

Friend, quoth the Judge, How do you know,
Whether you are defamed or no?
How can you prove that he must mean
You, rather than another Man?
Sir, quoth the Man it needs must be,
All Circumstances so agree,
And all the neighbours say 'tis Me
That's somewhat quoth the Judge, indeed;
But let this matter pass,
Since 'twas not *Aesop* 'tis agreed
But *Application* made the *Ass*!   (*PP* i.53)

Why study the works of extreme radical satirists in the Romantic? One answer lies in Marilyn Butler's statement 'Satire is a mode with which we do not as a rule associate the Romantic period'.[1] There has been a recent growth of interest in the variety and pervasiveness of satire at this time. Several books have uncovered connections between popular radical satire and the work of certain figures

[1] Marilyn Butler, 'Satire and the Images of Self in the Romantic Period: The Long Tradition of Hazlitt's *Liber Amoris*', in Claude Rawson (ed.), *English Satire and the Satiric Tradition* (Oxford, 1984), 209. Butler has done more than most to rectify this situation.

normally considered in terms of the literary mainstream.[2] This book can be used to develop work in this field. Byron and Shelley are particularly ripe for further analysis.

Shelley's attempts to write popular political satires directed at the Liverpool administration were frequently influenced by and modelled upon forms which had been taken up by extreme popular radical propagandists since the 1790s. His *A New National Anthem* addressed to 'Queen Liberty' of 1819 operates within a tradition of extreme radical appropriations of the national anthem which began in the mid-1790s. In 1793 Eaton had published *A New Song* in the form of a parodic national anthem celebrating Thomas Paine and singing the praises of Liberty in proto-Shelleian vein. In the same year Thomas Spence wrote a parodic national anthem in his journal *Pig's Meat* which anticipates the libertarian apocalypse of Shelley's conclusion with a vision of the Spencean Jubilee.[3]

In 1812 Shelley wrote and had published as a broadside for popular distribution *The Devil's Walk*. This social and political satire featuring a devil's tour through England was an early working of a device which Shelley was to develop at length and far more ironically in *Peter Bell the Third*. The earlier poem was written in imitation of Southey and Coleridge's *The Devil's Walk* of 1799, which in its turn is a late offshoot from the popular late eighteenth-century diabolical satires inspired by William Combe's *Diaboliad* and *The Devil Upon Two Sticks in England*. Shelley's version goes further than the generalized attacks upon corruption in Coleridge and Southey's poem. Shelley's description of the Regent mercilessly battens in on his corpulence to create a verse description of his bloated caricature image as it appeared in prints and satires throughout the second decade of the nineteenth century:

---

[2] Marilyn Butler's *Peacock Displayed* (London, 1979) and *Romantics, Rebels, and Reactionaries* indicated the critical latitude required if we are to understand the literary mechanisms of a society which could throw up, simultaneously, the satiric diversity of Byron, Gillray, Jane Austen, Blake, and Peacock. Bate's *Shakespearian Constitutions* revealed the widespread popularity of Shakespearian parody, and of the different publishing levels at which it operated, in the late 18th and early 19th cents. Vincent Caretta's *George III and the Satirists from Hogarth to Byron* (Athens, Ga., 1990) gives a useful sense of the thematic intermixture of verse and print satires 1780–1820, although the book is unbalanced. Caretta is unaware of the existence of extreme radical satire in his period, and so misses most of the fun. His index finds no space for the names of Spence, Eaton, Wooler, Hone, or Cobbett! Jon Mee's *Dangerous Enthusiasm* has examined Blake's Continent poems in terms of their methodological and intellectual links with the political satires of extreme radicals and the writings of religious enthusiasts in the 1790s.

[3] Shelley, *Poetical Works*, 574; *PP* ii. 287; *PM* i. 42–3.

Fat as the Prince's maudlin brain
Which, addled by some gilded toy,
Tired, gives his sweetmeat, and again
Cried for it, like a humoured boy.

For he is fat,—his waistcoat gay
When strained upon a levee day,
Scarce meets across his princely paunch;
And pantaloons are like half-moons
Upon each brawny haunch.[4]

The references to the Prince as a pampered boy and spoilt brat mirror standard images in the political caricatures of the day.[5] Shelley was not alone in seeing the potential of Southey and Coleridge's original as a vehicle for violent political satire. Byron was to attempt his own parody of the poem *The Devil's Drive: An Unfinished Rhapsody*. *The Devil's Walk* was also subsequently taken up in both loyalist and radical journals and a version of it attacking the loyalist Constitutional Association was written by Hone for his *Slap at Slop* in 1821. *The Devil's Walk* indicates the existence of a common currency for political satire that cut across literary and political barriers and appealed to loyalists, radicals, and major romantic poets alike.[6]

Shelley's attempt to write a popular parodic drama, *Swellfoot the Tyrant*, as a contribution to the Queen Caroline propaganda is closely related to the productions of the pamphlet, journal, and print satirists of the day. It was published anonymously for distribution during the crisis and then withdrawn because the Society for the Suppression of Vice threatened prosecution. Swellfoot almost obsessively puns on and plays with the conflation of the common people with pigs. This was one of the most constant and celebratory themes in radical satire from the early 1790s when satirists first began the delighted exploitation of Burke's reference to the 'swinish multitude'.[7] The piece teems with references to the nicknames and symbols which the scandal had generated in the prints and popular press. Even the form of Shelley's piece was fashionable, for the Queen's case had given rise to several other parodic dramas. A close

[4] Shelley, *Poetical Works*, 879.
[5] See *BMC*, no. 13764, *The Cradle Hymn*; no. 13843, *The Royal Cot*.
[6] Byron, *The Complete Poetical Works*, ed. Jerome McGann (Oxford, 1980), iii. 95; Hone, *A Slap at Slop*, 2^r.
[7] For the mass of porcine publications, see Smith, 79–85.

study of Shelley's only attempt to write an extended dramatic satire in relation to pro-Caroline propaganda is long overdue.[8]

The lines between Shelley's 'serious' works and the political parodies such as *Peter Bell the Third* or *Swellfoot* cannot always be easily drawn. *The Sensitive Plant*, for example, has now been enshrined as a distinguished example of what Donald Davie designated Shelley's urbane style.[9] The poem universalizes political issues in a way which the more explicit political parodies do not, yet it has not been observed that, written in 1819, it is composed in one of the most politicized forms of the day, the parodic fable.

The first five numbers of Eaton's journal *Politics for People* carried satiric political fables on the front page, and the journal as a whole is packed with them. They were favoured in radical broadsheet satire and feature in government evidence during the 1794 treason trials and remained a staple in the radical journals of the Peterloo period.[10] Dodsley's popular edition of Aesop was a best seller for fifty years after its publication in 1761. His introductory essay on fable, which Hone intended to quote ironically in his *History of Parody*, strenuously attempts to lay down rules which will uphold the hierarchical linguistic and social theory of the late eighteenth-century literary establishment: 'the language of the fable must rise and fall in conformity to the subject. A Lion when introduced in his regal capacity must hold discourse in a strain somewhat more elevated than a country Mouse.'[11]

Yet Dodsley's strictures and warnings against allowing a plain style to become vulgar only served to highlight the form's potential as a vehicle for radical satire. Eaton, Spence, and Wooler's parodic fables delight in ringing the changes: lions talk coarsely, behave tyrannically, and come to a sticky end, a splendid game-cock is beheaded and turns out to be 'a common tame scratch-dunghill pullet', an animated goitre

---

[8] Some elementary but useful spadework was done as long ago as the 1920s by N. I. White in his 'Shelley's *Swellfoot the Tyrant* in relation to Contemporary Political Satires', *PMLA* 36 (1921), 332–46. Carl Woodring, *Politics in English Romantic Poetry* (Cambridge, Mass., 1970), 269–73, makes no attempt at a detailed reading of *Swellfoot* in the context of Carolingian propaganda and concludes with the surprising assertion that '*Swellfoot* will never displace *The Rape of the Lock*, but there is fun in it.'

[9] Donald Davie, *The Purity of Diction in English Verse* (London, 1967), 146–56.

[10] See *PP* i. 25, 53, 69, 80–4; ii. 10–11. *BD* 23, (1817), 360–1; 27 (1817), 431–2; 39 (1817), 653–4; 6 (1818), 89–90; 22 (1818), 352. *A Complete Collection of State Trials*, xxiv (1818), 682–6.

[11] R. Dodsley, *Select Fables of Aesop and Other Fabulists* (London, 1781), p. lix.

sets himself up in fabular opposition to the healthy body.[12] Frequently the political fable will be accompanied by a parodic explanation disclaiming and ironically enforcing the political content. Eaton even wrote a fable celebrating the ability of fables to avoid libel prosecutions, which is quoted in full as the heading to this Conclusion.

A reading of *The Sensitive Plant* that placed it in the context of the radical appropriation of the fable would reveal Shelley's finger to have been firmly on the pulse of radical satire and parody yet again. Shelley was formally ambitious in ways that frequently link him with extreme radical journals and the gutter press. Why his attempts to write for this market were uniformly unsuccessful in publishing terms remains to be answered.

Byron might be considered in terms of a similar set of concerns. *Don Juan* is a parodic epic which the radical publishing environment responded to with impassioned alacrity. Apart from the plagiarisms of the anonymous first two cantos by radical publishers there were productions such as Hone's *Don Juan, Canto the Third!*, a fully fledged Byronic forgery which presents Don Juan doing the rounds of the radical London pressmen.

Byron's poem is full of minor parodies of forms long established as favourites in radical political satire. His suppressed dedication to the First Canto, reportedly hawked about the streets of London as a ballad, included an attack on the political apostasy of the Lakers in the form of an elaborate parody of *Sing a Song of Sixpence*. This nursery rhyme had already been absorbed into anti-state print satire and was to be used repeatedly by radicals during the Queen Caroline affair.[13] The First Canto of *Don Juan* also contained a parody of the Ten Commandments. Hone furiously excoriated Byron's publisher John Murray in an open letter for bringing out a blasphemous parody of precisely the text for which Hone was first tried on a charge of blasphemous libel in 1817. The Ten Commandments as they appeared in the Catechism had, as Hone well knew, been a staple of radical satire since the 1780s. The parodic and formal variety of *Don Juan* has a confidence in the variegated resources of the early nineteenth-century publishing world that places it happily in the company of Wooler and Hone's writings. Near the beginning of the First Canto

---

[12] For a discussion of the radical exploitation of fable, see Mark Philp on the 'dunghill pullet' in 'The Fragmented Ideology of Reform', 70–2.

[13] Marcus Wood, 'The Dedication to *Don Juan* and Nursery-Rhyme Parody: A New Satiric Context', *Byron Journal*, 20 (1992), 71–7.

of his masterpiece Byron struggles to find a fitting hyperbole with which to praise a somewhat dubious commodity, the virtue of Donna Iñez: 'In virtues nothing earthly could surpass her, Save thine "incomparable oil" Macassar'. In bowing, albeit archly, before the puffing skills of the celebrated advertiser of hair oil Byron proclaims his fellowship with 'the literature of the multitude' in a manner which would have delighted Hone but which Coleridge would have found reprehensible in a great poet.

All this shows how my work can be applied to more conventionally 'literary' areas. Until now it has been no part of this project to relate the political writings of canonical 'Romantic' authors to the more widely popular productions of radical publicists such as Spence, Eaton, Cobbett, Wooler, and Hone. This book has stressed the daring and even joyous nature of much radical propaganda and has examined that work in its own terms and not as a poor cousin to the canon. Not only can this work stand on its own two feet, but its formal richness makes special demands on the reader. To 'read' the works of Hone and Cruikshank demands the breaking-down of genre distinctions and notions of high and low art. Their texts are some of the most open in English. The temptation for the academic is to tie them down, or wrap them up neatly for storage in a prepared theoretical space. My intention has been to open them up. Hone conjoins, reinvents, but never drowns his sources. As a result his work emerges as virtually impossible to categorize in terms of style or genre. It is scrupulously classless and because of its unvarying basis in parody strangely authorless as well.

Hone made great claims for his pamphlets as an agent of change:

By showing what engraving on wood could effect in a popular way, and exciting a taste for art in the more humble ranks of life, they created a new era in the history of publication ... They are the parents to the present cheap literature, which extends to a sale of at least four hundred thousand copies every week ... Besides this ... my little pieces acquainted every rank of society, in the most remote corner of the British dominions, with the powers of Mr. George Cruikshank, whose genius had been wasted on mere caricature till it embodied my ideas and feelings.[14]

Hone's pamphlets did not single-handedly open the floodgates for cheap illustrated journalism, although their combination of type and wood-block in a single-page pamphlet certainly provided a pattern

[14] Hone, *Aspersions Answered*, 49.

for 'cheap literature" in the age of the steam press and machine-made paper. It is not true that Hone first set Cruikshank before the public. He had been working as the major illustrator for mainstream satiric journals such as *The Scourge* and *The Satirist* for several years before his association with Hone. Hone's work did, however, exert a decided influence on the forms and methods of radical satire in the six years following Waterloo.

Hone and Cruikshank's pamphlets strengthened and unified the satiric methods of the radical press. They took up the new publishing forms which the expanding children's book and advertising industries made available, and infused into these the iconographic richness of the satiric etching. They formed vital links between these areas of popular print culture and the major radical periodicals. The energy of their ridicule, and the multivalent iconographic and linguistic sources they incorporate, embodied and helped to inspire a new self-confidence in the radical press.

Hone and Cruikshank's collaborative work is part of the final flowering of English print satire and marks the point of its sudden demise. Within four years of the appearance of *The Political House* this type of illustrated pamphlet satire had virtually disappeared. The single-sheet satiric etching had gone into decline and by 1830 it was dead and replaced by the benign lithographs of John Doyle (H.B.) and his followers. It was not just print technology but the satiric spirit of the age that had changed. Popular illustrated journalism flourished but became increasingly kindly in its attitude towards the state.

The savage and violent energies of the gutter press no longer poured into satires attacking the government and monarchy but were absorbed by the expanding horror market which focused on sensational murders and sex crimes. The whimsical and charming social satire which was to become the predominant satiric diet in the respectable Victorian journals began to dominate in the 1820s. Cruikshank moved, as ever, with the times and was at the heart of these developments. He devoted himself increasingly to the illustration of cosy periodicals which specialized in gentle satires on fashion, food, the weather, the health of the nation, and the celebration of solid British activities such as equestrianism and pugilism. He also announced himself in 1823 as a children's book illustrator of genius with the etchings for the first English edition of *Grimm's Fairy Tales*. It was only on rare occasions such as the revolutions in central Europe in 1848 that a spark of Cruikshank's youthful satiric furore was revived.

Hone similarly moved towards the more balmy waters of the Victorian publishing mainstream with his very successful antiquarian anthologies *The Table Book* and *The Every-Day Book*. These publications introduced the British public to fundamental aspects of their radical heritage in the guise of antiquarian curiosities. They were not, however, confrontational or violently subversive in the manner of the earlier collaborative works. Hone and Cruikshank lost the essence of their former satiric being—the desire to glory in and imaginatively exploit unrespectability.

APPENDIX

A Transcription of the Original Manuscript Version of *The Late John Wilkes's Catechism of a Ministerial Member.*

This comprises Wilkes's eighteenth-century MS with Hone's MS deletions and additions. The latter were superscribed when Hone reworked the Wilkes MS for publication in 1816. Hone's alterations are printed in bold italics. Hone's deletions of Wilkes's MS are indicated by underlining, Hone's alterations to his own text by double underlining. Editorial comments are enclosed in angle brackets. Hone's occasional use of square brackets around some of his additions has been maintained.

[that is to say [an instruction
A Catechism/to be learned of every Person before

He be brought to be confirmed a Placeman or

Pensioner by the Minister

Question your
Q. What is thy name?

A. A place or Pensioner Lickspittle
  man

Q. Who gave you this name?

sureties to the ministry
A. My Godfathers and Godmothers in my Political

change of any formation change   member
Baptism wherein I was made a Lord of the <*sic*>

Majority   *Corruption*
Corruption, the Child of the Minister and a

Locust to devour the good Things of this Kingdom

                                        sureties
Q. What did your Godfathers and Godmothers then

for you?

A. They did promise and vow three Things in
                        Parliamentary Reformers
my Name : First that I should renounce Wilkes
    its their   *the Pomps*
and all his Works, The fruitless Honours and

                Popular favour
Vanities, of Patriotism/ and all the sinful lusts

of Independence.

Secondly that I should believe all the Articles

of the Court faith. And thirdly that, I should

                        sole
keep the Minister's holy will and commandments

And walk in the same all the Days of my Life

                    not   that
Q. And Dost not thou, think, that thou art bound to

believe and to do as they have promised for thee?

A. Yes verily for my own sake so I will and

Heaven born Ministry that they have
I heartily thank our / <u>dread</u> <u>Lord</u> <u>the</u> <u>Premier</u>

<u>that</u> <u>he</u> <u>hath</u> called me to this state of Elevation

through my own flattering cringing and bribery

shall   their successors   their
And I pray to <u>Heaven</u> to give me <u>its</u> Assistance

all the days of my life
that I may continue in the same/ <u>to my life's end</u>—
unto my life's end

<u>Catechist</u>

Q. Rehearse the Articles of thy Belief

[Answer
I believe <u>in</u> <u>black</u> <u>Harry</u> <u>the</u> <u>lord</u> Almighty, the
George,   the Regent/
Maker of <u>Pensioners</u> and <u>Placemen</u>. And in the
new streets   knights of the bath
the right honourable
<u>Lord</u> <u>May</u> James Murd
Mighty of Stane his sole creator and only dread
the minister   /   only of the bedchamber Lord,
<u>who</u> <u>was</u> <u>conceived</u> <u>by</u> <u>Jacobinism</u> <u>brought</u> <u>forth</u>
in Separate
copy
by Toryism and nursed by Despotism he suffered

under the Mayoralty of Fludger being mobed

hissed and pelted by the populace he was hung

up in effigy by the White Chaple Butchers and

consumed to Ashes in Jack Boots and a Judges

Wig—he fled an exile to Barages and was almost

buryed in Oblivion—The third Day he rose

again from the Dead and returned to England

He went up to Court and wispered pernicious

Counsel in the Sovereigns' Ear frightened by a

charge of Treason he returned to Barages for

the recovery of his digestion from thence he

shall come to punish Patriotism and to scourge

the Land. I believe in the Duke of Grafton the

Embezzlement of the Treasury the Inquisition

of Surgeons the forgiveness of Murder the

Resurrection of Bute and his Power everlasting

in

What dost thou chiefly learn by these Articles

of thy Belief?

A. First Learn to forswear all Conscience which

was never meant to trouble me nor the rest

of the tribe of Courtiers [Secondly, To swear Black

good pleasure of
is White and White is Black according to <u>the</u> <u>humour</u>

of the Ministers <u>and</u> / Thirdly, To put on the helmet

of Independence the only Armour against the

shafts of Patriotism.

sureties
Q. You said that your <u>Godfathers</u> <u>and</u> <u>Godmothers</u>

did promise for you that you should <u>Walk</u> <u>in</u>

keep
the Minister's Commandments tell me how

many there be?

A. Ten

Q. Which be they?

white   *answer*
<u>A.</u> The same to which the Minister for the Time

being always obliges all his creatures to swear

liege
I the Minister am the Lord thy God who brought

thee out of Want and Beggary into the House of

Commons.

                                        Patron
                        will   **me**
1 Thou shalt have none other Gods but mine
            supporting
            take   **measure**
2 Thou shalt not make to thyself any Graven

Image but mine, nor shalt thou frame the

  Clauses   **Bill in its progress to the Coms House**
Likeness/ of any Thing that is in Heaven above
                        beneath
    the Committee beneath below or where the Mace
or   in   the   Earth   Beneath   or   in   the   Waters

  is   **table**   **it be**
/ under the earth except / mine Thou shalt not
            nor any other of my real opponents
        M to Lord Cochrane nor shake hands with him / for I
bow down to them nor worship them for

  Lord   **Allow not**
thy God art a jealous Minister and visit the

forbid familiarity Majority with the Friends of the People
/ sins of the Father upon the Children unto the

                Cousins   **divide against**
the third and fourth / General of them that hate

me   **and**   **th tens th of thousands to**
and give places unto thousands / of them that

divide with me
Love me and keep my Commandments.

pension   *the*
3 rd. Thou shalt not take the Name of the Lord thy

Minister   *the Minister will force*
God in vain for I thy Lord will not hold him

to accept Chilterns   *Pensions*
guiltless that taken my Name in Vain—

head holiday on
4 th. Remember that thou keep holy the Ministers

speak for him in thy house
on his Levee Day on other days shalt thou / labour and

fetch and carry and he commandeth thee
/ do all that thou hast to do but the Levee

for   *glory glorification*   *Lord*
Day is / the Sabbath / of the Minister thy God in

in the house
it thou shalt do no manner of Work / but shalt

at his house home
wait upon him / thou and thy Daughter and

wife   *member*   *are*
thy Handmaid and the Stranger that is within

his influence
thy Gate for on other days the Minister is

except behind in the house
inaccessible / but delightet<h> in the Levee Day

Wherefore the Minister appointeth the Levee Day and chatteth
and for his amusement blesseth and Halloweth
thereon familiarly and is amused with it

Regent and the Helmets of the Lifeguards
5th. Honour the / <u>Minister</u> <u>and</u> <u>his</u> <u>Mistress</u> that they

stay
<u>Day</u> may be long in the Place which thy Lord

thy Minister giveth thee.

not call starving to death
6th. Thou shalt <u>do</u> <u>murder</u> <u>,</u> *<u>go</u> <u>to</u> <u>court</u>* Murder

not call Royal Gallivanting
7th. Thou shalt/ <u>commit</u> / Adultery

not say that Public to rob the Public is to
8th. Thou shalt Steal

9th. Thou shalt bear false Witness against the People

      not   *applause <u>praise</u>*
10th. Thou shalt / covet the Peoples <u>Houses</u> thou
                    good name
    not   *<u>praise</u> <u>esteem</u> <u>good</u> <u>name</u> <u>nor</u> <u>honour</u>*
shalt / covet the Peoples <u>Wives</u> <u>and</u> their <u>Daughters</u>

nor esteem <u>Rewards</u> <u>nor</u> <u>good</u> <u>name</u> or <u>Reverence</u>
and their <u>Maids</u> <u>and</u> <u>their</u> <u>men</u> <u>and</u> <u>their</u> <u>horses</u>

nor their reverence nor any reward
<u>and</u> <u>Asses</u> <u>and</u> <u>everything</u> <u>that</u> <u>is</u> <u>theirs</u>

Q. What dost thou chiefly learn by these Commandments?

A. I learn two Things my duty toward the

the Minister and my duty towards myself

Q. What is thy duty towards the Minister?

*receive **my** all from **him***
A. My duty towards the Minister is to believe in

trust him as much as I can
him to fear him to Honour him with all my Words

with all my bows with all my scrapes and all

my Cringes to flatter him to give him thanks

  give up   **soul to**
to put / my whole trust in him to Idolize

        obey
his Name and / his Word and serve him blindly

all the Days of his Political Life.

Q. What is thy duty towards thyself?

.

A. My duty towards myself is to love nobody but

myself and to do unto most Men what I

would not they should do unto me to sacrifice

to my own Interest even my Father and

Mother to pay little reverence to the King but

to compensate that omission by me servility

to all that are put in Authority under him

to lick the Dust under the Foot of my superiors

and to shake a Rod of Iron over the Backs of

my Inferiors, to spare the People by neither

Word or Deed to observe neither truth nor

Iustice in my dealings with them to bear them

Malice and hatred in my heart and where

their Wives and Properties are concerned to

to keep my Body neither in Temperance-

up
Soberness nor chastity but to give / a loose to

    to
my hands in picking and stealing and to my

   to   *and*
Tongue in evil speaking / lying and slandering of
their efforts to defend their liberty and recover their rights
                    privileges
never failing to appropriate their Goods to
       / *enjoy* / *envy*

the
my own use and to learn and later to get my

                      myself and   *people's labour*
Pension the Pensions of / my Colleagues / labour
own   living   out   of   theirs   and   to   do   my   Duty   in

that Department of Public plundering unto

which it shall please the Minister to call me

Q. My good Courtier, know this that thou art

not able of thyself to preserve the Minister's

favour nor to walk in his Commandments

                         protection favour
nor to serve him without his special / Grace

                         obtain
which thou must at all Time learn to call for
        memor   **application**
by diligent Prayer—Let me hear therefore if

      state rehearse   *memorial*
thou canst say the Ministers Prayer?

A. Our Lord who art in the Treasury whatsoever

be thy Name Thy Power be prolonged Thy will

be done throughout the Empire as it is in

each Session our usual sops
Parliament give us / <u>this</u> <u>Day</u> <u>our</u> <u>Daily</u> <u>Bread</u>

occasional absences on Divisions
and forgive us our <u>trespasses</u> as we promise

divide
not to forgive them that <u>Trespass</u> against

keep
thee Turn us not out of our Places but <u>lead</u>

us in<u>to</u> the House of Commons the Land of <u>the</u>

Pensions and Plenty deliver us from the People Amen

Q. What desirest thou of the Minister in this

Prayer? ***Memorial***

Patron
A. I desire my Lord the Minister our / <u>Political</u>

overstrained
Father who is the disposer of the Nation's <u>plundered</u>

Taxation to give his protection
Wealth / to send his Grace unto me and to all

vote for
Pensioners and Placemen that we may / <u>worship</u>

him serve him and obey him as far as we find

beseech
it convenient and <u>pray</u> <u>unto</u> the Minister

give
that he will <u>send</u> us all Things that be

reputation and appearance in the
needful both for our / Backs and Bellys and
House and but of it <u>and</u>
favourable
that he will be <u>gracious</u> to us and forgive us

<u>all</u> our negligences <u>in</u> <u>attending</u> <u>upon</u> <u>his</u>

<u>Levee</u> <u>and</u> <u>in</u> <u>remitting</u> <u>him</u> <u>the</u> <u>first</u> Fruits

<u>of</u> <u>our</u> <u>Places</u> <u>and</u> <u>Pensions</u> and that it will—

please him to serve and defend us in all

Dangers of Life and Limb from the People

natural
our / <u>everlasting</u> Enemies and that he will

help us in fleecing and grinding them and

out of ease for
this I trust he will do <u>of</u> <u>his</u> <u>infinite</u> <u>Love</u>

our support of him   ***corruption***
<u>to</u> himself and <u>his</u> <u>Suretie</u> / through our <u>bribery</u>

Influence
and <u>Corruption</u> and therefore I say Amen so be it.

Tests
Q. How many <u>Sacraments</u> hath the Minister ordained?

A. Two only as generally necessary to Elevation

(that is to say) Passive Obedience and Bribery—

Test

Q. What meanest thou by this word / Sacrament?

A. I mean an Outward visible sign of an inward—

intellectual
and Spiritual meanness ordained by the

Minister himself as a pledge to assure him thereof

Test

Q. How many parts are there in this Sacrament?

the

A. Two the outward and visible sign and / inward—

Spiritual Grace *Intellectual Meanness*

Q. What is the Outward and Visible sign or form of

Passive Obedience?

heels

A. Dangling at the Minister's Levee / whereby

the person is degraded beneath the baseness

of a Slave in the Character of a Pensioner

Placeman Expectant Parasite Toadeater or Lord

of the Bedchamber.

intellectual
Q. What is the inward and <u>Spiritual</u> Meanness?

subjection
A. A Death unto Freedom a <u>new</u> <u>Birth</u> unto

perpetual
/ Thraldom for being by Nature born <u>in</u>—

<u>Freedom</u> and the Children of Independence

we are hereby made Children of Slavery

submitting to the Test
Q. What is required of persons <u>going</u> <u>through</u> <u>the</u>

<u>Sacrament</u> of Passive Obedience.

Apostasy
A. <u>Repentance</u> whereby they forsake liberty and

faith whereby they steadfastly believe the

whom
Premises of the Minister made to them <u>in</u>

<u>that</u> <u>Sacrament</u> *submitting to that Test*

<u>*What is*</u>   *test*
Q. Why was the <u>Sacrament</u> of Bribery ordained?

support
A. For the continual <u>supply</u> of the Minister's—

Influence
<u>Extravagance</u> / and the feeding of us his needy

Creatures and Sycophants.

Q. What is the outward part or sign in the

Test
<u>Sacrament</u> of Bribery?

A. Bank Notes <u>and</u> <u>Guineas</u> which the Minister

hath commanded to be offered at his shrine

by his dependants.

Q. Why then are Beggars submitted to this—

Test
Sacrament when by reason of their poverty

they are not able to go through the necessary forms?

A. Because they promise them by their Sureties

which promise when they come to lucrative

Offices they themselves are bound to perform.

Q. What is the inward part or Thing signified?

Industry and Wealth <u>Property</u> <u>treasure</u>
A. <u>The</u> <u>sweat</u> / <u>and</u> / <u>Blood</u> of the People which are

had
verily and indeed taken and / received by the
this
Pensioners and Sinecurists Test on accepting their wages of
faithful in the Sacrament of Bribery and

in their
Corruption.

Q. What are the Benefits whereof you are—

partakers thereby?

A. The weakening and impoverishing the People

Liberty   Property
through the loss of their Blood and Treasure—

while our Wealth becomes enormous and our

Pride intolerable.

submit
Q. What is required of them who come to the—***Test***

Sacrament of Bribery and Corruption?

A. To examine themselves whether they repent them

Honour Independence
truly of any other former Signs of Grace and

Patriotism stedfastly purposing to be henceforward

Bill
Alderman Sir William Curtis Turtle
as Supple to the Minister as an Eelskin to draw on

and off like a Glove to crouch like a Spaniel to

purvey like a Jackall to Murder and Assassinate

With as little remorse as a Maquirk a W–y–th or a Bar–g–ton

<The remaining part of the MS is written on a separate sheet of smaller writing paper, and it is entirely in Hone's autograph.>

A. To examine them whether they repent them truly

    former   *henceforward*
of any former signs of / honour or patriotism steadfastly proposing /
to be faithful
/ towards the Minister
/ to be henceforward / to draw on and off to the Minister like his

glove; to crouch to him like a spaniel; to purvey for him

            Sir
like a jackall; to be as supple to him as / Alderman
      especially in the sinking Fund
Billy William   *the most lively*
Turtle:—to have / faith in nothing but the Funds / to believe

the words of   *alone only*
nobody but Lord Castlereagh / to have remembrance of nothing

<two words illegible> *the purpose* *to hate Mathew Wood the*
but what read is in the Courier O to have charity for

present Lord Mayor <u>well</u> *in and to his second Mayorality with all my*
<u>nobody</u> <u>but</u> <u>myself</u> <u>the</u> <u>great</u> <u>men</u> <u>of</u> <u>the</u> <u>earth</u>   <u>I</u> <u>to</u> <u>raise</u>

heart with all my mind with all my soul and with all my strength
up none that fall unless they be and<in> *the London*

to admire Sir John Silvester <one word illegible> *the recorder*
Gazette & and <<u>sic</u>> *to be in charity only with those who*

have something to give.

[Here <u>The</u> *endeth the Catechism].*

BIBLIOGRAPHY

PRIMARY SOURCES

Manuscripts

Bodl. (Bodleian Library, Oxford)

John Johnson Collection. Material has been used from the following main
    subject headings: 'Advertisers', 'Broadsides', 'Caricatures', 'Chapbooks',
    'Cruikshank', 'Human Freaks', 'Leaders of Reform', 'Penny Dreadfuls',
    'Street Ballads', 'Street Propaganda'.

BL (British Library)

Francis Place Papers: Add. MSS 27808–13, 27825, 27837–44.
William Hone Papers: Add. MS 4071, 40108–22.
'Satirical Songs and Miscellaneous Papers on the Return of Queen Caroline
    to England'.
'A Collection of Squibs on Buonaparte's Threatened Invasion'.
Francis Place Collection, vols. 18, 40, 46, folders 96, 204, 206–8, 212.

BM (British Museum, Department of Prints and Drawings)

Cruikshank Bequest; Box 22C, folder I B 4, sheet 1974 u 588; folder I B 10,
    sheets 1974 u 624 and 628; folder I B 20 u 844; folder I B 21, sheets 1974 u
    904 and 906. *BMC* (Collection of Political and Personal Satires).

Houghton Library, Harvard University

Widener Collection: collection of prints belonging to Captain Douglas.

New York Public Library

Berg Collection, George T. Lawley Collection, albums 1 and 2.

Saint Bride's Printing Library

Wilson Collection of Broadsides.

V & A (Victoria and Albert Museum)

Cruikshank Bequest, box I 92A, folders 9700, A–Z; box I 95, folders 9584,
    A–H; box I 96, folders 9958, 9997; box I 190, folders 9496A, 9503B.

Printed Material

A Collection of Pretty Poems for the Amusement of Children Six Feet High, probable ed. Christopher Smart (London: John Newberry, 1757).

A Peep into W———r Castle after the lost Mutton (London: W. Benbow, 1820).

A Political Alphabet (London: John Carpenter, 1830).

A Political and Satirical History of the Years 1756, 1757, 1758, 1759, and 1760. In a Series of One Hundred and Four Humorous and Entertaining Prints, 2 vols. (London, 1763).

Absconded in a Disconsolate State, Divers Persons Better Known than Trusted (London, 1820).

An Admirable Satire on the Death, Dissection, Funeral Procession and Epitaph of Mr Pitt (London, 1795).

The Anti-Gallican; or, Standard of British Loyalty, Religion, and Liberty. Including a Collection of the Principal Papers, Tracts, and Songs that have been Published on the Threatened Invasion (London, 1804).

Anti-Jacobin Review and Magazine.

A Slap at the Church.

Asmodeus; or, The Devil in London.

BAMFORD, SAMUEL, *Passages in the Life of a Radical* (1884) (Oxford: Oxford University Press, 1984).

BENTHAM, JEREMY, *Church of Englandism and its Catechism Examined* (London, 1818).

——— *Plan of Parliamentary Reform, in the Form of a Catechism* (London, 1817).

——— *Rationale of Judicial Evidence, Specially Applied to English Practice*, ed. J. S. Mill, 5 vols. (London, 1827).

BEWICK, THOMAS, *A Memoir of Thomas Bewick Written by Himself* (1862), ed. Iain Bain (Oxford: Oxford University Press, 1975).

The Black Dwarf.

BLAKE, WILLIAM, *Complete Writings*, ed. Geoffrey Keynes (Oxford: Oxford University Press, 1966).

British Review and London Critical Journal.

BROOM, HARRY, *The King in a Pickle! With a Cabinet of Curiosities* (London, 1820).

BYRON, GEORGE GORDON NOEL, LORD, *The Complete Poetical Works*, ed. Jerome K. McGann, 7 vols. (Oxford: Oxford University Press, 1980–93).

Catalogue of Books, Books of Prints, &c. Collected for a History of Parody, by Mr. William Hone, Containing an Extensive and Remarkable Assemblage of Extraordinary Parodies (London, 1827).

Catalogue of the Stock of Books of William Hone and of a Library in Fine Condition ... Which Will be Sold by Mr. Hone at Auction in his rooms (London, 1822).

Catalogue of the Valuable and Interesting Collection of Books Tracts, Ballads, and Prints of the Late Mr. William Hone (London, 1843).

COBBETT, WILLIAM, *Cobbett's Political Register, 1802–1835*, 89 vols.
—— *The Porcupine* (1880–1).
COLERIDGE, SAMUEL TAYLOR, *The Letters of Samuel Taylor Coleridge*, ed. E. L. Griggs, 6 vols. (Oxford: Clarendon Press, 1959).
—— *The Watchman* (London, 1796), repr. in *Collected works*, ed. Lewis Patton (London: Routledge & Kegan Paul, 1970).
—— *Omniana of S. T. Coleridge* (Oxford: Oxford University Press, 1917).
The Constitutional Apple Pie; or, Rhythmical Red Book (London: T. Hughes, 1820).
The Covent Garden Journal, and A Plan of the Universal Register Office, ed. Bertrand A. Goldgar (Oxford: Oxford University Press, 1988).

DEFOE, DANIEL, *A Hymn to the Pillory* (London, 1703).
—— *A Review*; repr. as *Defoe's Review*, 22 vols (New York: Columbia University Press, 1938).
—— *Jure Divino: A Satyr. In twelve books. By the author of The True-Born Englishman* (London, 1706).
DODSLEY, R., *Select Fables of Aesop and Other Fabulists* (London, 1781).

EATON, DANIEL ISAAC, *Politics for the People; or, A Salmagundy for Swine* (London, 1793–5); Greenwood repr., 2 vols. (New York, 1968).
—— *Trial of Daniel Isaac Eaton* (London, 1812).
Examination Extraordinaire of the Vice R——y of B——d——y Boro! Alias the Handsome Gentleman by John Bull (London, 1820).
The Examiner.

The Fallacy of French Freedom and Dangerous Tendency of Sterne's Writings (1799).
The Flying Post.
FOXE, JOHN, *The Acts and Monuments of John Foxe*, 4th edn. rev. corr. Josiah Pratt, 8 vols. (London: Religious Tract Society, 1877).

GAY, JOHN, *The Letters of John Gay*, ed. C. F. Burgess (Oxford: Oxford University Press, 1966).
The Gentleman's Magazine.
GOLDSMITH, OLIVER, *A History of the Earth and Animated Nature*, 8 vols. (London, 1774).
—— *Collected Works of Oliver Goldsmith*, ed. Arthur Friedman, 5 vols. (Oxford: Oxford University Press, 1965).
GROSE, FRANCIS, *A Guide to Health, Beauty, Riches and Honour* (London, 1785).
The Guardian of Education.

HARRINGTON, JAMES, *The Commonwealth of Oceana and A System of Politics*, ed. J. G. A. Pocock (Cambridge: Cambridge University Press, 1992).
HAZLITT, WILLIAM, *The Complete Works of William Hazlitt*, ed. P. P. Howe, 21 vols. (Bungay: J. M. Dent, 1930–4).
HOGARTH, WILLIAM, *Hogarth's Graphic Works*, ed. Ronald Paulson (Hartford, Conn.: Yale University Press, 1965).

Hogg, James, *The Poetical Mirror* (London, 1816); repr. ed. T. Earle Welby (London: Scholars Press, 1929).

Hunt, Leigh, *Leigh Hunt's Literary Criticism*, ed. L. H. and C. W. Houtchens (New York: Columbia University Press, 1956).

The Idler.

John Bull's Constitutional Apple Pie (London: J. Johnson, 1820).

Johnson, Samuel, *The Yale Edition of the Works of Samuel Johnson*, ed. W. J. Bate and Albrecht B. Strauss, 8 vols. (New Haven, Conn.: Yale University Press, 1969).

The London Magazine.
The Loyalist's Magazine; or, Anti-Radical.
The Loyal Man in the Moon.

The Magical Note and its Consequences (London, 1810).
The Men in the Moon; or, The 'Devil to Pay' (London: Dean & Munday [1820]).
The Monthly Magazine.

The New Daily Advertiser.
The New Italian Jugglers (London, 1820).
The Non Mi Ricordo Song Book (London, 1820).
The North Briton.

£0,000,000 Reward. Strayed and Missing, broadside (London, 1820).
The Observator.

Packwood, George, *Packwood's Whim* (London: printed for the author, 1796).

Paine, Thomas, *The Writings of Thomas Paine*, ed. M. D. Conway (1894–6).

Pangloss, Peter, pseud., *A New Favourite Royal Alphabet* (London: T. Dolby, 1821).

Peacock, Thomas Love, *The Novels of Thomas Love Peacock*, ed. David Garnett, 2 vols. (London: Rupert Hart-Davies, 1963).

Pig's Meat; or, Lessons for the Swinish Multitude, 3 vols. (London, 1793–6).

Place, Francis, *The Autobiography of Francis Place (1771–1854)*, ed. Mary Thale (Cambridge: Cambridge University Press, 1972).

The Political A Apple Pie (London: J. Johnson, 1820).
The Political Register.

Pope, Alexander, *The Prose Works of Alexander Pope 1711–1720*, ed. N. Ault (Oxford: Basil Blackwell, 1936).

The Post Boy.

The Quarterly Review.

The Quizzical Gazette Extraordinary and Wonderful Advertiser.

The Radical Chiefs, a Mock Heroic Poem (London: W. Turner, 1821).

The Radical Ladder; or, Hone's Political Ladder and his Non Mi Ricordo Explained and Applied, The Designs of the Radicals Developed and Their Plans Traced, A Satirical Poem With Copious Notes (London: W. Wright, 1820).

The Rambler.

The Rump Chronicle.

The Scot's Magazine.

The Self Afflicter. Lively Described in the whole course of the Life of Mr. John Lilburne, chapbook (1657).

SHELLEY, PERCY BYSSHE, *Poetical Works,* ed. Thomas Hutchinson, 2nd rev. edn. (Oxford: Oxford University Press, 1970).

——*Shelley's Prose,* ed. with intro. and notes by David Lee Clark (London: Fourth Estate, 1988).

SMART, CHRISTOPHER, *A Collection of Pretty Poems for the Amusement of Children Six Feet High* (London: John Newbery, c.1770).

SOUTHEY, ROBERT, *Letters from England,* ed. Jack Simmons (London: Cresset Press, 1951).

——*New Letters of Robert Southey,* ed. Kenneth Curry, 2 vols. (New York: Columbia University Press, 1965).

—— *Wat Tyler; A Dramatic Poem. A New Edition with a Preface Suitable to Recent Circumstances* (1817).

The Spectator, ed. Donald F. Bond, 5 vols. (Oxford: Oxford University Press, 1965).

SPENCE, THOMAS, *A Letter from Ralph Hodge to his Cousin Thomas Bull* (London, 1795).

——*The Coin Collector's Companion, Being a Descriptive Alphabetical List of the Modern Provincial Political and other Token Coinage* (London, 1795).

——*Pig's Meat; or, Lessons for the Swinish Multitude,* 3 vols. (London, 1793–6).

——*Pig's Meat: The Selected Writings of Thomas Spence,* ed. G. I. Gallop (Nottingham: Spokesman, 1982).

—— *The Political Works of Thomas Spence,* ed. H. T. Dickinson (Newcastle: Avero, 1982).

——'Selected Writings of Thomas Spence 1795–1814', in P. M. Kemp-Ashraf (ed.), *Essays in Honour of Willy Gallacher* (East Berlin: Humboldt Universität, 1966).

State Trials: A Complete Collection of State Trials, initially compiled by William Cobbett and continued by T. B. Howells, 34 vols. (1818–20).

STERNE, LAWRENCE, *Tristram Shandy,* ed. M. and J. New, 3 vols., The Florida Edition of the Works of Lawrence Sterne (Gainsville: Florida University Press, 1978–84).

STODDART, JOHN, *Slop's Shave at a Broken Hone* (London, 1820).

SWIFT, JONATHAN, *The Bickerstaff Papers,* ed. H. Davis (Oxford: Basil Blackwell, 1940).

SWIFT, JONATHAN, *Gulliver's Travels* (1726), ed. Harold Williams (Oxford: Basil Blackwell, 1941).

—— *Irish Tracts and Sermons*, ed. H. Davis (Oxford: Basil Blackwell, 1948).

—— *Miscellaneous and Autiobiographical Pieces*, ed. H. Davis (Oxford: Basil Blackwell, 1962).

The Tatler, ed. Donald F. Bond, 3 vols. (Oxford: Oxford University Press, 1987).

THOMPSON, JAMES, *Liberty, The Castle of Indolence*, ed. James Sambrook (Oxford: Oxford University Press, 1986).

The Total Eclipse: A Grand Politico-Astronomical Phenomenon, Which Occurred in the Year 1820 (London: Thomas Dolby, 1820).

The Trial of an Ox (Banbury, n.d.).

The Trial of Antichrist (London, 1806).

The Trial of Daniel Isaac Eaton (London, 1812).

The Triall of Lieut. Collonell John Lilburne (London, 1649).

The Trial of the Rev. Robt. Wedderburn (London, 1820).

The Tryal of William Whiston, Clerk (1740).

VAN BUTCHELL, MARTIN, *Martin Van Butchell's Diverting Pages* (1817).

The Verdicts of Three Honest Juries, broadside (1817).

WALPOLE, HORACE, *Horace Walpole's Correspondence*, ed. W. S. Lewis, 48 vols. (London: Oxford University Press, 1937–87).

WILKES, JOHN, *Essay on Woman* (1762).

The Wit of the Day; or, The Humours of Westminster (London, 1784).

Woolmer's Exeter and Plymouth Gazette.

YORK, HENRY READHEAD, *Letters from France in 1802*, 2 vols. (London, 1802).

The Publications of William Hone

Owing to the unusual and sometimes unique forms of Hone's publications, and the considerable bibliographic complexities surrounding their publication in terms of date, format, edition, authorship, printer, and publisher, in listing Hone's publications I have followed the policy adopted by Ann Bowden in her exemplary bibliography. I list alphabetically all of the titles cited or discussed in this book which Hone either wrote, edited, compiled, printed, or published. The available publication data accompanies the entries. Precise information regarding the location of Hone's early publications in major libraries and museums is to be found in Bowden's invaluable 'William Hone: Bibliographical Conspectus 1815–1821', pp. 531–9 of her thesis.

Ancient Mysteries Described, Especially the English Miracle Plays, Founded on Apocryphal New Testament Story, Extant Among the Unpublished Manuscripts in the British Museum; including notices of Ecclesiastical Shows, the Festivals of Fools and Asses —

the English Boy Bishop — the Descent into Hell — the Lord Mayors Show — the Guildhall Giants — Christmas Carols &c. (London: Printed for William Hone, 45, Ludgate Hill, 1823).

Another Ministerial Defeat! The Trial of the Dog, for biting the Noble Lord; with the Whole of the Evidence at Length (Printed by and for W. Hone, 67 Old Bailey, Three Doors from Ludgate-Hill, 1817), 8 pages, 2d.

The Apocryphal New Testament, Being all the Gospels, Epistles, and Other Pieces now Extant, Attributed in the First Four Centuries to Jesus Christ, His Apostles, and their Companions, and not Included in the New Testament, by its Compilers. Translated from the original tongues, and now first collected into one volume (William Hone, 1820).

A Political Catechism, Dedicated, Without Permission, to His Most Serene Highness Omar, Bashaw, Dey, and Governor, of the Warlike City and Kingdom of Algiers; The Earl of Liverpool; Lord Castlereagh, and Co. By an Englishman (London: Printed for one of the Candidates for the Office of Printer to the King's Most Excellent Majesty, and Sold by William Hone, 55, Fleet Street, and 67, Old Bailey, three Doors from Ludgate Hill, 1817). 8 pages. 2d.

The Appearance of an Apparition, broadside (London: printed for William Hone, 55 Fleet Street, 1816), 6d.

A Slap at Slop and the Bridge-Street Gang, 27 edns. (London: William Hone, 45 Ludgate Hill, 1821). 1s.

Aspersions Answered, an Explanatory Statement, Addressed to the Public At Large, and to Every Reader of the Quarterly Review in Particular (William Hone: London, 1824).

The Bank Restriction Barometer; or, Scale of Effects of the Bank Note System, and Payments in Gold. By William Franklyn, broadside (London: published by William Hone, Ludgate Hill, 1819). Published with the 'Bank Restriction Note'. 1s.

Buonaparte-phobia, or; Cursing Made Easy to the Meanest Capacity. A Dialogue Between the Editor of 'The Times', — Dr. Slop, My Uncle Toby, & My Father, 8 edns., broadside (London: printed for William Hone, 55 Fleet Street, 1815). 1s.

Buonaparte-phobia. The origin of Dr. Slop's Name, 2 edns. (London: printed by William Hone, 45 Ludgate Hill, 1820). 1s.

Don Juan, Canto the Third! (London: William Hone, Ludgate Hill, 1819). 3s. 6d.

The Every-Day Book; or, Everlasting Calender of Popular Amusements (London: William Hone, 1827).

The First Trial of William Hone, on an Ex-Officio Information At Guildhall, London, December 17, 1817, Before Mr. Justice Abbot for Publishing the Late John Wilkes's Catechism of a Ministerial Member, 20 edns. (London: printed by and for William Hone, 67 Old Bailey, 1817). 1s.

George Dandin, ou L'Echelle matrimoniale de la reine d'Angleterre; petit conte national, traduit de l'Anglais par lauterr de la maison politique que Jacques a batie, 2nd edn. (Paris: Pontieu, 1820).

Great Gobble Gobble Gobble, and Twit Twittle Twit, or Law Versus Common Sense, Being a Twitting Report of Successive Attacks on a Tom Tit, His Stout Defences & Final Victory. A New Song, with Original Music by Lay Logic Esq.re Student in the Law of Libel (London: Published by William Hone. No. 67 Old Bailey, 181), 4 pages, 2s.

Hone's Interesting History of the Memorable Blood conspiracy, Carried on by S. Mac-Daniel, J. Berry, J. Egan and J. Salmon, Thief-Takers, and their Trials and Sentences, in 1756, for Procuring two Boys to Committ a Robbery, in Order to get the Blood-Money; Also the Reasons for Which They were Suffered to Escape the Gallows, and Illustrative Legal and Critical Notes and Observations Applicable to Present Circumstances (London: Printed for William Hone, 55 Fleet Street, 1816), 32 pages with frontispiece by George Cruikshank. 1s. Frontispiece imprint: Published by W. Hone, 55 Fleet Street, September, 1816.

Hone's Reformist's Register and Weekly Commentary (1 Feb.–25 Oct. 1817), 2 vols. (London: printed by and for William Hone, at the Reformist's Register Office, 67 Old Bailey, 1817). 2d. per number.

The Late John Wilkes's Catechism of a Ministerial Member; Taken From an Original Manuscript in Mr. Wilkes's Handwriting, never before printed and adapted to the present Occasion. With Permission (London: printed for one of the Candidates to the Office of Printer to the King's Most Excellent Majesty, and sold by William Hone, 55 Fleet Street, and 67 Old Bailey, three doors from Ludgate Hill, 1817). 2d.

La Maison Politique que Jacques a Batie (Paris: Chez Rosa, Librarie, Palais-Royal, 1820).

The Man in the Moon &c. &c. &c., 28 edns. (London: printed by and for William Hone, 45, Ludgate Hill, 1820). 1s., coloured edn. 2s.

'Non Mi Ricordo!' &c. &c. &c. (London: Printed by and for William Hone, Ludgate Hill, 1820), 31 edns., 16 pages, 6d.

Official Account. Bartholomew Fair Insurrection; and the Pie-Bald Pony Plot! (London: printed by and for William Hone, Reformists' Register Office, 67 Old Bailey, 1817). 2d.

Official Account of the Noble Lords bite! and His Dangerous Condition, With Who Went to See Him, and What was Said, Sung, and Done, on the Melancholy Occasion. Published for the Instruction and Edification of All Ranks and Conditions of Men. By the Author of Buonaparte-phobia; or, Cursing Made Easy (London: Printed by and for W. Hone, 67 Old Bailey, Three Doors from Ludgate Hill, 1817), 16 pages, 4d.

The Political House that Jack Built, 54 edns. (London: printed by and for William Hone, Ludgate Hill, 1819). 1s., fine edn. 2s.

The Political Litany, Diligently Revised, to be Said or Sung, Until the Appointed Change Come (London: printed for one of the Candidates for the Office of Printer to the King's Most Excellent Majesty, and sold by William Hone, 55 Fleet Street, and 67 Old Bailey, Three Doors from Ludgate Hill, 1817). 2d.

The Political Showman — at Home! Exhibiting his Cabinet of Curiosities and Creatures — All Alive! By the Author of The Political House that Jack Built, 27 edns. (London, 1821). 1*s*.

The Printer's Address to the Queen, and Her Majesty's Tribute to the Press, in Answer, broadside (London: printed for William Hone, Ludgate Hill [,1820]). 1*s*.

The Queen's Matrimonial Ladder, A National Toy, with Fourteen Step Scenes; and Illustrations in Verse, with eighteen other Cuts, 44 edns. (London: printed by and for William Hone, Ludgate Hill, 1820). 'This pamphlet and the toy together, ONE SHILLING', fine coloured edn. 3*s*.

Remarkable Prophecies from the Revelation of St. John, Showing the Restoration of the Imperial Dignity in France, and its Duration until 1866 (London: W. Hone, 1816). 3*d*.

The Right Divine of Kings to Govern Wrong! Dedicated to the Holy Alliance. By the Author of The Political House that Jack Built, 8 edns. (London: printed for William Hone, 45 Ludgate Hill, 1821). 18*d*.

The Sinecurist's Creed, or Belief; as the same Can or May be Sung or Said Throughout the Kingdom. By Authority from Hone's Weekly Commentary, No. 2 (London: printed for one of the Candidates for the Office of Printer to the King's Most Excellent Majesty, and sold by William Hone, 55 Fleet Street, 1817). 2*d*.

The Table Book, 2 vols. (London: William Hone, 1827).

The Three Trials of William Hone, for Publishing Three Parodies; viz. The Late John Wilkes's Catechism, The Political Litany, and The Sinecurist's Creed; on Three Ex-Officio Informations, at Guildhall London During Three Successive Days, December 18, 19, & 20, 1817, 20 edns. (London: printed by and for William Hone, 67 Old Bailey, 1818). 4*s*.

Trial by Jury and Liberty of the Press, 7 edns. (London: printed by and for William Hone, 67 Old Bailey, 1818). 6*d*.

View of the Regent's Bomb, Now Uncovered, for the Gratification of the Public, in St. James's Park, Majestically Mounted on a Monstrous Nondescript, supposed to Represent Legitimate Sovereignty, broadside caricature (London: Printed for W. Hone, 55 Fleet Street, 1816).

The Whole Four Trials of the Thief Takers and Their Confederates ... Convicted at Hicks Hall and the Old Bailey, Sept. 1816. of a Horrible Conspiracy to Obtain Blood Money, and of Felony and High Treason (London: printed for William Hone, 55 Fleet Street, 1816). 2*s*. 6*d*.

The Whole Proceedings Before the Coroner's Inquest at Oldham, &c. on the Body of John Lees, who Died of Sabre Wounds at Manchester, August the 16, 1819 (London: printed for William Hone, Ludgate Hill, 1820). 12*s*.

The Will of a Great Personage who Died of 37 Mortal Stabs, on Friday, the 5th of April, 1816, at Twelve o'Clock at Night, broadside (London: Printed for W. Hone, 55 Fleet Street, 1816), 2*d*.

SECONDARY SOURCES

ALTICK, R. D., *The Shows of London* (Cambridge, Mass.: Harvard University Press, 1978).

ANDERSON, PATRICIA, *The Printed Image and the Transformation of Popular Culture* (Oxford: Oxford University Press, 1990).

ARASSE, DANIE, *La Guillotine dans la Révolution*, exhibition cat. (Paris: Institut fraçais de Florence, 1987).

ARNOTT, J. FULLERTON, and ROBINSON, J. W., *English Theatrical Literature: A Bibliography* (London: Society for Theatre Research, 1970).

L'Art de l'estampe et la Révolution française, exhibition cat. (Alençon: Musée Carnavalet, 1977).

ASHTON, JOHN, *English Caricature and Satire on Napoleon I* (London: Chatto & Windus, 1888).

ASPINALL, ARTHUR, *Politics and the Press* c.*1780–1850* (London: Home & Van Thal, 1949).

ASQUITH, IVON, 'Advertising and the Press in the Late Eighteenth and Early Nineteenth Centuries: James Perry and the *Morning Chronicle* 1790–1821', *Historical Journal*, 18 (1975), 703–24.

ATHERTON, HERBERT, M., *Political Prints in the Age of Hogarth* (Oxford: Oxford University Press, 1974).

BAER, MARC, *Theatre and Disorder in Late Georgian London* (Oxford: Oxford University Press, 1992).

BAKHTIN, MIKHAIL, *The Dialogic Imagination: Four Essays* (Austin: University of Texas, 1981).

BARHAM, R. H. DALTON, *The Life and Remains of Theodore Edward Hook* (London: Richard Bentley, 1848).

BARNARD, F. P., *Satirical and Controversial Medals of the Reformation: The Biceps or Double Headed Series* (Oxford: Oxford University Press, 1927).

BARRELL, JOHN, *The Birth of Pandora and the Division of Knowledge* (London: Macmillan, 1992).

—— *The Political Theory of Painting from Reynolds to Hazlitt* (London: Yale University Press, 1986).

BASTIAN, F., *Defoe's Early Life* (London: Macmillan, 1981).

BATE, JONATHAN, 'Shakespearian Allusion in English Caricature in the Age of Gillray', *Journal of the Warburg and Courtauld Institute*, 49 (1986), 196–210.

—— *Shakespearian Constitutions* (Oxford: Oxford University Press, 1990).

BAUDELAIRE, CHARLES, *Selected Writings on Art* (Cambridge: Cambridge University Press, 1981).

BAYLEN, D., NORBERT, J. and GOSSMAN (eds.), *A Biographical Dictionary of Modern British Radicals* (Brighton: Harvester, 1979).

BELL, R. C., *Commercial Coins 1787–1704* (Newcastle: Corbitt & Hunter, 1963).

—— *Specious Tokens 1784–1804* (Newcastle: Corbitt & Hunter, 1968).

——— *Tradesman's Tickets and Private Tokens 1785–1819* (Newcastle: Corbitt & Hunter, 1966).

BEURDELEY, MICHEL, *La France'a l'encan: exode des objets d'art sous la Révolution*, exhibition cat. (Fribourg: Office du Livre, 1981).

BLANCK, JACOB, 'A Twentieth Century Look at Nineteenth Century Children's Books', lecture, Simmons College, Boston, 27 Apr. 1954.

BOADEN, JAMES, *The Life of John Philip Kemble* (London, 1825).

BOIME, ALBERT, *Art in an Age of Revolution* (Chicago: University of Chicago Press, 1987).

BOULTON, JAMES, T., *The Language of Politics in the Age of Wilkes and Burke* (London: Routledge & Kegan Paul, 1963).

BOWDEN, ANN, 'William Hone's Political Journalism, 1815–1821', Ph.D. diss., University of Texas at Austin, 1975.

BRIGGS, ASA, *The Age of Improvement* (London: Longmans Green, 1959).

The British Numismatic Journal and Proceedings of the British Numismatic Society, vols. *1–3* (London: Harrison, 1904–6).

BROWN, J. A. C., *Techniques of Persuasion* (Harmondsworth: Penguin, 1963).

BROWN, LAURENCE, *A Catalogue of British Historical Medals* (London: Seaby, 1980).

BROWN, LUCY, *Victorian News and Newspapers* (Oxford: Oxford University Press, 1985).

BROWN, PHILIP ANTHONY, *The French Revolution in English History* (Edinburgh: C. Lockwood, 1918).

BRUNEL, CHRISTOPHER and JACKSON, PETER, 'Notes on Tokens as a Source of Information on the History of the Labour and Radical Movements', pt. 1, *Bulletin of the Society for the Study of Labour History*, 13 (1966), 26–37.

BRUTTINI, A., 'Advertising and Socio-Economic Transformations in England, 1720–1760', *Journal of Advertising History*, 5 (1982), 9–14.

BRYANT, ARTHUR, *The Age of Elegance* (Harmondsworth: Penguin, 1958).

BUCK, J. D.C., 'The Motives of Puffing: John Newberry's Advertisements', *SB* 30 (1977), 196–210.

BUTLER, MARILYN, *Burke, Paine, Godwin and the Revolution Controversy* (Cambridge: Cambridge University Press, 1984).

——— *Peacock Displayed: A Satirist in his Context* (London: Routledge & Kegan Paul, 1979).

——— *Romantics, Rebels, and Reactionaries: English Literature and its Background 1760–1830* (Oxford: Oxford University Press, 1981).

——— 'Satire and the Images of Self in the Romantic Period: The Long Tradition of Hazlitt's *Liber Amoris*', in Claude Rawson (ed.), *English Satire and the Satiric Tradition* (Oxford: Basil Blackwell, 1984), 209–23.

The Byron Journal.

CANNON, JOHN, *Parliamentary Reform 1640–1832* (Cambridge: Cambridge University Press, 1972).

CARNALL, GEOFFREY, *Southey and his Age* (Oxford: Oxford University Press, 1960).

CARRETTA, VINCENT, *George III and the Satirists from Hogarth to Byron* (Athens, University of Georgia Press, 1990).

CHASE, MALCOLM, 'The Concept of Jubilee in Late Eighteenth- and Early Nineteenth-Century England', *Past and Present*, 129 (1990), 132–47.

—— *The People's Farm* (Oxford: Oxford University Press, 1989).

CHEW, SAMUEL CLAGETT, *Byron in England: His Fame and after Fame* (London: John Murray, 1924).

CLAEYS, GREGORY, *Thomas Paine: Political and Social Thought* (Boston: Unwyn Hyman, 1989).

CLARK, ANNA, 'Queen Caroline and the Sexual Politics of Popular Culture in London, 1820', *Representations*, 31 (Summer 1990), 47–68.

CLARK, J. C. D., *English Society 1688–1832: Ideology and Social Structure during the Ancien Régime* (Cambridge: Cambridge University Press, 1985).

CLARKSON, THOMAS, *A History of the Abolition of the Slave Trade*, 2 vols. (London: 1808).

CLERK, CATHERINE, *La Caricature contre Napoleon* ([Paris]: Promodis, 1985).

CLEUGH, J., *The Divine Aretino* (London: Anthony Bond, 1965).

COHN, ALBERT MAYER, *A Bibliographical Catalogue of the Printed Works Illustrated by George Cruikshank* (London: Longmans, Green, 1914).

—— *George Cruikshank: A Catalogue Raisonnée of the Work Executed during the Years 1806–1877, with Collations, Notes, Approximate Values, Facsimiles and Illustration* (London: Bookman's Journal, 1924).

COLLET, C. DOBSON, *History of the Taxes on Knowledge: Their Origin and Repeal* (London: Watts, 1933).

COLLISON, R., *The Story of Street Literature, Forerunner of the Press* (London: Dent, 1973).

CONRAD, PETER, *Shandyism: The Character of Romantic Irony* (Oxford: Basil Blackwell, 1978).

The Cornhill Magazine.

COUPE, W. A., *The German Illustrated Broadsheet in the Seventeenth Century*, 2 vols. (Baden-Baden: Verlag Librarie Heitz, 1966–7).

—— 'Political and Religious Caricatures of the Thirty Years War', *Journal of the Courtauld and Warburg Institutes*, 25 (1975), 65–86.

CRIMMINS, JAMES, E., 'Religion, Utility and Politics: Bentham versus Paley', in Crimmins (ed.), *Religion, Secularization and Political Thought* (London: Routledge & Kegan Paul, 1990).

—— *Secular Utilitarianism, Social Science, and the Critique of Religion in the Thought of Jeremy Bentham* (Oxford: Oxford University Press, 1990).

CRUIKSHANK, DAN, and BURTON, NEIL, *Life in the Georgian City* (London: Penguin, 1990).

CUNNINGTON, PHYLLIS, and BUCK, ANN, *Children's Costume in England* (London: A. & C. Black, 1965).

DALTON, R., and HAMER, S., *The Provincial Token Coinage of the Eighteenth Century*, 3 vols. in 14 parts (London, 1910–18).

DANTO, ARTHUR, C., *The State of the Art* (New York: Prentice-Hall, 1987).

DAVENPORT, A., *The Life, Writings, and Principles of Thomas Spence* (London: Wakelin, 1836).

DAVIE, DONALD, *The Purity of Diction in English Verse* (London: Routledge, 1967).

DAWSON, P. M. S., *The Unacknowledged Legislator: Shelley and Politics* (Oxford: Oxford University Press, 1980).

DICKINSON, H. T., *British Radicalism and the French Revolution 1789–1815* (Oxford: Oxford University Press, 1983).

—— 'Popular Conservatism and Militant Loyalism' in Dickinson (ed.), *Britain and the French Revolution 1789–1815* (London: Macmillan, 1989).

DINWIDDY, JOHN, R., *Radicalism and Reform in Britain 1780–1850* (London: Hambledon Press, 1992).

DORKING, TAPRELL, *Ribbons and Medals: The World's Civil and Military Awards* (London: George Philip, 1974).

DOWDING, G., *An Introduction to the History of Printing Types* (London: Wace, 1961).

DOZIER, R. R., *For King, Constitution and Country* (Lexington: University Press of Kentucky, 1963).

DUNBAR, D. S., 'The Agency Commission System in Britain: A First Sketch of its History to 1941', *Journal of Advertising History*, 2 (1979), 19–20.

EATON, ANN THAXTER, 'Illustrated Books for Children before 1800', in *Illustrators of Children's Books 1744–1945*, comp. Bertha E. Mahony, Louise Payson Latimer, and Beulah Folmsbee (London, 1961).

—— *Treasure for the Taking* (London: George Harrap, 1947).

EHRENPREIS, IRVIN, *Swift: The Man, his Work, and the Age*, 3 vols. (London: Methuen, 1962–83).

EISENSTEIN, E. L., *The Printing Revolution in Early Modern Europe* (Cambridge: Cambridge University Press, 1983).

ELLIOTT, BLANCHE B., *A History of English Advertising* (London: B. T. Batsford, 1962).

ELLIOTT, R. C., *Satire and Magic* (Princeton, NJ: Princeton University Press, 1960).

ENGEN, R. K., *A Dictionary of Victorian Wood Engravers* (Cambridge: Chadwyck & Healey, 1985).

ESSICK, R. N., *William Blake, Printmaker* (Princeton, NJ: Princeton University Press, 1980).

EVANS, E. P., *The Criminal Prosecutiuon and Capital Punishment of Animals* (London: Faber & Faber, 1987).

EVANS, T., *A Brief Sketch of the Life and Times of Thomas Spence* (London, 1821).

EWING, ELIZABETH, *A History of Children's Costumes* (London: Batsford, 1977).

FEARN, M., ' "For Instruction and Amusement": The Publishing and Advertising of Nineteenth Century Children's Books', *Journal of Advertising History*, 5 (1982), 31–5.

FEATHER, JOHN (ed.), *Book Prospectuses before 1801 in the John Johnson Collection* (Oxford: Clarendon Press, 1976; Oxford Microfilm Publications, 1976).

FIGGINS, VINCENT, *Vincent Figgins: Type Specimens 1801–1805*, ed. with intro. by B. Wolpe (London: Printing Historical Society, 1967).

FITZGERALD, PERCY, H., *Samuel Foote: A Biography* (London: Chatto & Windus, 1910).

FOXON, D. F., *English Verse 1700–1750: A Catalogue of Separately Printed Poems with Notes on Contemporary Collected Editions*, 2 vols. (Cambridge: Cambridge University Press, 1975).

FREEMAN, R., *English Emblem Books* (London: Chatto & Windus, 1948).

French Caricature and the French Revolution, 1789–1799, exhibition cat. (Los Angeles: UCLA Press, 1988).

GARRETT, C., *Millenarians and the French Revolution in France and England* (Baltimore: Johns Hopkins University Press, 1975).

GASKELL, PHILIP, *A New Introduction to Bibliography* (Oxford: Oxford University Press, 1972).

GEORGE, MARY DOROTHY, *Catalogue of Political and Personal Satires: Preserved in the Department of Prints and Drawings in the British Museum* ([London: British Museum,] 1935–54).

—— *English Political Caricature 1793–1832: A Study of Opinion and Propaganda* (Oxford: Clarendon Press, 1959).

—— *Hogarth to Cruikshank: Social Change in Graphic Satire* (London: Allen Lane, 1967).

GILLILAND, CORY, 'Early American Copper Coinage in Relation to the Art and Taste of the Period', in *America's Copper Coinage* (New York: American Numismatic Society, 1985).

GODFREY, R., *English Caricature 1620 to the Present*, exhibition cat. (London: Victoria and Albert Museum, 1984).

GOMBRICH, E. H., *Meditations on a Hobby Horse* (Oxford: Phaidon Press, 1963).

—— and KRIS, E., *Caricature* (Harmondsworth: Penguin, 1940).

GOODWIN, ALBERT, *The Friends of Liberty: The English Democratic Movement in the Age of the French Revolution* (London: Hutchinson, 1979).

GORDON, L. L., *British Battle and Campaign Medals* (London: Lawrence Lee, 1979).

GRAY, NICOLETTE, *Nineteenth Century Ornamented Types and Title Pages* (London: Faber & Faber, 1976).

—— 'Slab Serif Type Design in England 1815–1845', *Journal of the Printing Historical Society*, 15 (1981), 1–36.

GREEN, THOMAS, *Verdict According to Conscience: Perspectives on the English*

Criminal Trial Jury 1200–1800 (Chicago: University of Chicago Press, 1985).

GREGG, PAULINE, *Freeborn John: A Biography of John Lilburne* (London: George Harrap, 1961).

HACKWOOD, FREDERICK WILLIAM, *William Hone: His Life and Times* (London: T. F. Unwin, 1912).

HAMILTON, HARLAN W., *Doctor Syntax: A Silhouette of William Combe Esq.* (London: Chatto & Windus, 1969).

HAMILTON, SINCLAIR, *Early American Book Illustrators and Wood Engravers*, 2 vols. (Princeton, NJ: Princeton University Press, 1968).

HAMILTON, WALTER, *George Cruikshank: Artist and Humorist* (London: Elliot Stock, 1878).

HANSARD, T. C., *Typographia* (London: 1825).

HARRISON, J. F. C., *The Second Coming: Popular Millenarianism* (London: Routledge & Kegan Paul, 1979).

HENRIQUES, URSULA, *Religious Toleration in England 1787–1833* (London: Routledge & Kegan Paul, 1961).

HERSBERG, OSCAR, 'The Evolution of Newspaper Advertising', *Lippincott's Magazine*, 60 (1897), 107–12.

HIBBERT, CHRISTOPHER, *George IV* (Harmondsworth: Penguin, 1976).

HILL, DRAPER, *Fashionable Contrasts* (London: Phaidon, 1966).

—— *Mr. Gillray the Caricaturist* (London: Phaidon, 1965).

HINDLEY, CHARLES, *The Catnach Press* (London: Reeves & Turner, 1869).

—— *The Life and Times of Jemmy Catnach* (London, 1878).

HINDLEY, D. and G., *Advertising in Victorian England* (London: Wayland, 1972).

The History of The Times: *'The Thunderer' in the Making, 1785–1841* (London: The Office of *The Times*, 1935).

HOBSBAWM, E. J., *The Age of Revolution 1799–1848* (London: Weidenfeld & Nicolson, 1962).

HOLE, ROBERT, 'British Counter-Revolutionary Propaganda in the 1790s' in Colin James (ed.), *Britain and Revolutionary France: Conflict, Subversion and Propaganda* (Exeter: University of Exeter, 1983).

—— *Pulpits, Politics and Public Order in England 1760–1832* (Cambridge: Cambridge University Press, 1989).

HONE, J. ANN, *For the Cause of Truth: Radicalism in London 1796–1821* (Oxford: Oxford University Press, 1982).

—— 'William Hone (1780–1832), Publisher and Bookseller: An Approach to Early Nineteenth Century London Radicalism', *Historical Studies*, 16 (Apr. 1974), 55–70.

HOUFE, SIMON, *A Dictionary of British Book Illustrators and Caricaturists 1800–1914* (Woodbridge: Antique Collector's Club, 1978).

How William Hone the Persecuted Publisher of Fleet Street, Beat the Bigots on his Three

Trials for Blasphemy, intro. Victor E. Neuberg (Newcastle upon Tyne, [n.d.]).

HUNT, J. W., *Reaction and Reform 1815–1841* (London: Collins, 1972).

HUTCHEON, LINDA, *A Theory of Parody* (New York: Methuen, 1985).

JACKSON, MARY V., *Engines of Instruction, Mischief and Magic: Children's Literature in England from its Beginnings to 1839* (Aldershot: Scholar, 1989).

JACKSON, PETER, *George Scharf's London* (London: Murray, 1987).

JAMES, LOUIS, 'An Artist in Time: George Cruikshank in Three Eras', *Princeton University Library Chronicle*, 25 (1973–4), 157–68.

—— *English Popular Literature 1819–1851* (New York: Columbia University Press, 1976).

JERROLD, BLANCHARD, *The Life of George Cruikshank in Two Epochs* (London: Chatto & Windus, 1898).

JOHNSON, A. F., *Type Designs: Their History and Development* (London: Grafton, 1934).

JONES, MARK, *The Art of the Medal* (London: British Museum, 1979).

—— *Medals of the French Revolution* (London: British Museum, 1977).

JONES, M. H., *Hannah More* (Cambridge: Cambridge University Press, 1952).

Journal of Advertising History.

KEMP-ASHRAF, P. M., *The Life and Times of Thomas Spence* (Newcastle: Frank Graham, 1983).

KINSLEY, W., 'The Dunciad as Mock Book', in J. A. Wynn and W. Kinsley (eds.),: *Pope: Recent Essays by Several Hands* (Hamden, 1964).

KLAUS, H. G., *The Literature of Labour* (Brighton: Harvester, 1985).

KLINGENDER, F. D., *Hogarth and English Caricature* (London: Pilot Press, 1944).

KNOX, T. R., 'Thomas Spence: The Trumpet of Jubilee', *Past and Present*, 76 (1977), 75–99.

KOLB, G. J., 'John Newberry, Projector of the Universal Chronicle: A Study of the Advertisements', *SB*, 11 (1977), 249–52.

KOSS, STEPHEN, *The Rise and Fall of the Political Press in Britain*, 2 vols. (London: Hamilton, 1981).

KRILL, J., *English Artist's Paper* (London: Victoria and Albert Museum, 1987).

KRIS, E., *Psychoanalytic Explorations in Art* (London: George Allen & Unwin, 1964).

KRUMBHAAR, E. B., *Isaac Cruikshank: A Catalogue Raisonnée* (Philadelphia: University of Pennsylvania Press, 1966).

LAFFIN, JOHN, *British Campaign Medals* (London: Abelard Schuman, 1964).

LAQUEUR, T. W., 'The Queen Caroline Affair: Politics as Art in the Reign of George IV,' *Journal of Modern History*, 54 (1982), 417–67.

LANGLOIS, CLAUDE, 'Counter-revolutionary Iconography', in *French*

Caricature and the French Revolution 1789–1799, exhibition cat. (Los Angeles: University of California Press, 1988).

LAVER, JAMES, *Children's Fashions in the Nineteenth Century* (London: B. T. Batsford, 1951).

LEECH, G. N., *English in Advertising* (London: Longmans, 1966).

LEHMANN, PAUL, *Die Parody in Mittelalter*, 2nd edn., rev. (Stuttgart: Anton Heiremann, 1963).

LEVÊQUE, JEAN JACQUES, *L'Art et la Révolution française 1789–1804* ([Neuchâtel:] Ides et Calendes, 1987).

LEWIS, J. N. C., *Printed Ephemera* (London: Faber & Faber, 1962).

LEWIS, LAWRENCE, *The Advertisements of the Spectator* (London: Archibald Constable, 1909).

LOBBAN, MICHAEL, *The Common Law and English Jurisprudence* (Oxford: Oxford University Press, 1991).

—— 'From Seditious Libel to Unlawful Assembly: Peterloo and the Changing Face of Political Crime *c.*1770–1820', *Oxford Journal of Legal Studies*, 10 (1990), 307–52.

McCALMAN, IAIN, *Radical Underworld: Prophets, Revolutionaries and Pornographers in London 1795–1840* (Cambridge: Cambridge University Press, 1988).

NEIL McKENDRICK, BREWER, JOHN and PLUMB, JOHN H. (eds.), *The Birth of a Consumer Society: The Commercialization of Eighteenth-Century England* (London: Europa, 1982).

MACKERNESS, E. D., 'End Paper Advertising', *Journal of Advertising History*, 5 (1982), 57–9.

MACKENZIE, E., *A Memoir of Thomas Spence* (Newcastle, 1836).

MACKENZIE, ROBERT SHELTON, 'George Cruikshank', *London Journal*, 6 (20 Dec. 1847), 177–82.

MACK, MAYNARD, *Alexander Pope: A Life* (New Haven, Conn.: Yale University Press, 1985).

McLEAN, RUARI, *George Cruikshank: His Life and Work as a Book Illustrator* (New York: Pellegrini & Cudahy [, n.d.]).

McLUHAN, MARSHALL, *The Mechanical Bride: Folklore of Industrial Man* (London: Routledge & Kegan Paul, 1967).

MAHONY, ROBERT, and RIZZO, BETTY, *Christopher Smart: An Annotated Bibliography 1743–1983* (New York: Garland, 1984).

MARLOW, JOYCE, *The Peterloo Massacre* ([London:] Rapp & Whiting, 1969).

MAYHEW, G. P., 'Jonathan Swift's Hoax of 1722 upon Ebeneezor Elliston', in A. N. Jeffares (ed.), *Fair Liberty Was all his Cry. A Tercentenary Tribute to Jonathan Swift* (London: Macmillan, 1967).

MEE, JONATHAN ANSON, *Dangerous Enthusiasm: William Blake and the Culture of Radicalism in the 1790s* (Oxford: Oxford University Press, 1992).

—— 'The Political Rhetoric of William Blake's Early Prophecies', doctoral diss., Cambridge University, 1989.

MOON, MARJORIE, *John Harris's Books for Youth 1801–1843* (Folkestone: Dawson, 1992).

MORISON, STANLEY A., *The English Newspaper: Some Account of the Physical Development of the Journals Printed in London between 1622 and the Present Day* (Cambridge: Cambridge University Press, 1935).

——*John Bell, 1745–1831* (Cambridge: printed for the author at Cambridge University Press, 1930; repr. New York, 1981).

——*Politics and Script* (Oxford: Oxford University Press, 1972).

MUIR, PERCY, *English Children's Books 1744–1945* (London: B. T. Batsford, 1954).

MUNTER, R., *The History of the Irish Newspaper* (Cambridge: Cambridge University Press, 1967).

NEVETT, T. R., *Advertising in Britain* (London: William Heinemann, 1982).

NEW, M. and J., 'Some Borrowings in *Tristram Shandy*', *SB* 9 (1976), 322–8.

NEWMARK, J. 'London's Early Advertising Agents', *Journal of Advertising History*, 9 (1986), 15–18.

——*Trade Tokens of the Industrial Revolution* (Aylesbury: Shire, 1981).

NICHOLS, JOHN, *Illustrations of the Literary History of the Eighteenth Century*, 8 vols. (London, 1817–58).

NORRIS, V. P., 'Advertising History according to the Textbooks', *Journal of Advertising History*, 4 (1981), 8–11.

OATES, J. C. T., *Shandyism and Sentiment* (Cambridge: Cambridge Bibliographical Society, 1968).

OGILVY, DAVID, 'A New Deal for your Clients', *Journal of Advertising History*, 3 (1980), 5–8.

OPIE, IONA and PETER, *The Lore and Language of Schoolchildren* (Oxford: Clarendon Press, 1959).

——(eds.), *A Nursery Companion* (Oxford: Clarendon Press, 1980).

——(eds.), *The Oxford Dictionary of Nursery Rhymes* (Oxford: Clarendon Press, 1952).

PATTEN, ROBERT L., *George Cruikshank: A Revaluation* (Princeton, NJ: Princeton University Press, 1974).

——*George Cruikshank's Life, Times, and Art*, i: *1792–1835* (London: Lutterworth, 1992).

PAULSON, RONALD, *Art and Revolution* (New Haven, Conn.: Yale University Press, 1983).

——*The Fictions of Satire* (Baltimore: Johns Hopkins University Press, 1967).

——*Hogarth: His Life, Art, and Times*, 2 vols. (New Haven, Conn.: Yale University Press, published for the Paul Mellon Centre for Studies in British Art, London, 1971).

——*Popular and Polite Art in the Age of Hogarth and Fielding* (Notre Dame, Ind.: University of Notre Dame Press, 1979).

——*Representations of Revolution* (New Haven, Conn.: Yale University Press, 1983).

——'The Severed Head', in *French Caricature and the French Revolution*, exhibition cat. (Los Angeles: University of California Press, 1988).

PENDRED, JOHN, *The Earliest Directory of the Book Trade*, ed. with intro. by Graham Pollard (London: Bibliography Society, 1955).

PHILIPPE, ROBERT, *Political Graphics: Art as a Political Weapon* (Oxford: Phaidon Press, 1982).

PHILIPSON, UNO, *Political Slang 1750–1850* (Lund: C. W. K. Gleerup, 1941).

PHILP, MARK, 'The Fragmented Ideology of Reform', in Philp (ed.), *The French Revolution and British Popular Politics* (Cambridge: Cambridge University Press, 1991).

——*Tom Paine* (Oxford: Oxford University Press, 1989).

PLUMB, J. H. 'The Commercialization of Leisure in Eighteenth-Century England', Stenton Lecture, Reading, 1972.

——'The First Flourishing of Children's Books', in G. Gottlieb (ed.), *Early Children's Books and their Illustration* (London: Oxford University Press, 1975).

——*Men and Places* (London: Penguin, 1966).

POLE, J. R., *Political Representation in England and the Origins of the American Republic* (London: Macmillan, 1966).

POLLOCK, JOHN, *Wilberforce* (London: Constable, 1977).

PORTER, ROY, 'The Language of Quackery in England 1660–1800', in Peter Burke and Roy Porter (eds.), *The Social History of Language* (Cambridge: Cambridge University Press, 1987).

PRESBREY, FRANK, *The Development and History of Advertising* (New York: Doubleday, 1929).

PROCHASKA, A. M. S., 'Westminster Radicalism 1807–1832', M.Phil. diss., Oxford University, 1975.

PROTHERO, IORWERTH, *Artisans and Politics in Early Nineteenth-Century London* (Folkestone: W. Dawson, 1979).

RAVEN, JAMES, *Judging New Wealth* (Oxford: Oxford University Press, 1992).

READ, DONALD R., *Peterloo: The Massacre and its Background* (Manchester: Manchester University Press, 1958).

REA, ROBERT R., *The English Press in Politics 1760–1774* (Lincoln, 1964).

REID, GEORGE WILLIAM, *Catalogue of Prints and Drawings in the British Museum. Division 1: Political and Personal Satires*, ii. (London: British Museum, 1870).

RICKWORD, EDGELL, *Radical Squibs and Loyal Ripostes: Satirical Pamphlets of the Regency Period 1819–1821* (Bath: Adams & Dart, 1971).

RIEWALD, J. G., 'Parody as Criticism', *Neophilologus*, 1 (1966), 125–9.

ROBINSON, J. W., 'Regency Radicalism and Antiquarianism: William Hone's Ancient Mysteries Described (1823)', *Leeds Studies in English*, 10 (1978), 1231–44.

ROGERS, PAT, *Grub Street: Studies in a Subculture* (London: Methuen, 1972).

ROLLESTON, F. R., *Some Account of the Conversion of the Late William Hone* (London: Keswick, 1853).

ROSCOE, S., *John Newberry and his Successors* (Wormley: Five Owls Press, 1973).

ROSE, MARGARET A., *Parody: Ancient, Modern, and Post-modern* (Cambridge: Cambridge University Press, 1993).

ROUTLEDGE, JAMES, *Chapters in the History of Popular Progress Chiefly in Relation to the Freedom of the Press and Trial by Jury* (London: Macmillan, 1876).

ROYLE, EDWARD, and WALVIN, JAMES, *English Radicals and Reformers 1760–1848* (Brighton: Harvester Press, 1982).

RUDÉ, GEORGE, *Wilkes and Liberty* (Oxford: Clarendon Press, 1962).

RUDKIN, OLIVE, *Thomas Spence and his Connections* (London: George Allen & Unwin, 1927).

RUSKIN, JOHN, *Works*, ed. E. T. Cook and A. Wedderburn, 39 vols. (London: George Allen, 1903–12).

RYSKAMP, CHARLES, Preface, in G. Gottlieb (ed.), *Early Children's Books and their Illustration* (London: Oxford University Press, 1975).

ST CLAIR, WILLIAM, 'William Godwin as Children's Bookseller', in Gillian Avery and Julia Brigg (eds.), *Children and their Books* (Oxford: Oxford University Press, 1989).

SAVAGE, WILLIAM, *Practical Hints on Decorative Printing* (London, 1822).

SAXL, F. S., 'Illustrated Pamphlets of the Reformation', *Lectures*, 2 vols. (London: Warburg Institute, 1957).

SCOUTEN, A. H. (ed.), *A Bibliography of the Writings of Jonathan Swift*; rev. edn. H. Teerink (Philadelphia: University of Pennsylvania Press, 1963).

SCRIBNER, R. W., *For the Sake of Simple Folk: Popular Propaganda for the German Reformation* (Cambridge: Cambridge University Press, 1981).

The Shadow of the Guillotine, exhibition cat. (London: British Museum, 1989).

SHEPARD, L., *The History of Street Literature* (Newton Abbot: David & Charles, 1973).

——*John Pitts, Ballad Printer* (Pinner: Private Libraries Association, 1969).

SHERBO, ARTHUR, 'Survival in Grub Street: Another Essay in Attribution', *Bulletin of the New York Public Library*, 64 (1975), 147–58.

SHERBURN, G., *The Early Career of Alexander Pope* (Oxford: Clarendon Press, 1934).

SHIELDS, ANTHEA, 'Thomas Spence and the English Language', *Transactions of the Philological Society* (1974–5), 33–65.

SIKES, HERSHEL, M., 'William Hone: Regency Patriot, Parodist, and Pamphleteer', *Newberry Library Bulletin*, 5 (July 1961), 281–94.

SMITH, HORACE and JAMES, *Rejected Addresses; or, The New Theatrum Poetarum* (London, 1812).

SMITH, NIGEL, *Perfection Proclaimed: Language and Literature in English Radical Religion* (Oxford: Oxford University Press, 1989).

SMITH, OLIVIA, *The Politics of Language 1791–1819* (Oxford: Oxford University Press, 1984).

SOUTHEY, ROBERT, *The Critical Heritage*, ed. Lionel Madden (London: Routledge & Kegan Paul, 1984).

SPATER, GEORGE, *William Cobbett: The Poor Man's Friend*, 2 vols. (Cambridge: Cambridge University Press, 1982).

STEVENSON, JOHN, 'The Queen Caroline Affair', in Stevenson (ed.), *London in the Age of Reform* (Oxford: Oxford University Press, 1977).

STONE, JULIUS, *Evidence: Its History and Policies*, rev. W. A. N. Wells (Sydney: Butterworth, 1991).

STRAUMANN, H., *Newspaper Headlines: A Study in Linguistic Method* (London: George Allen & Unwin, 1935).

THACKERAY, W. M., 'George Cruikshank', *Westminster Review*, 66 (1840), 1–42.

THOMPSON, E. P., *The Making of the English Working Class* (London: Victor Gollancz, 1966).

TRAUGOTT, JOHN, 'The Yahoo in the Doll's House: *Gulliver's Travels*, the Children's Classic', in C. Rawson (ed.), *English Satire and the Satiric Tradition* (Oxford: Oxford University Press, 1984).

TUER, A. W., *1,000 Quaint Cuts from Books of Other Days* (London: Field & Tuer [,1886]).

——*Pages from Forgotten Children's Books* (London: Leadenhall Press, 1898).

TURNER, E. S., *The Shocking History of Advertising!* (London: Michael Joseph, 1952).

VOGLER, RICHARD A., *The Graphic Works of George Cruikshank* (New York: Dover, 1979).

WARDROPER, JOHN, *The Caricatures of George Cruikshank* (London: Gordon Fraser Gallery, 1977).

——*Kings, Lords and Wicked Libellers: Satire and Protest 1760–1837* (London: John Murray, 1973).

WATERS, A. W., *The Trial of Thomas Spence in 1801* (Leamington Spa: Courier Press, 1917).

WELSH, C., *John Newberry: A Bookseller of the Last Century* (London: Grippen, Farren, Okeden, & Welsh, 1885).

WHINNEY, MARGARET, *Sculpture in Britain 1530–1830* (Harmondsworth: Penguin, 1964).

WHITE, R. J., *Waterloo to Peterloo* (London: William Heinemann, 1957).

WHITING, J. R. S., *Trade Tokens: A Social and Economic History* (Newton Abbot: David & Charles, 1971).

WICKWAR, WILLIAM HARDY, *The Struggle for the Freedom of the Press 1819–1832* (London: George Allen & Unwin, 1928).

WILBERFORCE, I. R. and S., *Life of William Wilberforce*, 5 vols. (London: 1838).

WILSON, KATHLEEN, 'Empire, Trade and Popular Politics in Mid-Hanoverian Britain: The Case of Admiral Vernon', *Past and Present*, 121 (1988), 74–111.

WOOD, JAMES PLAYSTEAD, *The Story of Advertising* (New York: Ronald Press, 1958).

WOOD, MARCUS, 'The Dedication to Don Juan and Nursery-Rhyme Parody: A New Satiric Context', *Byron Journal*, 20 (1992), 71–7.

—— 'Popular Satire in Early Nineteenth-Century Radicalism, with Special Reference to Hone and Cruikshank', Ph.D. diss., Oxford University, 1989.

WOODRING, CARL, *Politics in English Romantic Poetry* (Cambridge: Mass.: Harvard University Press, 1970).

WORDSWORTH, JONATHAN, WOOF, ROBERT, and JAYE, MICHAEL C., *William Wordsworth and the Age of English Romanticism*, exhibition cat. (New Brunswick: Rutgers University Press, 1987).

WRIGHT, THOMAS, *Caricature History of the Georges* (London: Chatto & Windus, 1865).

INDEX